The Economics of Regional Clusters

NEW HORIZONS IN REGIONAL SCIENCE

Series Editor: Philip McCann, *Professor of Economics, University of Waikato, New Zealand and Professor of Urban and Regional Economics, University of Reading, UK*

Regional science analyses important issues surrounding the growth and development of urban and regional systems and is emerging as a major social science discipline. This series provides an invaluable forum for the publication of high quality scholarly work on urban and regional studies, industrial location economics, transport systems, economic geography and networks.

New Horizons in Regional Science aims to publish the best work by economists, geographers, urban and regional planners and other researchers from throughout the world. It is intended to serve a wide readership including academics, students and policymakers.

Titles in the series include:

Industrial Agglomeration and New Technologies
A Global Perspective
Edited by Masatsugu Tsuji, Emanuele Giovannetti and Mitsuhiro Kagami

Incentives, Regulations and Plans
The Role of States and Nation-states in Smart Growth Planning
Edited by Gerrit J. Knaap, Huibert A. Haccoû, Kelly J. Clifton and John W. Frece

New Directions in Economic Geography
Edited by Bernard Fingleton

The Management and Measurement of Infrastructure
Performance, Efficiency and Innovation
Edited by Charlie Karlsson, William P. Anderson, Börje Johansson and Kiyoshi Kobayashi

Knowledge Externalities, Innovation Clusters and Regional Development
Edited by Jordi Suriñach, Rosina Moreno and Esther Vayá

Regional Knowledge Economies
Markets, Clusters and Innovation
Philip Cooke, Carla De Laurentis, Franz Tödtling and Michaela Trippl

Entrepreneurship, Industrial Location and Economic Growth
Edited by Josep Maria Arauzo-Carod and Miguel Carlos Manjón-Antolín

Creative Cities, Cultural Clusters and Local Economic Development
Edited by Philip Cooke and Luciana Lazzeretti

The Economics of Regional Clusters
Networks, Technology and Policy
Edited by Uwe Blien and Gunther Maier

Firm Mobility and Organizational Networks
Innovation, Embeddedness and Economic Geography
Joris Knoben

The Economics of Regional Clusters

Networks, Technology and Policy

Edited by

Uwe Blien

Institute for Employment Research and Technical University of Kaiserslautern, Germany

and

Gunther Maier

Vienna University of Economics and Business Administration, Austria

NEW HORIZONS IN REGIONAL SCIENCE

Edward Elgar

Cheltenham, UK • Northampton, MA, USA

Published by
Edward Elgar Publishing Limited
Glensanda House
Montpellier Parade
Cheltenham
Glos GL50 1UA
UK

Edward Elgar Publishing, Inc.
William Pratt House
9 Dewey Court
Northampton
Massachusetts 01060
USA

A catalogue record for this book
is available from the British Library

Library of Congress Control Number: 2008927699

ISBN 978 1 84720 515 5

Printed and bound in Great Britain by MPG Books Ltd, Bodmin, Cornwall

Contents

Contributors

Björn Alecke
Christoph Alsleben
Uwe Blien
Thomas Brenner
Martijn J. Burger
Juan C. Duque
Edward Feser
Peter Franz
Gerhard Heimpold
Simona Iammarino
Matthias Kiese
Stefan Köhler
Nicole Litzel
Gunther Maier
Philip McCann
Joachim Möller
Leonardo Monteiro Monasterio
Frank G. van Oort
Anne Otto
Otto Raspe
Sergio J. Rey
Martin T. W. Rosenfeld
Frank Scharr
André Torre
Gerhard Untiedt
Martin Wrobel

1. The starting point

Uwe Blien[*] and Gunther Maier[‡§]

1.1 AN ANALYTICAL MOTIVATION

"Space" is the *differentia specifica* for the research field of regional science. As compared to standard approaches of economics and other social sciences, regional science has to deal with all the complications that are generated by distance and proximity. In addition to the dimension that is always relevant in scientific research which is marked by "the arrow of time", in regional science we have to deal with the additional two dimensions that constitute a plane in a geometrical sense. In these dimensions many different relationships of social and economic agents are possible and many of them are described by the cluster term. As we will see below, sheer proximity (by forming an agglomeration) is relevant in some approaches of regional clusters, but in many other approaches, special "network" relationships are the focus of interest. These relationships could be of a manifold nature; their spatial character, however, is always constitutive for a complete description. It is particularly interesting how these network relations integrate with other relations and forces of economic life, including those of competition and domination.

Therefore, a book on regional clusters is relevant for many topics of regional analysis. Of course, this statement could be read the other way round: many topics of regional science are covered by a discussion of clusters. Therefore, our first motivation to publish a book about regional clusters is the promise that the field is of primary interest for regional analysis.

But this does not cover the complete analytical motivation of this book. It has to be added that the existence of clusters makes a difference for the fate of the regional economies affected. Many studies register a correlation between the existence of clusters and regional economic growth. This correlation is often positive, but in some cases it is negative. This requires additional research.

Finally, clusters are important simply because there is abundant evidence that they

* Institute for Employment Research (IAB), Nürnberg, Germany.

‡ Vienna University of Economics and Business Administration, Vienna, Austria.

§ The authors thank Stefan Fuchs (IAB), Joachim Möller (University of Regensburg) and Anne Otto (IAB Rheinland-Pfalz-Saarland) for fruitful discussions on the subject of regional clusters. Section 1.7 was written in cooperation with Anne Otto.

can be found empirically in economies. Their existence justifies an explanation. Some of the research providing empirical evidence is included in this book and more is quoted in the articles forming it. Therefore, clusters represent a phenomenon which is important to explain.

1.2 CLUSTER AS A MIRACLE TOOL OF REGIONAL POLICY?

There is a second motivation for this book that concerns the use of clusters in regional policy. Whereas in former times regional assistance was typically designed in a way affecting at least major parts of the economy of an underdeveloped area, recently the attention has shifted. Now, policy might be highly selective by concentrating on some cluster firms. Regional clusters are regarded as a tool that could be used to improve regional growth and to prevent the underdevelopment of regions. Regional policy not only assists special firms that form a regional cluster, in some cases measures are designed even to create one. As is shown in some articles of this book, one can have the impression that clusters are regarded as a tool which could be used to perform miracles. What other forms of regional policy could not accomplish, a cluster oriented regional assistance can – this is a widespread belief.

Obviously there are some empirical phenomena behind this belief. The "Silicon Valley" is legend and so are other examples of regions including a fast growing economy with a focus on a dominating industry. It would be a nice idea to start more of these clusters from scratch with the help of regional policy. The idea has materialized in many projects in Europe, whereas in the US, policy is holding its traditional distance from strategies of regional assistance but helping the formation of regional clusters indirectly.

In this book we do not intend to further broaden the "cluster hype". Instead, some of the authors try to develop rigorous tests of the success chances for this kind of regional policy. It is necessary first to look at the growth implications and at other direct consequences of clusters. If there is extra growth with clusters, are there any specific conditions to be met? What are the consequences for employment or does growth affect only the productivity dimension?

After finding answers to this first topic it is possible to approach the second research question. Is it possible to develop strategies of regional policy aiming at regional clusters and increasing regional growth of productivity and of employment? Or will this have detrimental consequences or lead to success only by chance? The results achieved so far nourish a more sceptical point of view. In this introductory chapter we will briefly turn to strategies of cluster policy in section 1.7, but before doing so, a clarification of the cluster notion is required.

1.3 WHAT IS A CLUSTER?

The cluster term is one of an inherently "fuzzy" character. Often the observer has the impression that every researcher has his or her own idea of what a cluster is. Even more, in some cases there is no explicit definition. It is not necessary that every researcher shares the same approach. But at least some basic ideas are required in order to come to a common level of understanding. In a first step, let us quote the definition of Porter (2003: 562), which is also used by Möller and Litzel (this volume): a cluster is "a geographically proximate group of interconnected companies, suppliers, service providers and associated institutions in a particular field, linked by externalities of various types." This definition indicates that a cluster is concentrated in a region, not distributed over the space. It may not be confined to only one industry but may include supply chains that connect firms of very different industries.

To open up a broad field of research it would be an advantage to use a definition even wider than the one given by Porter. In this respect the chapter by Iammarino and McCann (in this volume) is helpful. Referring to an earlier publication by Gordon and McCann (2000) they follow a transaction cost approach and develop a typology that covers many different research strategies. In this typology there are three basic forms of clusters: "They can be termed the *pure agglomeration*, the *industrial complex*, and the *social network*".[1] For all the three types geographical concentration is important. They represent different externalities of Porter's definition. We would like to use this typology as an extended definition and description of the cluster phenomenon and add only some aspects in the description of the types that could be of use in relation to empirical research.

It has to be emphasized that the first type, pure agglomeration, is a limiting case, which is often not regarded as a cluster. Agglomeration economics can be traced back at least to Alfred Marshall. The specific arguments he introduced included labour market pooling, use of nontraded inputs, and knowledge spillovers between firms. It is clear that this concerns mainly localization economies which are important for firms of the same industry. In Iammarino and McCann's the cluster as pure agglomeration includes also urbanization effects which refer to the sheer concentration of economic activity beyond the limits of one industry. This indicates a very wide definition of the cluster term. In fact, it is so wide that this special part of the definition is of little relevance for the papers collected in this book.

What is included and emphasized not especially by Iammarino and McCann but by other authors (for example by Möller and Litzel, this volume), is the existence of supply chains transcending single industries. This is often an important aspect. A large plant producing cars needs many other establishments as suppliers and these again need many others. Often these firms are not counted as being part of the automobile industry, but are categorized as producing electronics, chemicals and so on. To economize on transport costs and to satisfy the demands of just-in-time production a spatial concentration is advantageous for the supplychain. This is the basis of a powerful tendency towards regional concentration and towards cluster formation.

In Iammarino and McCann's terminology this case would be termed an industrial complex. These are of a more "organized" nature, as in the example of the automobile producing firm. In the interest of continuous production the duties of the numerous suppliers are exactly specified. Often there are expensive contractual fines if one of the

[1] Of course there is a completely different meaning of the cluster term. In this case it is aimed at groups or types in a set of objects. Statistical cluster analysis has been developed to identify these groups. This is not the intention of the cluster term used here.

suppliers is not able to deliver at the specified time in the defined quality. The firms at the centers of an industrial district can exert some power over the firms forming its periphery.

Networks as the third cluster type are of a more informal nature. Normally, network relationships are not as asymmetrical as are relationships between firms of an industrial district. Networks represent the most modern type of clusters. In former years Silicon Valley has been one of the paradigmatic cases. The network helps firms to save transaction costs. It facilitates finding solutions on all kinds of difficult technical problems by moving along the connections between network nodes. Transaction costs are saved and new solutions for efficient production are provided. An additional advantage of networks is their flexibility.

In all the cases covered by the definition of clusters the economic agents meant are mostly firms or establishments as part of firms. However, these are represented by human agents. Often their relationships are important for the character of the firms' relationships. For their stability it may be important that individual representatives can develop mutual trust. In the case of the cluster as network individual workers or experts may even represent nodes of the cluster. They may represent information or specialized abilities and they may form connections between otherwise independent firms.

At least in the case of the industrial district and the network, other forms of institutions than firms are subsumed under the cluster term too. An important point is that clusters are regarded as advantageous for innovative activity. Therefore, universities and research institutes may be very important. They may be linked to firms of a cluster by the supply or even by the exchange of high-skilled researchers. Apart from universities and research institutes other state institutions may be needed for the development of a favourable location. Assisting the development of appropriate infrastructure contacts between state institutions and the firms of a region is regarded as important. Agents of the state may additionally take over an active role in coining the cluster relationships between firms. State development agencies may set up cluster managers with their own offices to organize meetings and to establish contact.

1.4 CLUSTERS AND TRUST

The relationships of firms forming a cluster are interesting because they may be of a paradoxical nature. In standard economics these relationships are thought of as relying on competition. Every firm maximizes exclusively its own profit. The interests of other firms are neglected. If it is possible to use an advantage which is detrimental to another firm this advantage should be brought home. This assumption might be justified, since the imperative of profit maximization is rooted deeply in the institutional structure of a capitalist economy. A firm behaving differently risks its own demise. It is not able to secure an optimal rate of investment and it is in danger of a non-friendly takeover.

In a cluster of the network type, however, "trust" is important. At least in some respects it is crucial not to use advantages over others regarded as "unfair". From the participants of a relationship it is expected that they are reluctant to use a short-term advantage which could hurt the interests of others. Instead they may look at the middle- or long-run stability of the relationship. If a firm in a network is temporarily not able to pay a debt, it might be expected of the creditors to wait.

Trust can be a very powerful resource for economic success. Perkins (2000) describes the role of trust in the historical development of the highly successful Chinese community in several countries of South-East Asia. In a situation where the different states are not able or inclined to secure property rights mutual trust serves as a substitute, at least to some degree. In this case it was bound to the family connections of an ethnic minority. The example shows that it is not completely clear whether the reliance on trust is a contradiction to profit maximization or even its instrument. Research on clusters may help to clarify this issue. There is no general theory available at the moment, therefore it is an empirical question, which actions are classified as unfair and which not.

The reliance on relations of trust in a cluster has the additional consequence of reducing power. Firms restrict actions that could influence each other at least in some respects. Again, the degree to which this happens is an open question.

1.5 CLUSTER AND SPATIAL RELATIONSHIPS

It is obvious that the balance between actions which express competition and power on the one hand and actions based on relations of trust on the other hand, is a difficult one. Geographical proximity between firms might be important since it helps to establish and maintain trust. It is easier to monitor the behaviour of others who are close by. Additionally it is easier to establish a reputation for trustworthy behaviour, if the density of contact is higher because of sheer proximity. Apart from this, if people know each other they are more reluctant to put pressure on each other.

These are reasons why geographical proximity is correlated at least to some degree with "positive" relations in a population. But of course qualifications of this statement are required. The working of competition does not vanish, it is only partly suspended. Again, it has to be specified to what degree business relations are affected.

For many relations of trust face-to-face contact is important. A personal relationship can only be developed if the members of the network have relatively close contact with each other. After establishing the relationship immediate contact is no longer urgent, but it is still important to meet at intervals to maintain trust. This is one of the reasons for economic activity to be concentrated in particular places. It might seem cheaper to establish an internationally operating bank in a distant part of the world, but banks are concentrated in places which have high wages and high estate costs. London, New York and Frankfurt have the advantage that many relevant actors are available and can be contacted personally.

Proximity is not only important in network relationships which are based on trust. If the relevant actors are close to each other, the spreading of all kinds of information is facilitated. This saves transaction costs. Proximity is also important for the role cluster networks play in innovative activity. The combination of new solution is eased up if information about components is at hand.

In other types of clusters mentioned above (industrial district, agglomeration) distance is also important, partly for the reasons discussed, partly for other reasons. Proximity saves transport costs and facilitates the close coordination of activities. Especially in the case of the industrial districts both are relevant.

Technical progress has greatly reduced transport costs. Therefore, many properties of modern production processes are only possible under this condition. In many branches these processes span countries distributed over long distances. The importance of clusters is weakened in this respect. Transport costs are still not to be neglected, however.

Another tendency has been the rise of the internet and of other media of electronic communication. Obviously these tendencies are important for the distribution and transmission of information and for the maintenance of control. They could imply a significant decrease of transaction costs in the markets. At the moment surprisingly little empirical research about the impacts of these new media on the location decisions of firms is available. If an expectation can be formulated, then the new media will not form a complete substitute for immediate contact of the individual agents. Often, it still might be necessary to establish a relationship by personal interaction. In many cases the maintenance, however, can be done from the distance through email (and telephone) and maybe video-conferences. It will be necessary to follow these questions in new approaches of empirical research. The "death of distance" is not to be expected (Dohse et al. 2005).

1.6 CLUSTERS AND GROWTH

As we have seen, there are hopes that clusters will accelerate growth in a (regional) economy. This is based on the notion that clusters per se are advantageous for the usage of economic resources. By combining these resources more effectively clusters will lead to increases of productivity. Apart from this, clusters are regarded as advantageous for the promotion of innovation. In both views they will increase productivity. The most important mechanism considered to be working in favour of growth relies on the generation of knowledge spillovers between firms. One of the reasons why it might be worthwhile for a company to move to a place where many of its competitors are located is to benefit from the productive solutions developed by the other firms. In return the new firm might also contribute to this external effect. In the end the level of productivity in the respective location is raised.

It has to be emphasized, however, that the relation between cluster density and economic growth is a contingent one. Though there are numerous examples of positive effects of cluster development on regional growth, the literature describes counter examples showing that regional networks can hamper the growth of a region (for example, Grabher 1993b with respect to the Ruhr area in Germany). A network might block activities of outside actors and prevent growth by avoiding competition. Other types of clusters (industrial district and agglomeration) will have negative effects on regions if the leading firms or industries meet a crisis. Then they will tear down the economic development of the respective regions as they might have promoted it before. Therefore, for a region it is very important to specialize in the "right" clusters.

This is easy to request, but very difficult to fulfill. The agglomeration economies which constitute the foundation of the cluster concept imply that specific activities will be unevenly distributed among regions. Once a region has a higher concentration of an industry than competing regions, it will be more attractive to additional forms of that industry due to the agglomeration economies. Viewed from the other side, a region which tries to promote an industry cluster that is already successful in another region is at a severe disadvantage as it has to overcome the agglomeration advantage of its role model region. Viewed from a system theoretic angle, agglomeration economies introduce a nonlinearity into the economic system which may lead to undetermined long-term results of the growth process, path dependence and even chaotic behaviour (Maier and Sedlacek, 2005).

Even if clusters promote productivity growth there might be ambiguous effects on employment. Recent research on agglomeration effects showed that productivity growth may be accompanied by losses in employment. The theoretical argument runs as follows. If technical progress affects all factors of production (for example in the case of Hicks-neutral technical progress) or is at least not only capital-saving, it is possible to produce the same product with less and less labour. This is the labour-saving effect. But often, technical progress is accompanied by price decreases. In this case demand will expand and so does production. Since for higher output levels more labourers are required, there is a compensating effect of technical progress.

It can be shown that under very general circumstances the net effect of technical progress depends directly on the demand elasticity on the product market (Blien and Sanner 2006, starting from Appelbaum and Schettkat 1999). If product demand is elastic employment increases with technical progress; if demand is inelastic, however, employment decreases. A basic version of the theorem was used by Cingano and Shivardi (2004) to show how agglomerations affect productivity and employment growth. Typically, in recent times, metropolitan areas have relatively high rates of productivity growth. But they also reveal lower employment growth rates than the rural country. Therefore, with respect to clusters the conclusion is ambiguous. Even if clusters promote productivity growth they might be detrimental for employment.

1.7 CLUSTER POLICIES

Several chapters of this volume discuss cluster policies of the state. Therefore, after having clarified the cluster term, it is helpful to come back to this topic. A very general focus of many state policies in capitalist countries is the orientation towards economic growth. Often the mentioned positive relation between cluster density and productivity growth is taken for granted. This increases the pressure on all regions with relatively few clusters. In the time of globalization all regions are forced to imitate successful blueprints. As a consequence many governments and state agencies responsible for regions try to implement policies that should improve the scope and the strength of clusters or even create new ones. There are some common characteristics of these strategies (Raines 2001).

First, in cluster policies generally the support is concentrated on regional economic structures, especially on networks rather than on individual firms. Measures tend to provide common resources for a group of inter-related firms. This concerns specialized infrastructure or specific skills training programmes. The policy goal is to facilitate the development of a network rather than promote the growth of individual agents within a network. An important topic is to encourage linkages between and amongst firms and research institutions. This networking might not be generated automatically through the own interests of the firms involved because, especially with large networks, external effects might occur. It might not be profitable for individual firms to organize a network, though its effect on all firms of a region is large. Another case for state policy is the involvement of state institutions. Paradigmatic examples of clusters are those with a link to universities or other research institutions.

A second key element of cluster policy is that it is generally concerned with selected networks only. Usually the first stage of designing a cluster policy is the identification and choice of target clusters in the regional economies, targets which should be supported. The approach demands the concentration of policy resources in those parts of the region's industrial structure which are likely to show the greatest benefit, a form of "picking potential winners". For cluster policy targeting is a key element. This policy is favouring the development of a handful of sectors. By boosting the competitiveness of these sectors, a form of "growth pole" approach is effectively being followed. The aim whether explicit or not seems to be for these sectoral value chains to become "hubs" or "spines" around which wider economic development can take place.

The consequence of this feature of cluster strategies is that they are not neutral with respect to the industry structure of an economy. Firms have (dis-)advantages which arise whether they are members of a promoted cluster or whether they are not. Normally, a selectivity of this kind is regarded as highly problematic. Many of its forms are excluded by law in the European Union. Apart from this the identification of firms which could form a central focus of a region and successfully generate positive spillovers to other sectors is not easy. To manage cluster policy this identification has to be done by state bureaucrats. Why should they have more insights than market agents? Why should these agents not generate out of their own power the degree of networking that is required for the development of the cluster? Again, it has to be referred to external effects.

A third key element is that cluster policies emphasize the importance of enhancing innovation and learning within the cluster. In this respect, the policy overlaps with more traditional innovation assistance. What is perhaps new in the policy is the targeting on particular sectors rather than on the innovation system of a region as a whole. This is operating on the implicit principle that innovation is a function of specific networks which are a subset of the innovation system as a whole. Indeed, within such policies, clusters can be defined as networks which are bound and delimited by intensive and repeated knowledge transactions occurring far more often than in other parts of the economy, thereby requiring fewer policy resources to generate step-level changes in industrial competitiveness.

1.8 STRUCTURE OF THE BOOK

The thirteen chapters that form the remainder of this book can roughly be categorized in three groups. The first group is formed by Iammarino and McCann's and by Torre's chapter. These two chapters deal mainly with the definition of clusters and their classification. The concern about the fuzziness of the cluster term that is expressed in both these chapters reappears in other contributions throughout the book.

The second and by far the largest part of the book is formed by chapters 4 to 10. All these chapters analyse specific industry clusters, but apply a diverse set of methods and use information from different countries or regions. The chapter by Duque and Rey uses social network analysis methods for identification of clusters in San Diego County, California, USA. Brenner in his chapter derives a theoretical regional industry-size distribution and fits it empirically to data for Germany. This way he is able to statistically test for each industry whether spatial agglomerations exist and where they are located.

Chapter 6 by Rosenfeld, Franz and Heimpold looks at a part of Germany, the East German planning regions. They define criteria for the identification of economic development spots, a concept closely related to clusters, but less vaguely defined. In the empirical application, Rosenfeld et al. identify such economic development spots by use of descriptive statistical methods.

Monasterio in his chapter uses clusters as an explanatory variable for testing the effect of agglomeration and urban economies on individual wages in the Brazilian state of Rio Grande do Sul. As part of his research, he employs several spatial analysis techniques, in order to locate industrial clusters and calculate the market potential of the municipalities studied.

With chapter 8 by Möller and Litzel we return to Germany, more specifically the region of Eastern Bavaria. Möller and Litzel employ CORIS, a cluster-oriented regional information system that has been developed for their study area. On this basis they identify regional clusters, specialization of regions and the spatial concentration of value chains.

Van Oort, Burger and Raspe look at clusters from an urban perspective. In their analysis of the Dutch Randstad region they hypothesize that clusters in the context of a set of closely connected cities imply the cities to be specialized in different industries, while at the same time showing a marked degree of spatial and functional integration. They use various methods of analysis like count data regression analysis, social network analysis concepts and visualizations and a gravity model logic.

The chapter by Otto and Köhler deals again with Germany. It differs from the other such chapters in two ways. First, it concentrates on the role of start-up firms in the development of clusters. Second, it looks at three quite different clusters in the country, a growing, a mature, and a declining one. With this approach they demonstrate that life cycle aspects are important for the understanding of cluster development and that these should be taken into account more carefully.

The last group of chapters, chapters 11 to 14, deals explicitly with cluster policy. While cluster policy is discussed in many other chapters as well, in this group it constitutes the main focus. Chapter 11 by Feser is unique in this volume as it is the only one that explicitly deals with developing economies. Feser argues that for developing and transitioning economies a synergy leveraging approach is more defensible conceptually than a standard cluster policy approach. In this approach innovation policies should be designed to leverage synergies amongst businesses and non-market institutions as a means of improving policy efficacy.

Alecke, Alsleben, Scharr and Untiedt in their chapter challenge cluster policy from a different point of view. They apply the Ellison-Glaeser index to test for the degree of geographic concentration among sectors in the German economy. As it turns out technology oriented industries and knowledge intensive services are not among the most concentrated sectors. In fact their degree of geographic concentration is generally very weak. For cluster policy they draw the conclusion that aside from the long-established means of classical R&D policy, there seems to be little economic justification for an additional cluster policy on a regional level.

The remaining two chapters by Wrobel (chapter 13) and by Kiese (chapter 14) take on a similar perspective. They look at cluster policies that were implemented in the German states of Bremen and Lower Saxony, respectively. They show how political desire sometimes leaps ahead of scientific knowledge and blurs the theoretical concepts. Kiese also highlights the role of consultants who tend to sell cluster blueprints to policy makers. Both chapters clearly illustrate the strong dependence of cluster policy on the specific circumstances and the context of the region.

1.9 ACKNOWLEDGMENTS

The editors of this volume wish to thank the authors for their cooperation in the production process. Their professional quality as well as collegiate attitude made this process an enjoyable one. We also extend thanks for the patience that they were willing to exercise at times.

Besides the authors, a number of other people contributed to this book. Their input has greatly supported the editing process and substantially improved the quality of the manuscript. As editors of this book we are grateful for their contribution. Adam Goldstein has language-edited the whole text and his input proved to be essential for the readability of major parts of the manuscript. Monika and Marion Piber have helped with translations. Secretarial assistance has been provided by Ursula Grafeneder and Barbara Gaal. Rüdiger Cyprian helped with the index and proof-read part of the text.

In addition to the help provided by these colleagues, as editors of this book we also enjoyed the professional support provided by the publisher. Any remaining mistakes and errors are, of course, our responsibility.

REFERENCES

Appelbaum, E., Schettkat, R. (1999), 'Are prices unimportant?', *Journal of Post-Keynesian Economics*, **21** (3), 387–398.

Blien, U., Sanner, H. (2006), 'Structural change and regional employment dynamics', IAB Discussion Paper 6, Institute for Employment Research (IAB), Nürnberg, Germany.

Cingano, F. Schivardi, F. (2004), 'Identifying the sources of local productivity growth', *Journal of the European Economic Association*, **2** (4), 720–742.

Dohse, D. (2000), 'Technology policy and the regions – the case of the BioRegio contest', *Research Policy* **29** (9), 1111–1133.

Dohse, D., Laaser, C.F., Schrader, J.-V. (2005), 'Raumstruktur im Internetzeitalter: Tod der Distanz? Eine empirische Analyse', Kieler Diskussionsbeiträge 416/417, Kiel Institute for the World Economy, Kiel, Germany.

Gordon, I.R. and P. McCann (2000), 'Industrial Clusters: Complexes, Agglomeration and/or Social Networks?' *Urban Studies*, **3**, 513–532.

Grabher, G. (ed.) (1993a), *The Embedded Firm*, London and New York: Routledge.

Grabher, G. (1993b), 'The weakness of strong ties. The lock-in of regional development in the Ruhr area', in Grabher, G. (ed.), *The Embedded Firm*, London and New York: Routledge, 255–277.

Maier, G., Sedlacek, S. (eds) (2005), *Spillovers and Innovations. Space, environment and the economy*, Vienna: Springer.

Perkins, D.H. (2000), 'Law, family ties, and the East Asian way of business', in Harrison, L., Huntington, S.P. (eds) *Culture Matters. How Values Shape Human Progress*, New York: Basic Books, 232–243.

Porter, M.E. (2003), 'The Economic Performance of Regions', *Regional Studies*, **37** (6&7), 549–578.

Raines, P. (2001), 'The cluster approach and the dynamics of regional policy-making', Regional and Industrial Policy Research Paper 47, University of Strathclyde, Glasgow.

2. Innovation dynamics and the structure and evolution of industrial clusters

Simona Iammarino* **and Philip McCann**‡

2.1 INTRODUCTION TO GEOGRAPHY AND KNOWLEDGE SPILLOVERS

Over the last two decades, the interrelationships between industrial location behaviour, firm and industry technology, and innovation processes have come to be seen as essential features of regional development. In many arenas, analytical research and policy-thinking has focussed on understanding the factors that determine why particular types of technologies flourish in particular regions, and how this flourishing affects local economic growth. Lessons are often drawn from case-studies of particularly successful 'innovative' regions, which are then used to reformulate both industrial policy and regional policy. However, it is unclear to what extent simply observing the innovation performance of other localities is of much use in designing regional development policies. The reason is that many of these observations, comparisons, and policy arguments are based on analyses that take insufficient consideration of either the nature of innovation processes or the structural conditions under which technical–change occurs in the region. In order to explain the observed variety of geography-innovation outcomes it is necessary to take into account the nature of new knowledge in different industrial sectors. In particular, the dynamics of technological regimes, industrial structures and organisational practices all vary significantly across both sectors and activity types. But these variations are often overlooked in favour of stylised constructs, which appeal to consultants or government policy-makers longing for easy answers to complex problems. An example of this tendency can be found in the literature that

*SPRU, University of Sussex and University of Rome "La Sapienza". SPRU, University of Sussex, The Freeman Centre, Brighton, BN1 9QE, United Kingdom. Fax: +44 (0)1273 685865. E-mail: s.iammarino@sussex.ac.uk

‡Department of Economics, University of Waikato, Private bag 3105, Hamilton 3240, New Zealand: E-mail: pmccann@waikato.ac.nz, and Department of Economics, University of Reading, PO Box 219, Whiteknights, Reading RG6 6AW, United Kingdom. E-mail: P.McCann@reading.ac.uk

posits a positive relationship between innovation and industrial clusters.

Currently the most popular explanation of the benefits of industrial clustering focuses on the role played by localised external agglomeration economies. Underlying this thinking are Marshall's (1920) three explanations for the existence of positive agglomeration externalities, namely local information and knowledge spillovers, non-traded local inputs, and a skilled local labour pool. Two groups of literatures have developed here. Firstly, the so-called Marshall-Arrow-Romer (MAR) literature (Glaeser et al. 1992) focuses on processes of 'learning-by-doing' within a single localised industry. In addition to these localisation economies, however, a parallel stream of literature focussing on the role and importance of sectoral diversity and variety in agglomeration models has been developed both by the proponents of the new economic geography (Fujita et al. 1999; Fujita and Thisse 2002)) and also by proponents of more traditional approaches to urbanisation economies (Jacobs 1960; Glaeser et al. 1992). This diversity-variety literature suggests that inter-industry spillovers may be generally more important than intra-industry spillovers in spurring growth (Martin and Ottaviano 1999), although intra-industry effects may dominate certain sectors such as manufacturing (Henderson et al. 1995).

Models that posit industrial clustering as a central component of the regional innovation process are based on the idea that the knowledge and information required in the innovation process are systematically 'sticky' within particular clustered localities. Assessing the evidence regarding the geographical 'stickiness' of knowledge is complicated by the difficulties involved in measuring 'knowledge'. This requires the use of indirect techniques that track knowledge flows. The most widely used technique has been to observe the geography of patent generation and citations (Jaffe et al. 1993). This approach clearly points to the geographical stickiness of knowledge. However, there are other indirect arguments equally applicable to all sectors, which also point to the local stickiness of knowledge and the spatial limitations of knowledge flows. Over the last three decades, widespread technological development in ICT and transport has significantly reduced many aspects of spatial transaction costs, thereby potentially benefiting peripheral economies. Indeed, Glaeser (1998) argues that if we consider the changes in the transactions costs of goods-shipments alone, then the fact that transport costs have fallen by some 95 per cent during the twentieth century (Glaeser and Kohlhasse 2004), means that the transportation-costs rationale for industrial clustering and the existence of modern cities disappears. On the other hand, Gaspar and Glaeser (1998) argue that the facilitation of knowledge and information transfers continues to demand widespread and frequent face-to-face contacts amongst individuals, and that this demand constitutes a crucial factor in the generation of modern cities and industrial clusters.

Both the increasing localisation of knowledge and the continual localised growth of cities are occurring in a world also marked by increasing interconnectedness, both in terms of global trade flows and global information flows. In the modern competitive environment exhibiting both globalisation and localisation, global market competition, changes in demand, and technological change occur at incredibly high speed. Therefore, there are profound reasons to suppose that the relationship between innovation, geography and local economic growth may in reality be far more subtle, complex and varied than the simple Marshallian agglomeration model suggests. In research fields concerned with issues relating to technology, the original Marshallian-Arrow-Romer stream of literature and the diversity literature on urbanisation economies (Jacobs 1960) have both therefore been broadened to include technological indices as endogenous variables for explaining local economic growth (Acs 2002; Jaffe et al. 1993). Examples of such indices include local patent counts, local R&D expenditures, and local R&D employment. These models are also extended to include various alternative measures of knowledge creation and innovation.

Nonetheless, by confining their focus to localised spillover effects, such neoclassical interpretations have failed to fully consider other possible mechanisms underlying spatial agglomeration (Breschi and Lissoni 2001; Autant-Bernard et al. 2003). In particular, production function-based models do not give a full account of the diversity of industrial cluster types that exist. Nor do they tackle issues such as the evolution of clusters and the disruptive changes imposed by technological progress and globalisation processes on agglomeration economies (Guerrieri et al. 2001; Hilpert 2003). On the other hand, evolutionary growth theories do attempt to place technological regimes and creative destruction at the centre of their analyses, but when applied to clustering many of these evolutionary models have also failed to incorporate an understanding of the price system for providing a brake on the system when congestion factors start to bite.

For this reason, in order to identify the relationship between clusters and innovation, it is necessary to consider the variety of relationships, as well as the ways in which these geography–industry relationships relate to innovation processes. Without such a careful assessment, the literature on regional innovation will remain largely stylised. In order to accomplish this we extend a transactions costs classification of industrial clusters into a knowledge typology of clusters. Here we follow Pavitt's (1984) classic taxonomy of the sources of innovation. Our arguments show that the transactions costs classification and the knowledge taxonomy are broadly consistent, and that these classification systems can offer real insights into the micro-foundations, nature, and evolution of clusters.

2.2 A TRANSACTIONS COSTS CLASSIFICATION OF CLUSTER TYPES

A transactions costs approach can be adopted to highlight three stylised sets of geography–firm–industry organisational relationships. This transactions costs classification of cluster types was originally developed by Gordon and McCann (2000), and has since been used elsewhere (McCann 2001; Simmie and Sennet 1999; McCann and Sheppard 2003; McCann and Shefer 2004; McCann and Mudambi 2004, 2005). These classifications are not explanatory theories, but they are based on the implicit assumptions underlying most of the existing literature on agglomeration and clustering phenomena. They are not meant to represent any particular geographical category or place, but rather distinguish clusters on the basis of the cluster's composition of firms, the nature of their relations, and transactions undertaken within the clusters.

Characteristics	Pure agglomeration	Industrial complex	Social network
Firm size	atomistic	some large firms	variable
Characteristics of relations	non-identifiable fragmented unstable and frequent trading	identifiable stable and frequent trading	trust loyalty joint lobbying joint ventures non-opportunistic
Membership	open	closed	partially open
Access to cluster	rental payments location necessary	internal investment location necessary	history, experience, location necessary but not sufficient
Space outcomes	rent appreciation	no effect on rents	partial rental capitalisation
Example of cluster	competitive urban economy	steel or chemicals production complex	new industrial areas
Analytical approaches	models of pure agglomeration	location–production theory, input–output analysis	social network theory (Granovetter)
Notion of space	urban	local or regional but not urban	local or regional but not urban

Table 2.1: Industrial clusters: a transactions costs perspective

The three types can be termed the 'pure agglomeration', the 'industrial complex', and the 'social network'. They are depicted in Table 2.1.

In the model of *pure agglomeration*, inter-firm relations are inherently transient. Firms are essentially atomistic, in the sense of having no market power, and they will continuously change their relations with other firms and customers in response to market arbitrage opportunities, thereby leading to intense local competition. As such, there is no loyalty between firms, nor will relations be long-term. The external benefits of clustering accrue to all local firms simply by reason of their local presence. The cost of membership of this cluster is simply the local real estate market rent. There are no free riders, access to the cluster is open, and consequently growth in the local real estate rents serves as the best indicator of the cluster's performance. This idealised type is best represented by the Marshall (1920) model of agglomeration described in section 2.3, and it is the notion of clustering underlying models of new economic geography (Krugman 1991; Fujita et al. 1999), irrespective of whether the agglomeration is driven by economies of localisation or urbanisation. The conception of space in these models is essentially urban space insofar as this type of clustering only exists within individual cities.

The *industrial complex* type is characterised primarily by long-term stable and predictable relations between the firms in the cluster. This type of cluster is most commonly observed in industries such as steel and chemicals, and is the type of spatial cluster typically discussed by classical (Weber 1909) and neo-classical (Moses 1958) location–production models, representing a fusion of locational analysis with input–output analysis (Isard and Kuenne 1953). Component firms within the spatial grouping gain membership by undertaking significant long-term investments, particularly in terms of physical capital and local real estate. Access to the group is therefore severely restricted by both high entry and exit costs. The rationale for spatial clustering in these types of industries is that proximity minimises inter-firm transport transactions costs. Rental appreciation is not a feature of the cluster, because the land, which has already been purchased by the firms, is not for sale. The notion of space underlying the industrial complex model is local, but not necessarily urban. These types of complexes can exist either within or outside of an individual city. This pattern of clustering is actually the only explicitly spatial element in the transactions costs approach of Williamson (1975), who focuses primarily on the types of flow-process scale economies that firms can realise in vertically integrated production complexes. Such thinking has often formed the basis for policies aimed at fostering industrial enclaves, particularly in developing economies (Isard, Schooler and Vietorisz 1959), and in sectors such as petrochemicals. However, this transaction-cost logic is equally applicable to any type of modern industry operating just-in-time (JIT) delivery systems, such as automotives, electronics, supermarket retailing, and distribution.

The third type of spatial industrial cluster is the *social network* model. This is associated primarily with the work of Granovetter (1973), and is a response to the hierarchies model of Williamson (1975). The social network model argues that mutual trust relations between key decision making agents in different organisations may be at least as important as decision-making hierarchies within individual organisations. These trust relations will be manifested by a variety of features, such as joint lobbying, joint ventures, informal alliances, and reciprocal arrangements regarding trading relationships. One key feature of such trust relations is an absence of opportunism, in that individual firms will not fear reprisals after any reorganisation of inter-firm relations. Inter-firm cooperative relations may therefore differ significantly from the organisational boundaries associated with individual firms, and these relations may be continually reconstituted. All of these behavioural features rely on a common culture of mutual trust, the development of which depends largely on a shared history and experience amongst decision-making agents. This social network model is essentially aspatial, but from the point of view of geography it can be argued that spatial proximity will tend to foster such trust relations and a local business environment marked by confidence, risk-taking and cooperation. Spatial proximity is therefore necessary but not sufficient to acquire access to the network. Membership of the network is only partially open, in that local rental payments will not guarantee access, although they will improve the chances of access.

The geographical manifestation of the social network model is the so-called 'new industrial areas' model (Scott 1988), which has been used to describe the characteristics and performance of areas such as the Emilia-Romagna region of Italy and Silicon

Valley (Scott 1988; Saxenian 1994; Castells and Hall 1995). More recently, the trust embodied in the social network approach has been used to explain the relations between social capital, creativity and space (Glaeser et al. 2000; Glaeser et al. 2002; Caves 2000; Florida 2002, 2005a,b; Scott 2000), although untangling these issues is complex (Glaeser 2004). In the social network model space is once again local, but not necessarily urban.

In reality, all spatial clusters or industrial concentrations will contain characteristics of one or more of these ideal types, although one type will tend to be dominant in each cluster. Therefore, from an empirical and policy perspective, it is necessary to determine which of the typologies best reflects an individual cluster. This will allow for the design of the appropriate empirical testing and policy evaluation without any arbitrary presuppositions regarding the form of a particular cluster. In light of the arguments presented here, it is clear that most cluster discussions in both the academic and the policy literature adopt a rather general and stylised model of local economic geography, which is a hybrid composite description based on different understandings of knowledge, information, inter-firm relations and transactions costs. These cluster approaches tend to be largely unconcerned with the actual detailed interplay between industries and geographical systems, or of the specific evolutionary features of different clusters or locations. Such lack of precision explains the recent hectic efforts to identify localised knowledge spillovers, irrespective of the characteristics of any functional dimension of knowledge processes, or of the relevant industry and cluster types. As they cannot provide an independent accurate assessment of the nature of a cluster, such hybrid analyses can easily lead to the adoption of bad public policies.

An advantage of the transactions costs classification scheme is therefore that it provides an organising framework to deal with the diversity of spatial concentrations we observe, a diversity which is often overlooked by many hybrid descriptions of clusters. On the other hand, if our objective is to understand the evolution of these various cluster types in different localities and sectors, then a description of the relations between the actors within the cluster is only part of the solution. It is also necessary to consider issues relating to the nature of knowledge and information. Therefore, a weakness of the transactions-costs framework is that hierarchies (particularly, but not exclusively, firm structures) are viewed and reduced to a consequence of changes in transaction costs, whereas dynamic factors such as learning, accumulation, and knowledge creation are largely ignored. However, this type of transactions costs perspective offers possibilities for including a technical change component as an additional explanation for the diversity of spatial cluster types.

2.3 THE FIRM AND KNOWLEDGE INFLOWS AND OUTFLOWS

In order to begin to understand why particular types of clusters will emerge in particular situations, we must consider the perceived costs and benefits to the individual firm of spatially grouping its activities with those of other potential competitor and collaborator firms. Perceptions of possible benefits deriving from local knowledge and information spillovers are central in understanding firm behaviour vis-à-vis clusters.

We can split knowledge spillovers into two types, namely knowledge inflows and knowledge outflows. Regarding knowledge inflows, we may safely assume that all firms regard knowledge inflows positively. However, unintentional knowledge outflows can have both positive and negative effects on the firm. The private effect of an unintentional knowledge outflow on the owner firm is a leakage of its valuable intellectual capital, and this would always be viewed negatively (Grindley and Teece 1997). On the other hand, the potentially positive effect of an unintentional knowledge outflow is the public good aspect of knowledge (d'Aspremont et al. 1998). This would be important in situations where local knowledge outflows contribute to a virtuous cycle by strengthening the local knowledge base of the location, thereby making it a more attractive location for other knowledge-bearing firms, leading to larger knowledge inflows in the future. This is a classic idealised evolutionary process (McCann and Mudambi 2004, 2005). The firm's view of the net benefits of knowledge spillovers, allowing for both knowledge outflows and knowledge inflows, will therefore depend on its assessment of how these two processes are likely to affect it. Obviously, however, the structure and organisation of an industry will affect the firm's perceptions of knowledge outflows. For example, we can consider the case of a broadly competitive market structure, which is characterised by a large number of firms, each with a relatively small market share and profits. In this case, competitor firms will have less to lose from knowledge outflows and more to gain from inflows stemming from a strong clustered location. In such a situation the public good aspect of local knowledge will predominate and knowledge outflows will be viewed as generally positive (Jaffe et al. 1993; Saxenian 1994). In the transactions costs model of Table 2.1, this combination of features is exhibited by the pure agglomeration type.

In an oligopolistic industry structure, on the other hand, which is characterised by a few large firms, each with a large market share and considerable strategic interdependence, firms often perceive knowledge outflows to industry rivals as extremely costly in terms of lost competitive advantage. The reason is that in these circumstances the private good aspect of knowledge is generally the dominant consideration. In situations where any knowledge outflows from a firm are more valuable to its competitors than are any potential knowledge inflows to the firm from its competitors, firms will perceive the overall net effect of unintended knowledge outflows as being negative (McCann and Mudambi 2004, 2005). This will lead the firm to avoid locating in clusters characterised by pure agglomeration. On the other hand, depending on the transportation costs, the same firms may consider locating in complexes characterised by stable, planned and long-term inter-firm relationships.

This argument provides a powerful counter-argument to Porter's account of industrial clustering. This is because if we apply the Akerlof (1970) market-for-lemons model, industrial clusters that include large oligopolistic competitors will be plagued by adverse selection and should either fail to form, or become concentrations of mediocrity, unless the clustering of firms exhibits the characteristics of an industrial complex as described in Table 2.1. This counter-argument to the Porter logic appears to explain the empirical finding that many of the largest firms do not co-locate their knowledge creation activities with those of their competitive rivals (Cantwell and

Santangelo 1999; Simmie 1998). From this perspective, the only possible reason why such a firm would locate in either a pure agglomeration or a social network cluster would be to facilitate the recruitment of specialist labour. However, oligopolistic firms are often able to hire appropriate specialist labour by simply locating within the same broad regional vicinity as other firms (Cantwell and Iammarino 2003), rather than within the same urban location. The inter-firm spillover arguments implicit in the pure agglomeration and social network models of industrial clustering therefore largely do not apply to oligopolistic multinational or multiplant firms (Arita and McCann 2002, 2004, 2006), unless the firm undergoes almost complete hierarchy fragmentation. Horizontal diversification and decentralisation is presently common among multinational and multiplant oligopolistic firms, but this is quite a different phenomenon from the levels of corporate fragmentation that would be required in order for these firms to benefit from local knowledge and information spillovers.

Similar arguments are also pertinent in the case of the social network model, which is assumed to operate on the basis of 'trust' relations. However, knowledge spillover arguments fail to specify the conditions under which such trust relationships will emerge. Consequently, they remain largely opaque (Iammarino and McCann 2006). If the firms in a cluster are small, then the arguments for pure agglomeration may be largely applicable in the case of the social network, although distinguishing between the two becomes problematic. However, if some of the firms in the cluster are large, then it is not clear how such a social network would evolve.

The development of clusters in general, and also of particular types of clusters, is not an automatic phenomenon. This is because all clusters must possess a certain degree of logic of a form broadly consistent with one of the three transactions costs types. If no such logic exists, then no cluster emerges, while if a particular logic is dominant, then a particular type of cluster will emerge. According to the evolutionary economics view, cluster types are heterogeneous and path dependent (Dopfer et al. 2004; Iammarino 2005). Historical contingency explains the actual existence of selection mechanisms in socio-economic processes, in which change is neither solely based on structural elements subject to general rules, nor purely driven by random effects. At each point in time in a system's evolution, a number of paths are theoretically possible, but only a few will be chosen by actors because each path must conform to the logic of socio-economic dynamics (Schwerin and Werker 2003). As such, clusters can be viewed as acting as a selection mechanism that may provide conditions favourable to meet the new requirements of technical change, that is, the social capabilities for institutional change. Moreover, not only do the characteristics of the selection environment and their changes influence the actors, but the latter also change the environment (Cohen and Levinthal 1990; Lambooy and Boschma 2001). In this evolutionary view, growth opportunities are therefore assumed to be shaped and constrained by path dependency, that is, by the inheritance of local structural characteristics from past knowledge accumulation and learning, and these may often be geographically determined (Boschma 2005).

2.4 AN EXTENDED (PAVITT-BASED) TECHNOLOGICAL CLASSIFICATION OF CLUSTER DIVERSITY

To discuss the evolutionary dynamics of spatial agglomerations, the transactions costs classification elaborated in Table 2.1 can be revised and extended along the lines of the classic Pavitt (1984) taxonomy of the sources of innovation among industry types (Iammarino and McCann 2006). This is presented in Table 2.2. Adapting the Pavitt (1984) taxonomy to the case of cluster taxonomy allows us to identify the main features of the nature of knowledge, technological regimes and industrial and governance structures implied by the three original transactions costs cluster types. Table 2.2 therefore represents an extension of the transactions costs cluster classification presented in Table 2.1, in which the underlying knowledge conditions of the cluster are now made explicit. This allows us to take into account the diverse ways in which firms may interact with the industrial and technological environment, and the multiple linkages between knowledge conditions and economic growth.

In the model of pure agglomeration, where the notion of space is essentially urban, knowledge is explicit and codified. It is available to any actor and organisation, and generally produced by public institutions outside firms' boundaries. Variety and promiscuity are distinctive features of cities. The combination of different streams of knowledge occurs across a broad range of sectors (often termed 'Jacobs externalities') and individual linkages or relations are unpredictable, due to the low degree of cumulativeness. Innovative firms in such settings are often operating in knowledge-intensive business services (Iammarino and McCann 2006).

The industrial complex is associated primarily with cumulative learning from sources inside the industry and the firm, such as in-house R&D, and on the basis of knowledge which is specific to industrial applications. Such environments generally exhibit low entry possibilities and high industry concentration. Large incumbents account for most of the sector's innovative activity. These firms can profit from their innovations in part because they have the potential to exclude rival firms from using the new product and processes they have generated. In these situations, information based on non-transferable experience is an important input in generating innovative activity, and the incumbent firms tend to have the innovative advantage over new firms because innovation is relatively routinised and processed within the existing hierarchical bureaucracies. As such, lead firms play a crucial role and power asymmetry is central to the value chain and the system of innovation governance (Iammarino and McCann 2006). Once the different types of cluster are distinguished in terms of technological regimes, structures and governances, as well as their transactional relations, the social network model appears as a relatively homogenous and consistent analytical category. Thus, we are able to split the single transactions costs social network typology into two subcategories, namely the 'new social network' category and the 'old social network' category (Iammarino and McCann 2006).

In the new social network model, technological opportunities arise mainly from sources outside the firm and the industry sector, such as academic research. In this type of technological environment knowledge tends to be both generic and non-systemic. There also tends to be high rates of market entry and exit, high volatility of market

Characteristics	Pure agglomeration	Industrial complex	Social network	
			New SN	Old SN
Nature of technical knowledge	codified, explicit and mobile, transmitted by way of information	mixed, routinised, R&D-intensive, based on non-transferable experience	tacit, new, sticky and leaky, transmitted within cognitive networks	mixed, mature, incremental, transmitted within localised networks
Technological trajectory	oriented to processes, problem-solving	oriented to complex products, cost-cutting	oriented to radically new products	oriented to processes, customer-driven
Dynamics	stochastic	strategic	mixed	mixed
Sources of innovation	external to the firm	internal to the firm	mixed	external to the firm
Appropriability of innovation returns	low, perfect or monopolistic competition	high, private creation of new knowledge, oligopolistic competition	mixed, public-private creation of new knowledge	low, collaboration and competition
Technological opportunities	medium	low	very high, uncertain	low
Degree of cumulativeness	low	high	low	high
Knowledge base	diversified	specialised	research-based	specialised along filière
Modes of governance	market	hierarchies	relational networks	social and historical networks
Examples of industrial specialisation	finance, banking, insurance, business services, retailing	steel, chemicals, automotive, pharmaceuticals, machine tools, medical instruments, ICT hardware	SME high-tech clusters in general purpose technologies	Customised traditional goods textiles, footwear, furniture, tourism
Example of cluster	'Silicon Valley' (California)	'Silicon Glen' (Scottish Electronics Industry)	'Silicon Fen' (Cambridge UK)	Italian industrial districts (Emilia-Romagna)
Pavitt classification	Supplier dominated firms	Production intensive firms	Science-based firms	Supplier dominated firms

Table 2.2: Industrial clusters: knowledge, technology and innovation dynamics

shares, and a low level of market concentration. In this environment, the tacit and sticky nature of knowledge requires geographical proximity. On the other hand, factors such as the relatively 'leaky' character of new knowledge, the openness of the innovation system, and the related emergence of new rules, standards, blueprints and verification procedures all point to the importance of external sources of technical knowledge, which may not necessarily be localised (Iammarino and McCann 2006). As such, innovation is frequently associated with a high level of uncertainty regarding both technology and demand, as well as a high level of market turbulence. As a consequence, lower survival of new firms is likely to be associated with higher innovativeness and growth of surviving firms (Alchian 1957). Innovations therefore come primarily from non-routinised knowledge, with start-ups playing an important role and small firms accounting for the bulk of innovative activity (Iammarino and McCann 2006).

In the old social network type, there is not necessarily any clear hierarchical structure. The overall coordination of the innovation system relies on a mix of cooperation and competition (Iammarino and McCann 2006). Knowledge is largely codified and mature, and it develops along trajectories that are mainly oriented toward process innovation. Knowledge transmission occurs essentially by way of personal contacts, social and political lobbying, and backward and forward linkages. Moreover, from a geographical perspective the new and old social networks differ fundamentally from one another in terms of the governance and evolution of innovation (Simmie et al. 2004). In the latter case networks are based mostly upon geographical proximity, whereas relational and organisational proximity often form the basis for new social networks. On the other hand, old social networks are also usually rooted in historical experience, whilst new social networks rely on various kinds of communities of practice, which do not necessarily require spatial proximity (Iammarino and McCann 2006).

The classifications presented in Table 2.1 and Table 2.2 offer a structure for interpreting the critical issues of knowledge spillovers and innovation. Indeed, all three categories in Table 2.1 are predicated on the existence of knowledge spillovers and all three categories of Table 2.2 are predicated on the existence of innovation, although the innovation system differs in scope and nature across the cluster typologies. Both our transactions costs-based taxonomy and our new extended technology and knowledge-based classification system identify the distinctive evolutionary characteristics of clusters, and they thereby help to clarify debates and discussions about whether and how knowledge spillovers will occur in a given context.

2.5 FURTHER EMPIRICAL ISSUES

This chapter has argued that in order to understand the relationship between innovation and clustering it is first necessary to correctly identify the types of transactional relationships that predominate in a particular cluster, as well as the sources of innovation. This is because the nature of the activities, the transactions, the operations, the inter-firm relations, and the organisations and institutions specific to a certain socio-economic context are the factors which define the economic geography of space. Thus, the notions of space that emerge from the different cluster types in Tables 2.1 and 2.2 are not clear-cut. Although the pure agglomeration model is essentially urban, both the industrial complex and the social networks models can assume different configurations, from strictly defined localised agglomerations to broad, administrative regional units. However, if classificatory efforts such as our own taxonomies cannot rigorously represent any particular space–innovation structure, it follows that the spatial unit of analysis for any possible policy-making cannot be easily predetermined. This is because the region is not synonymous with cluster, nor with a local labour system, nor with a local innovation system. Regions are administrative and political definitions, whereas clusters and innovation systems are defined by the geography of knowledge spillovers and networks of externalities, the scope of which can vary considerably.

In terms of understanding potential policy roles regarding clusters and innovation, the question then remains, which spatial area defines the economic geography of innovation? The embedded questions that arise here are essentially the following. At what levels of spatial concentration are knowledge spillovers generated? And is there a correct spatial unit of analysis for the operation of innovation systems and the implementation of innovation policy?

Regarding the level of spatial concentration over which knowledge spillovers are generated, the first problem relates to the types of firms which are operating. There is much evidence which suggests that the spatial extent over which informal knowledge is shared between actors can vary between industries and organizations, depending on the firm's technological profile and the nature of its required knowledge and information inputs. A general observation is that larger and more technologically advanced firms typically have critical relationships with customers, suppliers and local inputs which extend over much larger geographical scales than do smaller firms or firms which are less technologically advanced (Arita and McCann 2000; Cantwell and Iammarino 2003; Gordon and McCann 2005a,b). As such, the critical geographical extent of knowledge spillovers may not be independent of the objects of our analysis, and this requires careful analysis of issues of industrial organisation.

The second problem regarding spatial units, and in particular the correct spatial unit of analysis and policy implementation, is a statistical problem. Inter-industry knowledge spillovers and intra-industry spillovers, which are perceived as being the drivers of urbanisation economies based on variety and also localisation economies based on specialisation, are usually proxied by available indicators such as population density, employment intensity, or relative local employment specialisation or diversity. However, these simple measures are themselves often very sensitive to the particular spatial definitions employed. The problem here is that changing the spatial aggregation of the geographical unit of observation, such as from urban centres to metropolitian areas, to local labour systems, to regional systems, to provinces and finally to countries, itself affects the results in terms of the inferred presence or absence of spillovers and the extent of spatial concentration of innovative activities. Similarly, even with the same overall geographical area, changing the actual boundary definition of the sub-regions will also affect the calculated results. In fact, any estimates based on the sub-division of a given spatial area into different sized spatial units will to some extent suffer from the modifiable areal unit problem (Openshaw and Taylor 1979).

Both of these two empirical issues require us to consider carefully the local economic context, and in particular, to identify the types of firms operating locally. Identifying the characteristics of the firms, their transactions, and their relations with other firms will then allow us to make realistic assessments of how the firms will most likely perceive the effects of unintended outward knowledge spillovers. On this basis we can then begin to make predictions regarding the types of local innovation behaviour, and the modes of local innovation generation. These predictions themselves can then help to define the most appropriate spatial scope of analysis.

2.6 CONCLUSIONS

All industrial clusters can be characterised in terms of their transaction costs and relational characteristics, as described in Table 2.1, and also in terms of their technological regimes and knowledge characteristics, as depicted in Table 2.2. Theories of innovation and technical change have taught us that innovators tend to emerge in locations where technological opportunities are the highest. Under conditions of high opportunity, high appropriability and high cumulativeness, innovators will tend to be geographically concentrated, giving rise to emergent clusters. However, the particular form of innovation system that emerges in a particular locality will also depend on the nature of knowledge embodied and exchanged in both the industry and the firms. As such, a careful assessment of industry transactions, relations, and knowledge outflows is essential for understanding cluster–innovation dynamics.

REFERENCES

Acs, Z. (2002), *Innovation and the Growth of Cities*, Cheltenham, UK and Northampton, MA, USA: Edward Elgar.

Akerlof, G.A. (1970), 'The market for lemons: quality uncertainty and the market mechanism', *Quarterly Journal of Economics*, **84**, 488–500.

Alchian, A.A. (1957), 'Uncertainty, evolution and economic theory', *Journal of Political Economy*, **58**, 211–221.

Arita, T. and P. McCann (2000), 'Industrial alliances and firm location behaviour: some evidence from the US semiconductor industry', *Applied Economics*, **32**, 1391–1403.

Arita, T. and P. McCann (2002), 'The spatial and hierarchical organization of Japanese and US multinational semiconductor firms', *Journal of International Management*, **8** (1), 121–139.

Arita, T. and P. McCann (2004), 'Industrial clusters and regional development: a transactions costs perspective on the semiconductor industry', in H.L.F. de Groot, P. Nijkamp, R.R. Stough (eds), *Entrepreneurship and Regional Economic Development: A Spatial Perspective*, Cheltenham, UK and Northampton, MA, USA: Edward Elgar.

Arita, T. and P. McCann (2006), 'Clusters and regional development: some cautionary observations from the semiconductor industry', *Information Economics and*

Policy, **18** (2), 157–180
Autant-Bernard, C., V. Mangematin and N. Massard (2003), 'Creation and growth of high-tech SMEs: the role of the local environment', in J. Leage-Hellman, M. McKelvey, A. Rickne (eds), *The Economic Dynamics of Biotechnology: Europe and Global Trends*, Cheltenham, UK and Northampton, MA, USA: Edward Elgar.
Boschma, R.A. (2005), 'Proximity and innovation: a critical assessment', *Regional Studies*, **39** (1), 61–74.
Breschi, S. and F. Lissoni (2001), 'Knowledge spillovers and local innovation systems: a critical survey', *Industrial and Corporate Change*, **10** (4), 975–1005.
Cantwell, J.A. and S. Iammarino (2003), *Multinational Corporations and European Regional Systems of Innovation*, London and New York: Routledge.
Cantwell, J.A. and G.D. Santangelo (1999). 'The frontier of international technology networks: sourcing abroad the most highly tacit capabilities', *Information Economics and Policy*, **11**, 101–123.
Caves, R.E. (2000), *Creative Industries*, Cambridge MA: Harvard University Press.
Castells, M. and P. Hall (1994), *Technopoles of the World: The Making of the 21st Century Industrial Structures*, London: Routledge.
Cohen, W.M. and D.A. Levinthal (1990), 'Absorptive capacity: New perspective on learning and innovation', *Administrative Science Quarterly*, **35**, 128–152.
d'Aspremont, C., S. Bhattacharya and L.-A. Gerard-Varet (1998), 'Knowledge as a public good: efficient sharing and incentives for development effort', *Journal of Mathematical Economics*, **30** (4), 389–404.
Dopfer, K., J. Foster and J. Potts (2004), 'Micro-meso-macro', *Journal of Evolutionary Economics*, **14**, 263–279.
Florida, R. (2002), *The Rise of the Creative Class*, New York: Basic Books.
Florida, R. (2005a), *The Flight of the Creative Class*, New York: Harper Collins.
Florida, R. (2005b), *Cities and the Creative Class*, New York: Routledge.
Fujita, M., P. Krugman and A.J. Venables (1999), *The Spatial Economy*, Cambridge, MA: MIT Press.
Fujita, M. and J.-F. Thisse (2002), *Economics of Agglomeration*, Cambridge, MA: Cambridge University Press.
Gaspar, J. and E.L. Glaeser (1998), 'Information technology and the future of cities', *Journal of Urban Economics*, **43**, 136–156.
Glaeser, E.L. (1998), 'Are cities dying?', *Journal of Economic Perspectives*, **12** (2), 139–160.
Glaeser, E.L. (2004), *Book review of Richard Florida's 'The Rise of the Creative Class'*, http://post.economics.harvard.edu/faculty/glaeser/papers.html
Glaeser, E.L. and J. Kohlhasse (2004), 'Cities, regions and the decline of transport costs', *Papers in Regional Science*, **83** (1), 197–228.
Glaeser, E.L., H.D. Kallal, J.A. Schinkmann and A. Shleifer (1992), 'Growth in cities', *Journal of Political Economy*, **100**, 1126–1152.
Glaeser, E.L., D.I. Laibson, J. Scheinkman and C.L. Soutter (2000), 'Measuring trust', *Quarterly Journal of Economics*, **115**, 811–46.
Glaeser, E.L., D.I. Laibson and B. Sacerdote (2002), 'An economic approach to social

capital', *Economic Journal*, **112**, 437–58.

Gordon, I.R. and P. McCann (2000), 'Industrial clusters: complexes, agglomeration and/or social networks?' *Urban Studies*, **3**, 513–532.

Gordon, I.R. and P. McCann (2005a), 'Innovation, agglomeration and regional development', *Journal of Economic Geography*, **5** (5), 523–545.

Gordon, I.R. and P. McCann (2005b), 'Clusters, innovation and regional development: an analysis of current theories and evidence', in C. Karlsson, B. Johansson, R. Stough (eds), *Industrial Clusters and Inter-Firm Networks*, Cheltenham, UK and Northampton, MA, USA: Edward Elgar.

Granovetter, M. (1973), 'The strength of weak ties', *American Journal of Sociology*, **78**, 1360–1380.

Grindley, P.C. and D.J. Teece (1997), 'Managing intellectual capital: licensing and cross-licensing in semiconductors and electronics', *California Management Review*, **39** (2), 8–41.

Guerrieri, P., S. Iammarino and C. Pietrobelli (eds) (2001), *The Global Challenge to Industrial Districts. The case of Italy and Taiwan*, Cheltenham, UK and Northampton, MA, USA: Edward Elgar.

Henderson, J.V., A. Kuncoro and M. Turner (1995), 'Industrial development in cities', *Journal of Political Economy*, **103**, 1067–1085.

Hilpert, U. (ed.) (2003), *Regionalisation of globalised innovation. Locations for advanced industrial development and disparities in participation*. London: Routledge.

Iammarino, S. (2005), 'An evolutionary integrated view of regional systems of innovation. Concepts, measures and historical perspectives', *European Planning Studies*, **13** (4), 495–517.

Iammarino, S. and P. McCann (2006), 'The structure and evolution of industrial clusters: transactions, technology and knowledge spillovers', *Research Policy*, **35** (7), 1018–1036.

Isard, W. and R. E. Kuenne (1953), 'The impact of steel upon the greater New York-Philadelphia industrial region', *Review of Economics and Statistics*, **35**, 289–301.

Isard, W., E.W. Schooler and T. Vietorisz (1959), *Industrial Complex Analysis and Regional Development*, New York: John Wiley and Sons.

Jacobs, J. (1960), *The Economy of Cities*, New York: Random House.

Jaffe, A.B., M. Trajtenberg and R. Henderson (1993), 'Geographic localization of knowledge spillovers as evidenced by patent citations', *Quarterly Journal of Economics*, **63**, 3, 577–598.

Krugman, P. (1991), 'Increasing returns and economic geography', *Journal of Political Economy*, **99** (33), 483–499.

Lambooy, J.G. and R.A. Boschma (2001), 'Evolutionary economics and regional policy', *The Annals of Regional Science*, **35**, 113–131.

Marshall, A. (1920), *Principles of Economics*, 8th edition, London: Macmillan.

Martin, P. and G.I.P. Ottaviano (1999), 'Growing locations: industry location on a model of endogenous growth', *European Economic Review*, **43**, 281–302.

McCann, P. (2001), *Urban and Regional Economics*, Oxford: Oxford University Press.

McCann, P. and R. Mudambi (2004), 'The location decision of the multinational enterprise: some theoretical and empirical issues', *Growth & Change*, **35** (4), 491–524.

McCann, P. and R. Mudambi (2005), 'Analytical differences in the economics of geography: the case of the multinational firm', *Environment and Planning A*, **37** (10), 1857–1876.

McCann, P. and S. Shefer (2004), 'Location, agglomeration and infrastructure', *Papers in Regional Science*, **83** (1), 177–196.

McCann, P. and S. Sheppard (2003), 'The rise, fall and rise again of industrial location theory', *Regional Studies*, **37** (6&7), 649–663.

Moses, L.N. (1958), 'Location and the theory of production', *Quarterly Journal of Economics*, **73**, 259–272.

Nelson, R.R. and S.G. Winter (1982), *An Evolutionary Theory of Economic Change*, Cambridge, MA: Harvard University Press.

Openshaw, S. and P.J. Taylor (1979), 'A million or so correlation coefficients: three experiments on the modifiable areal unit problem', in Wrigley, N. (ed.), *Statistical Applications in the Spatial Sciences*, London: Pion.

Pavitt, K. (1984), 'Sectoral patterns of technical change: Towards a taxonomy and a theory', *Research Policy*, **13**, 343–373.

Saxenian, A. (1994), *Regional Advantage. Culture and Competition in Silicon Valley and Route 128*, Cambridge MA & London: Harvard University Press.

Schwerin, J. and C. Werker (2003), 'Learning innovation policy based on historical experience', *Structural Change and Economic Dynamics*, **14**, 385–404.

Scott, A.J. (1988), *New Industrial Spaces*, London: Pion.

Scott, A.J. (2000), *The Cultural Economy of Cities*, London: Sage.

Simmie, J. (1998), 'Reasons for the development of "islands of innovation": evidence from Hertfordshire', *Urban Studies*, **35** (8), 1261–1289.

Simmie, J. and J. Sennet (1999), 'Innovative clusters: theoretical explanations and why size matters', *National Institute Economic Review*, **4/99** (170), 87–98.

Simmie, J., C. Siino, J.M. Zuliani, G. Jalabert and S. Strambach (2004), 'Local innovation system governance and performance: a comparative analysis of Oxfordshire, Stuttgard and Toulouse', *International Journal of Technology Management*, **28** (3–6), 534–559.

Weber, A. (1909/1929), *Theory of the Location of Industries*, trans. .J. Friedrich, Chicago: University of Chicago Press.

Williamson, O.E. (1975), *Markets and Hierarchies*, New York: Free Press.

3. First steps towards a critical appraisal of clusters

André Torre*

3.1 INTRODUCTION

The essential character of the geographical concentrations of populations and economic activities, phenomena of polarized economic development and the spatial concentration of companies has often remained inconceivable for mainstream economists, and for a simple reason: it is impossible to systemically account for the forces of concentration in a model characterized by equilibrating effects, which rules out the possibility of medium-term development of one part of the economy at the expense of another. It was not until Krugman's revolutionary work (1991) that consideration of spatial polarization was finally introduced into the rubric of mainstream economics.

Parallel to this movement in geographical economics (which included endogenous growth theories) path-breaking work by Porter (see, for example, 2000) thrust clusters into the spotlight by stressing how the spatial concentration of innovation and research activities relates to local development processes. Porter's work met with even greater response than Krugman's, since its implications are not confined to economics. Rather they directly apply to the work of policy makers at the local as well as at the national level. Today clusters are the basis of local and even national policies in many countries such as the United Kingdom, Germany, and the Netherlands. For example, in France cluster concepts were the basis of recent reflections about the "Systèmes Locaux de Production" (Local Systems of Production) and the new "Pôles de compétitivité" (Poles of competitiveness). Clusters are also often regarded as important development tools by advocates of a globalized economy (see OECD, 2001 and 2005, World Bank, 2002).

While the contribution of the New Economic Geography is quite easily understandable, Porter's contribution is less clear. At first sight it is rather surprising that the work was so celebrated. In fact, Porter's theses show an astonishing similarity with already established concepts from various branches of spatial and industrial analysis: growth poles, industrial districts, milieux and local production systems on the production side, and technopoles, technological districts and innovating milieux in the

* UMR SAD-APT Agro Paris Tech 16, rue Claude Bernard F. 75231 Paris Cedex 05.

field of innovation all preceded the idea of clusters. That begs the question of whether the concept represents simple tracing, imitation, or a revival of arguments explaining spatial concentration factors and the resulting advantages.

The success of the cluster concept remains a topic of reflection and debate (see Lorentzen, 2005). One can appreciate the belated rediscovery of already well established evidence, especially its application by public policy, but one can also wonder about its conceptual validity and its normative character. In other words, if we already adhere without reservation to the idea that space is polarized, what is the added value of the explanations of this polarization advanced in the cluster approach? And, consequently, how can we evaluate arguments in favour of such concentrations and policies to promote them?

This chapter seeks to question the relevance of the cluster concept by unpacking its theoretical premises and by critically evaluating the concept's efficacy in local economic development policies. The discussion begins with an examination of definitional issues, and then goes on to explore why this loosely defined concept has enjoyed so much popularity. We then clarify the concept's underlying premises regarding knowledge transmission before discussing the disadvantages of cluster-based development policies. The discussion concludes by highlighting the greater explanatory power of more traditional factors for understanding processes that concentrate research and innovation activities.

3.2 ELEMENTS OF DEFINITION

Since Porter (1990, 2000) revived the term "cluster" which had already been employed by Schumpeter, its popularity has soared. The concept is amenable to local development and regional planning specialists, who recognize it as a powerful tool of policy intervention, but the term also causes some consternation to academics, who struggle to agree on its definition.

Indeed, if clusters constitute a new way of qualifying localized structures of innovation activity, it is neither easy to define its precise contents, nor to distinguish them clearly from existent concepts such as innovative milieux, technopoles, technological districts.... Porter's own definition provides little help: a cluster is "... a group of geographically closed firms and associated institutions, interconnected within a particular field and linked by common elements and complementarities". The same could be said regarding most localized agglomerations of firms. Along these lines, Feser (1998) notes, "in spite of the intense interest in industrial clusters in the policies of economic development in Europe and in North America, there is little consensus on the definition that specifies clusters, the dynamics which underlies their growth and their development, as well on the initiatives aiming at forming and reinforcing them". However, the cluster concept continues to grow in popularity and seldom has an economic concept caused such passions, particularly one from the framework of territorial policies.

Initially, the concept of cluster was applied to the so-called success stories, the best-known example of which is Silicon Valley. Within limited geographical space there exist many small, high-tech electronics companies, which are bound together by confidence and commercial relations. This results in an extremely high-performing local network of producers. Technological innovation and high profit rates pervade this system, which is characterized by close relations with external actors such as local public authorities, venture capitalists and business angels. The success of Nokia illustrates another facet of clusters, one which is more directly centred on relationships of technical complementarity and subcontracting at the local level. The Finnish cluster, which was formed around a single leading company in mobile telephony, focuses above all on the exploitation and the development of information and communication technology. This competence is shared by all the local firms and has been nurtured by the authorities via technological policies favouring R&D and the development of human resources. Extremely competitive on an international level, the cluster is based on a localized network connecting Nokia and its equipment suppliers. Similarly, a group of firms of less importance knew how to create niches, particularly in the field of telecommunication, and then to develop a powerful local web of high-tech companies related to the centre of the system.

Soon, the concept of clusters opened up in all directions; towards less high-tech industries, systems with less favourable performance, and local and national economic policy (OECD, 2001 and 2005). From the point of view of development policies, the creation of synergies between local companies is always beneficial insofar as the expeditious circulation of knowledge ensures the proper operation of organized systems. Therefore, any policy seeking to promote inter-firm networks appeared valid because it was thought that enhanced competitiveness was the necessary result. A widespread assumption developed that "local networks" are prima facie superior to other forms of organization. Though admissible as an advertising argument aimed at attracting companies or subsidies to a given location, this simplistic position is obviously not supported from the point of view of the scientific analysis. Other evidence is essential.

3.3 THE REASONS FOR SUCCESS

Why has the cluster concept experienced so much popularity and success in both academic and political spheres? It is certainly not due to the clarity or precision of its definition. Indeed, the concept is characterized by a substantial degree of vagueness and inaccuracy, which has often been pointed out in the literature (see for example Martin and Sunley, 2003, or Taylor, 2005). This vagueness increases proportionately with the number of reformulations proposed. Not only has it proven impossible to assign precise and well-ordered analytical substance to the concept of clusters, but also it has been noticed – as Porter himself seems to recognize – that the substance varies significantly depending on the public authority or decision maker implementing it. Moreover, as the term does not specify a coherent and precisely limited geographic area, studies vary widely in their spacial conception of clusters, from the reach of innovation activities, to districts, and sometimes even regions.

Following Martin and Sunley (2003), it is reasonable to suppose that the success of the cluster concept derives in large part from its deliberately vague character (see however the attempt of Dunning, 2000). This permits the term to correspond to various types of localization as well as adapt easily to a great number of policy circumstances and situational constraints. The successive refashioning of an already soft concept furthermore allows it to keep up with changing trends and thereby remain "marketable". This vagueness – whether desired or inadvertent – constitutes an asset when one tries to popularize policies with trendy and versatile catchwords.

From a scientific point of view it can be argued that the concept of clusters is so successful because it rests on four major theoretical pillars, which, according to the literature on innovation processes and policies, identify numerous performance advantages in localized network formations:

- Cluster theories relate to the concepts of the knowledge economy, or "new economy", and directly address the issue of dissemination of knowledge on the local level, underlining the crucial character of the interactions between the network members. Knowledge does not circulate in the air, as implied by Marshall's argument, but is rather exchanged between agents or groups located within a geographical space through the relations between them. This is particularly true for academic research, whose repercussions seem largely local (Acs, 2000).
- Cluster theories apply the concept of network externalities to the local and inter-company level, which connects the idea of the cluster to the literature on transport and communication infrastructures. The benefit drawn from the cluster formation by any member of the network is directly related to the presence of other members, thereby integrating the participants in a community of shared interests.
- Clusters address the concept of vertical integration. Clusters represent a sort of quasi-integration, which grants individual firms collective market advantages due to the pooling of certain infrastructures and reduced transaction costs between actors using the same production process. Non-commercial inter-firm relations are particularly important in this respect (Karlsson, 2005). Commercial relations, however, are not to be neglected. As performance criteria they have always been at the centre of attention paid to clusters, in particular when clusters were used as development tools.
- Lastly, clusters are also related to processes of globalization insofar as they are not presented as closed, isolated systems, but rather as localized structures for enhancing competitiveness in a global economy. Cluster formations maintain an outward orientation, either through individual agents or through the fact that they are part of larger national development policies. They also act as agents of globalization by profiting from the comparative advantages afforded by localized positive externalities while simultaneously stimulating competition also between companies and institutions searching for new markets.

Furthermore, the literature states that the ability to form a cluster often depends upon the presence of certain local structural conditions. These include in particular the divisibility of the value chain, whereby various firms can best make use of their respective competences, the presence of low transport costs (to ensure the commercialization of the production), the existence of local knowledge-exchange relationships grounded in trust, and the ability of the system to adequately react to market changes (flexibility of the production processes). The presence of these elements is necessary but not sufficient.

3.4 AN UNDERLYING HEROIC THEORETICAL HYPOTHESIS

As we have seen, the cluster concept speaks in one way or another to four venerable literatures within economic and organizational science. This explains much of its popularity with researchers, but it does not really illuminate the analytical underpinnings of the approach nor the subjacent premises on which it rests. These premises are grounded above all in the dynamics of innovation in a knowledge economy. To better understand the nature of clusters, it is necessary to reconsider the theoretical premises underlying this approach and analytically explore the rationale for promoting a particular organization of economic activity. Justifications for clusters rest on a view in which innovation is generated primarily by knowledge transfer through face to face relations. Such a conception of innovation activity requires the co-localization of research and development activities. It thereby justifies the existence of clusters and provides the rationale of promoting them.

The theoretical foundation of this approach can be summarized as follows. The ability to innovate is increasingly tied to one's capacity to produce and adapt knowledge, especially scientific knowledge resulting from public or private research. It is within this context that one can speak of a knowledge economy (Foray, 2000), an economy based primarily on the evolution and rapid renewal of knowledge. However, innovation-related knowledge exhibits a particular characteristic: its imperfect appropriability. While a traditional private good becomes the exclusive property of the person who owns or manufactured it, the same does not apply to knowledge, as its creators have difficulty laying claim to it. This is the case with other (semi)public goods as well: they can be reproduced or imitated. Therefore a system of patents guaranteeing the protection of new knowledge was set up in order to keep innovators from being immediately deprived of the results or benefits of their work.

Nonetheless, the limits of patents are evident. They cannot protect the entire process of innovation because they act ex post and do not necessarily protect all of the constituent knowledge processes. In fact, knowledge's imperfect appropriability (including the case of already existing patents) results in numerous spillover effects, which spread from one innovative firm to other companies of the same sector, or connect alternatively researchers from various organizations. These are the celebrated knowledge spillover effects, which benefit those companies that possess a basis of knowledge compatible with that of the innovators. They also support the development of contemporary economies, which is highlighted for example by the theory of endogenous growth.

So far nothing has been said regarding the spatial scope of these knowledge dissemination processes. They can easily take place between very distant firms, for example by the means of the Internet, telephone, fax, or technical manuals. However, empirical observations show a tendency towards spatial concentration of research and innovation activities. Innovation is disproportionately concentrated in certain areas of a small number of countries, and furthermore within particular and clearly delimited geographical locales, such as technopoles, cities, science parks, and university campuses. The knowledge economy approach attributes this co-localization of research and innovation activities to the knowledge spillovers it engenders. The form of knowledge and the modes by which it diffuses inevitably lead to the agglomeration of those economic actors who want to profit from it. Actors who are too far from the source of knowledge production are assumed to be incapable of reaping its benefits.

The argument in favour of spatial concentration rests on the particular characteristics of knowledge, which can be divided, according to Polanyi (1962), into two distinct but often complementary categories: tacit knowledge and codified knowledge. The latter includes written sources – at least those that are readily accessible in handbooks or publications. It can spread over substantial distances without difficulty, and thus be reproduced or duplicated by people completely unfamiliar with the initial process of its creation.[1] Tacit knowledge, on the other hand, cannot cope with distance. It can only be copied by means of observation, practice, or learning, and since it is encoded in human beings and their daily behaviour it can only be transmitted via face to face contacts. The role of tacit knowledge in the co-localization of research activities and innovative enterprises is clearly evident. It is only within spatially anchored communities that tacit knowledge can really be transmitted and transferred. Hence it is necessary to organize innovation at the local level, to support spatial connections, and to create and promote clusters.

This line of reasoning suffers from an important analytical flaw. The argument is based on the idea that spillover effects occur as a result of the public character of knowledge, that is, the inability of its producers to appropriate it as private. But, it is simultaneously maintained that it is the tacit character of this knowledge (that is, strongly appropriated and not easily transmissible) that produces the need for face to face relations. Thus, there are two contradictory theses, the first of which explains the dissemination of innovations and knowledge, and the second of which incompatibly explains the delimitation of its diffusion to the local level. To take one example, absolute adherence to the tacit knowledge view of diffusion, which relies on face to face relations, would necessarily prohibit any possible diffusion and thereby remove incentives for other innovating firms to co-locate. Nonetheless, it is exactly this argument which is most often advanced in support of policies seeking to promote the polarization of research and innovation activities.

To make the matter clearer, let's return to the logic of the innovation argument. It is said that the presence of tacit knowledge justifies the need for geographical proximity in innovation activities. Indeed, this knowledge is presumably appropriable and not easily transmissible. This would justify the need for face to face relations, and thus for geographical proximity. At the same time, the argument relies on the idea of geographical spillovers, the mechanisms by which knowledge is diffused in space. But why does knowledge spread? Because it is de facto public property that cannot be appropriated. Therefore, it diffuses to other companies, including competitors.

[1] Note that this interpretation goes in the direction of patentability and the attribution of specific property rights to individuals or legal entities.

There are two ways to resolve the logical contradiction between the appropriability of knowledge implied in spillovers and the non-appropriability of tacit knowledge. (1) Either tacit knowledge is appropriable, and consequently there are no localized spillover effects because knowledge cannot be diffused. In this case, companies cannot benefit from each other, whether they are proximate or remote. Tacit knowledge then becomes a regular, private good which is not an object of diffusion processes. We are then left with codified knowledge, for which distance is irrelevant. Therefore it cannot be used to justify the need for geographical proximity. (2) The other resolution is to view knowledge (tacit and codified) as a non-appropriable good. In this case it can diffuse regardless of the distance involved. Thus, either we adhere to the hypothesis of tacit "knowledge", which means sacrificing the idea of spillovers, or we preserve the hypothesis of non-appropriable knowledge. In the first case, we get knowledge goods, exchanged on markets like traditional goods, and which are not externalities any longer. In the second case we forget about tacit knowledge, which is in contradiction to non-appropriability, and admit that knowledge diffuses irrespective of distance.

3.5 DISADVANTAGES OF CLUSTERS, OR THE NEGATIVE EFFECTS OF GEOGRAPHICAL PROXIMITY

To continue our evaluation of clusters, we will now critically analyse the empirical phenomenon and policies promoting them. Clusters do in fact exist, and they possess many of the advantages often cited in the literature or in policy documents. On the other hand, reference is rarely made to potential disadvantages of spatial agglomerations of firms, particularly firms involved with innovation processes.

Proper evaluation of cluster policies should take into account the negative dimensions of geographical proximity. This concern is largely neglected in the literature with the exception of works such as Boschma (2005) or Torre and Rallet (2005), who show that combining various forms of proximity creates disadvantages. If we concentrate only on geographical proximity and its connection to clusters, it appears that high concentrations of innovative firms will likely give rise to various problems. These problems, which may undermine cluster policies aimed at promoting knowledge transfer, can be subsumed under three categories.

First, there are difficulties associated with opportunistic behaviour within a local system of innovation. Above, we examined arguments that suggest (a) proximity leads to diffusion of innovations and knowledge at the local level, and (b) that this diffusion promotes development of the system as a whole. However, it is important to note that the opposite result is always possible. Indeed, and as the business intelligence literature shows, geographical proximity between competitors can adversely impact firms that develop top-level innovations. This is particularly true for clusters where similar activities take place, that is, clusters dedicated to a single industrial activity and its derivatives, or when firms with complementary activities related to the same production network are co-located. In this case, knowledge leaks, industrial espionage, and poaching of specialist employees are all facilitated by close proximity. These practices, which are extremely common within technopoles, for example, do not enhance the local system. They endanger the effort of innovation and threaten the expected benefits. They may discourage firms from seeking to innovate, or lead them to relocate to more favourable areas.

Secondly, there is the risk that the system will fall prey to negative lock-in. Although the process of spatial lock-in has often been praised, this feedback mechanism can also induce a regressive spiral. Two negative scenarios are possible. The first is connected to the rigidity of the productive trajectories, which occurs when a formation is more attuned to its internal rules and processes than to external demands and conditions. Thus we note the existence of local systems which are plagued by excessive specialization or trapped in mono-activity. This makes them vulnerable to changes in the competitive situation and product-cycle hazards. This inability to adopt to new innovations is responsible for the death of "mature" clusters, an ironic fate for formations intending to be innovative. The second scenario involves the development of exclusivity. This risk, which tends to affect "small" clusters, leads the cluster to shun new entrants (either companies or scientists) and thus hampers the renewal of human capital.

Lastly, as Bathelt et al. (2004) underline, it is quite possible that the internal bonds between cluster members are only marginally favourable to the transfer of knowledge or innovation. In fact, as these authors note, the dynamic clusters run a risk of routinizing or banalizing internal relations while emphasising exchanges with the outside. In this case, the local relations often rest on weak ties. The firms, who share a common knowledge base, confine their interactions to the execution of routine tasks. This level of weak exchange (or local buzz) may favour the cohesion of the system, but is not a sufficient basis on which to build meaningful synergies in innovation and research. On the contrary, exchanges with the external, distant actors (or global pipeline) can turn out much more advantageous for innovation policy since they act as conduits for introducing radical innovations from afar. On this level there are the strong ties between organizations with different competences.

3.6 RETURN TO THE CONCEPT OF CLUSTER

In light of the foregoing discussion, it will be useful to briefly return to the concept of "the cluster" and its multitudinous meanings. In fact, the term "cluster" often leads to confusion because it relies on expansive definitions. In order to impart some structure into this vagueness, we propose unpacking the definition of cluster into its two basic dimensions. The objective here is to take the cluster approach seriously while imparting some needed coherence. The two basic, irreducible analytical components of the cluster concept are: (1) the relations between productive agents are localized; (2) they are organized. From this postulate, we can build a table (adapted from Feser, 1998), which seeks to identify the various forms of clusters encompassed by Porter's original concept, and to exclude other types of local organizational models from this definition.

		Organization of the inter-firm relations	
		Strong	Weak
Localization of inter-firm relations	Strong	1. Cluster à la Porter	3. Cluster tied to a resource or to local history
	Weak	2. Cluster without definite local base	4. Sparse activities

Table 3.1: Where are the clusters today?

Box 1 represents the conception of clusters outlined by Porter, since it simultaneously combines high degrees of localization and organization with the existence of what could be called geographical and organized proximities (see below). Box 2, characterized by strong inter-firm relations but weak local embeddedness, corresponds to the definition of an industry cluster analysed at the national or regional level. Box 3, which associates weak internal local bonds with a strong spatial concentration of firms, includes many production systems that fall outside the realm of Porter's initial conception. But it is in fact members of this group which are most often targeted by innovation policies seeking to create synergies at the local level. Certain poles of competitiveness are found in this category. The same applies to "clusters" identified in various emerging markets. Cases falling within Box 4 are of little interest since this category does not integrate either of the two components of the cluster concept.

This categorization highlights all the difficulties involved in the analysis of clusters. In the canonical definition they should correspond only to box 1, but it is clear that today the definition often also extends to boxes 2 and 3. Moreover, we should not neglect the fact that clusters sometimes follow a dynamic life-cycle, which leads them from their formation to maturity through successive stages reflecting transformations in the internal organization of production and innovation. Following the OECD, we can imagine that burgeoning clusters focus on establishing relations between local actors and formulating network practices aimed at enhancing the production of incremental innovations. Only later will companies develop complementary activities and participate in collective training in the context of the production of strongly conceptualized innovations. In all cases, the normative dimension that today is connected with the concept of clusters forces us to identify different categories and to identify stages of growth and modes of evolution.

3.7 TOWARDS AN ANALYSIS OF CLUSTERS BY RETURNING TO THE FUNDAMENTALS OF ECONOMICS

It is evident that the precise definition and the demarcation of clusters pose problems and that they remain largely irreducible in an analytical approach, irrespective of whether they are the conditions of knowledge circulation, the delimitation of geographical borders or the type of relevant technologies. Although it is quite difficult to deny the concentration of laboratories and innovating companies in the same geographical areas, and even the existence of numerous clusters, it is possible that the latter are simply a consequence of policies aimed at their creation. In other words, the spatial concentration of innovation and research activities in specific areas is an irrefutable fact. But from a theoretical point of view we continue to lack valid explanations.

Clusters do exist, their number is on the rise, and cluster related policies continue to gain ever more importance. What are the reasons for such a success? It is important to provide an explanation for the existence of clusters and for their success. Such an explanation should not limit itself to policy-relevant cases, but should go further to uncover the economic and social conditions necessary for the generation and the reproduction of innovations. If such an analytical perspective is adopted, then it appears that the bases of clusters rest on three factors typical of more traditional economic analysis.

- First, economic relations are embedded in social networks, and the latter often have strong territorial bases. From this perspective, localized networks of innovation are not attributable to the functional necessity of face to face contacts in order to exchange knowledge. Rather, they exist because co-operation is established between researchers or engineers who belong to different organizations but have graduated from the same university or belong to the same social or family network (Grossetti and Bes, 2001). Geographical proximity is more an economic cause of spatial agglomeration than a social effect deduced from the embedding of economic relations in inter-individual relations. In other words, it is not enough to put two agents face to face within the same space to obtain synergies; it is also necessary that they belong to the same network or share common frameworks. Moreover, it is clear that the passage of time and the history of the localized system largely condition the success of local interactive processes.
- Second, the geographical framework of economic interactions is largely conditioned by the interplay of institutions. However, today geographical proximity seems to be a powerful factor for legitimizing these institutions (self-valorization of the local). Thus local development policies institutionally produce geographical proximity as a privileged mode of economic interaction. The quest for synergies between local actors has become the basis of most local development policies. Evidence for this can be found in the proliferation of technopoles, technological parks or poles of competitiveness, which are created with large public subsidies. Such programs often lead to a co-localization of the agents without accompanying synergy effects. In fact, recent investigations of inter-firm co-operation show that firms tend to cooperate with organizations not located in the same area (Freel, 2003; Tether, 2002), and that proximate interactions are relatively weak.
- Third we must be aware that very often traditional economic factors can explain the success of local agglomerations, even in the absence of any strong synergies

(see Gordon and Mc Cann, 2005). We will mention just three of them. The first rests on attractive real estate prices: often real estate prices are kept artificially low by public authorities in order to attract companies or research laboratories. The second factor is the set of financial and fiscal advantages (tax rebates, temporary or full tax relief, tax exemptions etc.) offered by local communities in order to attract firms. A third factor that should not be neglected is the argument about local labour markets, as put forward by the New Geographical Economy (Krugman, 1991). It is obvious that companies seek the proximity of firms working in the same field (or in related sectors) in order to access the pool of skilled local labour. This point is particularly applicable to the case of most qualified engineers and star scientists.

3.8 CONCLUSION

This work has sought to reconsider the definition of clusters and to contribute some insights regarding the reasons for their popularity amongst academics and policy makers. After having cast a critical eye on the theoretical bases and policy applications of the cluster concept, the conclusion drawn from this analysis is that the existence and popularity of clusters stem from three essential factors, none of which have anything to do with the transmission of innovations. The first factor is the embedding of economic relations in highly localized social networks. The second is the role played by institutions in constituting a particular spatial framework of economic interaction. Last is the localized attraction of certain places that offer favourable land prices, taxation or local labour markets.

Nonetheless, the fact that cluster concepts reflect the organized character of innovation at the local level and imply policies to enhance this organization means that their success is not due to chance. Supported by public initiatives such as the stipulation of standards, support for start-up companies, R&D or technology transfer, and innovation policies, clusters can be regarded as a driving force of regional and even national systems of innovation. Given this result we should ask the following. Aren't clusters most useful as tools of public policy, where these local systems reveal their full potential and show their real usefulness? Shouldn't the primary interest in clusters be in their operational character? This is what the success of cluster-based policies suggests.

REFERENCES

Acs, Z. (2002), *Innovation and the Growth of Cities*, Cheltenham, UK, and Northampton, MA, USA: Edward Elgar.

Bathelt, H., A. Malmberg and P. Maskell (2004), 'Clusters and knowledge: local buzz, global pipelines and the process of knowledge creation', *Progress in Human Geography*, **28** (1), 31–56.

Boschma, R.A. (2005), 'Proximity and innovation: a critical assessment', *Regional Studies*, **39** (1), 61–74.

Dunning, J. (2000), *Regions, Globalization and the Knowledge-Based Economy*, Oxford: Oxford University Press.

Feser, E.J. (1998), 'Old and new theories of industry clusters', in Steiner, M. (ed.), *Clusters and Regional Specialisation*, London: Pion Ltd.

Foray, D. (2000), *L'Économie de la connaissance, Repères*, Paris: La Découverte.

Freel, M. (2003), 'Sectoral pattern of small firms innovation, networking and proximity', *Research Policy*, **32**, 1–20.

Gordon, I. and P. McCann (2005), *Clusters, innovation and regional development*, mimeo, London: London School of Economics.

Grossetti, M. and M.P. Bes (2001), 'Encastrements et découplages dans les relations science-industrie', *Revue Française de Sociologie*, **42** (2), 327–355.

Karlsson, C., B. Johansson and R. Stough (eds) (2005), *Industrial Clusters and Inter-Firm Networks*, Cheltenham, UK, and Nothampton, MA, USA: Edward Elgar.

Krugman, P. (1991), 'Increasing returns and economic geography', *Journal of Political Economy*, **99** (3), 483–499.

Lorenzen, M. (ed.) (2005), 'Clusters and change: endogenous and exogenous influence on regional growth dynamics', *European Urban and Regional Studies*, special issue.

Martin, R. and P. Sunley (2003), 'Deconstructing clusters: chaotic concept or political panacea?', *Journal of Economic Geography*, **3** (1), 5–35.

OECD (2001), *Innovative Clusters, Drivers of National Innovation Systems*, Paris: OECD.

OECD (2005), *Business Clusters, Promoting Enterprise in Central and Eastern Europe*, Paris: OECD.

Polanyi, M. (1962), *Personal Knowledge: Toward a Post-critical Philosophy*, London: Routledge and Kegan.

Porter, M. (1990), *The Competitive Advantage of Nations*, New York: The Free Press.

Porter, M. (2000), 'Locations, clusters and company strategy', in Clark, G., M. Feldman, M. Gertler (eds), *The Oxford Handbook of Economic Geography*, Oxford: Oxford University Press.

Taylor, M. (2005), 'Clusters: the mesmerizing mantra', communication at the colloquium *Regional Growth Agendas*, 28–31 May, Aalborg, Denmark.

Tether, B.S. (2002), 'Who co-operates for innovation, and why? an empirical analysis', *Research Policy*, **31**, 947–996.

Torre, A. and A. Rallet (2005), 'Proximity and localization', *Regional Studies*, **39**, 47–60.

World Bank (2002), http:/www.worldbank.org/poverty/scapital/whatso.htm

4. A network based approach towards industry clustering

Juan C. Duque*[*] and Sergio J. Rey[‡]

4.1 INTRODUCTION

Industry cluster identification has become an important research topic in regional science, partly as a response to the growing demand by policymakers for analytical tools that provide a better understanding of a regional economy. While there is generally wide agreement that industrial clusters are important for economic development programs, there is much less consensus on how a region's industrial clusters should be identified. Three sequential questions must be answered in order to carry out an industry cluster analysis: First, which cluster typology do we want to identify? Secondly, what information source will be used to obtain the measurement variable? And thirdly, what is the appropriate methodological approach? These questions have been answered in different ways by different researchers and policy analysts, resulting in a great deal of variation in the implementation of cluster identification methods in practice.[1]

The main objective of this paper is to provide a detailed description of a new approach to identify industry clusters and interindustry networks, based on input-output tables. The goal is to outline an efficient algorithm using readily available data so that the method can be replicated in any region, thereby allowing for comparative studies of industrial clusters over space and time.

This new method draws on concepts from network analysis theory. It can be divided into two main blocks: data reduction and network partitioning. Data reduction begins by representing industries and products/services flows as a directed graph, where the links are represented as arrows indicating the direction of the flows. Based on several assumptions about how industries are related into a supply chain, the initial graph is then converted into an undirected graph by transforming products/services flows into relative weights. The second reduction is formulated as a minimization

[*] Regional Analysis Laboratory (REGAL), San Diego State University.

[‡] Regional Analysis Laboratory (REGAL), San Diego State University and Regional Economics Applications Laboratory (REAL), University of Illinois.

[1] For overviews on regional cluster research see Steiner, 1998; Bergman and Feser, 1999.

problem, resulting in a minimum spanning tree (MST) for a subset of the initial graph edges. The final clusters are obtained by selectively deleting edges in the MST, such that each cluster contains a core industry.

The paper is organized as follows. Section 4.2 provides a general description of different typologies of industry clusters. Section 4.3 contains a detailed explanation of the implemented methodology for clustering identification. Section 4.4 presents the results of applying this methodology using input-output tables for San Diego County in 2002. Final comments are provided in Section 4.5.

4.2 CLUSTER DEFINITION

4.2.1 Cluster typology

There are many different ways to define an industry cluster. A broad and oft-cited definition of industry clusters comes from Porter (1990):

> "a cluster consists of industries linked through vertical (buyer-supplier) or horizontal (common customers, technology, channels) relationships"
>
> *Porter (1990, p. 149)*

Several variants have emerged from this core idea, each of which pays special attention to specific industry characteristics. This gives rise to different cluster typologies. A brief description of some of the most representative cluster typologies follows:

Regional industry clusters

In this typology, the spatial location of industries is an important characteristic. According to Bergman and Feser (1999), regional clusters are "cluster[s] whose elements share a common regional location, where region is defined as a metropolitan area, labor market, or other functional economic unit."

Functional clusters

In this case, what matters is what companies produce. Thus, companies producing or offering similar products or services belong to the same clusters. The US Census Bureau has adopted this concept in order to define the North American Industry Classification System (NAICS).

Value-added industry clusters

This typology focuses on products/services flows through companies, rather than location or activity. According to Czamanski (1971), an industry cluster is "a subset of industries of the economy connected by flows of goods and services stronger than those linking them to the other sectors of the national economy."

The methodology proposed in this paper focuses on identifying industry clusters. From this perspective, industries will tend to occupy a common cluster in cases where there is a high transaction flow between them. Variables such as geographical location and main activity can then be used *a posteriori* in order to characterize the clusters.

4.2.2 Measurement variable

Since interindustry transactions are the main component of the cluster typology we utilize, our methodology relies on a regional input-output model.

An input-output model portrays each industry's interactions with the regional economy as a linear equation:

$$X_i = \sum_{i=1}^{n} z_{i,j} + \sum_{l=1}^{m} y_{i,l} \tag{4.1}$$

where X_i is total gross output (in monetary values) for sector i, $z_{i,j}$ is interindustry deliveries to sector j by sector i, and $y_{i,l}$ is delivery to final demand component l by sector i. This equation provides a detailed accounting of the distribution of an industry's output. At the same time, a second identity describes the industry's input (that is, purchasing) structure:

$$X_j = \sum_{i=1}^{n} z_{i,j} + VA_j \tag{4.2}$$

where *VA* is industry value added, which typically consists of labor compensation, indirect business taxes, and profits. For each industry in the economy $i = 1, 2, \cdots, n$, equations 4.1 and 4.2 are equal, hence input equals output for all industries. Combining all these equations, we can represent the system as:

$$X = Z\tau + Y \tag{4.3}$$

where X is a $nx1$ vector of gross industry outputs, Z is an nxn interindustry flow matrix, τ is a $nx1$ vector of ones, and Y is an $nx1$ vector of final demands. From the perspective of industry cluster analysis, the matrix Z provides a detailed description of the interindustry linkages that exist in the economy. As such, the identification methods suggested in the literature focus on extracting information from Z to define groups of industries that constitute clusters. The manipulation of the flow matrix differs, however, across the various cluster design methodologies.

4.2.3 Three approaches for exploring Z

Since the early seventies input-output tables (I/O tables) have become an important instrument for identifying industry clusters (Streit, 1969; Czamanski, 1971; Roepke et al., 1974). This section provides a brief description of three of the most general methodological approaches. The commonality among these three methodologies is that they all extract core information from the intricate structure of interindustry relationships (Z).

Principal components and factor analysis

The basic objectives of the "principal components" methods are data reduction and interpretation. The first objective reflects the potentially large amount of redundant information on interindustry relationships contained in a regional input-output table. To deal with this prospect, the original transaction matrix is manipulated to generate a set of "components" that summarize the main structure of the interindustry flows, while minimizing the redundancy of the information contained in each component.

Once the components are identified, the second objective, interpretation of the components, is addressed. Each component forms the basis for a cluster. The assignment of individual industries to the appropriate cluster is carried out according to a particular decision rule. In some instances, the principal components analysis is extended into a factor analysis. The extension creates a new set of components from the original components, manipulating the latter in order to simplify the assignment of industries to clusters. In what follows we label these approaches as principal components factor analysis (PCFA).

One advantage of PCFA is that it allows one to identify relationships that otherwise are not visible in the transactions matrix. This is particularly attractive when considering large transaction matrices for which a visual inspection of direct linkages is virtually impossible. Slater (1977) and Latham (1976) have argued, however, that PCFA tends to produce groupings of industries that have similar input and sales profiles, rather than clusters of industries with strong internal linkages. In other words, these methods tend to stress complementary linkages rather than vertical (forward and backward) linkages. Moreover, Latham (1976) and Harrigan (1982) have also criticized principal components because it fails to identify and include the industry that is the source of the complementarity for a cluster.

ÓhUallacháin (1984) suggests that these criticisms are somewhat misplaced. With regard to principal component's focus on complementary rather than vertical linkages, ÓhUallacháin (1984) argues that this should be seen as a strength rather than a limitation of the approach, since existing methods failed to identify complementary linkages. Furthermore, it is fairly straightforward to extend principal components to identify the sources of the commonalities for specific clusters.

Multivariate statistical clustering

The main idea behind multivariate clustering (MVC) methods is to group together a set of objects for which measurements on a number of variables (characteristics) are available, such that the members of a cluster are similar to each other but distinct from those objects outside the cluster. There are a wide number of algorithms that have been suggested in the literature, but they all essentially share the same characteristics: [a] an objective function that specifies the criterion used to form the groups; and [b] a measure of similarity (or dissimilarity) between the objects under consideration.

Two general classes of clustering algorithms exist. The first class is known as partitioning methods. These algorithms divide the dataset into k clusters, where the value of k is specified by the user. Objects are assigned to one of the k clusters according to some objective function. The second set of clustering algorithms is hierarchical. These algorithms yield an entire hierarchy of clusters from the original objects in the data set. There are two subclasses of hierarchical algorithms. Agglomerative methods start with n objects or clusters and proceed in an iterative fashion by combining the two most similar clusters into a new aggregate cluster. This process continues until ultimately all the original objects belong to a single cluster. The second subset are divisive hierarchical methods, which work in the opposite direction. Here a single aggregate cluster is decomposed beginning with the subdivision of the cluster into two groups with maximum dissimilarity. The process is repeated for each of the derived subgroups until there are n clusters remaining.

The results of the application of a clustering algorithm can be conveniently summarized in a dendrogram, which is a two-dimensional tree graph displaying the outcome of the sequential clustering process. This allows the analyst to view the nesting of different sub-clusters within aggregate clusters, providing important insights into the overall inter-relatedness of the different clusters. This is a distinct advantage over the other multivariate cluster methods, the outcome of which is a set of mutually exclusive (and possibly exhaustive) clusters.

The use of multivariate clustering for the identification of industry clusters has been rather limited. Blin and Cohen (1977) apply a hierarchical clustering algorithm to an 83 sector US I/O table, however they were interested in questions related to aggregation errors in I/O analysis, rather than the question of identifying industry clusters per se.

Bergman et al. (1996) correctly point out that statistical cluster analysis yields mutually exclusive groups of industries. They suggest, however, that while this aids interpretation, it is unrealistic in the context of regional industry cluster analysis since industries tend to belong to multiple clusters due to the complexity of interindustry linkages. Nonetheless, retaining the full set of analytical results allows one to gain important into the relationship between clusters. This is one advantage of MVC over PCFA.

Network analysis

The final class of cluster identification methods derives from the field of graph theory. In a series of papers, Campbell (1972, 1975) proposes applying a number of graph theoretic concepts to the study of interindustry relationships at the regional scale. Applied to interindustry analysis, a graph is defined as a set of nodes (industries) that are connected by edges (flows of products/services). In a directed graph, a distinction is made between forward and backward linkages, while in an undirected graph representation, no such distinction is made. Graph theory offers a wealth of measures to analyse the structure of an interindustry economy, whether the linkages are portrayed as a directed or as an undirected graph.

Unfortunately, graph theoretic concepts have only been extended to cluster identification in one study. Since this methodological approach can be approached as a complex combinatorial problem, the challenge has been to find time-efficient algorithmic solutions. Network analysis is an interesting methodological approach given that the final solution can provide clear information about how industries are related within each cluster. Also, graph theory provides a wide variety of visualization tools that are useful for better understanding the cluster dynamics.

4.3 METHODOLOGY

This section presents a new method for identifying industry clusters. It draws on network analysis theory and relies on regional I/O tables as the data source.

4.3.1 Overview

The methodology can be divided into two main components, data reduction and network partitioning. Data reduction starts by representing industries and products or services flows as a directed graph, with arrows indicating the direction of flows.

Based on several assumptions about how industries are related within a supply chain, the initial graph is converted to an undirected graph by transforming products/services flows into relative weights. These weights can be used to measure the importance of each link in the network.

Next, threshold points are defined in order to delete weak links. There is not a unique threshold point. Rather, each industry has a specific threshold point based on its relationships with other industries.

The second reduction is more intensive. In this step, a subset of the most important links in the graph are identified. This subset has to satisfy three important conditions: first, the number of links must be equal to the number of industries minus one; second, these links must connect all the industries into a single cluster; and third, this subset must represent the optimal solution for a given objective function. The model is formulated as a minimization problem, such that the final graphical representation conforms to what is known in graph theory as a Minimum Spanning Tree (MST).

Deleting a link from the MST implies breaking the connected network into two disconnected sub-networks (clusters).[2] This process shapes the second portion of this methodology, the network partitioning.

The first step in network partitioning involves selecting a subset of industries that play an important roll in the economy. These "core industries" are chosen by ranking all industries according to three different criteria: transaction volume, adjusted transaction volume and market power. This step is also useful in order to identify the appropriate number of clusters.

Finally, when the subset of core industries has been fixed, the MST is broken into disconnected clusters (sub-networks) such that each cluster contains one core industry.

Given this general overview, we now turn to a more detailed description of each step in the methodology.

---

[2]This type of graph is known as a "Forest", which is a vertex-disjoint union of trees that results from deleting links from a spanning tree.

Decile	Transaction volume (in per cent)
10th	97.88
20th	99.60
30th	99.90
40th	99.97
50th	99.99
60th	100.00

Table 4.1: Analysis of transaction volume by decile

Reduction

Given an interindustry transaction matrix $Z_{n,n}$, where index n is the number of industries, and elements $z_{i,j}$, represent sales from industry i to j (with $i, j = 1, 2, \cdots, n$), it is possible to represent this information in a directed network where each node represents an industry, and links represent transactions between industries. A complete representation of interindustry transactions can generate a highly intricate network, with a huge number of interindustry links. But empirical evidence shows that a significant portion of the interindustry transactions occur within a small subset of links. Table 4.1 presents the distribution of transactions across deciles of links for the San Diego Economy. As shown in the table, 10 per cent of the links account for 97.88 per cent of all the interindustry transactions.

The reduction process sequentially reduces the information of the I/O table, until only the most important information remains. In order to carry this simplification, it is necessary to make some assumptions regarding the characteristics of interindustry relationships. These assumptions are described below, along with descriptive statistics confirming that the data satisfy these assumptions.

> ***Assumption 1: in a supply chain the products/services flow in one direction.***
> *Given two industries i and j, and transactions $z_{i,j}$ and $z_{j,i}$, there exists a dominant transaction such that $z_{i,j} >> z_{j,i}$ if i supplies j or $z_{j,i} >> z_{i,j}$ if j supplies i.*

Table 4.2 shows the relative difference between opposite flows (RFD) estimates as follows:

$$\text{RFD}_{i,j} = \frac{abs(z_{i,j} - z_{j,i})}{z_{i,j} + z_{j,i}} \tag{4.4}$$

The results indicate large differences between opposite flows. In fact, 72.2 per cent of the RFD values are between 90 per cent and 100 per cent.

Given the satisfaction of this assumption it is possible to simplify Z by taking into account only the dominant transaction flow in each industry dyad. So, we apply the following transformation: $Z_{i,j} = \max(Z_{i,j}, Z_{j,i})$.

Relative difference (in per cent)	Industries (in per cent)
0–10	2.10
10–20	2.10
20–30	2.20
30–40	2.30
40–50	2.50
50–60	2.80
60–70	3.30
70–80	4.20
80–90	6.40
90–100	72.20

Table 4.2: RFD distributions

At this point, two industries, i and j, are connected by a link representing a transaction between i and j, or *vice versa*. This transaction has differing relative weight for i and j. Thus, transaction $z_{i,j}$, which represents the output of industry i directed to industry j, has relative weight $RW_{i,j}^{out}$ measured as the ratio between $z_{i,j}$ and i's output for all other industries:

$$RW_{i,j}^{out} = \frac{z_{i,j}}{\sum_{j=1}^{n} z_{i,j}} \tag{4.5}$$

At the same time, $z_{i,j}$ represents an input for industry j, with relative weight $RW_{i,j}^{inp}$ equal to:

$$RW_{i,j}^{inp} = \frac{z_{i,j}}{\sum_{i=1}^{n} z_{i,j}} \tag{4.6}$$

where, $0 \leq RW_{i,j}^{out}, RW_{i,j}^{inp} \leq 1$ and $\sum_{j=1}^{n} RW_{i,j}^{out} = 1$, $\sum_{i=1}^{n} RW_{i,j}^{inp} = 1$.

Then, for each transaction (link) there are two values measuring its relative weight, $RW_{i,j}^{out}$,$RW_{i,j}^{inp}$. These two values can be understood as a weight range of $z_{i,j}$. Since the main objective of this reduction process is to identify the most important links, the second assumption defines the relative weight as the maximum relative weight reached by $z_{i,j}$ ($MRW_{i,j}$).

> ***Assumption 2: maximum relative weight.***
> *The maximum relative weight reached by $z_{i,j}$ ($MRW_{i,j}$), is equal to $max(RW_{i,j}^{out}, RW_{i,j}^{inp})$*

This assumption makes it possible to introduce two additional simplifications in the graphical representation:

1. Directed links representing transactions between industries can be transformed into undirected links weighted as $MRW_{i,j}$

2. Those links with MRW lower than a threshold point can be excluded from the analysis. This threshold can be different for each industry. Thus, the threshold point for industry i (TP_i) is equal to the average MRW of all links involving industry i (L_i).

$$TP_i = \frac{\sum_j MRW_{i,j}}{L_i} \tag{4.7}$$

   The decision rule in order to delete weak links is: delete link (i, j) iff $TP_i \geq MRW_{i,j} \leq TP_j$. Otherwise, keep the link.[3]

   Another reduction then occurs after this first filtering process. The idea now is to bring the current network to its maximal reduction level, without generating a disconnected network.

3. Spanning tree: given a connected, undirected network $(G(V, E), \omega : E)$, a spanning tree is a sub-network that connects all the nodes together. This sub-network must contain $(n - 1)$ links.

According to the description above, a network can have many possible spanning trees. Link weights $(\omega : E)$ can be used in order to formulate a function that helps us to choose the most appropriate spanning tree.

In our industry cluster problem this function can be formulated as the sum of the weight of the links in the spanning tree. Given that the greater weight $(MRW_{i,j})$ indicates a stronger link, the optimal spanning tree will be the one with a total weight greater than or equal to every other feasible solution. This solution is known in the literature as the maximum spanning tree.

Since $0 \leq MRW_{i,j} \leq 1$, it is possible to estimate its dual value as $MRW'_{i,j} = 1 - MRW_{i,j}\ \forall i, j$. Thus, the maximum spanning tree using $MRW_{i,j}$ is equal to the minimum spanning tree using $MRW'_{i,j}$. This transformation does not imply any change in the final solution, but it does make it possible to apply one of the most popular algorithms for solving this kind of combinatorial problems: Kruskal's Algorithm (Procedure 4.1).[4]

Kruskal's Algorithm requires $O(m \log(n))$ time, where m is the number of links and n the number of nodes. This gives more sense to the filtering procedure using threshold points.

An important property of the spanning trees is that the elimination of one link at a time implies the partition of the network into disconnected sub-networks (forest). Thus, in order to design k industry clusters, it is necessary to delete $(k - 1)$ links from the minimum spanning tree. But which links to eliminate? This leads to the second part of the industry clusters definition, the partition process.

[3]This initial reduction should not lead to any disconnected network. If this happens, it is necessary to decrease the value of L_i until no disconnection occurs.

[4]Although it is possible to formulate the algorithm as a maximization problem, we preferred to retain Kruskal's original formulation.

Procedure 4.1: KRUSKAL'S ALGORITHM $(G(V,E),\omega : E)$

comment: Compute the minimum spanning tree (T)

$T \leftarrow \phi$
$E1 \leftarrow E[G]$
while $|T| \leq (|V[G]| - 1)$
do
- From $E1$ select an edge (i,j) with minimum value w
- $E1 \leftarrow E1 - \{(i,j)\}$
- **if** $V(i)$ and $V(j)$ do not belong in the same tree
  then unite the trees $V(i)$ and $V(j)$ into a single tree $T \leftarrow T \bigcup \{(i,j)\}$

return (T)

Partition

Since the current objective function minimizes the total weight, the elimination of $(k-1)$ links with the highest weights appears as the best alternative for cluster design. The downside is that this approach tends to generate singleton clusters, which are clusters with only a single industry. These run counter to the main objective of regional cluster analysis and are therefore problematic. To avoid singletons we base the partitioning process on the following criterion: *An economically representative cluster must contain at least one industry that plays an important role in the supply chain. These industries are called "core industries."* The next section presents the procedure to identify these industries based on the available information about transaction flows.

Core industries Several factors can be used to determine whether an industry qualifies as a "core industry." We utilize three different factors: *transaction volume*, as a measure of size; *adjusted transaction volume*, in order to incorporate information about concentration of transactions; and finally, an approximation of *market power* based on information about relative weights location ($RW^{out}_{i,j}$ or $RW^{inp}_{i,j}$).

a. Transaction volume (TV)**:** This measure focuses on industry size, measured as the ratio between the transactions made by industry i, and the total transaction volume between all the industries. Thus, the greater the ratio the more qualified the industry is to be a core industry.

$$TV_i = \frac{\sum_{j=1}^{n} z_{i,j} + \sum_{j=1}^{n} z_{j,i}}{\sum_{i,j} z_{i,j}} \tag{4.8}$$

However, it is not enough simply to qualify as a core industry. TV_i does not provide information about the structure of these transactions. How many industries are related with industry i? In other words, how concentrated are those flows?

b. Adjusted transaction volume (TVa): A core industry must play an important roll in the supply chain. It is expected that such an industry should be related to many other industries in the economy. In order to incorporate this idea, the transaction volumes (TV_i) are adjusted by including a measure of how concentrated the flows are. The idea is to give more weight to those industries related to many other industries.

$$TVa_i = \frac{2 \cdot TV_i}{\left(GINI_i^{out} + GINI_i^{inp}\right)} \tag{4.9}$$

where $GINI_i^{out}$ is the Gini coefficient for transactions from i to other industries (output). And, $GINI_i^{inp}$ is the Gini coefficient for transactions from other industries to i (input).

c. Market power (MP): The last factor seeks to incorporate some measure of market power. A core industry does not have to be a very large industry. It is possible that certain industries play a vital role in supply chains without moving lots of money through the chain.

This methodology uses maximum relative weights ($MRW_{i,j}$) as a proxy for market power. The procedure is as follows:

Let's suppose a transaction $z_{i,j}$ from i to j, with $RW_{i,j}^{out} = 0.8 > RW_{i,j}^{inp} = 0.3$. In this case $z_{i,j}$ represents 80 per cent of the sales of industry i and 30 per cent of the purchases of industry j. This means that industry i strongly depends on j. The higher the dependence of i, the higher the power of j. In this case the market power is located in industry j. Then, 0.8 is allocated to j and 0.0 is given to i.

If the same decision rule is applied to every link in the reduced network,[5] then the industries with highest accumulated values can be labeled as core industries in terms of market power. These decision rules are formulated in Procedure 4.2.

Finally, vectors TV, TVa and MP are summarized into a single vector by applying principal component analysis.[6] The first factor scores (s_i) can then be used as final measures in order to identify core industries. The higher the score value, the higher the odds of becoming a core industry.

Since each cluster must contain one core industry, factor scores are useful for identifying the appropriate number of clusters (k). The steps are shown in Procedure 4.3. The input for this procedure is a matrix $S_{n\times 2}$. The first column contains industry IDs and the second column contains the factor scores. S is sorted in descending order by the second column (scores). With this input, the procedure estimates the distances between every pair of consecutive values in order to identify potential cutting points that divide the vector into two subsets such that the first k industries are isolated from the remaining $n - k$ industries. Rather than generating a single value, the procedure, instead, returns a vector $K_{((n-1)\times 1)}$ with potential values of k sorted by suitability.

This output can be used along with other criteria to determine the total number of clusters.[7] Once k is chosen, the core industries are the first k industries in S: $S_{((1:k),1)}$.

[5] Which is the graph $G(V, E), \omega : E$ used as input in Procedure 4.1.

[6] Based on correlation matrix and unrotated factor solution.

[7] In the application we use two additional criteria to define the final number of clusters: [1] Information

Final step: Deleting $k-1$ links Once the core industries have been defined, the final step is to delete $k-1$ links such that each core industry is assigned to a different cluster.

There exist several solutions that satisfy this constraint, but adhering to the principle of minimizing the total weight means eliminating the links with the highest values.

Procedure 4.4 entails a simple modification to the original Kruskal's Algorithm in order to make the final partition (F).

Procedure 4.2: MARKET POWER $(G(V,E), RW^{inp}_{i,j}, RW^{out}_{i,j}, MRW_{i,j})$

---

comment: Compute the market power for each industry (p_i)

MAKESET(P) with elements p_i $(i = 1 \dots |V[G]|)$
for each edge $(i,j) \in E[G]$

$$\textbf{do}\begin{cases}\textbf{if } RW^{out}_{i,j} > RW^{inp}_{i,j}\\ \quad\textbf{then } p_j \leftarrow p_j + MRW_{i,j}\\ \quad\textbf{else if } RW^{out}_{i,j} < RW^{inp}_{i,j}\\ \quad\textbf{then } p_i \leftarrow p_i + MRW_{i,j}\\ \quad\textbf{else if } RW^{out}_{i,j} == RW^{inp}_{i,j}\\ \quad\textbf{then } \begin{cases} p_i \leftarrow p_i + (MRW_{i,j}/2)\\ p_j \leftarrow p_j + (MRW_{i,j}/2)\end{cases}\end{cases}$$

return (P)

Procedure 4.3: SORT K $(S_{(n\times 2)})$

---

comment: Generate as sorted list of potential values of k

$d \leftarrow zeros((n-1),1)$
for $k \leftarrow 1$ **to** $(n-1)$
  do $d_{(k,1)} \leftarrow S_{((k+1),2)} - S_{(k,2)}$
$K \leftarrow \phi$
for $l \leftarrow 1$ **to** $n-1$

$$\textbf{do}\begin{cases}K \leftarrow K \bigcup \{argmax(d_k)+1\}\\ d_{argmax(d_k)} \leftarrow -\infty\end{cases}$$

return (K)

From this list (K), the analyst can select a convenient value of k^*.

about internal and external linkages, and [2] Direct inspection.

Procedure 4.4: FOREST $(T, \omega : E, C)$

comment: Create a forest (F) of k trees, s.t. each tree contains a core industry $c_i \in C \in V[T]$

$$
\begin{array}{l}
F \leftarrow \phi \\
E1 \leftarrow E[T] \\
C1 \leftarrow C \\
\textbf{while } |F| \leq (|V[G]| - (k-1)) \\
\quad \textbf{do} \begin{cases} \text{From } E1 \text{ select an edge } (i,j) \text{ with minimum value } w \\ \textbf{if } |\{i,j\} \bigcap C1| == 1 \\ \quad \textbf{then} \begin{cases} F \leftarrow F \bigcup \{(i,j)\} \\ E1 \leftarrow E1 - \{(i,j)\} \\ C1 \leftarrow C1 \bigcup (\{i,j\} - C1 \bigcap \{i,j\}) \end{cases} \end{cases} \\
\textbf{return } (F)
\end{array}
$$

4.3.2 Special case: avoiding large clusters

In some cases, one encounters an industry (m) that acts as a magnet attracting many industries into a single cluster. This often occurs with industries like wholesale trade, where many industries converge to supply and/or purchase products/services. This section explains how to deal with this situation without having to exclude any industry from the final solution.

The main assumption in this case is that there exist internal links between industries connected to m. In other words, although several industries converge at m, it is expected that every single industry does not supply/purchase all the products/services flowing through m. Subsets of industries supplying (purchasing) a subset of products/services is a more logical transactional pattern. This concept is made clearer in Figure 4.1.

Under this assumption, it can be feasible to break m into different complementary pieces such that $m = m_1 \bigcup m_2 \bigcup m_3 \bigcup \cdots$. Each piece is then the portion of m containing subsets of connected suppliers/buyers. Procedure 4.5 contains the steps to break m.

As can be seen, the original transaction matrix Z is resized without loss of information $(Z2)$. It is also important to note that the number of pieces into which m is broken (s) is not defined *a priori*.

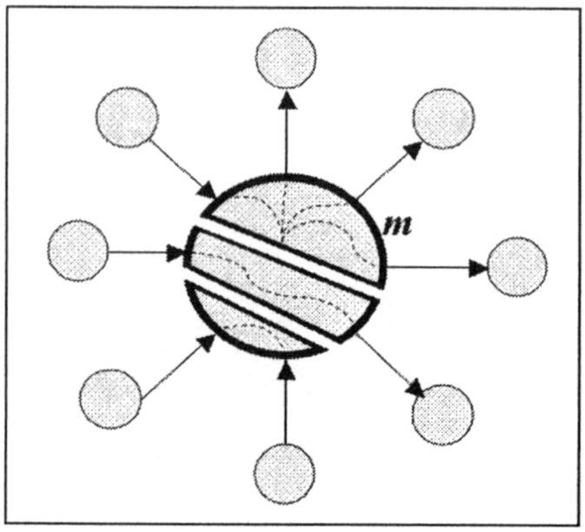

Figure 4.1: Large cluster and internal relationships

Procedure 4.5: BREAK BIG CLUSTERS (F, Z, m)

comment: Break a big cluster into smaller subclusters

$Z1_{(n,n)} \leftarrow Z$
$Ids \leftarrow \phi$
$n \leftarrow |V[F]|$
for $i \leftarrow 1$ **to** n
  do { **if** there exist a path in F connecting industries i and m
    then $Ids \leftarrow Ids \bigcup i$
$Z2_{((n-1),(n-1))} \leftarrow$ Remove Row m and Column m from $Z1$
Using $Z2$, solve the Industry Cluster to get $F2$ with k trees
Identify the trees (t_l) in which Ids was broken up $(Ids = \bigcup_{l=1}^{s} V[t_l])$
for $l \leftarrow 1$ **to** s
  do $Ids_l \leftarrow V[t_l]$
$Ids_{s+1} \leftarrow V[F2] - Ids$
$Z2 \leftarrow Z2.resize((n+s),(n+s))$
for $i \leftarrow 1$ **to** $(s+1)$
  do for $r \leftarrow 1$ **to** $(n-1)$
    do { **if** $r < m\ .AND.\ r \in Ids_i$
      then { $Z2_{(r,(n-1+i))} \leftarrow Z1_{(r,m)}$; $Z2_{((n-1+i),r)} \leftarrow Z1_{(m,r)}$ }
      else if $r > m\ .AND.\ r \in Ids_i$
      then { $Z2_{(r,(n-1+i))} \leftarrow Z1_{((r+1),m)}$; $Z2_{((n-1+i),r)} \leftarrow Z1_{(m,(r+1))}$ }
return $(Z2)$

4.4 INDUSTRY CLUSTERS IN SAN DIEGO COUNTY

4.4.1 Introduction

In this section the cluster identification method outlined in section 4.3 is applied to the case of San Diego County. An I/O table containing transactions between 499 industries was obtained from IMPLAN 2002. The discussion includes three sections: [1] Number of clusters to designate, [2] The special case of the "wholesale trade" industry, and [3] Presentation of results.

4.4.2 Number of Clusters

A three step process was used to determine the most suitable number of clusters: [1] Factor score analysis; [2] Proportion of "weak" clusters in the economy; and [3] Direct inspection.

Factor Scores Analysis

The factor score analysis (introduced in Section 4.3.1) was applied as the first of the three criteria to define the number of clusters.

Figure 4.2 shows the top scoring 100 industries in the factor analysis. The y-axis indicates the factor scores, with rankings descending on the x-axis from 1 to 100.

Applying Procedure 4.3 yields a list of the first twenty suggested numbers of clusters: 2, 4, 3, 5, 7, 11, 8, 12, 18, 23, 21, 10, 44, 15, 20, 17, 40, 45, 58, 31. As can be seen, the initial values are too small, which can lead to clusters with a large number of industries. This is, then, the first piece of information to determine the number of clusters.

Proportion of Weak Clusters in the Economy

The second step was to run the clustering model for values of k ranging from 2 to 100, and then analyse the internal and external linkage characteristics of each solution. The idea is to designate a number of clusters by which the final solution is meaningful in terms of these two criteria.

Internal Linkages Two measures of internal cohesion were implemented: the share of interindustry purchases made by the cluster that are produced by other cluster members (Purchase Share), and the share of interindustry sales by the cluster that are purchased by cluster members (Sales Share). The former measure gives a relative indication of the importance of backward linkages in the supply chain for the cluster, while the latter measure reflects the relative importance of the cluster as an internal sales market for member industries.

To provide a classification of the clusters based on their internal linkages, the purchase and sales shares for each cluster were compared to the average measure for all of the clusters. Given these averages, individual clusters were classified with respect to their internal interindustry linkages according to the following rules. If the purchase

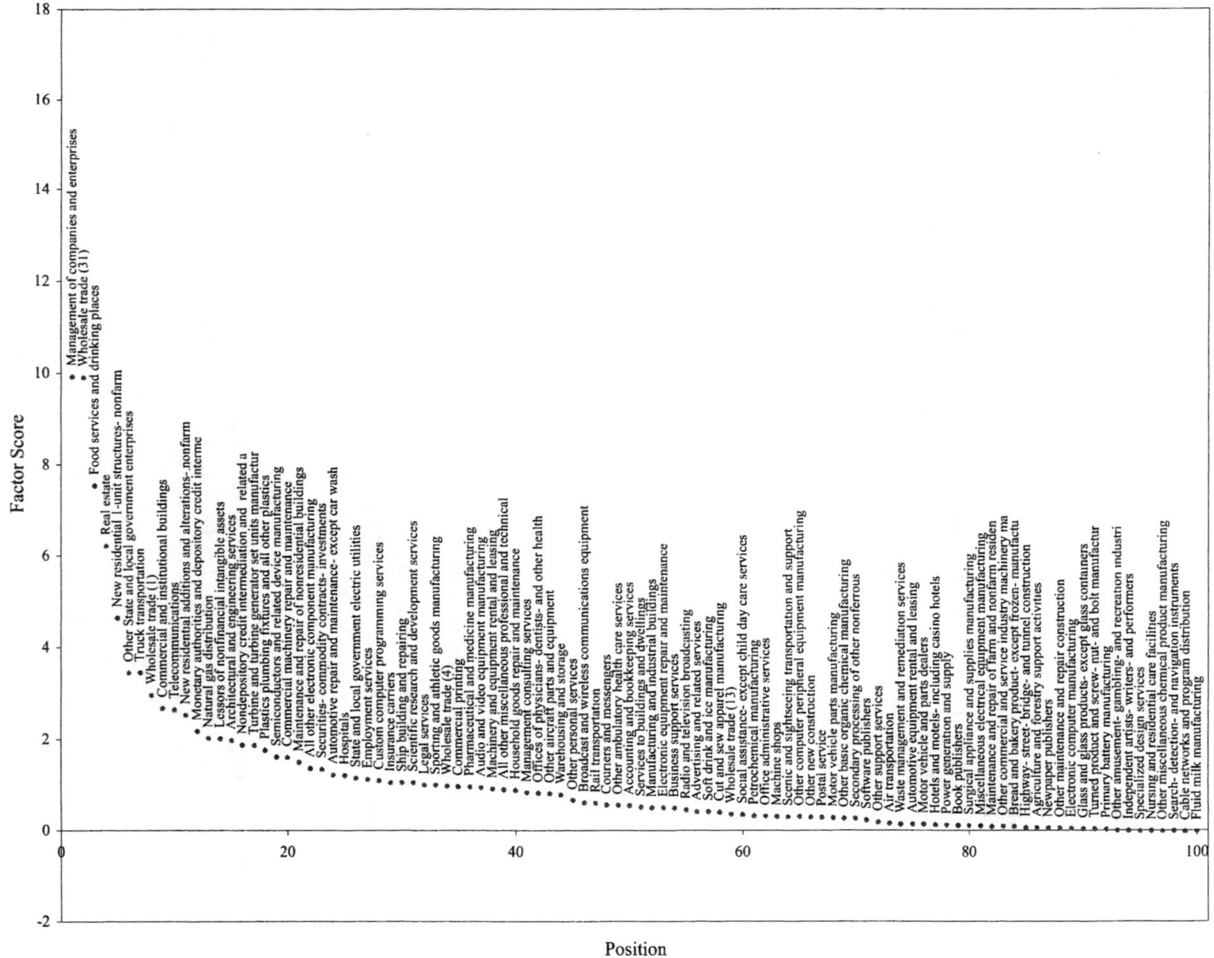

Figure 4.2: Factory scores of each industry

share was above the purchase share average (ICP), but the sales share was below the sales share average (ICS), the cluster was classified as having "purchase" oriented internal linkages. If the purchase share was below the ICP and the sales share was above ICS, the linkages were classified as "sales" oriented. If both the purchase and sales shares were above the ICP and ICS values, respectively, the internal linkages were classified as "strong." And, if both measures were below average, the cluster has "weak" internal linkages.

The equations to estimate the intra-cluster purchase and sales coefficients are:

$$ICP1_c = \frac{\sum_{i \in C}^{n} \sum_{j \in C}^{n} Z_{i,j}}{\sum_{i=1}^{n} \sum_{j \in C}^{n} Z_{i,j}} \tag{4.10}$$

$$ICS1_c = \frac{\sum_{i \in C}^{n} \sum_{j \in C}^{n} Z_{i,j}}{\sum_{i \in C}^{n} \sum_{j=1}^{n} Z_{i,j}} \tag{4.11}$$

where $Z_{i,j}$ is interindustry deliveries to sector j by sector i, with i, j = indices of industries (total number = n). $i \in C$ indicates that industry i is a member of cluster C.

One possible criticism of the $ICP1_c$ and $ICS1_c$ measures is that they treat within-industry and between-industries flows identically in measuring interactivity. Clearly, between-industries flows are more important to interactivity than are within-industry flows. To allow for a more refined measure of interactivity, a second set of intra-cluster linkages was estimated, $ICP2_c$ and $ICS2_c$, where the within-industry flows are excluded from the analysis (it is $Z_{i,i} = 0$ for $i = 1, \cdots, n$).

External Linkages A second set of cluster diagnostics can be used to characterize the importance of the cluster to the larger economy. As with the intra-cluster linkage measures, both backward and forward indices are developed for the extra-cluster linkages. These are based on the Leontief inverse for the regional input-output matrix:

$$L = (I - A)^{-1} \tag{4.12}$$

where A is the regional input-output matrix in the form of direct coefficients. The global intensity of this matrix is:

$$v = \sum_{i=1}^{n} \sum_{j=1}^{n} l_{ij} \tag{4.13}$$

This measure of global intensity is used to fix the limits of the two measures of global linkages for each industry. The first is the power of dispersion for the backward linkages (BL):

$$BL_j = \frac{\frac{1}{n} \sum_{i=1}^{n} l_{ij}}{\frac{v}{n^2}} \tag{4.14}$$

Industries for which the power of dispersion for backward linkages is greater than one produce an above average increase in activity for the regional economy when the industry experiences a unit increase in its final demand. These industries can be viewed as output drivers for the regional economy due to their reliance on locally produced inputs. A BL for the cluster is calculated as the weighted average of the individual BL measures for the industries in the cluster, with the weights based on the industry's share of total cluster output:

$$BL_c = \sum_{i \in C} BL_i \frac{X_i}{\sum_{j \in C}^{n} X_j} \tag{4.15}$$

The forward linkage of the cluster is captured by the index of the sensitivity of dispersion:

$$FL_j = \frac{\frac{1}{n}\sum_{i=1}^{n} l_{ji}}{\frac{v}{n^2}} \tag{4.16}$$

An industry with a forward linkage coefficient greater than one is considered to have an above average sensitivity to unit changes in aggregate final demands. High FL coefficients indicate that the sector plays a strategic enabling role as a core supplier of inputs to other industries. Like the backward linkage coefficient, the forward linkage measure for the entire cluster is calculated as a weighted average of the indices for each sector in the cluster. Clusters with $FL_c > 1$ display an above average sensitivity to unit changes in all sectors' final demand.

Considering forward and backward external linkages, each cluster can be categorized as one of four types: *Key clusters* are clusters that have backward and forward external linkage coefficients exceeding 1; *Driver clusters* are clusters with a backward coefficient greater than 1 and a forward coefficient less than 1; *Enabler clusters* are clusters with a backward coefficient less than 1 and a forward coefficient greater than 1; and *Weak clusters* are clusters with both forward and backward coefficients less than 1.

In order to define k, the second criterion was that the final solution must not contain more than 50 per cent "weak" clusters on either the internal or external measures.

Figure 4.3 shows the proportion of "weak" clusters in each solution ranging from 2 to 100. As can be seen, the greater the number of clusters, the greater the ratio of "weak" clusters in the solution. Excluding $k = 1, 2, 3$, the ratio of "weak" industries reaches 50 per cent at $k = 37$ and $k = 43$. This information, together with the results obtained from the factor scores analysis, will be combined in the next, and final, step to determine the number of clusters.

Direct Inspection At this point, after applying the factor score analysis and the proportion of weak clusters criterion, the set of potential values of k has been reduced to some value between 37 and 44. Note that $k = 44$ is the first value of k in the factor score analysis which is closest to the range $[k = 37, 43]$ obtained from the proportion of weak clusters criterion.

Careful inspection of the solutions from $k = 37$ to $k = 44$ is the final step in determining the most suitable number of clusters. After this inspection, we settle on $k = 43$ as the best number of clusters. Values of k less than 43 imply merging sets

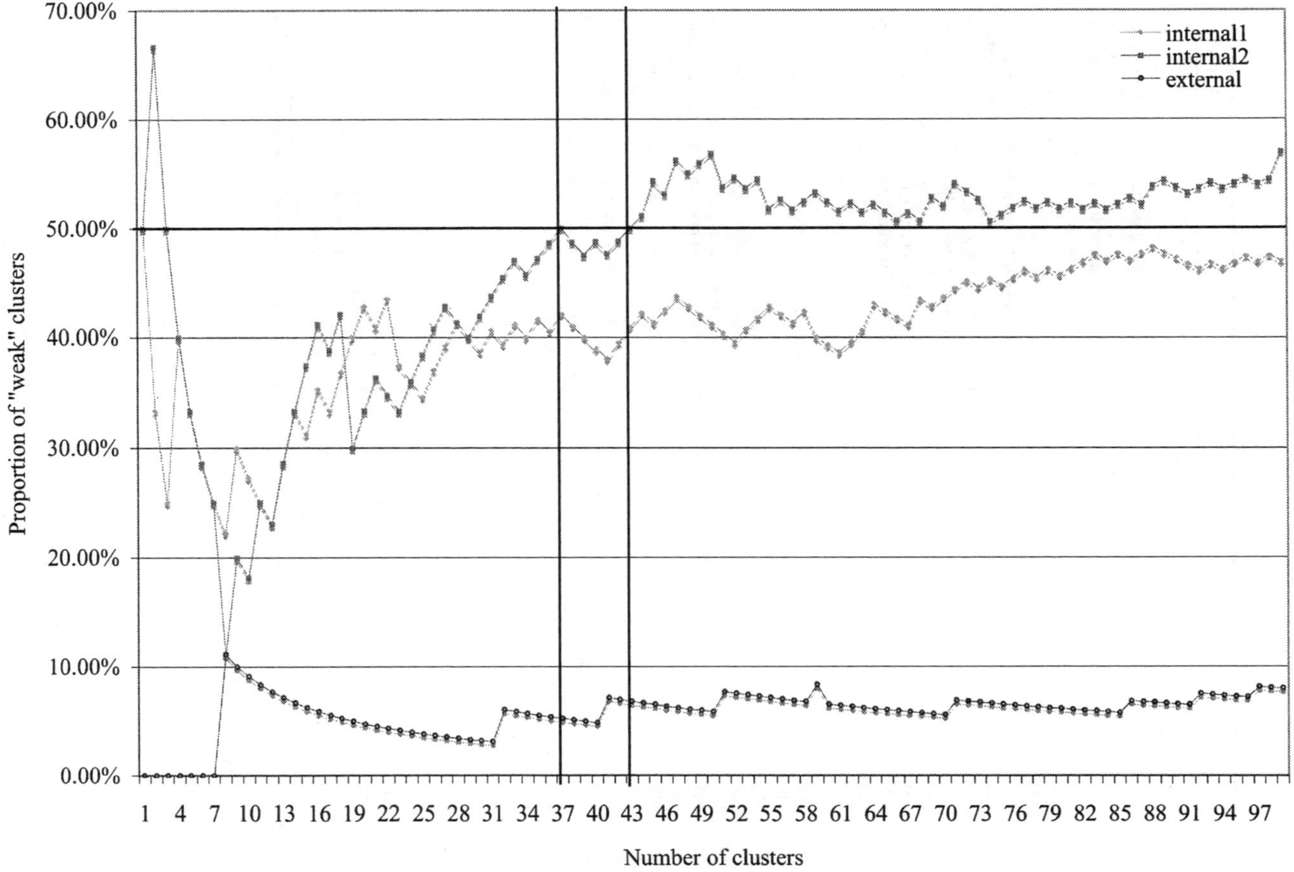

Figure 4.3: Percentage of "weak" cluster in each solution

of industries that reduce the specificity of the clusters. On the other hand, values of k greater than 43 lead to the creation of singletons, which is undesirable in a cluster analysis.

Cluster Id	Industry Id	Description
1	451	Management of companies and enterprises
2	530	Wholesale trade 31
3	481	Food services and drinking places
4	431	Real estate
5	33	New residential 1-unit structures nonfarm
6	499	Other State and local government enterprises
7	394	Truck transportation
8	500	Wholesale trade 1
9	38	Commercial and institutional buildings
10	422	Telecommunications
11	35	New residential additions and alterations nonfarm
12	430	Monetary authorities and depository credit interme
13	31	Natural gas distribution
14	436	Lessors of nonfinancial intangible assets
15	439	Architectural and engineering services
16	425	Nondepository credit intermediation and related a
17	285	Turbine and turbine generator set units manufactur
18	177	Plastics plumbing fixtures and all other plastics
19	311	Semiconductors and related device manufacturing
20	485	Commercial machinery repair and maintenance
21	43	Maintenance and repair of nonresidential buildings
22	312	All other electronic component manufacturing
23	426	Securities commodity contracts investments
24	483	Automotive repair and maintenance except car wash
25	467	Hospitals
26	498	State and local government electric utilities
27	454	Employment services
28	441	Custom computer programming services
29	427	Insurance carriers
30	357	Ship building and repairing
31	446	Scientific research and development services
32	437	Legal services
33	381	Sporting and athletic goods manufacturing
34	503	Wholesale trade 4
35	139	Commercial printing
36	160	Pharmaceutical and medicine manufacturing
37	309	Audio and video equipment manufacturing
38	434	Machinery and equipment rental and leasing
39	450	All other miscellaneous professional and technical
40	486	Household goods repair and maintenance
41	444	Management consulting services
42	465	Offices of physicians dentists and other health
43	353	Other aircraft parts and equipment

Table 4.3: Core Industries

Table 4.3 shows the 43 core industries. Section 4.4.4 provides a general description of those 43 clusters.

4.4.3 The Case of Wholesale Trade Industry

As discussed in Section 4.3.2, certain industries may act as magnets attracting many industries into the same cluster. This is the case of the wholesale trade industry, where

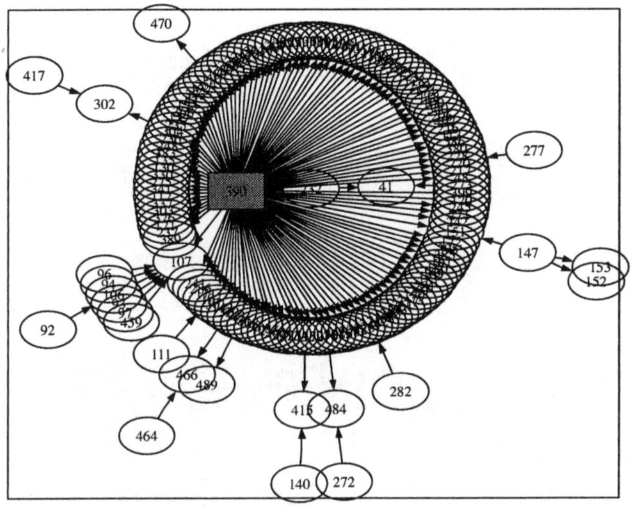

Figure 4.4: "Wholesale trade" cluster

many industries converge to provide and/or obtain products/services. This kind of cluster creates problems for the analysis.

Figure 4.4 shows the original "Wholesale trade" industry surrounded by 143 strongly related industries.[8] To allow this large cluster not only means making an extreme generalization; it also makes it difficult to find other underlying supply chains.

Figure 4.5 contains the graphical representation after applying the Procedure 4.5 to break the original "Wholesale trade". The procedure returned 31 pieces coded from 500 to 530. As can be seen, once the big industry is broken, the other surrounding industries are attached to the piece with which they are most closely related, creating small sub-clusters. In the final solution, these sub-clusters can be assigned to other clusters, or they can become independent clusters.

4.4.4 General Characteristics

Table 4.4 describes several characteristics of the 43 industry clusters, with measures such as size of the clusters (Size); share of the total transactions generated by each cluster (Output); share of total employment held by each cluster (Employ.share); and the values for internal and external linkages, including each cluster's classification.

Size

The cluster size, measured as the number of industries in the clusters, varies from one (known as singletons) to fifty nine. 56 per cent of the clusters contain between 2 and 10 industries per cluster.

---
[8] Almost 33% of the total sample of industries included in this study.

Id	Core	Size	Output	Employ. share	ICP1	ICS1	Type	ICP2	ICS2	Type	BL	Fl	Type
1	451	14	0.0628	0.0216	0.1112	0.0388	weak	0.0981	0.0342	weak	1.0194	7.0090	key
2	530	1	0.0673	0.0266	0.1167	0.0542	weak	0.0000	0.0000	weak	0.9954	10.1868	enabler
3	481	56	0.0526	0.0999	0.3081	0.4156	strong	0.2000	0.2698	strong	1.0898	1.5708	key
4	431	36	0.1492	0.1895	0.3625	0.3609	strong	0.2087	0.2078	strong	1.0211	4.2478	key
5	33	25	0.0433	0.1373	0.1675	0.3317	sales	0.1646	0.3259	strong	0.9971	0.9447	weak
6	499	6	0.0264	0.0064	0.3192	0.1826	purchase	0.1645	0.0941	purchase	0.9939	3.4922	enabler
7	394	3	0.0213	0.0130	0.1906	0.0860	weak	0.0400	0.0181	weak	1.0090	2.5909	key
8	500	59	0.0188	0.0147	0.2291	0.2802	purchase	0.2090	0.2556	strong	1.0197	1.0369	key
9	38	21	0.0122	0.0409	0.1170	0.5105	sales	0.0716	0.3127	sales	1.0776	0.8774	driver
10	422	7	0.0515	0.0259	0.3954	0.3448	strong	0.0526	0.0459	weak	0.9877	2.8777	enabler
11	35	4	0.0014	0.0091	0.0264	0.3088	sales	0.0260	0.3037	sales	1.0793	0.7911	driver
12	430	1	0.0219	0.0080	0.1164	0.0985	weak	0.0000	0.0000	weak	1.0501	3.0451	key
13	31	8	0.0107	0.0059	0.3675	0.2679	purchase	0.2544	0.1855	strong	0.8452	2.2934	enabler
14	436	3	0.0236	0.0027	0.2468	0.0465	purchase	0.2019	0.0380	purchase	0.8831	2.5969	enabler
15	439	11	0.0438	0.0421	0.2118	0.1558	purchase	0.1427	0.1049	purchase	0.9952	1.8195	enabler
16	425	5	0.0252	0.0081	0.1286	0.0694	weak	0.0391	0.0211	weak	0.9947	2.9224	enabler
17	285	18	0.0090	0.0042	0.3152	0.6425	strong	0.0559	0.1139	weak	1.0435	0.9731	driver
18	177	5	0.0112	0.0024	0.0777	0.0295	weak	0.0331	0.0126	weak	1.0479	2.0511	key
19	311	12	0.0201	0.0070	0.2498	0.3901	strong	0.1734	0.2708	strong	1.1671	1.3128	key
20	485	16	0.0142	0.0128	0.0569	0.0718	weak	0.0538	0.0679	weak	1.1663	1.1078	key
21	43	3	0.0191	0.0117	0.1116	0.0401	weak	0.1077	0.0387	weak	1.0232	2.0214	key
22	312	3	0.0128	0.0037	0.2276	0.1929	purchase	0.0761	0.0645	weak	1.1954	2.1550	key
23	426	2	0.0351	0.0169	0.5511	0.5894	strong	0.2544	0.2721	strong	1.1875	2.3192	key
24	483	10	0.0060	0.0185	0.1354	0.3158	sales	0.1248	0.2912	strong	1.0361	1.2147	key
25	467	6	0.0049	0.0182	0.1123	0.6427	sales	0.0767	0.4388	sales	1.1230	0.8217	driver
26	498	5	0.0119	0.0007	0.0060	0.0012	weak	0.0059	0.0011	weak	0.8888	1.7691	enabler
27	454	5	0.0350	0.0425	0.1085	0.0409	weak	0.0813	0.0307	weak	0.9610	1.9732	enabler
28	441	14	0.0161	0.0274	0.1194	0.1270	weak	0.0525	0.0558	weak	0.9599	1.7970	enabler
29	427	2	0.0296	0.0145	0.7166	0.6255	strong	0.4894	0.4272	strong	1.0650	1.7817	key
30	357	14	0.0018	0.0079	0.1000	0.4924	sales	0.0802	0.3950	sales	1.0230	0.8083	driver
31	446	7	0.0060	0.0298	0.0474	0.1213	weak	0.0410	0.1049	weak	0.9649	1.4352	enabler
32	437	1	0.0222	0.0128	0.1390	0.0475	weak	0.0000	0.0000	weak	0.9510	2.5463	enabler
33	381	9	0.0023	0.0037	0.2816	0.8375	strong	0.2538	0.7548	strong	1.0485	0.8176	driver
34	503	19	0.0060	0.0027	0.3853	0.2040	purchase	0.3730	0.1975	strong	0.9785	0.9568	weak
35	139	7	0.0122	0.0049	0.3049	0.1634	purchase	0.2767	0.1483	purchase	1.0218	1.3572	key
36	160	2	0.0125	0.0031	0.3557	0.7742	strong	0.0003	0.0007	weak	1.2418	1.1890	key
37	309	10	0.0050	0.0069	0.1964	0.7388	sales	0.1892	0.7116	strong	1.0840	0.8761	driver
38	434	6	0.0185	0.0054	0.1435	0.1157	weak	0.0632	0.0509	weak	1.1861	1.7698	key
39	450	1	0.0066	0.0022	0.0144	0.0037	weak	0.0000	0.0000	weak	0.9395	1.9327	enabler
40	486	6	0.0037	0.0026	0.1072	0.1183	weak	0.0964	0.1064	weak	1.0551	1.0251	key
41	444	1	0.0166	0.0100	0.0442	0.0115	weak	0.0000	0.0000	weak	0.9523	2.1172	enabler
42	465	7	0.0032	0.0383	0.1129	0.9317	sales	0.0555	0.4584	sales	0.9896	0.8048	weak
43	353	16	0.0265	0.0259	0.2320	0.2553	purchase	0.1599	0.1760	strong	1.0534	1.1914	key

Table 4.4: General characteristics

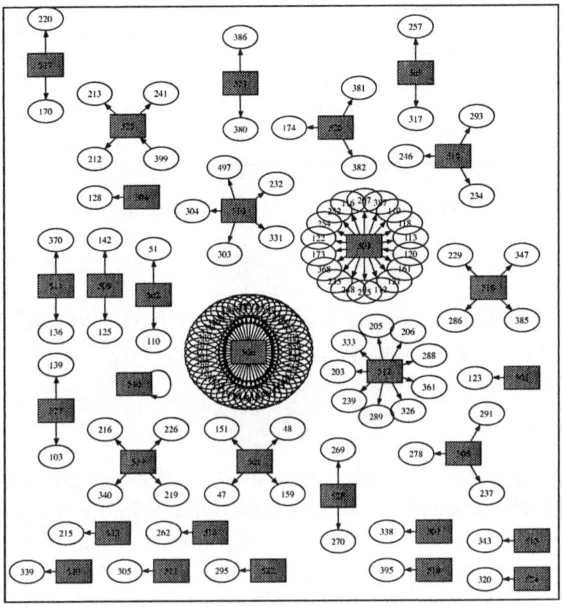

Figure 4.5: "Wholesale trade" cluster broken into smaller clusters

There are only five singletons: "Wholesale trade 31" (Id = 2), "Monetary authorities and depository credit intermediation" (Id = 12), "Legal services" (Id = 32), "All other miscellaneous professional and technical services" (Id = 39), and "Management consulting services" (Id = 41). These industries interact with too many industries, which makes it difficult to assign them to one specific cluster.

On the other hand,"Wholesale trade 1" (Id = 8), related to apparels, book and stationaries; and "Food services and drinking places" (Id = 3), related to food and drinks products, are the two largest clusters in the economy, with 59 and 56 industries respectively.

Output Share

The output share is estimated as the ratio between the output of each cluster and the total output generated by all the industries in the economy. The average output share per cluster is 2.33 per cent, with values ranging from 0.14 per cent to 14.92 per cent.

The largest cluster, in terms of output share, is "Real estate" (Id = 4), with 14.92% of the total output. Thirty-six industries are included in this cluster. Their common factor is that they are related to facilities built for different purposes: leisure, culture, education, sports, farming, healthcare, and so on.

"New residential additions and alterations nonfarm" (Id = 11), is the smallest cluster. The four industries included in this cluster are primarily engaged in making additions or alterations of residential units.

	Size	Output Share	Employment Share
Size	1.000		
Output Share	0.341	1.000	
Employment Share	0.549	0.769	1.000

Table 4.5: Correlations between size, output share and employment share

Although the largest and the smallest clusters are both involved in a common sector, construction, each one is focused on different activities.

Employment Share

The largest cluster in terms of employment share is "Real estate" (Id = 4). This cluster accounts for 18.95 per cent of the total employment in the economy. The smallest cluster in terms of employment share is "Semiconductors and related devices manufacturing". This cluster accounts for 0.7 per cent of the total employment.

Table 4.5 presents a correlation matrix of size, output share and employment share. As can be seen in the table, there exists a close relationship between output generation and employment share. The correlation coefficient between these two variables is 76.9 per cent. Interestingly, there is not a strong relationship between the number of industries in the cluster and its capacity to generate output and employment. This suggests that the algorithm results in clusters that capture different aspects of the regional economy.

Internal and External Linkages

Table 4.4 presents the two measures of internal linkages: intra-cluster purchase coefficient (ICP) and intra-cluster sales coefficient (ICS). Each one of these measures was estimated with and without the intra-industry transactions. The table also contains two measures of external linkages, backward and forward linkages (BL and FL respectively).

Table 4.6 shows the percentage of clusters assigned to each category. According to the internal linkages, including intra-industry transactions, thirty-nine per cent of the industries were classified as "weak" clusters, while the remaining 61 per cent are roughly equally distributed between "strong," "purchase" and "sales" oriented clusters. The same classification process was then applied with intra-industry transactions excluded. The table shows that this exclusion leads to an increase in the percentage of "weak" clusters from 39 per cent to 49 per cent, as well as an increase in the percentage of "strong" clusters from 21 per cent to 30 per cent.

With regard to the external linkages between each cluster and the rest of the economy, only 7 per cent of the industries were classified as "weak" clusters; 44 per cent as "key" clusters; 33 per cent as "enabler" clusters and the remaining 16 per cent as "driver" clusters. It is important to note the very high value given to the forward link-

Category	Internal 1[1]	Internal 2[2]	External
Weak	39.53%	48.84%	
Strong	20.93%	30.23%	
Sales	18.60%	11.63%	
Purchase	20.93%	9.30%	
Weak			6.98%
Key			44.19%
Enabler			32.56%
Driver			16.28%

[1] $avg(ICP1) = 0.20, avg(ICS1) = 0.28$
[2] $avg(ICP2) = 0.12, avg(ICS2) = 0.18$

Table 4.6: Cluster classification according to the internal and external linkages

ages of "Wholesale trade 31," one of the five singletons in the analysis. This confirms the important role that this industry plays in enabling the rest of the economy.

Table 4.7 shows the average cluster size and output per cluster type. The results show some evidence of a relationship between the size and the types of internal linkages. As can be seen, "strong" clusters are considerably bigger, in terms of industries per cluster, than "weak" clusters. This relationship is not as strong in the case of external linkages.

Finally, Figure 4.6 presents an example of a graphical representation of the final clusters. The squared box represents the core industry and the arrows represent products/services flows.[9]

4.5 FINAL COMMENTS

This paper introduces a new approach for identifying industry clusters based on graph theory. Since it relies on readily available data, the approach can be used to compare regional industrial clusters across space and time. Additionally, the reliance on network based constructs provides useful visualization and numerical measures that can help improve our understanding of how industries are related within and between clusters.

We illustrated the approach with a case study of San Diego County, California, where 499 industries were aggregated into 43 industry clusters. The industry "Wholesale trade" was subjected to special treatment in order to avoid generating a very large cluster. The results also show the ability of the methodology to design balanced clusters in terms of internal and external linkages.

Further research will be carried out in three directions. The first task is to design a methodology to determine the most suitable geographical unit of study, in order to

[9] The graphs for each cluster, including additional comments, are available from the authors upon request.

Type	Average Size	Average Output
	Internal1	
strong	16.00	0.0402
purchase	14.67	0.0201
sales	12.13	0.0097
weak	5.53	0.0223
	Internal2	
strong	20.31	0.0312
purchase	6.75	0.0265
sales	10.4	0.0047
weak	5.90	0.0222
	External	
key	13.63	0.0288
driver	11.71	0.0052
enabler	5.36	0.0259
weak	17.00	0.0175

Table 4.7: Average size and average output per cluster type

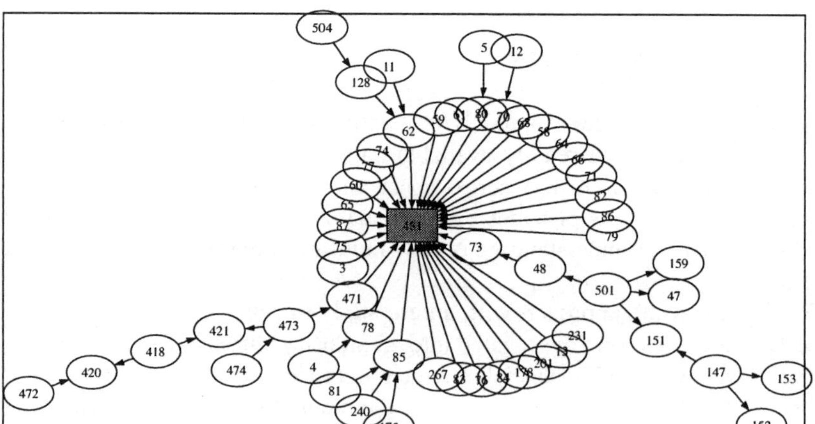

Figure 4.6: Network representation of cluster "Food services and drinking places"

avoid artificial breaks in the supply chains. At present, the geographical boundary of the regional economy is specified exogenously and the clusters determined within this constraint. We are exploring ways to simultaneously determine both the geographical extent and industrial composition of clusters. Second, it is necessary to explore the possibility of designing *fuzzy clusters*, where the industries can belong to more than one cluster. And third, one needs to design a dual version of the methodology in which the network reduction process focuses on designing industry clusters based on weak links, rather than strong links. This will allow an alternative perspective on cluster networks.

REFERENCES

Bergman, E.M. and E.J. Feser (1999), 'Industrial and regional clusters: concepts and comparative applications', *The Web Book of Regional Science*, www.rri.wvu.edu-/WebBook/Bergman-Feser/contents.htm.

Bergman, E., E. Feser and S. Sweeney (1996), *Targeting North Carolina manufacturing: Understanding the state's economy through industrial cluster analysis*, Institute for Economic Development, University of North Carolina at Chapel Hill.

Blin, J. and C. Cohen (1977), 'Technological similarity and aggregation in input-output systems', *The Review of Economics and Statistics*, **29**, 82–91.

Campbell, J. (1972), 'Growth pole theory, digraph analysis and the interindustry relationships', *Tijdschrift Voor Economie en Social Geografie*, **62**, 69–87.

Campbell, J. (1975), 'Application of graph theoretic analysis to interindustry relationships', *Regional Science and Urban Economics*, **5**, 91–106.

Czamanski, S. (1971), 'Some empirical evidence of the strengths of linkages between groups of related industries in urban-regional complexes', *Papers, Regional Science Association*, **27**, 137–150.

Czamanski, S. and L. Ablas (1979), 'Identification of industrial clusters and complexes: a comparison of methods and findings', *Urban Studies*, **16**, 61–80.

Harrigan, F. (1982), 'The relationship between industrial and geographical linkages', *Journal of Regional Science*, **22**, 19–31.

Latham, W.R. (1976), 'Needless complexity in the identification of industrial complexes', *Journal of Regional Science*, **16**, 45–55.

ÓhUallacháin, B. (1984), 'The identification of industrial complexes', *Annals of the Association of American Geographers*, **74**, 420–436.

Porter, M.E. (1990), *The Competitive Advantage of Nations*, New York: Basic Books.

Roepke, H., D. Adams and R. Wiseman, (1974), 'A new approach to the identification of industrial complexes using input-output data', *Journal of Regional Science*, **14**, 15–29.

Slater, P.B. (1977), 'The determination of functionally integrated industries in the United States', *Empirical Economics*, **2**, 1–9.

Steiner, M. (1998), *Clusters and regional specialization: on geography, technology, and networks*, London: Pion.

Streit, M.E. (1969) 'Spatial association and economic linkages between industries', *Journal of Regional Science*, **9**, 177–188.

5. Industry-specific spatial agglomerations in Germany

Thomas Brenner[*‡]

5.1 INTRODUCTION

Localized clusters and industrial districts have attracted much attention in recent years. They have been identified as centres of economic growth, leading policy makers to support their emergence. This in turn has triggered a scientific literature that seeks to identify these local clusters and industrial districts (Sforzi 1990, Isaksen 1996, Paniccia 1998, Braunerhjelm and Carlsson 1999, Brenner 2004, Sternberg and Litzenberger 2004 and Brenner 2006). Different studies utilize somewhat different approaches to examine a variety of geographical areas.

Most of these approaches operationalize the concept of clusters and industrial districts on the basis of the relative share of industries in each region. If this share exceeds a certain threshold in a region, the region and industry are then subject to further analysis. Various additional conditions are also sometimes specified: Sforzi (1990) and Paniccia (1998), for example, argue that small firms must dominate a region in order for it to be called an industrial district. In contrast, Isaksen (1996) examines the relationship between those industries that are found to exceed the threshold. Only if some related industries are concentrated in the same region does he then talk about a local cluster.

Three studies have been conducted on the case of Germany, so far (Brenner 2004, Sternberg and Litzenberger 2004 and Brenner 2006). Sternberg and Litzenberger (2004) apply an approach similar to that of Isaksen (1996) and Braunerhjelm and Carlsson (1999). They analyse the regional shares of industries and define a cluster index. All regions with a cluster index above 4 in a particular industry are defined as regional clusters. Brenner (2004 and 2006) takes a somewhat different approach, though it too is based on the relative share of industries in regions. Here, a distribution function of relative activity is fitted and a test is then conducted to determine whether this distri-

[*] Philipps-Universität Marburg, Marburg, Germany

[‡] I want to thank Dirk Fornahl, Ulrich Witt and the participants of the ETE-Workshop in Jena and the Workshop on Spatial Econometrics in Kiel for helpful comments and discussions and the German Federal Ministry for Education and Research for financial support. The usual disclaimer applies.

bution function is bimodal. If it is bimodal then all regions that fall in the group of higher activity are considered local industrial clusters.

Brenner's approach has the advantage that no arbitrarily set threshold is used. At the same time, it could be criticized on a similar basis insofar as three arbitrarily chosen functional forms are fitted to the empirical distribution of industry-specific activities. Furthermore, Brenner uses administrative districts rather than labour market areas, which Sforzi (1990) has shown to be feasible. Sternberg and Litzenberger (2004) use 'Raumordnungsregionen' for Germany, which of all the regional classifications most closely approximate labour markets areas.

Hence, this paper utilizes Brenner's general approach, but modifies it in two ways. First, a fourth functional form is added and a test is conducted on each to determine whether it contributes significantly to describing the empirical data. Second, 'Raumordnungsregionen' are used as spatial units instead of administrative districts. Aside from these two modifications we replicate Brenner's (2006) procedure and apply it to the same data. We obtain information about which industries exhibit spatial agglomerations and in which regions these agglomerations are located.

The paper proceeds as follows. In Section 5.2 various alternative distributions are deduced on the basis of theoretical considerations. The empirical data used and the methods used to fit the various theoretical distributions to the data are presented in Section 5.3. Section 5.4 applies the method to 198 industries in Germany and presents the results. A conclusion follows in Section 5.5.

5.2 THEORETICAL SPATIAL DISTRIBUTION OF INDUSTRIES

It is not the intention of this paper to develop a model that explains the spatial distribution of industries. Such a complex task goes well beyond the scope of this paper. Our goal is merely to identify existing industry-specific spatial agglomerations. To this end, we define a theoretical distribution of industry-specific activity across regions. Although we derive functional forms for this distribution from certain theoretical considerations, the aim is not to supply a comprehensive justification for each function, but rather to identify a set of plausible functions that can then be tested empirically.

5.2.1 Binomial distribution

Although Ellison and Glaeser (1997) develop finally a somewhat different index, their initial argument is based on the assumption that firms are randomly and independently located in space. Eventually they reject this null hypothesis for most industries, but the assumption remains a useful starting point.

Such an assumption leads to the prediction of a regional industry-size distribution following a binomial distribution. This prediction first of all holds for measuring industry-size by the number of firms. When we assume each firm to contain the same number of employees, it also holds for the number of employees. So, our first functional form to consider is the binomial distribution. Let us denote the number of employees in an industry i by e_i. Let us consider one region r. The likelihood of any of these e_i employees in the considered industry to be located in region r depends on the size of the region. Even if employees locate randomly in space, they should end up in large regions with a higher probability. We denote the size of a region r by s_r, where s_r has to be defined such that

$$\sum_{r} s_r = 1 \tag{5.1}$$

holds. This implies that the probability of each employee to be located in region r is given by s_r. If we assume that the employees are randomly distributed in space, the probability of finding $e_{i,r}$ employees from industry i in region r is given by

$$P(e_{i,r} = e) = Bnm(e_i, e, s_r) = \frac{e_i!}{e! \cdot (e_i - e)!} \cdot s_r^e \cdot (1 - s_r)^{e_i - e} . \tag{5.2}$$

The shape of the binomial distribution is depicted in Figure 5.3.

5.2.2 Exponential distribution

The above model assumes that the propensity of firms to locate in a certain region depends only on the size of the regions. However, in reality other local factors are also involved. Resources such as human capital, natural endowments, and infrastructure all matter (see, for example, Ellison and Glaeser 1999). It is unclear, however, what local resources are more important and their relative importance also varies across industries. Hence it is impossible to fully account for local resource factors in the analysis of each industry.

However, general knowledge about local resources can be used to refine the regional industry-size distribution function. One local resource which all economists consider important is human capital. One measure for a region's human capital is the number of students who are trained there. The distribution of the number of students per inhabitant in Germany's administrative districts is depicted in Figure 5.1. A statistical analysis shows that the shape of this distribution is best fitted by an exponentially decreasing function.

This suggests that the exponential function, given by

$$P(e_{i,r} = e) = (1 - \xi) \cdot \xi^e \tag{5.3}$$

where ξ is a parameter, might describe the regional industry-size distribution adequately. However, we do not claim that the number of students is the decisive factor even if we find the exponential function to be an adequate representation of the regional industry-size distribution. This is because other local factors might be similarly distributed in space. Furthermore, Bottazzi, Dosi, Fagiolo, and Secchi (2005) find a similar functional form for specific parameter values in their model of interdependent firm location.

5.2.3 Erlang-n-distribution

Bottazzi, Dosi, Fagiolo and Secchi (2005) find quite different shapes of distributions in their analysis. Besides a distribution that looks similar to a binomial distribution and

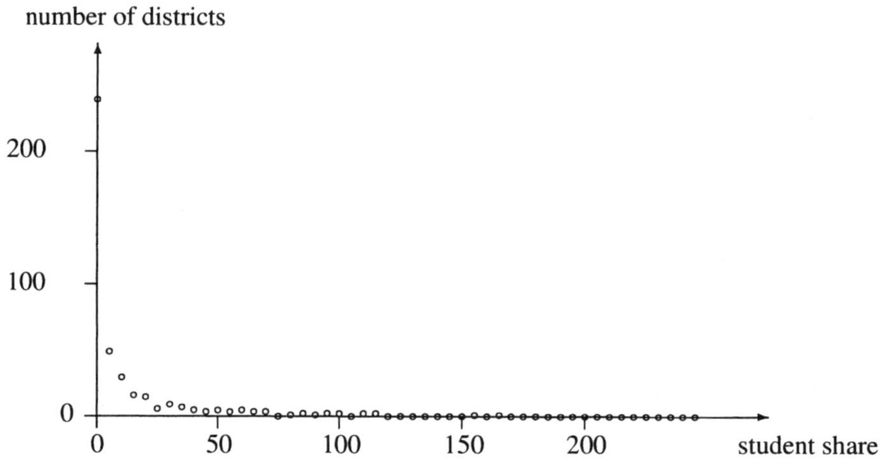

Figure 5.1: For each number of students per 1000 inhabitants (horizontal axis) the number of administrative districts in Germany (vertical axis) that contain approximately this number of students is depicted.

two distributions that look similar to an exponential distribution, there is a third type of distribution that starts from a low value, increases first and then decreases similarly to an exponential function (Bottazzi et. al. 2005, Figure 2).

A similar distribution also attains in the case of the number of business service firms. These firms are usually seen as a local factor that influences the location of manufacturing firms. Their distribution among the 441 administrative districts in Germany is presented in Figure 5.2. While the binomial distribution is rejected as an adequate description of this distribution, the Erlang-n-distribution ($n = 2$) fits the distribution well. Mathematically the Erlang-n-distribution ($n = 2$) is given by

$$P(e_{i,r} = e) = \frac{(1-\xi)^2}{\xi} \cdot e \cdot \xi^e \tag{5.4}$$

where ξ is a parameter.

Again, the above arguments should not be interpreted as claiming that specific factors or dependencies cause specific distributions. The idea is rather to find some distributions which might plausibly fit the data. We could continue the above process and find additional functions, but the current three are plausible and representative of the different kinds of shapes that can be expected (see Figure 5.3). Only one specific shape needs to be added.

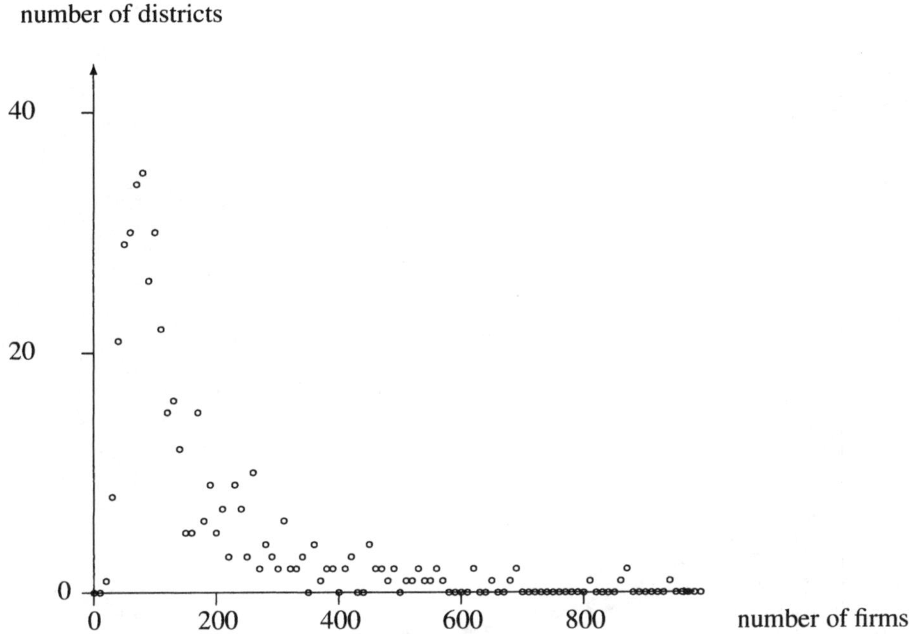

Figure 5.2: For each number of service firms that provide services to other firms, for example legal firms, marketing firms, PR consultants and so on (horizontal axis), the number of administrative districts in Germany (vertical axis) that contain approximately this number of firms is depicted.

5.2.4 Agglomeration

Once again, we do not intend to offer a causal model of local agglomerations or clusters. What we do claim is that if local agglomerations or clusters exist, we should observe a small number of regions that contain a very high level of activity in the industry under consideration. The observed activity level in these regions should clearly exceed that in other regions (see Brenner 2001 and 2004 for a theoretical analysis) such that they fall outside of the regional industry-size distribution as described by the above functions. Brenner (2004) therefore argues that the regional industry-size distribution should contain a second peak.

This second peak can be modelled in a variety of ways. It is, however, clear that an additional function is needed in order to model such a second peak containing a number of firms or employees quite above the average number predicted by the other functions. In order to avoid introducing another functional form, one of the above functions is used. The Erlang-n-distribution ($n = 2$) is perfectly suited to describing

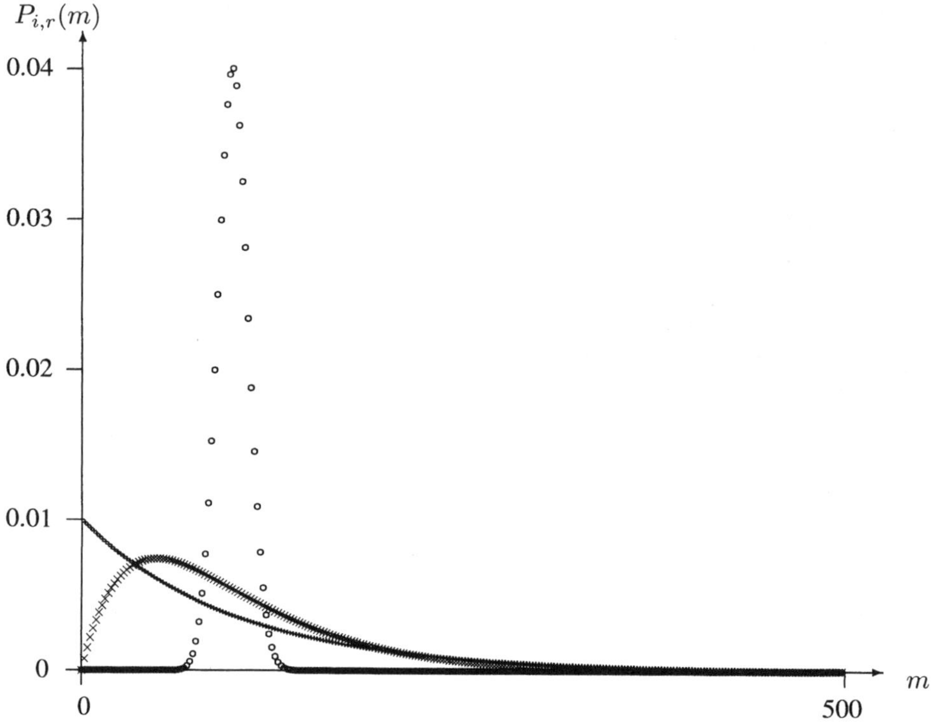

Figure 5.3: Theoretically predicted regional industry-size distribution for the number of firms or employees according to a binomial distribution (o), an exponential distribution (+), and an Erlang-n-distribution (×). The parameters of the distributions are chosen such that they lead to the same average number.

such a second peak because it starts from a value of zero and increases until reaching its maximal value and then decreases exponentially.

Therefore, in order to model the second peak, we shift the Erlang-n-distribution to higher values of e, the number of employees:

$$P(e_{i,r} = e) = \begin{cases} \frac{(1-\xi)^2}{\xi} \cdot (e - e_0) \cdot \xi^{e-e_0} & \text{if} \quad e > e_0 \\ 0 & \text{if} \quad e \leq e_0 \end{cases} \tag{5.5}$$

where ξ is a parameter and e_0 denotes the number of employees at which the function begins.

5.2.5 Complete function

Thus far we have formulated four functions that might describe the empirical regional industry-size distribution. The first one, the binomial distribution, is based on a clear modelling of the underlying processes. The other functional forms have been obtained on the basis of some plausible arguments. Hence the binomial distribution does not contain a free parameter, whereas the other functions do. We therefore alter the binomial distribution to include a free parameter: we define the probability of firms or employees locating in a certain region r by $\xi_1 \cdot s_r$ instead of s_r.

Furthermore, the binomial distribution above depends on the size of the region under consideration. The same can be expected to hold for the whole regional industry-size distribution. We therefore define the parameters for all of the other functions to also depend on the size of the region. The combined function is given by

$$\begin{aligned} P(e_{i,r} = e) &= \mu_1 \cdot Bnm(M_i, e, \xi_1 \cdot s_r) + \mu_2 \cdot (1 - \xi_2(s_r)) \cdot \xi_2(s_r)^e \\ &+ \mu_3 \cdot \frac{[1 - \xi_3(s_r)]^2}{\xi_3(s_r)} \cdot e \cdot \xi_3(s_r)^e \\ &+ \begin{cases} \mu_4 \cdot \frac{[1-\xi_4(s_r)]^2}{\xi_4(s_r)} \cdot (e - e_0(s_r)) \cdot \xi_4(s_r)^{e-e_0(s_r)} & \text{if} \quad e \geq e_0(s_r) \\ 0 & \text{if} \quad e < e_0(s_r) \end{cases} \end{aligned} \tag{5.6}$$

μ_1, μ_2, μ_3, and μ_4 determine to what extent each of the functions contributes to the total distribution. Their sum must be one. ξ_1, $\xi_2(s_r)$, $\xi_3(s_r)$, $\xi_4(s_r)$, and $e_0(s_r)$ are the parameters of the various functions. We obtain a function that increases linearly in s_r if each term increases linearly in s_r. While the binomial distribution already satisfies this condition, the other three terms in Equation (5.6) must be further modified.

The average expected value for the exponential distribution, the second term in Equation (5.6), is given by

$$\frac{\xi_2(s_r)}{1 - \xi_2(s_r)} . \tag{5.7}$$

We would like this average expected value to equal

$$\xi_2 \cdot s_r . \tag{5.8}$$

Equating (5.7) and (5.8), we obtain

$$\xi_2(s_r) = \frac{\xi_2 \cdot s_r}{1 + \xi_2 \cdot s_r} . \tag{5.9}$$

Hence, we define $\xi_2(s_r)$ by Equation (5.9). The same is done for the third term in Equation (5.6), the Erlang-n-distribution. We obtain

$$\xi_3(s_r) = \frac{\xi_3 \cdot s_r}{2 + \xi_3 \cdot s_r} . \tag{5.10}$$

The average expected number of firms according to the last term in Equation (5.6) is given by $e_0(s_r) + \frac{2\cdot\xi_4(s_r)}{1-\xi_4(s_r)}$. There are several ways to make this value linearly dependent on s_r. The most obvious is to assume that the first term, $e_0(s_r)$, is a linear function of s_r,

$$e_0(s_r) = e_0 \cdot s_r \ , \tag{5.11}$$

and that the second term also depends linearly on s_r, which is reached by

$$\xi_4(s_r) = \frac{\xi_4 \cdot s}{2 + \xi_4 \cdot s_r} \ . \tag{5.12}$$

Hence, we finally obtain an Equation (5.6) with nine parameters that are independent of the size of the region, although the resulting distribution shows the requested dependence on the regions' sizes. Four parameters represent the relative contribution of each function, μ_1, μ_2, μ_3, and μ_4, and five parameters determine the exact shape of the functions, ξ_1, ξ_2, ξ_3, ξ_4, and e_0.

5.3 DATA AND EMPIRICAL METHOD

The aim of this paper is to identify industrial agglomerations in Germany. The distributional function developed above is fitted to the empirical data on 198 industries in Germany. The resulting functional form is used to identify agglomerations. The necessary steps are described in detail below. First, however, we describe the data that we use in the analysis.

5.3.1 Empirical data

The data used in this study were collected by the German Federal Institute for Labour. The dataset contains the number of employees for each 3-digit industry[1] and each of the 97 'Raumordnungsregionen'[2] in Germany as of 30 June 2003. The number of employees in a certain industry is defined as the sum of all persons employed at firms classed within this industry. Self-employed persons and one-person firms are not included in the data.

The analysis is restricted to 198 of the 222 industries at the 3-digit level. We exclude all industries that contain less than 100 firm sites because the spatial distribution of an industry with less than 100 firms leads to few statistically significant results. Furthermore, we exclude those industries that represent single households and general state expenditure. Of the included industries, ten belong to agriculture and mining, 95 are manufacturing industries, and 93 are service industries. The industries are denoted

[1] Industries are classified according to the WZ93-classification, which was the standard classification of industries in Germany at the time the data was collected.

[2] 'Raumordnungsregion' are the kind of regions used in German statistics that come nearest to labour market areas. They take into account the commuting of people. However, they do not split the 440 German administrative regions ('Kreise') and do not include areas from different states, which makes them different from what real labour market areas would be in some cases.

by i ($\in \{1,2,...,N_i\}$, $N_i = 198$). The regions are denoted by r ($\in \{1,2,...,R\}$, $R = 97$).

The size of each of the 97 regions is calculated on the basis of total employment in the region. We define

$$s_r = \frac{\sum_{i=1}^{N_i} e_{i,r}}{\sum_{r=1}^{R} \sum_{i=1}^{N_i} e_{i,r}} \, . \tag{5.13}$$

Using the number of employees as a measure for the size of a region allows the results to be interpreted in relative terms. The regional industry-size distribution represents to what extent a region's share of an industry diverges from the pattern expected on the assumption that the industrial structure is exactly the same in each region.

5.3.2 Fitting the model to the data

In a first step the complete distribution (5.6) is fitted to the empirical data. To this end, the parameter set that maximizes the negative log-likelihood value is calculated:

$$L_i = -\ln\left[\prod_{r=0}^{R} P(e_{i,r} = e)\right] \, . \tag{5.14}$$

The parameter sets that maximize L_i are calculated numerically using the direction set method (according to Powell). Because local maxima exist for the log-likelihood function, 1000 different starting points for the parameters are randomly chosen. A repetition shows that the resulting parameter values are reliable. The maximal log-likelihood values are denoted by $\hat{L}_i$.

The ranges of the parameters have to be restricted. Obviously, all of them should be positive. Furthermore, the condition $\mu_1 + \mu_2 + \mu_3 + \mu_4 = 1$ must be satisfied. In addition, the last term in Equation (5.6) requires specific consideration. If we restrict the parameters of this term only by requiring $\mu_4 > 0$, $\xi_4 > 0$, and $e_0 > 0$, the second peak of the distribution might move into the range of the first peak. The whole purpose of this term was to produce a second peak. Therefore, two restrictions are necessary.

First, $e_0 \cdot s_r$ sets a minimum number of employees that must be located in region r if this region falls into the second peak of the distribution and is to qualify as an industrial agglomeration. As argued above, this number has to be high, usually high enough so that no region would contain such a number of employees under normal conditions. For each value of e_0, the number of regions that can be expected (according to the first three terms) to contain more than $e_0 \cdot s_r$ employees without industrial agglomeration can be calculated. This number is denoted by $n_{norm}(e_0)$. The value will never be zero because the other parts of the distribution decrease exponentially and therefore never reach a value of zero. However, according to the above argument the value should be small compared to the number of regions that contain industrial agglomerations according to the clustering part of the distribution. The condition

$$\frac{n_{norm}(e_0)}{R} < 0.2 \cdot \mu_4 \tag{5.15}$$

is used here. This implies that the share of the distribution explained by the last term in Equation (5.6) has to be five times as large as the share of regions that are expected to have more than $e_0 \cdot s_r$ employees on the basis of the other terms.

Second, if local agglomerations are a distinctive phenomenon, they should be the exception to the rule. We would not talk about 'local industrial clusters' if they occurred in most of the regions. Hence, the share of the regions that contain an agglomeration has to be small. We use 10 per cent as a maximum number. This implies that $\mu_4 \leq 0.1$ has to be satisfied.

5.3.3 Adequacy and functional forms

Of course, a distribution function can always be fitted to empirical data with the help of the maximum likelihood method. Since we obtain values for the parameters independent of how good the fit is, it is necessary to conduct two additional analyses.

First, a Komolgorov-Smirnov test is conducted to check whether the empirical distribution is adequately described by the model used. The above distribution is rejected by the Komolgorov-Smirnov test for 30 of the 198 industries. We continue our analysis only for those 168 industries for which the theoretical distribution fits the empirical data. This reduces the number of industries in agriculture and mining from 10 to 8, the number of manufacturing industries from 95 to 92, and the number of service industries from 93 to 68.

The theoretical distribution is mainly rejected for service industries. A possible reason for this is that service industries might be even more uniformly distributed in space than predicted by a random distribution. Some services have to be provided very near to the customer. Hence, they follow strongly the population numbers and thus the size s_r of the regions. This leads to a regional industry-size distribution with a very sharp peak, that cannot be represented by the above theoretical distribution. We can conclude that an additional term is necessary to describe especially some of the service industries.

Second, some of the terms in the theoretical distribution might be superfluous. In order to test this we eliminate each of the functional forms once and fit the remaining theoretical distribution to the empirical data. If the eliminated part is necessary, the fit should become much worse.

The likelihood ratio test is used to check whether eliminating one part of the theoretical distribution (5.6) worsens the fit significantly. The log-likelihood ratio is given by

$$\lambda_k = 2\ln[\hat{L}_i(\mu_k = 0)] - 2\ln[\hat{L}_i] \tag{5.16}$$

if the k-th functional form is eliminated. λ_k measures this difference in the fitting of the data. If one of the first three functions in Equation (5.6), namely the binomial, the exponential, or the Erlang-n-distribution, is eliminated the number of parameters that are fitted to the empirical data is reduced by two. In this case the likelihood ratio test leads to a rejection (significance level of 0.05) of the hypothesis that eliminating the respective part does not change the adequateness of the theoretical distribution if

$\lambda_k > \lambda_{c,1} = \lambda_{c,2} = \lambda_{c,3} = 2.99$ (see Mittelhammer 1996). In the case of the agglomeration part, the number of parameters is reduced by three, so that the hypothesis of this part being unnecessary can only be rejected for $\lambda_k > \lambda_{c,4} = 3.91$. Hence, the likelihood ratio test allows for each part of the theoretical distribution to check whether this part is necessary. If $\lambda_1 > 2.99$, $\lambda_2 > 2.99$, $\lambda_3 > 2.99$, and $\lambda_4 > 3.91$, the complete theoretical distribution describes the empirical data significantly better than any reduced form. This is tested for each industry separately.

If not all parts of the theoretical distribution are proved to be necessary, the theoretical distribution is reduced successively. First the part with the lowest value of λ_k and $\lambda_k < \lambda_{c,k}$ is eliminated. Then, the procedure is repeated with the remaining parts of the theoretical distribution. One part is eliminated, the remaining function is fitted to the empirical data and the likelihood ratio is calculated. Again, it might result that all remaining parts contribute significantly to the fit with the empirical data. In this case the procedure stops. Otherwise the insignificant part with the lowest value of the likelihood ratio is eliminated. This procedure is repeated until every elimination leads to a significant reduction of the fit or only one part or one part and the agglomeration part remain. We obtain a theoretical distribution that describes the empirical data sufficiently well. This theoretical distribution might consist of all four functional forms or of only some of them. The results might differ between industries.

5.3.4 Identification of spatial agglomerations

The last part, the agglomeration part, of the theoretical distribution has been introduced to represent the spatial agglomerations of an industry. We argued that if agglomerations in space exist, there should be a group of regions that contain much more economic activity in the industry than the other regions. This group of regions is represented in the regional industry-size distribution by the agglomeration term. Hence, the identification of these regions with agglomerations is straightforward and proceeds in two steps.

First, spatial agglomerations, as they are defined here, only exist if the agglomeration term significantly contributes to the description of the empirical spatial industry-size distribution. The above described analysis provides us with knowledge about whether the agglomeration term matters in each industry.

Second, for each industry in which the agglomeration term matters the parameter $e_0(s_r)$ of the agglomeration term informs us about the minimal number of employees that the agglomerations in this industry contain. Hence, all regions that contain more than $e_0(s_r)$ employees are called spatial agglomerations of the respective industry.

5.4 STUDY OF GERMANY

The empirical method, which is described above, is applied to the employment numbers of the 168 3-digit industries in Germany for which the theoretical regional industry-size distribution is confirmed by the Komolgorov-Smirnov test. As a result we obtain for each studied industry information about whether each of the functional terms in the theoretical distribution is relevant. We also obtain the values of the parameters.

We proceed in two steps. First, we identify all industries in which regional agglomerations occur and discuss the parameters that characterize these agglomerations. Second, we identify the location of all industry-specific agglomerations.

5.4.1 Industries with regional agglomerations

The set up of the theoretical distribution and the above arguments make the identification of industries with regional agglomerations easy. If there are agglomerations in an industry as we defined them above, the agglomeration term in the distribution has to play a role. While fitting the theoretical distribution to the empirical data, we check for the importance of each term. A likelihood ratio test is used to check whether eliminating a term decreases the goodness of the fit significantly. It is important to notice that by this we can be sure (on a 5 per cent significance level) that the agglomeration term matters in those cases in which it remains in the analysis. We can, however, not be sure that it does not matter if it is removed. Hence, we are rather conservative in identifying industry-specific agglomerations and it can be expected that too few such agglomerations are identified.

First, we give an overview of the industries that show spatial agglomerations, meaning that the agglomeration term plays a role. To this end, all 168 studied industries are categorized into classes of industries. The results for these classes of industries are presented in Table 5.1. In total, for 120 industries regional agglomerations are found. Most of them belong to the manufacturing sector, while for the service industries such agglomerations can often not be confirmed. This confirms the usual focus of the research into agglomeration and clustering on the manufacturing sector. Nevertheless, for quite a number (39) of service industries the existence of regional agglomerations is shown by this study.

Besides identifying the industries in which regional agglomerations exist, the analysis provides us with knowledge about the values of the parameters of the theoretical distribution that is fitted to the empirical data for each industry. The minimal number of employees that have to be present in a region to be called an agglomeration is given by $e_0(s_r)$. This means that the threshold for calling a concentration of employment in an industry an agglomeration is empirically determined in this approach. It results from fitting the parameter $e_0(s_r)$ to the empirical data. We are especially interested in how much more employees have to be located in region than we would expect according to the size of the region and industry to call it an agglomeration. This is given by the value:

$$\phi_i = \frac{e_0(s_r)}{e_i \cdot s_r} = \frac{e_0}{e_i} \,. \tag{5.17}$$

We find that this value differs very much between the studied industries. In the literature sometimes agglomerations of industries are identified mainly based on the relative size of the industry in a region. The value that is analysed is employment ratio:

$$\rho_r = \frac{e_{i,r} \cdot e_{tot}}{e_r \cdot e_i} \tag{5.18}$$

where e_{tot} defines the total employment in the country. ρ_r corresponds to the value of ϕ_i, meaning that in the above approach all regions are defined as containing an industry-specific agglomeration for which $\rho_r > \phi_i$ holds. In the literature usually regions are defined to contain an industry-specific agglomeration or cluster if the value ρ_r exceeds a certain ad-hoc defined value, for example 3 (see Isaksen 1996). The approach taken here differs from the approaches in the literature because the threshold ϕ_i is empirically estimated. The value for each industry is given in the appendix.

The values that we find range from 1.3 to 103.1. However, most values are between 3 and 20 (see Table 5.2). Hence, the threshold results, in general, to be much higher in this approach than in the literature. Since the value is empirically estimated here, we conclude that it is set too low in the literature. However, two features have to be added here.

First, in most industries only one agglomeration is identified. This is partly caused by the choice of the theoretical regional industry-size distribution. We added to this distribution one mathematical term that describes the existing agglomerations. This term is able to describe a number of agglomerations at the same time only if these agglomerations are relatively similar in size. Otherwise, it will only be able to capture one of them, which will always be the largest of them. Hence, the approach taken here might underestimate the number of agglomerations and, thus, overestimate the threshold value ϕ_i. In the industries in which several agglomerations are identified, the threshold value ϕ_i ranges mainly between 3 and 10.

Second, in service industries we find sometimes very low values of ϕ_i, even if only one agglomeration is identified (see, for example, the industry 'Wholesale of household goods' with $\phi_i = 2.6$). This shows that service industries are often very uniformly distributed in space. If then one region has a somewhat higher share of the employment in this industry, it is identified as containing an agglomeration in this industry. This shows that the approach used here takes into consideration the overall distribution of an industry in space. If the distribution is quite uniform, regions with a low employment ratio might already have been identified as containing an agglomeration. If an industry is distributed in space quite unequally, large concentrations are necessary to make an agglomeration. Table 5.2 shows that the service industries are, on average, much more uniformly distributed than the manufacturing industries.

5.4.2 Regional agglomerations

All industry-specific agglomerations that are identified by the above procedure are listed in the appendix. As mentioned above, for most industries we find exactly one agglomeration (see Table 5.3). This is partly caused by the method applied. The method is rather conservative. It tends to identify too few agglomerations in too few industries. Hence, the agglomerations that are identified are very reliable, but there might exist more agglomerations than are identified here.

The identified agglomerations are not equally distributed in space. Most industry-specific agglomerations are found in East Baden-Württemberg (9 agglomerations). Next come Hamburg, Frankfurt and two regions in the West of Bavaria (see Figure 5.4). This corresponds quite well with the economically very active regions.

Class	Number of industries	Passing the Komolgorov-Smirnov test	Cluster term is important
Agriculture, etc.	6	4	3
Mining and quarrying	4	4	4
Primary sector	**10**	**8**	**7**
Food products, etc.	8	7	7
Textiles and leather	11	11	8
Wood and products	5	5	3
Paper, etc.	5	5	4
Chemicals, etc.	9	9	7
Non-metallic products	7	6	4
Metals and products	12	11	8
Machinery and equipment	7	7	6
Electrical and optical equip.	15	15	14
Transport equipment	8	8	6
Manufacturing n.e.c.	8	8	7
Manufacturing sector	**95**	**92**	**74**
El., gas and water supply	4	4	1
Construction	5	2	1
Wholesale, etc.	19	13	8
Hotel and restaurants	5	2	0
Transport, etc.	12	10	6
Financial intermediation	5	3	3
Business activities, etc.	22	22	12
Social services and education	11	4	3
Unions and organizations	3	2	2
Services to leisure activities	7	6	3
Service sector	**93**	**68**	**39**
Total	**198**	**168**	**120**

Table 5.1: Classes of industries and the number of industries within these classes for which the Komolgorov-Smirnov test confirms the adequateness of the theoretical distribution and the agglomeration term is relevant.

ϕ_i	1-2	2-3	3-4	4-5	5-6	6-8	8-10	10-15	15-20	20-50	50-105
Agric. & mining	-	-	-	-	1	-	1	2	-	2	1
Manufacturing	1	1	7	3	4	14	6	16	7	13	3
Services	-	5	10	8	5	5	2	3	1	1	-

Table 5.2: Frequency with which the threshold ϕ_i falls into certain ranges.

Number of identified agglomerations	1	2	3	4	5	6	7	9	10	13
Agric. & mining	7	-	-	-	-	-	-	-	-	-
Manufacturing	54	3	5	4	-	1	3	1	1	2
Service	31	4	1	-	2	-	1	1	-	-

Table 5.3: Number of industries for which certain numbers of agglomerations are identified.

However, regions like Munich and Stuttgart show up with less agglomerations (4 and 3, respectively) than expected. Some of the regions with a large number of agglomerations are quite small regions in terms of population. We find that it is much easier for such small regions to be identified as containing an industry-specific agglomeration because a somewhat higher number of employees in an industry is sufficient. Large regions with a high activity, such as Munich or Stuttgart, require a quite dominating position of an industry to be identified as agglomeration. This is caused by the fact that the analysis is done in relative terms.

Furthermore, Figure 5.4 does not show a clear geographic tendency, such as a north–south or east–west gradient in the number of agglomerations. This contrasts with the usual findings of economic analyses in Germany, which most of the time find a north–south and an east–west difference. Here, no such obvious difference is found, beside the fact that all regions with 6 or more agglomerations are located in the former West Germany.

This changes somewhat if we only consider agglomerations in manufacturing industries (see Figure 5.5). Some domination of the south becomes visible, in line with the well-known higher industrial activity in Bavaria and Baden-Württemberg. Some regions change their position dramatically by this restriction to manufacturing industry. Notably Frankfurt is completely empty if only the manufacturing sector is considered. All industry-specific agglomerations in Frankfurt belong to service industries.

Obviously, the service sector shows a different distribution in space. There are more agglomerations in the north and also in the former East Germany (see Figure 5.6). However, in total the number of agglomerations in service industries is much less and the picture is less homogeneous.

In all these analyses, however, we have to keep in mind that for some industries a lot of agglomerations are identified while for most industries only one agglomeration is identified by the above approach. Hence, the industries with a large number of agglomerations have a comparably strong impact on the geographic distribution of agglomerations.

5.5 CONCLUSIONS

This paper identifies industry-specific agglomerations in Germany. It has been argued that if local clusters exist, they should represent local agglomerations of employment

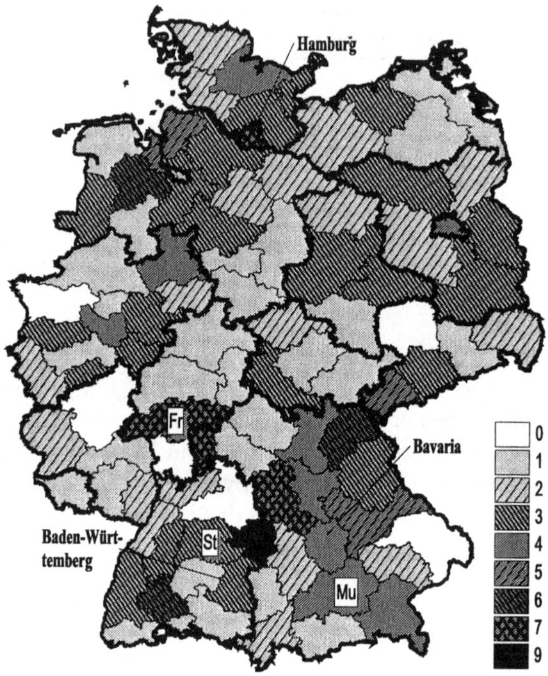

Note: Cities mentioned in the text are marked as **Fr** (Frankfurt), **Mu** (Munich), and **St** (Stuttgart). Thicker lines mark the borders of German federal states.

Figure 5.4: Number of agglomerations in each region.

in the respective industries. A method has been developed, based on the fitting of a theoretical regional industry-size distribution to empirical data, to identify such industry-specific agglomerations. This method has been applied to Germany on the level of 3-digit industries. 198 different industries are studied, including manufacturing as well as service industries.

We find that most manufacturing industries are concentrated in space and that the existence of agglomerations can be proved. Far from all, but still more than half, of the service industries are also geographically concentrated and local agglomerations can be proved to exist. How employment is distributed in space differs very much between industries. As a consequence, the concentration of employment in a region that is necessary to be exceptional differs strongly between industries. Only such exceptional concentrations are called agglomerations here. Thus, the threshold of the employment ratio that is required for an agglomeration depends crucially on the industry studied. We find values ranging from 1.3 to 103.1.

Finally, the geographic distribution of agglomerations in Germany is studied. We find most agglomerations in manufacturing industries in the south of Germany, espe-

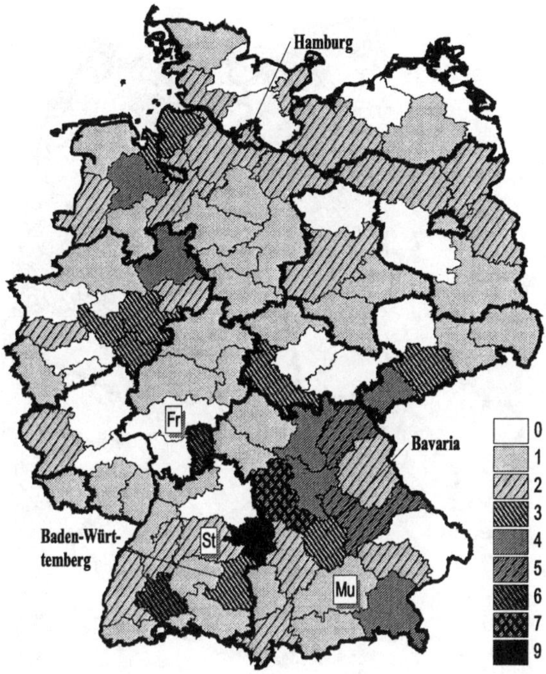

Note: Cities mentioned in the text are marked as **Fr** (Frankfurt), **Mu** (Munich), and **St** (Stuttgart). Thicker lines mark the borders of German federal states.

Figure 5.5: Number of agglomerations in the manufacturing sector in each region.

cially in Bavaria and Baden-Württemberg. The agglomerations in service industries are rather located in the north of Germany and the former East Germany, except for the top position of Frankfurt.

APPENDIX

Here, all industries that are confirmed to show agglomerations in Germany are listed. In addition, for each industry the critical value ϕ_i is listed in brackets and all regions that are identified to contain an agglomeration in this industry are given.

Growing of crops; market gardening; horticulture (5.6): Oldenburg

Growing of crops combined with farming of animals (mixed farming) (12.9): Altmark

Fishing, fish farming and related service activities (37.0): Bremerhaven

Extraction and agglomeration of peat (50.9): Emsland

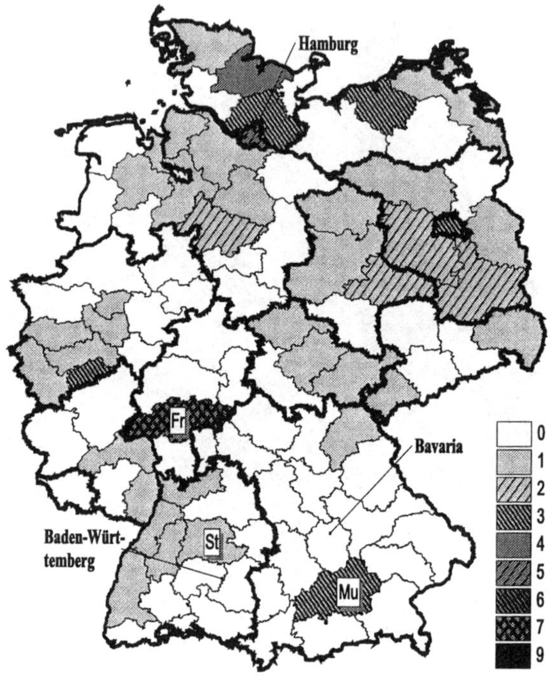

Note: Cities mentioned in the text are marked as **Fr** (Frankfurt), **Mu** (Munich), and **St** (Stuttgart). Thicker lines mark the borders of German federal states.

Figure 5.6: Number of agglomerations in the service sector in each region.

Quarrying of stone (10.5): Ingolstadt

Quarrying of sand and clay (9.2): Oberpfalz-Nord

Other mining and quarrying n.e.c. (21.3): Bayerischer Untermain

Production, processing and preserving of meat and meat products (5.2): Oldenburg

Processing and preserving of fish and fish products (103.1): Bremerhaven

Processing and preserving of fruit and vegetables (12.0): Schleswig-Holstein Ost

Manufacture of dairy products (9.9): Hamburg-Umland-Süd, Lüneburg, Allgäu, Südostoberbayern

Manufacture of grain mill products, starches and starch products (6.7): Schleswig-Holstein Ost, Oldenburg, Emsland, Ingolstadt

Manufacture of prepared animal feeds (42.7): Bremen-Umland

Manufacture of beverages (7.4): Trier

Preparation and spinning of textile fibres (15.6): Hochrhein-Bodensee, Oberfranken-Ost

Textile weaving (25.3): Oberfranken-Ost

Finishing of textiles (14.9): Oberfranken-Ost

Manufacture of made-up textile articles, except apparel (9.2): Südwestsachsen

Manufacture of knitted and crocheted fabrics (16.9): Chemnitz-Erzgebirge, Neckar-Alb

Manufacture of leather clothes (16.1): Südostoberbayern

Manufacture of other wearing apparel and accessories (13.5): Bayerischer Untermain

Manufacture of footwear (37.1): Westpfalz

Sawmilling and planing of wood; impregnation of wood (8.2): Ostwürttemberg

Manufacture of builders' carpentry and joinery (7.5): Trier

Manufacture of wooden containers (3.4): Lüneburg, Mittelhessen, Osthessen, Südthüringen, Westmittelfranken, Regensburg

Manufacture of pulp, paper and paperboard (6.4): Emsland, Aachen, Bayerischer Untermain

Publishing (3.1): Hamburg

Printing and service activities related to printing (3.5): Schleswig-Holstein Süd-West

Reproduction of recorded media (6.4): Westmecklenburg, Mecklenburgische Seenplatte, Bremen-Umland, Hannover

Manufacture of refined petroleum products (19.7): Uckermark-Barnim

Manufacture of basic chemicals (22.4): Rheinpfalz

Manufacture of paints, varnishes and similar coatings, printing ink and mastics (6.8): Lausitz-Spreewald

Manufacture of soap and detergents, cleaning and polishing preparations, perfumes and toilet preparations (6.4): Düsseldorf

Manufacture of other chemical products (6.8): Göttingen

Manufacture of man-made fibres (26.1): Südostoberbayern

Manufacture of plastic products (4.9): Westmittelfranken

Manufacture of glass and glass products (11.1): Oberpfalz-Nord

Manufacture of non-refractory ceramic goods other than for construction purposes; manufacture of refractory ceramic products (24.3): Oberfranken-Ost

Manufacture of bricks, tiles and construction products, in baked clay (13.9): Landshut

Manufacture of cement, lime and plaster (12.2): Schleswig-Holstein Süd-West, Oderland-Spree, Arnsberg

Manufacture of tubes (10.7): Siegen

Other first processing of iron and steel (12.4): Siegen

Casting of metals (8.9): Arnsberg

Manufacture of steam generators, except central heating hot water boilers (12.8): Westmittelfranken

Forging, pressing, stamping and roll forming of metal; powder metallurgy (11.0): Bochum/Hagen

Treatment and coating of metals; general mechanical engineering (7.3): Schwarzwald-Baar-Heuberg

Manufacture of cutlery, tools and general hardware (6.1): Düsseldorf, Ostwürttemberg

Manufacture of other fabricated metal products (8.3): Siegen

Manufacture of other general purpose machinery (5.4): Donau-Iller (BW)

Manufacture of agriculture and forestry machinery (14.1): Bayerischer Untermain

Manufacture of machine tools (6.2): Nordschwarzwald

Manufacture of other special purpose machinery (4.5): Ostwürttemberg

Manufacture of weapons and ammunition (42.7): Südheide

Manufacture of domestic appliances n.e.c. (3.2): Bielefeld, Ostwürttemberg, Donau-Iller (BW), Würzburg, Industrieregion Mittelfranken, Westmittelfranken, Augsburg, Regensburg, Südostoberbayern

Manufacture of office machinery and computers (18.3): Paderborn

Manufacture of electric motors, generators and transformers (12.7): Industrieregion Mittelfranken

Manufacture of electricity distribution and control apparatus (3.5): Bielefeld, Unterer Neckar, Stuttgart, Ostwürttemberg, Schwarzwald-Baar-Heuberg, Oberfranken-West, Donau-Iller (BY)

Manufacture of insulated wire and cable (4.2): Bremerhaven, Oldenburg, Bochum/Hagen, Schwarzwald-Baar-Heuberg, Industrieregion Mittelfranken, Westmittelfranken, Regensburg

Manufacture of accumulators, primary cells and primary batteries (30.5): Ostwürttemberg

Manufacture of lighting equipment and electric lamps (34.1): Arnsberg

Manufacture of electrical equipment n.e.c. (10.6): Oberfranken-West

Manufacture of electronic valves and tubes and other electronic components (7.9): Oberes Elbtal/Osterzgebirge, Oberpfalz-Nord, Regensburg

Manufacture of television and radio transmitters and apparatus for line telephony and line telegraphy (6.4): Schleswig-Holstein Nord

Manufacture of television and radio receivers, sound or video recording or reproducing apparatus and associated goods (18.5): Hildesheim

Manufacture of medical and surgical equipment and orthopaedic appliances (9.5): Schwarzwald-Baar-Heuberg

Manufacture of industrial process control equipment (22.4): Mittlerer Oberrhein

Manufacture of optical instruments and photographic equipment (32.0): Ostwürttemberg

Manufacture of watches and clocks (67.8): Schwarzwald-Baar-Heuberg

Manufacture of motor vehicles (10.0): Braunschweig, Ingolstadt, Landshut

Manufacture of parts and accessories for motor vehicles and their engines (5.1): Nordhessen, Saar, Ostwürttemberg, Bayerischer Untermain

Manufacture of railway and tramway locomotives and rolling stock (25.5): Prignitz-Oberhavel

Manufacture of aircraft and spacecraft (2.5): Hamburg, Bremen, Ost-Friesland, Bremerhaven, Hamburg-Umland-Süd, Bodensee-Oberschwaben, Augsburg, Ingolstadt, München, Allgäu

Manufacture of motorcycles and bicycles (3.3): Oldenburg, Osnabrück, Berlin, Halle/Saale, Bielefeld, Bochum/Hagen, Nordthüringen, Südthüringen, Chemnitz-Erzgebirge, Südwestsachsen, Donau-Iller (BW), Bayerischer Untermain, Main-Rhön

Manufacture of other transport equipment n.e.c. (11.4): Münster

Manufacture of furniture (5.6): Bielefeld, Paderborn, Oberfranken-West

Manufacture of jewellery and related articles (48.8): Nordschwarzwald

Manufacture of musical instruments (18.6): Südwestsachsen

Manufactures of games and toys (1.3): Südthüringen, Chemnitz-Erzgebirge, Südwestsachsen, Stuttgart, Ostwürttemberg, Schwarzwald-Baar-Heuberg, Bayerischer Untermain, Oberfranken-West, Oberfranken-Ost, Industrieregion Mittelfranken, Westmittelfranken, Regensburg, Oberland

Miscellaneous manufacturing n.e.c. (12.2): Westmittelfranken

Recycling of metal waste and scrap (7.3): Magdeburg

Recycling of non-metal waste and scrap (3.1): Westmecklenburg, Prignitz-Oberhavel, Uckermark-Barnim, Oderland-Spree, Magdeburg, Dessau, Oberlausitz-Niederschlesien

Steam and hot water supply (17.5): Mittleres Mecklenburg/Rostock

Site preparation (5.0): Ostthüringen

Sale of motor vehicle parts and accessories (4.7): Rheinpfalz

Sale, maintenance and repair of motorcycles and related parts and accessories (5.1): Dessau

Wholesale of agriculture raw materials and live animals (6.0): Oldenburg

Wholesale of household goods (2.6): Schleswig-Holstein Süd

Wholesale of machinery, equipment and supplies (3.0): Schleswig-Holstein Süd

Other wholesale (3.7): Düsseldorf

Retail sale of second-hand goods in stores (6.6): Schleswig-Holstein Nord

Retail sale not in stores (5.9): Nordschwarzwald

Sea and coastal water transport (20.7): Schleswig-Holstein Ost, Hamburg-Umland-Süd

Non-scheduled air transport (11.0): Hamburg, Lausitz-Spreewald

Cargo handling and storage (6.7): Bremerhaven

Other supporting transport activities (11.4): Rhein-Main

Activities of travel agencies and tour operators; tourist assistance activities n.e.c. (2.9): Rhein-Main

Telecommunications (3.6): Schleswig-Holstein Mitte

Other financial intermediation (6.0): Rhein-Main

Insurance and pension funding, except compulsory social security (3.0): Hamburg, Köln, München

Activities auxiliary to financial intermediation, except insurance and pension funding (9.4): Rhein-Main

Letting of own property (3.9): Berlin

Renting of automobiles (3.9): Hamburg, Mittleres Mecklenburg/Rostock

Renting of other machinery and equipment (3.9): Havelland-Fläming

Renting of personal and household goods nec (2.6): Schleswig-Holstein Mitte, Schleswig-Holstein Süd, Bremen-Umland, Rhein-Main, Mittlerer Oberrhein

Hardware consultancy (6.1): Stuttgart

Software consultancy and supply (4.1): Unterer Neckar

Data processing (4.0): Hannover

Maintenance and repair of office, accounting and computing machinery (4.5): München

Other computer related activities (9.7): Mittelthüringen

Research and experimental development on natural sciences and engineering (4.6): Aachen

Research and experimental development on social sciences and humanities (5.1): Schleswig-Holstein Mitte, München

Advertising (3.6): Hamburg

Provision of services to the community as a whole (5.7): Südheide

Adult and other education (2.8): Mittleres Mecklenburg/Rostock, Vorpommern, Prignitz-Oberhavel, Havelland-Fläming, Altmark, Magdeburg, Dessau, Dortmund, Südwestsachsen

Veterinary activities (4.9): Oderland-Spree

Activities of business, employers' and professional organizations (4.5): Bonn

Activities of trade unions (2.6): Schleswig-Holstein Mitte, Hannover, Berlin, Bochum/Hagen, Rhein-Main

Activities of other membership organizations (3.2): Bonn

Radio and television activities (10.9): Rheinhessen-Nahe

News agency activities (3.3): Hamburg, Lausitz-Spreewald, Berlin, Bonn, Rhein-Main, Oberlausitz-Niederschlesien, Oberfranken-Ost

Other recreational activities (4.3): Nordthüringen

REFERENCES

Bottazzi, G., G. Dosi, G. Fagiolo and A. Secchi (2005), *Sectoral and Geographical Specificities in the Spatial Structure of Economic Activities*, Pisa: Sant' Anna School of Advanced Studies.

Braunerhjelm, P. and B. Carlsson (1999), 'Industry clusters in Ohio and Sweden, 1975-1995', *Small Business Economics*, **12**, 297–293.

Brenner, T. (2001), 'Self-organisation, local symbiosis of firms and the life cycle of localised industrial clusters', *Papers on Economics & Evolution*, **103**, Jena: Max-Planck-Institute.

Brenner, T. (2004), *Local Industrial Clusters: Existence, Emergence and Evolution*, Routledge: London.

Brenner, T. (2006), 'An identification of local industrial clusters in Germany', *Regional Studies*, **40**, 991–1004.

Ellison, G. and E.L. Glaeser (1997), 'Geographic concentration in U.S. manufacturing industries: a dartboard approach', *Journal of Political Economy*, **105**, 889–927.

Ellison, G. and E.L. Glaeser (1999), 'The geographic concentration of industry: does natural advantage explain agglomeration?', *American Economic Review*, **89**, 311–316.

Isaksen, A. (1996), 'Towards increased regional specialization? the quantitative importance of new industrial spaces in Norway, 1970-1990', *Norsk Geografisk Tidsskrift*, **50**, 113–123.

Mittelhammer, R.C. (1996), *Mathematical Statistics for Economics and Business*, New York: Springer.

Paniccia, I. (1998), 'One, a hundred, thousands of industrial districts. Organizational variety in local networks of small and medium-sized enterprises', *Organizational Studies*, **19**, 667–699.

Sforzi, F. (1990), 'The quantitative importance of Marshallian industrial districts in the Italian economy', in F. Pyke, G. Becattini and W. Sengenberger (eds), *Industrial Districts and Inter-Firm Co-operation in Italy*, Geneva: International Institute for Labour Studies, 75–107.

Sternberg, R. and T. Litzenberger (2004), 'Regional clusters in Germany: their geography and their relevance for entrepreneurial acitivities', *European Planning Studies*, **12**, 767–792.

6. Sectoral concentration, business networks and innovative competences in East Germany – an empirical approach to identify economic clusters

Martin T. W. Rosenfeld*, Peter Franz* and Gerhard Heimpold*

6.1 INTRODUCTION

In recent years, politicians and other regional policy actors have increasingly emphasized the attractiveness of their regions by pointing out their potential to work as economic clusters. This has created a certain "cluster euphoria", currently observable in many countries. The trend is based on popular case studies of economically successful clusters – like Silicon Valley – whose success policy makers would like to replicate in other regions. The euphoria on the political front conceals the fact that researchers in regional economics have not yet developed a universally accepted procedure to identify regional clusters. With the exception of numerous case studies there are only a few papers that systematically analyze whole regions or a national economy for potential economic clusters. And even those studies that take all German regions into account (Sternberg, Litzenberger 2004; Brenner 2003; Krätke 2005), differ considerably with regard to methods and results.

What most scholars in regional economics agree on, however, is the hypothesis that spatial concentration of companies and their economic activities are important factors for regional economic growth. This spatial concentration generates agglomeration benefits such as reduced transport and production costs. Especially important are lower information costs, facilitating collaborative research and development between companies. Apart from this general agreement, researchers disagree about the degree of spatial proximity required for the members of a cluster to reap the benefits of

*Halle Institute for Economic Research (IWH), Halle (Saale)

agglomeration. We therefore find great variations in the measurement and definition of clusters. Another point which makes the various definitions of clusters arbitrary and vague is the uncertainty as to the frequency and intensity of mutual relations between companies that is necessary in order to classify them as a cluster. Furthermore, it is still an open question whether the lessons learned from case studies of high-technology clusters can be transferred to other technologies and industries.

For this reason the Halle Institute for Economic Research (IWH) conducted a study for the Federal Office for Building and Regional Planning. The study extends across all planning regions in the new German Länder. The transformation of the East German economy after the German unification might be of special interest for emerging regional clusters. In the study presented in this chapter, three essential aspects of regional clusters are identified. These aspects are explained in section 6.2. When a region features all three aspects in an interrelated fashion, we define this region as an Economic Development Spot (EDS), which can be expected to generate high growth dynamics in the future. The second part of the paper then explains the methods used for identifying EDS empirically. The findings on East German EDS are presented in section 6.3 and their political implications are discussed in section 6.4.

6.2 OPERATIONALIZATION OF ECONOMIC DEVELOPMENT SPOTS (EDS)

According to Porter (1998), one must account for three distinct dimensions when attempting to identify those spatial concentrations that might qualify as clusters (which we call EDS). They include (a) spatial proximity between businesses from the same industry or affiliated industries, (b) co-operative market and non-market relations between these businesses, and (c) the presence of universities and other scientific institutions, industrial associations, and so on, which produce impulses for innovations.[1] We followed this definition, operationalizing the three elements that constitute an economic cluster as shown in Table 6.1.

The following sections explain the methods used for identifying spatially concentrated industries, business networks, and spatially concentrated innovative competences.

6.2.1 Spatially concentrated industries

For this study, we utilize indicators measuring the absolute concentration of industries. To show the absolute spatial concentration of an industry, we calculated the ratio of economic activities of this industry in a certain sub-region to the economic activities in this industry in the region as a whole (that is, the sum of all sub-regions). The seven counties (Kreise) or Free Towns (kreisfreie Städte) in which the absolute concentration of economic activities was highest were classified as containing spatially concentrated

[1] Since it is still unclear whether the three elements used as operationalisation together are sufficient for creating a cluster, we use the term EDS instead of "cluster".

Constituting elements of economic clusters	Operationalization
(a) spatial proximity between businesses from the same industry or from affiliated industries	spatially concentrated industries
(b) co-operative market as well as non-market relations between these businesses	existence of one or more business networks
(c) the presence of universities and other scientific institutions, industrial associations, etc. which provide impulses for innovations	spatially concentrated innovative competences

Source: IWH.

Table 6.1: Constitutive elements of economic clusters and their operationalization

industries.[2] For measuring spatial concentrations, various indicators can be used, for example, value added, sales, number of employees, or number of companies. For the IWH study we use employment data from the statistics of employees subject to social security contributions. The data are classified by counties and Free Towns as well as by industry (NACE two digit numbers). By using industry data that is already based on two digit number classification, it was possible measure the concentration of economic activities of affiliated industries – one element of EDS.

6.2.2 Business networks

Co-operative market as well as non-market relations between businesses represent another element of EDS. Indicators for such relations are the existence of value added chains and business networks. Analysing value added chains would require in-depth interviews with firms. This may be a suitable approach for case study research focussed on individual economic clusters (cf. for instance, the study presented by Scheuplein 2002, on the film industry cluster in the Potsdam-Babelsberg region), but it is simply not practical for an investigation that covers a large territory (in this case: East Germany as a whole). Therefore, only the existence of business networks is used to gauge relations between businesses. Typical characteristics of each network were analysed, especially the type of industry to which the members of the network belong. With this method we attempt to examine whether there are coincidences between the identified spatially concentrated industries and the business networks; such coinci-

[2]Determining the number of production locations (counties, Free Towns) to include is a somewhat subjective process. By focusing on only the n (in this case seven) most important production locations we do not take into account how the economic activities of an industry are spread across all sub-regions (here 118 counties and Free Towns). It can be assumed that economic activities of certain industries are highly concentrated in a small number of counties or Free Towns when they depend on local sources of raw materials or other natural conditions. Activities of those industries for which there is demand in all regions, such as food or construction, are probably spread more evenly across regions. With this in mind, we also measured relative industry concentrations using the Gini coefficient. The findings regarding the relative concentration of industries are included in the full paper (see Rosenfeld et al. 2006).

dences indicate cluster qualities of industry agglomerations.

Identifying business networks requires the operationalization of networks. Ideally, an investigation of networks should cover formal and informal networks. Doing this would have meant conducting interviews among the East German firms to get information regarding their inter-firm relationships. The inherent challenges of an East Germany-wide investigation make the identification of informal business networks impossible in the context of this study. We therefore decided to concentrate on formal networks that present themselves as such, for example through internet presentations, by appointing network managers, or by publishing contact information. We recorded only networks consisting of at least three partners, at least one of which had to be a private enterprise. The other partners could also be public scientific institutions.

We identified formal business networks through a two-step process. First, publicly available information about existing business networks was analysed. The internet platforms of various government-sponsored support programmes for business networks or innovation networks (for example, InnoRegio, NEMO, InnoNet) proved to be particularly useful. We also used information from existing network databases for the Länder Brandenburg[3] and Saxony[4], as well as from the websites of individual networks. Second, questionnaires were sent out to ministries of the East German states, chambers of commerce, and to regional development agencies in order to identify additional networks receiving support from these agencies. Through this method we also found several networks that developed without government support.

6.2.3 Spatially concentrated innovative competences

The term spatially concentrated innovative competences has only recently entered the vocabulary of regional economics and politics. Its use marks a change of perspective in regional economics. While the traditional approach identifies the growth potential of a region by considering its basic location factors such as infrastructure and the availability of human capital, additional factors such as specific entrepreneurial skills, the existence of scientific institutions and the quality of the human capital in a region have recently started to play a more prominent role.

Three elements are important for establishing spatially concentrated innovative competences:

Innovative actors: There must be entrepreneurs in a region who are able to create innovative products and processes with high market potential. Entrepreneurial activities are frequently supplemented by activities of scientific and innovation related institutions such as technology parks.

Common technology: The economic activities in a spatially concentrated field of innovative competences do not necessarily originate from companies in the same

[3]Cf. http://www.kooperationsnetze.brandenburg.de/. The current version of this database includes networks in Berlin, too.

[4]Cf. http://www.sachsen.de/de/wu/wirtschaftsfoerderung/netzwerke/index.html. The network database published by the State Ministry for Economic Affairs and Labour in Saxony is based on a survey by Prof. Dr. Roland Schöne, Technische Universität Cheminitz, Institut für Mittelstandsentwicklung i.G. (cf. Schöne, no year).

industry; manufacturing and service companies and research institutions, however, focus on the same general type of technology.

Spatial concentration within a region: Innovation activities are usually not spread evenly across a region, but are spatially concentrated in a small number of subregions, so externalities that depend on short distances (knowledge spillovers) can take place.

Concerning the operationalization of the concept of spatially concentrated innovative competences, the authors decided to use the patent application statistics classified by county and technological field (Greif, Schmiedl 2002). The analysis was conducted for a period of six years taking into consideration that innovative competences are represented by relatively steady innovation activities. This also reduces the effects of short term fluctuations in the number of patent applications. The frequency of patent applications per technological field and county was calculated for every planning region for the period from 1995 to 2000. We consider a planning region to possess innovative competences as soon as 50 or more patent applications were filed in one technological field in the period observed, that is, on average more than eight per year.

The higher the number of patent applications, the more knowledge has been generated with potential for commercial use. The higher the number of registered patents, the more likely that patent applications were filed by a larger number of companies and research institutions instead of just one source.

6.3 EMPIRICAL FINDINGS ON THE LOCALIZATION AND NATURE OF ECONOMIC DEVELOPMENT SPOTS (EDS)

The indicators developed in section 6.2 formed the basis for an empirical study by the IWH conducted in 2004 in all 23 East German planning regions. The results of this study are summarized in the following map (Figure 6.1). Concentrations of economic activities that qualify as EDS are marked with a black pin. The map also shows regional concentrations of competences, which can be interpreted as potential EDS (marked with a white pin), concentrations which might develop into fully fledged EDS. When a region features any two of the three elements constituting economic clusters, we speak of a potential EDS. To keep the map simple, we included potential EDS only in those planning regions where just one or no EDS proper was identified. In regions with more than one EDS there is usually also a larger number of potential EDS. Presenting them all on the map would overload it.

In total we identified 42 EDS in East Germany. The map suggests there are a lot more of them in the south than in the north of East Germany, a distribution pattern similar to other indicators of economic activity. A more detailed analysis reveals three types of regions: Type I regions contain one or more EDS. Regions which merely contain one or more potential EDS, that is, areas with any two of the three elements constituting economic clusters, are classified as type II regions. Finally, in type III regions there are neither EDS nor potential EDS. Some of the three elements of economic clusters might exist in type III regions, but there is no inter-relationship between them. According to this typology, we classified the East German regions as follows:

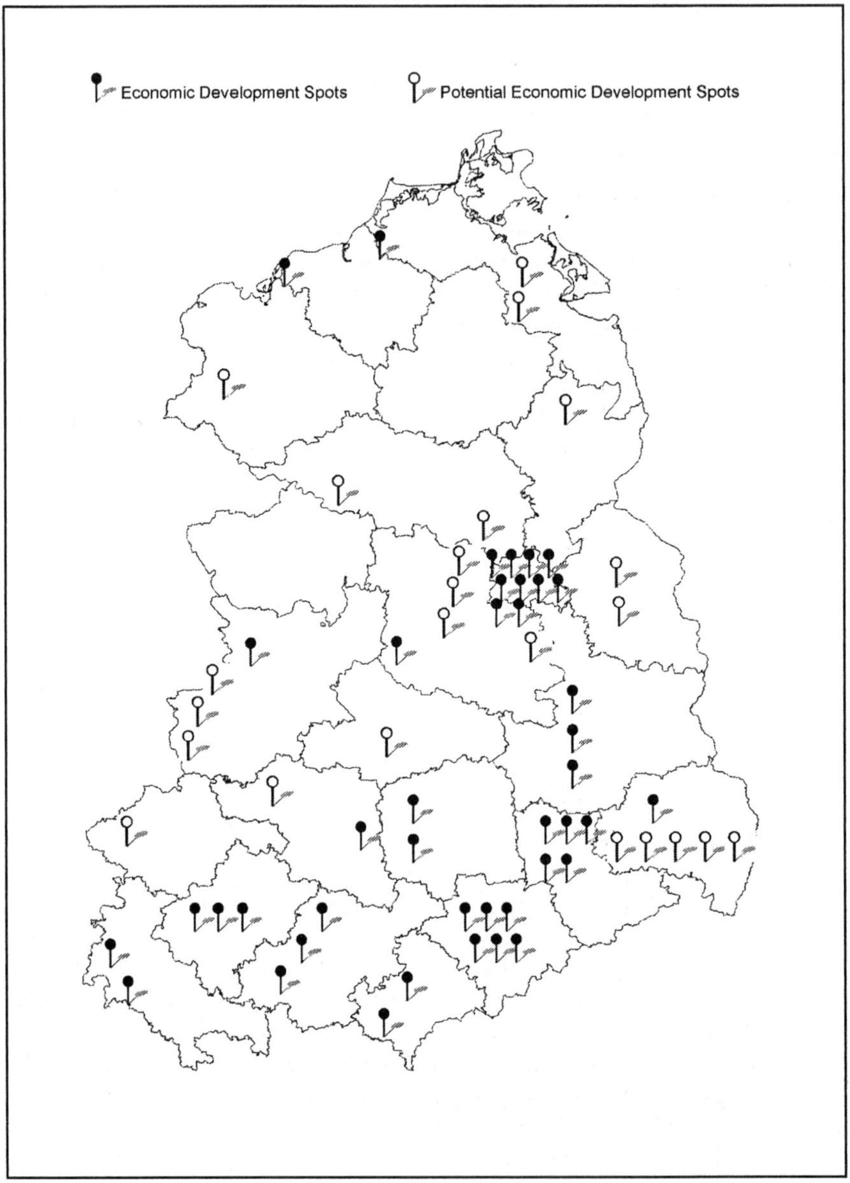

Source: IWH.

Figure 6.1: Regional pattern of Economic Development Spots and Potential Regional Development Spots in the East German planning regions

Of the 23 planning regions 14 qualify as type I regions, that is, they contain at least one EDS. In ten of the 14 regions in this group we identified more than one EDS. Scientific institutions are involved in most of the 42 EDS. We already mentioned the uneven distribution across East Germany. To be more specific, EDS are most common in Saxony (especially in the Upper Elbe Valley and in the Chemnitz Region), Thuringia (except Northern Thuringia), and Berlin including the surrounding regions of Brandenburg. These regions are generally characterized by a high population density and can therefore be described as agglomeration areas.

The (for the most part sparsely populated) northern regions have very few EDS or even potential EDS (type II regions). Seven regions qualify as type II regions: Western Mecklenburg, Western Pomerania, Prignitz-Oberhavel, Uckermark-Barnim, Oderland-Spree, Dessau and Northern Thuringia.

We identified only two type III regions, that is regions where neither potential nor fully-fledged EDS exist. These two regions are the Altmark (in the north of Saxony-Anhalt) and the Mecklenburgische Seenplatte (the lake district of the Land Mecklenburg-Western Pomerania).

6.4 CONCLUSIONS AND IMPLICATIONS FOR REGIONAL POLICY

The purpose of our study was to empirically identify EDS, comprehensively covering a larger economic area, in order to shed new light on the issue of economic clusters. The findings only partly correspond to the picture drawn in the political and public discussion about East German clusters, which often appears influenced by wishful thinking!

Further studies should try to determine whether and to what extent the identified EDS actually have the economic effects that the literature usually attributes to clusters, and whether they contribute to higher economic growth in their regions compared to other regions. Future studies should also verify reported distribution patterns of regional clusters with the help of additional indicators. In particular, the third element of our EDS (patent applications) has to be critically reviewed. Patents are not the only indicator of innovations; in the service sector, for example, innovations are often not patentable. On the basis of additional indicators, the presented results would probably have to be modified.

The policy makers responsible for regional policy and particularly for the economic recovery of East Germany will not be willing to wait until satisfactory answers to these questions have been found. They want to take economic policy measures now. Some recommendations for such measures can be made on the basis of our findings:

1. One obvious regional policy strategy for type II regions is to ensure that the one lacking element of a full EDS can be established. The innovation competence in a region, for example, could be strengthened by establishing or expanding educational or scientific institutions (matching the existing spatially concentrated industries). Relationships between existing research institutions and actors in local industry concentrations can be intensified through a region-specific network

management. It first has to be determined, however, whether the companies of an industry concentrated in that region can be expected to remain there in the long term. When firms' locations are contingent, that is, not tied to regional resources such as raw materials, labour with specific skills, or convenient transport links, promoting the lacking element of an EDS cannot contribute to a bright future for the respective industry in that region. The strategy of adding the missing element is also problematic in regions where this means spatially concentrating industries to complement the existent concentration of innovation competence and networks. Supplementing these elements by selectively setting up "suitable" businesses is bound to fail in many cases simply because the number of companies willing to relocate is limited. Pushing such business relocations with higher investment grants might be a waste of public resources, since the investor would have invested even without subsidies from the government. The best strategy for type II regions that lack a spatial concentration of industries is to pursue its general development policy and to merely draw particular attention to the special competence available in a region (in the sense of the constituting elements of an EDS) and to directly contact companies which are complementary to the existing regional economic structure.

2. Type I regions, especially those with more than one EDS, are probably already favourably equipped with economic growth factors. As mentioned before, the population density in these regions is high. It is possible that the EDS in these areas will develop positively without any government interference. Other IWH studies have shown, however, that East German industry centres are still considerably short on growth factors compared to West Germany (cf. Rosenfeld and Heimpold 2004; Franz 2003). It therefore seems plausible that type I regions still require regional policy support as well. Such measures should selectively support (and stabilize) existing EDS or their constituent elements. However, the preceding cautions regarding potentially misguided policies still apply. The potential EDS existing in type I regions can also be strengthened by supplementing them with the appropriate missing elements of an EDS; this is the same strategy that also seems obvious for type II regions and has been discussed above.

3. Finally, what can regional policy do for type III regions? These regions tend to be rural, peripheral areas with a low population density. It would be very risky to establish "artificial" concentrations of industries there as there are no regional business networks or spatially concentrated innovation competences to link to, and little regional potential to draw on; the likelihood of failure is very high. It therefore seems more reasonable to ensure that peripheral regions will be able to profit from the spillover effects of the centres to a greater extent than they do now. One option, for example, is improving the transport infrastructure, which allows people in the respective areas to commute to jobs outside their home regions.

REFERENCES

Brenner, T. (2003), 'An identification of local industrial clusters in Germany', Jena *Max Planck Institute of Economics, Papers on Economics & Evolution*, **304**.

Franz, P. (2003), 'Wie schneiden die großen ostdeutschen Städte im gesamtdeutschen Vergleich ab? Daten zu ihrer wirtschaftlichen und finanziellen Lage', *Raumforschung und Raumordnung*, **61** (3), 160–169.

Greif, S. and D. Schmiedl (2002), *Patentatlas Deutschland - Ausgabe 2002*, München.

Krätke, S. (2005), 'Wissensintensive Wirtschaftsaktivitäten im Regionalsystem der Bundesrepublik Deutschland: Clusterpotenziale und Beitrag zur regionalen Wirtschaftsleistung', in H.J. Kujath (ed.) *Knoten im Netz. Zur neuen Rolle der Metropolregionen in der Dienstleistungswirtschaft und Wissensökonomie*, Münster, 159–201.

Porter, M. (1998), 'Clusters and competition: new agendas for companies, governments and institutions', in: M. Porter (ed.), *On Competition*, Boston, 197–287.

Rosenfeld, M.T.W. and G. Heimpold (2004), 'Stand und Tendenzen regionaler Disparitäten im wiedervereinigten Deutschland', in F. Gerlach, A. Ziegler (eds), *Neuere Herausforderungen der Strukturpolitik*, Marburg, 73–95.

Rosenfeld, M.T.W., P. Franz, J. Günther, G. Heimpold, Gerhard, F. Kronthaler (2006), 'Ökonomische Entwicklungskerne in ostdeutschen Regionen. Branchenschwerpunkte, Unternehmensnetzwerke und innovative Kompetenzfelder der Wirtschaft', *IWH-Sonderheft* 5/2006, Halle (Saale).

Scheuplein, C. (2002), 'Identifizierung und Analyse von Produktionsclustern. Das Beispiel der Filmwirtschaft in Potsdam-Babelsberg', *Raumforschung und Raumordnung*, **60** (2), 123–135.

Schöne, R. (no year), *Netzwerkuntersuchung. Netzwerkkooperationen von KMU als ein Lösungsansatz für die Regionalentwicklung (Untersuchungszeitraum 1.7. 2001 bis 31.1.2002). Eine Bestandsaufnahme im Freistaat Sachsen mit Schlussfolgerungen und Empfehlungen.* Abschlussbericht (überarbeitete Fassung). Im Auftrag des Sächsischen Staatsministeriums für Wirtschaft und Arbeit. Technische Universität Chemnitz, Institut für Mittelstandsentwicklung i. G., Professur Erwachsenenbildung und betriebliche Weiterbildung, in: http://www.sachsen.de/-de/wu/wirtschaftsfoerderung/netzwerke/download/complete.pdf, accessed April 13, 2005.

Sternberg, R. and T. Litzenberger (2004), 'Regional clusters in Germany - their geography and their relevance for entrepreneurial activities', *Planning Studies*, **12**(6), 767–791.

7. Clusters and the spatial structure of wages in Rio Grande do Sul (Brazil): a multilevel approach

Leonardo Monteiro Monasterio[*‡]

7.1 INTRODUCTION

The purpose of this paper is to test whether a spatial wage structure exists in the state of Rio Grande do Sul, Brazil. Inspired by the New Economic Geography approach (henceforth referred to as NEG), the study aims to measure the effects of locational factors on wages.

The state of Rio Grande do Sul occupies an area of approximately 300,000 km^2 (roughly the size of Italy) and has around 10 million inhabitants. Its socioeconomic indicators are relatively high compared to Brazil as a whole (see Figure 7.1). The service sector represents the largest portion of the state's economic activity (44 per cent of its GDP), followed by manufacturing (41 per cent), and agriculture (15 per cent). However, there are huge regional disparities. The economic history of the different regions has produced a range of features which even today shape public concerns and policies. Reduction of the regional inequalities within the state is usually at the top of the political agenda (although, in practice, public policies are often responsible for increasing these disparities!). Nevertheless, about 61 per cent of the state's industrial production is concentrated in the regions around the axis Porto Alegre–Caxias do Sul.

A wide range of academic literature[1] has been devoted to regional issues in Rio Grande do Sul. Despite the quality of this literature, modern methods of spatial analysis are almost unknown among local researchers, and there are few studies that apply quantitative geographical methods to economic issues. Recently there have appeared interesting long-term studies on the quantitative indicators of industrial concentration (Lautert, 2004), but no explicit spatial analyses. Among the few studies that apply exploratory analysis of spatial data (ESDA) techniques to the economic issues of Rio Grande do Sul is the recent paper by Ruiz and Domingues (2005).

* Department of Economics, Federal University of Pelotas (Brazil)
‡ This research was supported by CNPq.
[1] See Alonso et al. (1994).

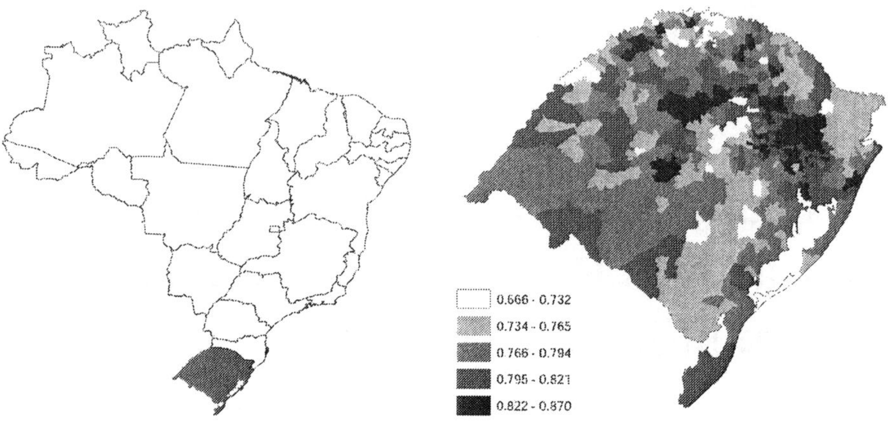

Figure 7.1: Location of Rio Grande do Sul in Brazil (left) and human development index, Rio Grande do Sul, 2000 (right)

The present study extends this previous work by applying quantitative analytical methods. The first part of the paper uses several spatial analysis techniques in order to identify the industrialized and high market potential areas of the state. Spatial smoothing, ESDA, and implicit spatially constrained clustering techniques are applied to the 467 municipalities of Rio Grande do Sul.

This information is relevant to the second part of the study, which uses census data to estimate the impact of agglomeration economies on individual wages across the population of the state. The specific purpose is to test the prediction of a spatial wage structure in line with NEG models (Krugman, 1991; Hanson 1997, 1998, 2000). Is labour productivity (and hence the wages) of workers located near the core of the economy higher than on the periphery? Classical regression provides unreliable hypothesis testing for such questions because of the data's hierarchical structure (Browne and Rasbash, 2004). The spatial determinants of wages are therefore estimated using a multilevel analysis. The regressions considered the individual and municipality levels, and included demographic, occupational, and locational variables. The results suggest that NEG predictions of a spatial wage pattern do indeed exist in Rio Grande do Sul.

The basic source of data is the sample of the Demographic Census of 2000 (IBGE, 2002). This dataset is considered one of the best available sources in Brazil. One of its main features is that it includes the "informal" sector of the economy, which is very important because of the particularly large number of workers it employs in Brazil.[2] After selecting only individuals with the appropriate traits, the sample was reduced to 54,715 manufacturing workers.

[2] It has been suggested that, in Brazil, 54 per cent of the workforce is employed in the informal sector of the economy (Gonzales et al. 2002).

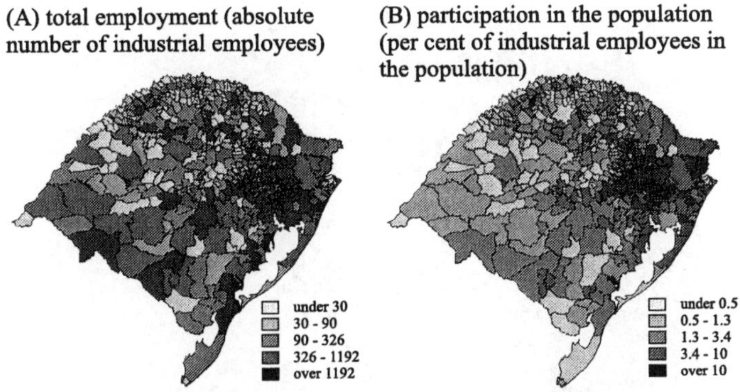

Figure 7.2: Industrial employment in Rio Grande do Sul, 2000

7.2 SPATIAL INDUSTRIAL CLUSTERS IN RIO GRANDE DO SUL

7.2.1 Spatial Distribution of Manufacturing Employees

Exploratory Spatial Data Analysis is a set of techniques used to describe spatial distribution, uncover patterns of spatial correlation or clusters, and identify outliers (Anselin, 1998). This section will begin with very simple data visualization methods before applying more sophisticated techniques.

Figure 7.2 depicts the spatial distribution of manufacturing employment, and its representation in the total working population.

The absolute data map creates an illusion that manufacturing employment is well distributed across space. The rate map, on the other hand, indicates that the eastern part of the state seems more industrialized than the western part. One problem with such data visualization is that the population of municipalities varies widely. The smallest has about 1,000 inhabitants, whilst Porto Alegre has more than 1.3 million. As is widely known, this fact makes the variance of the rate amongst the smallest municipalities higher than the largest ones.

In order to reduce the heteroskedasticity of the data, a process of data smoothing is applied. The chosen process goes like this:

$$\text{Smooth}_i = \frac{\sum_{j=1}^{R} w_{ij}\text{Employment}_j}{\sum_{j=1}^{R} w_{ij}\text{Population}_j} \tag{7.1}$$

The contiguity matrix was calculated based on a distance band criterion. Distance bands are created by drawing a radius around each municipality centroid and counting every other centroid as a neighbour. The program Geoda 0.95 (Anselin, 2004) internally computes the minimum distance necessary to guarantee that each municipality has at least one neighbour; that is, there are no "islands" in the binary contiguity

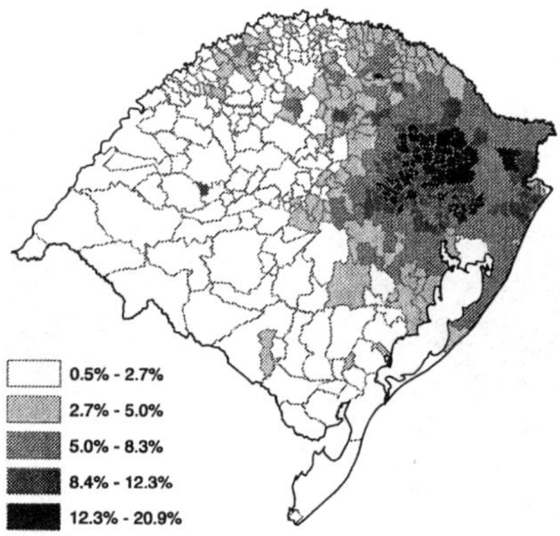

Figure 7.3: Smoothed participation of industrial employment in the population, Rio Grande do Sul, 2000

matrix. This criterion results in a highly connected matrix, with an average of 69 neighbours per municipality. Another departure from the usual procedures is that the w matrix is row standardized, but the values of the main diagonal are set as being equal to 1. This places more weight on the employment density of the unit during the spatial smoothing process. Figure 7.3 depicts the outcome of the smoothing procedure.

As expected, the distribution is smoother, and the data appear much more clustered than in Figure 7.2.

7.2.2 Indicators of Global and Local Spatial Autocorrelation

Moran's I

Is the level of manufacturing employment in the municipalities of Rio Grande do Sul spatially correlated with neighbouring municipalities? Moran's I will be used to evaluate the global autocorrelation of the data (O'Sullivan and Unwin, 2003, p. 197):

$$I = \frac{n}{\sum_{i=1}^{n}(y_i - \bar{y})^2} \frac{\sum_{i=1}^{n}\sum_{j=1}^{n} w_{ij}(y_i - \bar{y})(y_j - \bar{y})}{\sum_{i=1}^{n}\sum_{j=1}^{n} w_{ij}} \tag{7.2}$$

where:

n ... number of spatial units
$y_{i,j}$ ... value of variable y in i or j
$\bar{y}$ ... y average
w_{ij} ... element i, j from the same W matrix explained above.

Using spdep, the spatial econometrics package for R, the Moran I statistic was calculated as 0.33. Hence, H_0 (no spatial autocorrelation) was refuted in favour of H_1 (positive autocorrelation). The Moran scatterplot in Figure 7.4 provides additional information on the spatial structure of the data.

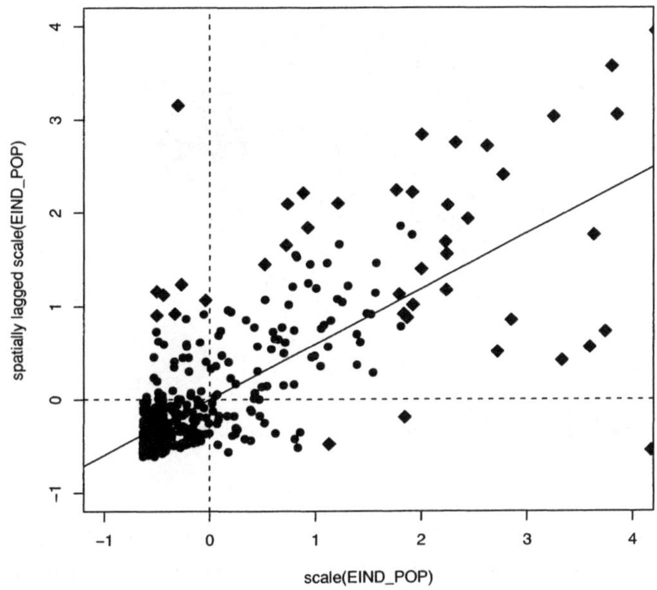

Figure 7.4: Moran scatterplot for the participation of industrial employment in the population, Rio Grande do Sul, 2000

Local Indicators of Spatial Association

The Moran's I statistic indicates global autocorrelation, but is not able to distinguish which areas exhibit correlation with their neighbours. Local tests of autocorrelation were developed in order to solve this. Anselin (1995) established that a Local Indicator of Spatial Association (LISA) should have two properties: (a) show which units have similar values to those of their neighbours; (b) the sum of the individual LISA should be proportional to the global indicator of spatial autocorrelation. Local Moran's I (I_i) has both properties (O'Sullivan and Unwin, 2003, p. 203–204):

$$I_i = z_i \sum_{j \neq i}^{n} w'_{ij} z_j \tag{7.3}$$

$$z_i = \frac{y_i - \bar{y}}{s} \tag{7.4}$$

where

z ... standardized values of y
w' ... normalized values of the W matrix.

Intuitively, the value of a local Moran's I is equal to the value of the attribute in place i multiplied by the weighted average of its neighbours. Values of I_i greater than 0

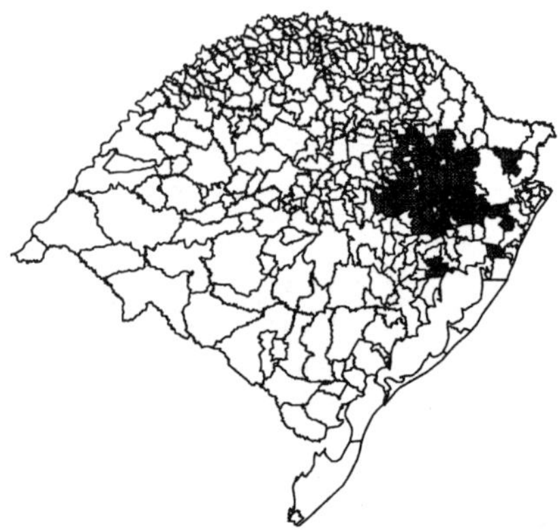

Figure 7.5: Moran's high-high industrialization clusters

suggest positive spatial autocorrelation, whilst those lower than 0 indicate negative spatial autocorrelation. In the present case, the I_i were calculated using the spdep package.[3]

In spdep, the values of Moran's I_i are compared to an analytical reference distribution. The map in Figure 7.5 highlights the areas of High-High clusters, that is, those areas where the place's value and the weighted average of its neighbours are both high.

7.2.3 Market Potential

The market potential of a region was defined by Harris (1954) as:

$$\mathrm{MP}_i = \sum_{j=1}^{R} \left(\frac{M_j}{D_{ij}} \right) \tag{7.5}$$

that is, MP_i , the market potential of i, is the sum of the demand in all places j (M_j) weighted by the inverse of the distance (D_{ij}). Previous regional studies of market potential were more interested in issues concerning manufacturing location. Not surprisingly, they found that manufacturing was concentrated near areas of high market potential (Brakman et al., 2003, p.36).

In this study, market potential will be calculated by using two techniques, the first of which reproduces Harris's (1954) concept. In the second, the Euclidian distance to the economic centre of the state is estimated. Using GDP by municipality as the weighting variable, this centre was calculated as follows:

$$x_m = \frac{1}{n} \sum_{i=1}^{n} \left(x_i \frac{\mathrm{GDP}_i}{\sum_{i=1}^{n} \mathrm{GDP}_i} \right), \quad y_m = \frac{1}{n} \sum_{i=1}^{n} \left(y_i \frac{\mathrm{GDP}_i}{\sum_{i=1}^{n} \mathrm{GDP}_i} \right) \tag{7.6}$$

[3] Geoda and ArcGis use permutations to generate the reference distribution. This produces different results not in the values of the I_i, but in their statistical significance.

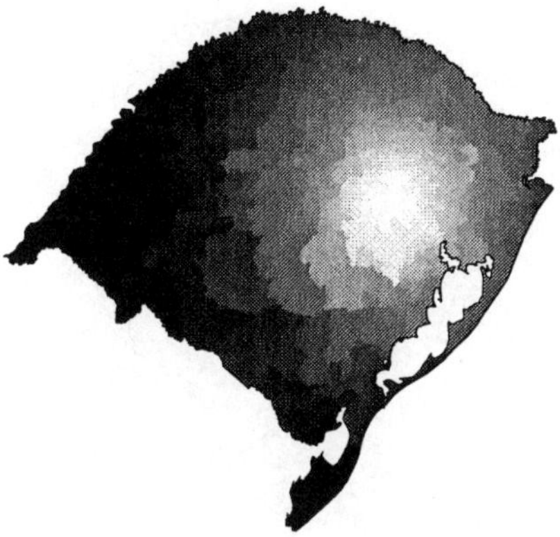

Note: Darker colours represent longer distances

Figure 7.6: Distribution of the Euclidian distance to the economic centre

where x_i and y_i are the latitudes and longitudes of the centroids of each municipality. Using GDP data for 2001 (FEE, 2003), the resulting centre is latitude 29.5923 South and longitude 52.0526 West. This position corresponds roughly to Santa Cruz do Sul, a town with a number of modern tobacco processing units.

Figure 7.6 shows the distribution of Euclidian distances from the centroid of each municipality to the economic centre of the state, while Figure 7.7 represents the market potential. It is clear that the latter statistic provides a richer portrait of the economy of Rio Grande do Sul than the former. The industrial core, that is, the area from Porto Alegre to Caxias do Sul, has a high market potential, but towns in the hinterland, such as Santa Maria, Pelotas and Rio Grande also show above average values.

7.2.4 Implicit Spatially Constrained Clustering

Implicit spatially constrained cluster analysis is a simple way of including spatial dimensions in clustering methods. The survey by Duque and Raúl-Ramos (2005) describes the various methods available, with their strengths and weaknesses. Although other methods are more sophisticated than implicit spatially constrained analysis, this method generates a regionalization which is satisfactory for the purposes of this study. The method is quite straightforward: the Cartesian coordinates of the centre of the spatial unit, properly transformed, are incorporated among the variables considered in the clustering algorithm. In the present study, latitude and longitude (standardized, of course) of the centre of each municipality were treated as variables with the same weight as the economic ones (Calciu, 1996). The obvious criticism against implicit clustering is that there are no guarantees that contiguous regions will emerge. Fortunately, non-contiguity was not a major issue amongst the clusters identified here.

The clara (clustering for large applications) algorithm in R was applied. This is a partitioning clustering method that is able to deal with very large datasets. The algorithm works roughly in two steps. First, it takes a sample of the data and applies a

Note: Darker colours represent higher levels of market potential

Figure 7.7: Market potential

clustering method (PAM: partition around medoid), which creates k medoids. Then, each observation is assigned to its nearest medoid. The process is repeated t times and the sum of the dissimilarities between the observations and their closest medoid is the algorithm's criteria to find the best solution. In the present study, the Euclidian distances were used in order to calculate the dissimilarities between observations and the value of t was set to five.

Only four variables were used to locate the industrial clusters: latitude and longitude of the centroid of the municipality, market potential, and manufacturing employment in the working population (spatially smoothed), as calculated in previous sections of this paper. There are a variety of criteria for selecting the optimum number of clusters. For the purposes of this study it was decided to consider the average size of the silhouette. In this case, the highest average size of the silhouette was reached with $k = 3$. The resulting map is the depicted in Figure 7.8

There are three basic clusters. One includes the industrial core of the state, the so-called Porto Alegre–Caxias do Sul axis. The municipalities in this cluster are the most industrialized, and/or are close to the most economically dynamic areas of the state, with high market potential. The two other clusters correspond, in general, to the non-industrialized municipalities and are far from the industrial core. The cluster in the south includes the municipalities of what is called the "Campanha" of Rio Grande do Sul, and is usually considered to be the state's main regional problem. The northern cluster consists of the "Planalto" region. The clusters identified are roughly contiguous, but not completely so. The spatially constrained implicit clustering method does not, in fact, guarantee contiguity. For instance, Rio Grande and Pelotas, both situated in the south of the state, were included in the cluster of the industrial core. Although this breaks the spatial contiguity of the cluster, it makes economic sense. This area has an important industrial base, and the population of both municipalities (about 500,000 inhabitants) provides a sizeable market.

7.3 MANUFACTURING WAGES IN RIO GRANDE DO SUL

In this section the impact of locational variables on manufacturing wages in Rio Grande do Sul is estimated by using a multilevel approach that utilizes the proxies calculated in the previous section. It is appropriate, however, to present an overview of the theories guiding the econometric tests.

7.3.1 Theoretical Overview

The main hypothesis is that locational externalities generate higher labour productivity and hence higher wages. Although this was a longstanding intuition, it was formalized and developed by New Economic Geography. Krugman, Fujita, Venables, and Thisse, for example, constructed models that explain the formation of a centre–periphery distribution of economic activity. In the long run, and with the right parameters, nominal wages would be higher in the centre and lower outside it. In other words, salaries would be positively related to market potential.

One of the criticisms of NEG is that it is difficult to test its models. Many do not have unique equilibrium solutions, and can only be solved by simulation, or by use of demand variables that are not easily available. However, this kind of criticism is no longer valid. Head and Mayer (2004) have pointed out that there are a considerable number of empirical studies inspired by NEG. There are of course still many problems in the literature, one of which is how to rule out alternative explanations of the results.[4] Nevertheless, it is important to stress that NEG models, especially those related to the wage equation, have received substantial empirical support.

Gordon Hanson (1997; 1998) was one of the first economists to test an NEG model. His 1998 paper tests the Krugman (1991) model as developed by Thomas (1997). The model starts with two identical agents who consume two types of goods: manufactured goods and housing services. There is monopolistic competition, increasing returns on the production of manufactured goods, and iceberg transport costs. Adopting plausible parameters, production is concentrated in few locations.

Intuitively, agglomeration is a consequence of companies trying to reach local markets, reduce transport costs and minimize fixed costs. On the other hand, the centripetal forces are the high level competition near the centre and higher wages (Hanson, 1998). According to this approach, agglomeration economies make it possible to pay higher wages, which can be balanced against the higher costs of living, and/or losses in well-being of living near industrial areas (Brakman et al., 2003, ch. 3).

Hanson (1998) modifies the Krugman (1991) model with the aim of estimating its structural parameters. Hanson's econometric regression, using data from continental USA counties, gives strong support to the predictions of the model: increasing returns on manufacturing together with higher wages near the economic centre.

This paper does not perform a similar structural test of the Krugman (1991) model, since the lack of data makes it difficult to replicate Hanson's tests. In other words, the choice of variables and the research objectives follow the logic of Hanson's paper, but

[4] Fingleton (2004) compares two non-nested models (NEG and Urban Economics) to explain local wage rates in Great Britain. In this case, the empirical test supports the Urban Economics model.

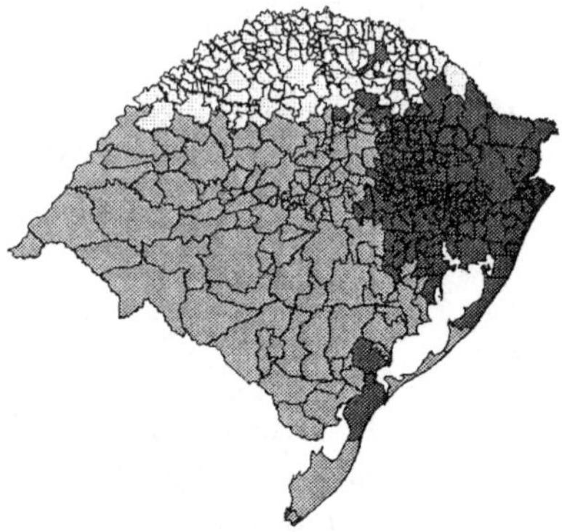

Figure 7.8: Implicit clustering regionalization clara ($k = 3$)

the results cannot be compared with his, nor understood in a structural way. Instead of using data from municipalities, an estimate will be made using individual census data. The research strategy is to estimate a wage regression (Mincer, 1974) and include locational and occupational proxies.

Classical econometrics ignores the possibility that there are grouping effects among individuals. An intuitive example comes from the performance of pupils. Their grades depend on personal efforts or qualities, but also on variables related to their class, school and even educational district. Research on multilevel econometrics has shown that the covariance between the error terms of two pupils from the same class would be non-zero. Hence, traditional OLS results in unreliable hypothesis testing (Browne and Rasbash, 2004).

The present data have a clear hierarchical structure. The wages of workers do not depend exclusively on their personal and occupational characteristics, but also on the location of firms and possible grouping effects. Unfortunately, IBGE census data provide no information about firms. Therefore the study will consider just two levels: the individual (level 1) and the municipality (level 2).

$$w_{ij} = \beta_{0j} + \beta_1 x_{ij} + \beta_2 x_{ij} + \ldots \beta_n x_{ij} + \phi_1 y_{ij} + \phi_2 y_{ij} + \ldots \phi_m y_{ij} + e_{0ij} \quad (7.7)$$

$$\beta_{0j} = \beta_0 + u_{0j} \quad (7.8)$$

where:

w_{ij} ... hourly wage of person i in municipality j.
β_{0j} ... intercept for the jth municipality
x_i ... vector including individual characteristics that may impact the productivity of work or wages.

y_n ... vector with measurable locational aspects of the municipality where the individual i works.
e_{0ij} ... error term of the first level
β_0 ... average intercept for all municipalities
u_{0j} ... error term of the second level.

Both error terms are assumed to be $N(0, \sigma^2)$. The multilevel regression estimates not only the β coefficients, called fixed parameters, but also the variance of the error of both levels (σ^2_{u0}, σ^2_{e0}). These parameters are called random parameters. The correlation between the wages of two workers in the same municipality is given by:

$$\rho = \frac{\sigma^2_{u0}}{\sigma^2_{e0} + \sigma^2_{u0}} \tag{7.9}$$

7.3.2 Variables and Sources

Individual variables based on a sample of 10 per cent of the total population of the 2000 Brazilian National Census (IBGE 2002):

- Schooling: number of complete years of study;
- Age: measured in years;
- Dummies for the colour of individuals: the criterion adopted mirrors the official one, that is, self-identification of colour (yellow, white, native Brazilian, brown, and black);[5]
- Dummy for gender;
- Dummies for occupations: 3 digit index based on the Brazilian Classification of Occupations (CBO).[6]

Locational Variables:

- AGGLOMERATION (smoothed): see section 1.1
- MARKET POTENTIAL: see section 1.3
- REGIONAL CLUSTERS: see section 1.4
- URBANIZATION RATE: share of the population of a municipality living in urban areas in 2000. Source: PNUD (2003).
- URBAN POPULATION: total population living in urban areas in 2000. Source: PNUD (2003).

[5]Although it may sound politically incorrect to use colours to express ethnic features, these categories are officially adopted by the Brazilian Federal Statistical Institute (IBGE). Ethnic relations and definitions are especially complex in Brazil. In fact, more than 70 per cent of self-identified white Brazilian males have at least 10 per cent of genes of African origin (Pena and Bortolini, 2004, p. 43).

[6]Muendler (2006) provides definitions and converters between the CBO and the international classification system (ISCO-88).

7.3.3 Estimation and Results

The selected sample from the Census data for Rio Grande do Sul considers manufacturing workers in formal employment, who are literate, and between 18 and 65 years old. The use of these criteria reduced the sample to exactly 54,715 individuals. The strategy of the analysis was to include all the demographic and occupational data available as explanatory variables in the Mincerian regression.

The data bank of municipal data used in the first section of the study was merged with the individual data according to the individual's place of work (not the place of residence). All regressions were carried out using *R* 2.4.0 (2006) and lme4 package for multilevel estimation. The models were fitted by maximizing the restricted log-likelihood.

Model I is just a baseline, but it supports the hypothesis concerning gender and racial discrimination in the job market. Women's wages are about 23 per cent lower than men's, and black or brown individuals receive 10 per cent and 6 per cent less wages than white individuals respectively, controlling for age and schooling. Obviously, the results may also be influenced by non-observable parameters, such as varying levels of educational opportunity across gender and racial groups.[7]

Model II adds locational variables to Model I. Even when controlling for individual traits, wages are higher in locations with higher market potential, that is, in industrialized and more urbanized clusters. All estimators for locational dimensions have the expected signs, and are statistically significant. In Model III, the non-significant variables from Model II, Planalto and Urban Population, are removed. The results are very similar to the previous model, with no major changes in the values the estimators. Nevertheless, Akaike and Schwarz criteria indicate Model III is the preferred model.

Model III shows that working in a municipality located in the Campanha cluster reduces wages by 3.5 per cent. Based on Model III, the marginal effect of an increase of 1 per cent in the market potential or in the agglomeration is estimated to generate an increase of 0.2 per cent and 0.8 per cent in wages respectively. A hypothetical increase of 1 per cent in the urbanization rate of the municipality corresponds to an increase of 0.06 per cent in individual salaries.

Models II and III also suggest that ρ, the correlation between the wages of two workers from the same municipality, is around 7 per cent $((0.013 + 0.174)/0.174)$. This percentage indicates the share of wage differential that arises from the characteristics of municipalities, even when locational factors are controlled.

It is important to stress that the results refer to nominal and not to real wages. As indicated above, one of the conditions of equilibrium of the model is that there are no differences in real wages among similar individuals.[8]

---

[7] The estimators associated with the dummies for occupation, age and education were omitted from Table 7.1, but are available upon request.

[8] Miranda et al. (2002) run Mincerian regressions for individuals using a different dataset and dummy variables for the Southeastern and Northeastern regions of Brazil. They found that it would be necessary to establish a price index 60 per cent higher in the Southeast in order to equalize real wages between the regions. The authors took this result as an indication of regional differences in Brazil, and do not make any reference to New Economic Geography models.

	MODEL I	MODEL II	MODEL III
CONSTANT	1.256*** (10.52)	-2.050*** (-4.87)	-1.950** (-5.83)
WOMAN	-0.256*** (-57.09)	-0.256*** (-57.34)	-0.256*** (-57.34)
BLACK	-0.100*** (-11.20)	-0.100*** (-11.24)	-0.100*** (-11.25)
YELLOW	-0.045 (-0.71)	-0.044 (-0.70)	-0.044 (-0.70)
BROWN	-0.062*** (-8.00)	-0.061*** (-7.87)	-0.061*** (-7.87)
NATIVE BRAZILIAN	-0.037 (-1.14)	-0.037 (-0.97)	-0.037 (-0.98)
MARKET POTENTIAL		0.163*** (7.12)	0.155*** (10.24)
AGGLOMERATION (SMOOTHED)		0.784*** (3.12)	0.765*** (4.00)
CAMPANHA		-0.037* (-1.65)	-0.035* (-1.69)
PLANALTO		-0.010 (-0.35)	
URBANIZATION RATE		0.066*** (2.43)	0.061*** (3.79)
URBAN POPULATION		-0.002 (-0.24)	
Random Effects			
Second Level σ^2_{u0}	0.032	0.012	0.013
First Level σ^2_{e0}	0.174	0.174	0.174
Akaike Information Criterion	61861	61673	61657
Schwarz Information Criterion	63653	63518	63484
Log-Likelihood	-30730	-30630	-30623

Note: Age, education and occupational dummies were included in all models. t values between parentheses: * significant at 0.10; ** significant at 0.05; *** significant at less than 0.001.

Table 7.1: Econometric results – dependent variable: log of wage per hour in main occupation

7.4 FINAL REMARKS

This paper has aimed to test the effects of location on manufacturing wages in present-day Rio Grande do Sul. Several analytical techniques were used to highlight the spatial patterns of the distribution of industrial activity in the state. They have shown the degree of clustering in this sector and have estimated the market potential of each municipality.

Regression analysis using individual census data suggests that "space matters" in terms of the wages of workers. The results support the hypothesis of New Economic Geography, which asserts that nominal wages, with the proper controls, would be lower in places with lower market potential, low urbanization, low agglomeration economies, and far from the economically dynamic regions of the state.

One of the contributions of this paper is to highlight the usefulness of multilevel analysis and of merging spatial data and individual data. This has made it possible to estimate the effects of agglomeration, urbanization economies and market potential on the wages of manufacturing workers. Nevertheless, one should exercise caution when interpreting the results. Hanson (2000) draws attention to the problems involved with measuring agglomeration economies and their effects. In particular, unobserved exogenous local variables may complicate efforts to understand precisely how agglomeration economies work.

Apart from technical issues, the results of the study are important to policymakers concerned about the regional economic disparities within the state. In order to facilitate the development of effective regional policies, the measurement of agglomerative forces is relevant to decisions concerning which sectors and locations should receive further public incentives.

REFERENCES

Anselin L. (2004), *Geoda: geodata analysis software*, University of Illinois, Urbana-Champaign.

Anselin L. (1995), 'Local Indicators of Spatial Association - LISA', *Geographical Analysis*, **27**, 93–115.

Anselin L. (1998) 'Exploratory spatial data analysis in a geocomputational environment', in P. Longley, S. Brooks, R. McDonnell, W. Macmillan (eds) *Geocomputation: A Primer*, New York, NY: Wiley and Sons, 77–94.

Alonso J., M. Benetti and P. Bandeira (1994), *Crescimento econômico da regiâo sul no Rio Grande do Sul: causas e perspectivas*, Porto Alegre, Brazil: Fundaçâo de Economia e Estatística Siegfried Emanuel Heuser.

Brakman, S., H. Garretsen and C. Van Marrewijk (2003), *An introduction to Geographical Economics*, Cambridge: Cambridge University.

Browne, W. and J. Rasbash (2004), 'Multilevel modelling', in M. Hardy and A. Bryman (eds) *Handbook of Data Analysis*, London: Sage Publications.

Calciu, M. (1996), 'Une méthode of classification sous contrainte of contigué en géomarketing', *Cahiers of recherche of l'IAE de Lille* (96/5). Université des Sciences et Technologies de Lille.

Duque J.C., R. Ramos and J. Surinach (2005), *Supervised regionalisation methods: a survey*. Unpublished manuscript.

FEE (Fundação de Economia e Estatística) (2003), *PIB Municipal do RS - 1985-01*, CD-ROM, Porto Alegre, Brazil: FEE.

Fingleton B. (2004), 'The new economic geography versus urban economics: an evaluation using local wage rates in Great Britain', in European Regional Science Association, *ERSA conference papers*, Porto, Portugal.

Gonzales, R. H. et al. (2002), *A informalidade no mercado de trabalho brasileiro e as políticas públicas do governo federal*, Brasília: MTE.

Hanson G. (1997), 'Increasing returns, trade and the regional structure of wages', *Economic Journal*, **107** (440), 113–33.

Hanson G. (1998), *Market potential, increasing returns, and geographic concentration*, National Bureau of Economic Research Working Paper 6429. Cambridge, MA.

Hanson G. (2000), *Scale economies and the geographic concentration of industry*, National Bureau of Economic Research, Working Paper 8013. Cambridge, MA.

Harris C. (1954). 'The market as factor of localization of the industry in the United States', *Annals of the Association of American Geographers*, **39** (4), 315–348.

Head K. and T. Mayer (2004), 'The empirics of agglomeration and trade', in V. Henderson and J.F. Thisse (eds) *Handbook of Regional and Urban Economics*, Amsterdam: Elsevier North-Holland, 2609–2669.

IBGE (2002), *Censo Demográfico 2000: Microdados da Amostra – RS – 2ª edição*, On CD-ROM. Brasília, DF, Brazil: INGE.

Krugman P. (1991), 'Increasing returns and economic geography', *Journal of Political Economy*, **99** (3), 483–499.

Lautert V. (2004), 'A dinâmica da concentração geográfica na indústria do Rio Grande do Sul (1872-2000)', in *II Encontro de Economia Gaúcha Conference Papers –* May 20th and 21th. Porto Alegre, RS, Brazil.

Mincer J. (1974), *Schooling, experience and learning*, New York, NY: Columbia University.

Miranda R., C. Oliveira, M. Almeida, M. Mac Dowell and R. Ellery jr. (2002), 'Regional wage difference in Brazil: is there a regional problem?' *II Encontro Brasileiro de Estudos Regionais e Urbanos Conference Papers.*

Muendler, Marc (2006), *Resources for research on Brazil*, available from http://www.-econ.ucsd.edu/muendler/html/brazil.html.

O'Sullivan D. and D. J. Unwin (2003), *Geographic Information*, Hoboken, NJ: Analysis Wiley.

Pena S. and M.C. Bortolini (2004), 'Pode a genética definir quem deve se beneficiar das cotas universitárias e demais ações afirmativas?' *Estudos Avançados*, **18** (50), 31–50.

PNUD (2003), *Atlas do Desenvolvimento Humano no Brasil*, CD-Rom. Brasília: PNUD.

R Development Core Team (2006), *R: A language and environment for statistical computing*, Vienna, Austria: R Foundation for Statistical Computing, http://www.R-project.org.

Ruiz R. M. and E. P. Domingues (2005), 'Corredores Industriais na Região Sul', *VIII Encontro de Economia da Região Sul Conference Papers.*

Thomas A. (1997), *Increasing returns, congestion costs and the geographic concentration of firms*, mimeo, Washington: International Monetary Fund.

8. Measuring specialisation and concentration in regional clusters – an empirical analysis for Eastern Bavaria

Joachim Möller* **and Nicole Litzel**‡

8.1 INTRODUCTION

What is a cluster? Is it more than just a fashionable brand used for a strand of regional politics and economic development? A prerequisite of a brand is a definition and a clear shape. Clusters have not attained these sharp outlines yet. Despite a vast literature on the topic, an unequivocal definition that also includes a mode of operationalisation and falsification is still missing, as are methodical frameworks for cluster identification and empirical analysis.

Being such a soft concept, the term "cluster" is very broadly used and can be interpreted in nearly as many different ways as there are users. It is also a rather attractive concept: clusters are embraced in a vast spectrum of contexts from highly formalised models of regional economic theory (see Fujita et al. 1999, chapter 16) to practical training units for business development institutions. Undoubtedly, the concept is in vogue, thereby making it a ripe target for criticism. On the other hand it can be seen as a good example of new results of applied research quickly finding their way into practical economic policy.

Cluster phenomena are manifold and can be observed - be it in the geographic concentration of companies, in the functional specialisation of regions, in cooperation between companies and even competitors, as well as in strong networks linking research institutions and companies. The description of localisation economies - standing at the core of cluster theory - dates back to the work of Marshall (1890).

Nonetheless, empirical studies using sound scientific methods are scarce. It is still an open question if clusters really do have a positive effect on the "fitness" of companies and regions. Many results are either based on more or less anecdotal evidence

* Institute for Employment Research (IAB) and University of Regensburg
‡ University of Regensburg

or rely on statistical data with thin cluster-specific information. Considering the hefty sums – usually from public sources – invested in network development and support programmes, more reliable measures for gauging the effects and benefits of policies would constitute a valuable contribution.

An obstacle on the way to conduct sound empirical studies is the lack of suitable data. The official industry classifications are based on branches and can therefore only partially support value-chain-oriented studies. Input–output tables depicting trade links between industries could be applied to aspects of cluster analysis if they had a regional focus, a prerequisite for location-based studies. In addition, the analysis of cluster structures requires data at the company level. Cluster phenomena are observed by looking at the links between firms, suppliers, customers, their research and development partners, and other network connections.

Adding a company-based, cluster-oriented information system to the existing industry-level data would greatly contribute to our ability to study cluster structures. Of course, the systematic collection of this type of information requires a considerable amount of work, beginning with an identification of regional clusters. For many purposes such databases with company-specific information exist, but they are rarely systematic, lacking data on backward and forward linkages. They are also often not publicly accessible.

Thanks to a local initiative of public institutions and private companies, a cluster-oriented regional information system[1] was created in 2000 for Eastern Bavaria, consisting of the districts of Upper Palatinate and parts of Upper Franconia and Lower Bavaria. Further work is currently being carried out in the European Metropolitan Region Nuremberg and in the economic space along the Danube from Regensburg to Passau at the Austrian border.

The idea of this paper is to use the cluster-specific information collected in CORIS in order to contribute to the quantification and operationalisation of cluster phenomena, focusing on measurements of regional specialisation and spatial concentration of economic activities.

8.2 CLUSTERING PHENOMENA

According to Feser and Sweeney (2002, p. 111), "... industry clusters are typically defined as significant geographic concentrations of major end-market industries, their extended supply chains, other sectors that share close technological or human capital affinities, and various specialized supporting institutions". Alternatively, a cluster can be understood as "... a geographically proximate group of interconnected companies, suppliers, service providers and associated institutions in a particular field, linked by externalities of various types" (Porter 2003, p. 562). Examining these statements, it is clear that clusters can encompass a variety of things and that a precise definition is lacking. But there is overwhelming evidence for the existence of this phenomenon of clustering. Indeed the most powerful argument for such an approach to understanding regional economies is that clusters are simply there.

[1] Available under the brand CORIS at www.coris.eu.

New Economic Geography provides a justification why clusters – although differing largely in their phenotype and being so difficult to grasp by hard statistics – have become a dominant feature of our thinking about regional economic development. One theoretical backbone is the interrelationship between economies of scale, transport costs in the widest sense and externalities of market size. How can it be advantageous to locate where others are? New Economic Geography[2] discusses models based on monopolistic competition. They explain the phenomenon of clustering through the interactions of companies and consumers and the existence of scale economies and transport costs (Dixit and Stiglitz 1977, Ethier 1982). Krugman's core–periphery model (1991b) with its modifications and expansions[3] represents an important step in explaining the concentration and aggregation of production under certain parameter settings. The interaction of choice of location, production and consumption can lead to a self-reinforcing process of production centralisation. The focus here is on the vertical integration along a value chain. Companies are grouped not only by their industry affiliation, but by the industries they are connected with. These forward and backward linkages (Hirschman 1958) are externalities occurring through increasing demand or production in the market and are characteristic for the dynamics of clustering.

In the Dixit-Stiglitz world of New Economic Geography, a major benefit of agglomerating economic activity is the variety of inputs available in the vicinity at low transport costs. Finding accurate inputs spurs productivity. However, for increasing the probability of good matches, "blurred" and unspecific diversity is not helpful. The nature of the input diversity has to correspond to the companies' fields of activity, or their specialisations. In other words, what counts is variety focused on a specific value chain. This is closely related to the concept of functional specialisation at the regional level, a notion that has been coined to indicate the loosening of the traditional clear-cut borders of industrial branches, which are now often crossed by more and more complex customer–supplier relationships. Hence diversity meets specialisation.

Neglecting the borders of different industries along the lines of input-output linkages and between productive units on the one hand, and supporting services on the other appears to be quite typical for clustering. It can therefore be understood as a holistic form of regional specialisation combining the actions of different players along a – by integration of production and outsourcing possibly sliced (for example Ethier 1982, Feenstra 1998) – value chain including the cooperation of firms and research units and other supporting institutions. This new approach takes the edge out of the dichotomy between diversity and specialisation postulated in former studies (for example Glaeser et al. 1992).

Functional specialisation also plays a role in grasping major trends in structural development of the economy. Several empirical studies show for instance that the specialisation of regions measured by the spatial concentration of certain production activities using conventional industry classifications has been declining (Kim 1995 for the USA, Möller and Tassinopoulos 2001 and Haas and Südekum 2005 for Germany).

---

[2]See, for example, Krugman 1991a, Ottaviano and Puga 1997, Fujita et al. 1999, Fujita and Thisse 2002, Head and Mayer 2004.

[3]See, for example, Krugman and Venables 1995, Helpman 1998, Puga 1999, Forslid and Ottaviano 2003.

Seen in isolation these results indicate a growing geographic spread of horizontally interlinked companies and could be used as an argument against clustering.

However, taking into account intersectoral specialisation changes the picture. A decline of industry-based specialisation might well be compatible with a growing importance of functional specialisation.[4]

The advantages of functional specialisation of a region (and thereby clustering) are based on three lines of arguments: input sharing, labour market pooling and knowledge spillovers.[5]

All in all, one can conclude that economic theory provides powerful theoretical arguments for the existence of clustering. For empirical analysis, however, the fuzziness of cluster concepts remains, a fact well recognised in the literature (for a critical view see for example, Martin and Sunley, 2003). As Enright (2003, p. 101), for instance, bemoans: "Despite all the research that has been done, the variety of regional clusters still poses a problem of definition. Similar terminology is used for clusters with widely different characteristics. 'Cluster' terminology seems so embedded that one despairs of redefining or sharply defining the term." He suggests a range of criteria to provide a useful and applicable classification for various types of clusters. Unfortunately, most of these criteria, or cluster dimensions as Enright puts it, remain fuzzy as well.

Enright (2003) offers some evidence of the variety of specific clusters along these dimensions on the basis of a questionnaire sent to 160 cluster experts worldwide. These dimensions cover aspects like geographic scope, density, breadth, depth and stage of development of the clusters. Moreover, characteristics of firms forming the clusters like geographic span of sales, technological activity, innovative capacity, and ownership structure all play a role in classification. It turns out that existing clusters vary widely with respect to all of these dimensions. Concerning geographical scope, for example, ". . . the cluster can spread across provincial or national borders, spread through a state or province, be located in city, or even highly localized within a city." (Enright 2001, p. 3)

The underlying problem is that economic spaces are byproducts of historical processes of business formation, growth and decline. They reflect economic and political history, regional circumstances like accessibility and market potential, availability of natural resources, artisan traditions, impacts of economic policy and so on. Additionally, the value-added chains in which regions typically specialise differ substantially in their complexity and in their requirements for technology, skills and logistics. The conglomeration of all these diverse forces makes the resulting structure of each economic space as idiosyncratic as any organic structure, or, as Guinet (2003, p. 154) puts it: "A cluster is always a singularity in the economic space. (. . .) Clusters are inherently different between countries (or regions), between technological areas, and

[4]A new variant of functional specification is described by Duranton and Puga (2005). They observe an important change in the division of labour between cities of different size. "Cities shift from specialising by sector – with integrated headquarters and plants – to specialising mainly by function – with headquarters and business services clustered in larger cities, and plants clustered in smaller cities" (Duranton and Puga 2005, p. 343). The authors find evidence for this hypothesis by investigating the spatial dispersion of occupations and skills.

[5]For details see, for example, Marshall 1890, Rosenthal and Strange 2003, Duranton and Puga 2003 or Baptista 2003.

ultimately between individual clusters themselves."

This variety hampers the operationalisation of clustering as a workable empirical concept. It seems that a passepartout is illusionary. However, the situation is not as bad as it seems at first glance. In the following section we argue that there are strategies for identification of clusters and that objective measurement concepts do exist at least for certain cluster dimensions. Instead of presenting a comprehensive strategy, we demonstrate how empirical methods can be applied if a suitable database for a regional economy is available. It is argued that the empirical analysis of cluster phenomena should be based not only on secondary statistical sources but also on data collected using a region-specific survey design.

8.3 IDENTIFICATION OF REGIONAL CLUSTERS AND BUILDING A DATABASE

For the analysis in this paper it is necessary to obtain a cluster-oriented regional database that does not structure a region according to the usual statistical industry classification, but along regional value chains or clusters. Inherent in this approach is the recourse to firm-specific data. For Eastern Bavaria, such information has been collected.

8.3.1 Methodology of cluster identification

To identify regional clusters we developed a methodology to systematically register the value-chain-oriented structures and functional specialisation in an economic space. The survey is conducted along the core competencies of individual companies and institutions and their interactions that can be observed. Firm-specific and cluster-relevant data are collected and backed by geographic information.

The methodology involves several interconnected elements. To gain initial insight into the economic structures and identify some leading companies in the region, in-depth interviews with experts from different institutions are conducted. In the following step, members of the managing board of the leading companies are interviewed as well, leading to information about further relevant firms and institutions in the region, which are then also considered for interviews. Since many different fields of interest have to be taken into account, a detailed manual for each type of interview has been developed.

After this stage, a rough outline of the region's main value chains is visible – including first indications about the segments covered by regional competencies – and a share of the relevant companies and institutions are identified. The geographic boundaries of the cluster-specific economic space also begin to shapen. These often span administrative borders and should if possible be defined by functional considerations.[6]

[6]Feser et al. (2001) also work on the conceptual problem of clusters neglecting administrative borders. As a basis for further quantitative and qualitative analyses they develop a methodology that combines a non-spatial technique revealing inter-industry links with an analysis of employment patterns in economic space.

Cluster	Criteria				
	Concen-tration	Pole companies	Pool workforce	Support. inst.	Networks
AUT	++	+++	++	++	+++
EE	+	+++	+++	++	++
S-MAC	++	++	+++	++	++
PLA	+	++	++	+	o
P&C	++	+++	+++	+++	+
G	++	+++	+++	++	+
IT	++	o	+	++	++
LOG	+	++	+	+	+
BIO	+++	o	++	++	++
(FPT)	++	+	+	o	o

Table 8.1: The set of cluster criteria and their application to Eastern Bavarian data

We then develop a company survey on the basis of the information acquired in the interviews regarding cluster potential, inter-firm linkages, and the location's strengths and weaknesses. The questionnaire focuses on deepening the cluster-specific information. It contains sections inquiring about customer–supplier relationships and co-operations, joint projects, for example in the development of human capital or research, functional versus industry affiliation, products and services offered, core competencies, innovations, company size by turnover and number of employees, company structure and so on. The detailed firm-specific information is complemented by a focused analysis of secondary statistical data.

For the identification of cluster potential in a region we developed a set of five criteria to which the data apply. Table 8.1 gives an overview of these criteria and to what extent they are evidenced by different fields in our reference region, Eastern Bavaria. The nine value chains we identified in the Eastern Bavarian economic space as clusters operate in the Automotive Industry [AUT], Electronics & Electrical Engineering [EE], Specialised Automation [MAC], Plastics Industry [PLA], Biotechnology [BIO], Information Technology [IT], Glass & Glass Processing Industry [G], Porcelain & China [P&C] and Logistics & Specialised Trade [LOG]. After the first expert interviews some other industries, for instance food processing technology [FPT], were considered as well, but the data could not support their inclusion as clusters.

The first collection of data was carried out in 2000 and 2001. The information system is constantly updated, offering the opportunity to trace developments in the regional economic structure. Consequently, two new clusters – Sensors and Renewable Primary Products – will be included in the information system soon.

We used five criteria to identify clusters. In the next section we describe them with reference to examples from Eastern Bavaria.

First, we consider the economic activities in the region and see whether we can identify particular elements. Along with that comes a structuring of each value chain according to the main competencies covered by the regional players. Especially when using the database for economic policy guidelines and network management, it is useful to move beyond the simple categories of producer, supplier, and institution in order to further differentiate the various parts of the value chain. In some clusters it is possible to refer to the NACE codes for a description of the various functions, but for others it makes sense to depict them in more detail. Taking the automotive industry, for instance, the NACE codes DM.34.00 cover manufacture of motor vehicles (DM.34.10), manufacture of bodies (coachwork) for motor vehicles (DM.34.20) and manufacture of parts and accessories for motor vehicles and their engines (DM.34.30). In CORIS the automotive industry is divided up into ten categories: car manufacturers, first tier suppliers of plastics, electronics, metals and further systems, second tier suppliers of plastics, electronics and further components, further suppliers of services and machinery, supporting institutions and services. This is one strategy to shed some light on the hierarchical structures in a value chain and at the same time to further describe and analyse the region's economic competencies.

Second, we look for the existence of leading companies in the industries under consideration. We speak of a leading company if a local firm shows at least two of the three following characteristics: it is highly dynamic and leads in the development of technologies and manufacturing processes (technology leader); it has a leading market position in certain segments (market leader); its name is closely connected to a certain product or technology at a national and/or international level (image). For Eastern Bavaria, qualifying firms in the automotive industry include the producer BMW (including process and product optimisation, but no further R&D), leading first tier suppliers like Siemens VDO, Webasto, Grammer and Harman/Becker (all of them with either headquarter or R&D facilities) and further pole companies in other parts of the value chain.

Third, the phenomenon of labour market pooling is taken into account. Can the existence of a specialised workforce be observed? In some areas an obvious pooling of skills is found, for instance highly specialised craftsmen in glass and porcelain, or engineers in electronics and robotics. Interviews reveal that employers are aware of the improved possibilities for skill matching in a functionally specialised region (as observed as well by Andersson et al. 2004). Also, there is evidence of poaching incidents as described by Combes and Duranton (2001) and Fosfuri and Rønde (2003). Indications for a trade-off between pooling and poaching can be derived from a range of cooperation projects that include the intense cross-company exchange of employees.

Fourth, we examine supporting institutions and their sectoral importance. Vital contributors to cluster structures include universities and universities of applied sciences with cluster-relevant faculties and fields of research and the willingness to cooperate, research institutes, technical and vocational schools, technology transfer institutions, regional development agencies, working committees and network management organizations. All of these can be found in the economic space analysed: namely an internationally renowned vocational school for a broad range of glass applications, faculty chairs for special fields in biochemistry, in logistics, and in psychology for the development of man–machine interfaces, and network management agencies for biotechnology, sensors and information technology.

The last criterion is the evidence of cooperation between firms and between companies and institutions. Joint actions in the sense of coopetition, described by Brandenburger and Nalebuff (1996) as the cooperation between competitors, are also of some importance. In Eastern Bavaria the latter can be observed in joint R&D projects undertaken by porcelain manufacturers – usually fierce competitors in the end markets – and research institutions, as well as in a mutual purchase group and a cross-company trainee-programme. Many different kinds of cooperation occur in managed networks such as the "cluster initiative" in Security IT or the strategic partnership in sensor technology. Another example is the microsystems laboratory at the Regensburg University of Applied Sciences, which enables joint research projects with electronics companies. Lastly, there are also several instances of collaborative development projects between producers and suppliers, often involving exchange of personnel.

8.3.2 Database

We use data collected in the cluster-oriented regional information system CORIS[7] for Eastern Bavaria. Firm-level data stem from the implementation of the methodology described above, to which we append geographic information. A company survey conducted in the region in 2001 led to 315 questionnaires returned. The information obtained was added to the results of more than 100 in-depth interviews with experts of regional economic structures and company representatives. Further information was garnered from media reports and internet research. Also, companies and institutions are invited to submit their indications with an online questionnaire.

Roughly 1,400 online entries of firms and institutions are available and updated on a regular basis. For the following analysis we use only company information. Since some of them are affiliated with more than one cluster, the total number of observations is 1,433. All company database entries include an indication of size – either the exact number of employees at the location or the company's placement in employment size categories. In the latter cases we used the mean of the class as indicator for the size of the firm.

8.3.3 Evidence on functional specialisation

The company survey conducted in Eastern Bavaria included two questions aimed at highlighting divergences between a company's official industry classification and its functional affiliations in regional value chains. The outcomes are depicted in figures 8.1 and 8.2.

The answers to the question "Which industry is your company working in?" reveal that electrical engineering dominates with nearly one third of all employees in the region. The second largest industry is automobile construction with more than 20 per cent, followed by metals and mechanical engineering (see Figure 8.1).

[7] available under http://www.coris.eu

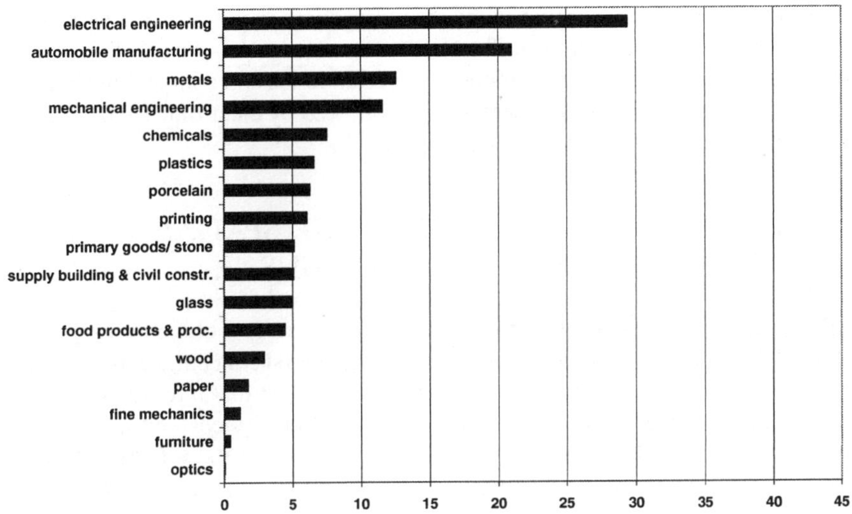

Source: Eastern Bavarian company survey, companies weighted by number of employees

Figure 8.1: Industrial affiliation of companies

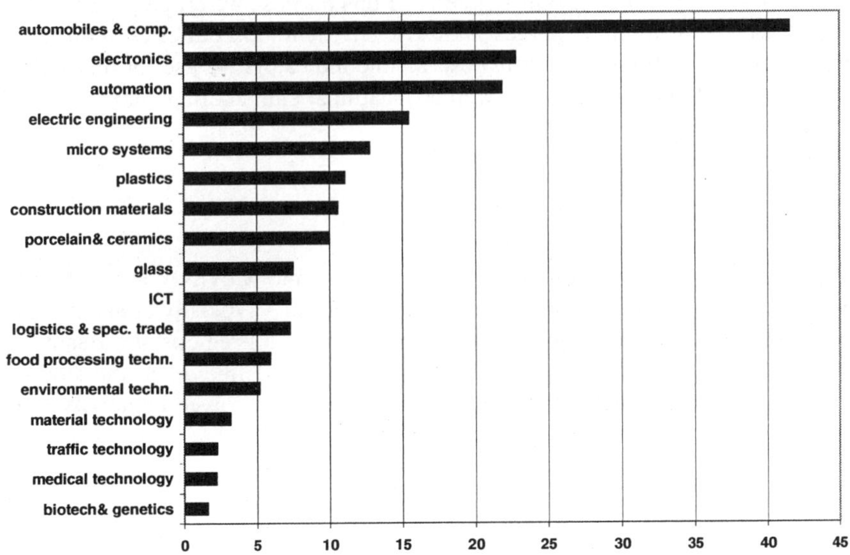

Source: Eastern Bavarian company survey, companies weighted by number of employees

Figure 8.2: Industries and functional specialisations

In order to capture the complexity of functional affiliations, the question "Which industry is your company working in, be it as a producer, a supplier or a service company?" offered firms the option of choosing more than one industry. The results of this question suggest the dominant industry is automobiles and components with more than 40 per cent of employees connected to it, followed by electronics and automation with roughly one fifth of employees (see Figure 8.2).

8.4 SPECIALISATION OF REGIONS AND SPATIAL CONCENTRATION OF VALUE CHAINS

The phenomenon of clustering stands in close relation to two classic concepts in regional analysis, the specialisation of regions and the spatial concentration of economic activities. Regional specialisation is understood as the fact that a region has comparative advantages in the production of certain goods and services and uses – relative to other regions – a high share of its productive capacities in these fields. Concentration of an activity in space implies that production of a certain kind is not distributed "evenly" in space, that is, according to population density, for instance. Although the two concepts differ, they are interrelated to some extent. Specialisation typically entails concentration and concentration brings about specialisation.

Having collected data based on the concept of clustering we can apply indicators previously developed to measure specialisation and concentration in space. The results are compared to corresponding indicators using traditional industry classification in the region (source: Federal Labour Office). For this purpose we employ the 79 2-digit industries, as well as the nine biggest industries in the region out of all industries. In the following sub-sections we briefly describe the indicators we use for measurement (Krugman and Herfindahl indices as well as locational Gini coefficients).

8.4.1 Specialisation of regions

Measurement concepts

Let x_{ir} be the number of firms for measuring economic activity i in sub-region r, where the latter is taken as a spatial unit at NUTS3 level – typically counties – in the current context. Furthermore, let $x_{i.}$ denote activity i in all regions, $x_{.r}$ denote total activity in sub-region r and $x_{..}$ overall activity. Moreover define a_{ir} as the total share of activity i in region r and A_{ir} as the share of the region involved in activity i in the aggregate:

$$a_{ir} = \frac{x_{ir}}{x_{.r}} \quad \text{and} \quad A_{ir} = \frac{x_{ir}}{x_{i.}}. \tag{8.1}$$

In addition we use the share of region r across all activities and the share of activity i in total aggregate activity across all regions:

$$a_r = \frac{x_{.r}}{x_{..}} \quad \text{and} \quad A_i = \frac{x_{i.}}{x_{..}}. \tag{8.2}$$

We can then define measures of specialisation of a region according to the Krugman and Herfindahl indices as

$$\text{SPEC}_r^K = \sum_i |a_{ir} - A_i| \quad \text{and} \quad \text{SPEC}_r^H = \sum_i a_{ir}^2. \tag{8.3}$$

A third possibility for measuring regional specialisation is offered by the modified Gini coefficient. Calculate the Balassa index

$$B_{ir} = \frac{A_{ir}}{a_r} = \frac{a_{ir}}{A_i}, \tag{8.4}$$

then form pairs composed of the share of an activity in total economic activity of a region, a_{ir}, and the share of the corresponding activity in total economic activity, A_i. Sort these pairs in ascending order and denote the resulting sequences by a tilde. The cumulated ordered shares are given as

$$\tilde{s}_{jr} = \sum_{i=1}^{j} \tilde{a}_{ir} \quad \text{and} \quad \tilde{S}_{jr} = \sum_{i=1}^{j} \tilde{A}_i \quad \text{for} \quad j = 1, \ldots, I. \tag{8.5}$$

Plotting $\tilde{S}_{jr}$ on the horizontal and $\tilde{s}_{jr}$ on the vertical axis yields a quasi Lorenz curve. The modified Gini coefficient as a measure of regional specialisation can then be calculated as

$$\text{SPEC}_r^G = 1 - \sum_{i=1}^{I} (\tilde{s}_{i-1,r} - \tilde{s}_{ir})\tilde{A}_i \quad \text{with} \quad \tilde{s}_{0r} = 0. \tag{8.6}$$

A Gini coefficient value of zero indicates no specialisation, while a value of one indicates perfect specialisation.

Specialisation by firms

We measure economic activity by the number of firms weighted by the number of employees.[8] Figure 8.3 depicts the results for the Lorenz curves for regional specialisation using conventional industry statistics for the nine biggest industries in the region, whereas Figure 8.4 gives the results using data from CORIS, which is based in the concept of functional specialisation.

In order to obtain more quantitative information on the degree of specialisation, we calculated the Gini coefficients, the Herfindahl and the Krugman indices. Again, we compared the results for specialisation indicators obtained by the cluster-based data with an indicator of specialisation using official statistics for the nine biggest industries in the region. The results are depicted in Figures 8.5, 8.6 and 8.7.

Three main conclusions can be drawn. First, the Lorenz curves clearly indicate differences in specialisation between the sub-regions in our sample. Both graphs in

[8] For some of the firms only employment categories are available. In these cases we used the mean of the class as indicator for the size of the firm.

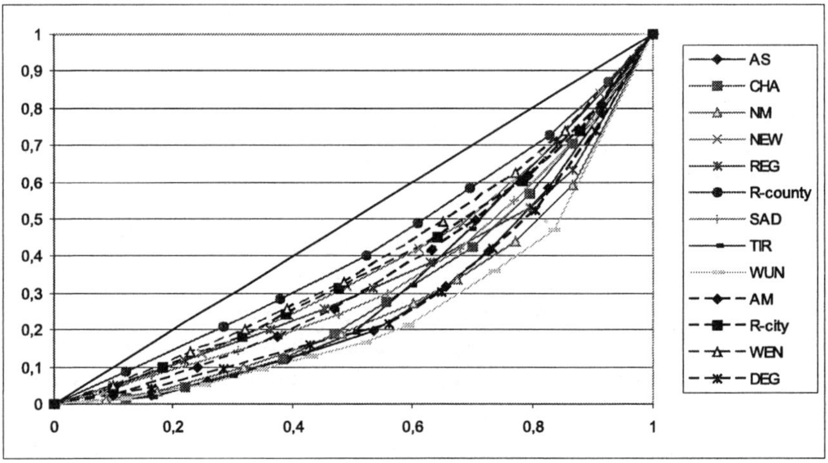

Source: Federal Labour Office, industry size by number of employees

Figure 8.3: Lorenz curves of regional specialisation for 13 counties in Eastern Bavaria using the nine biggest industries

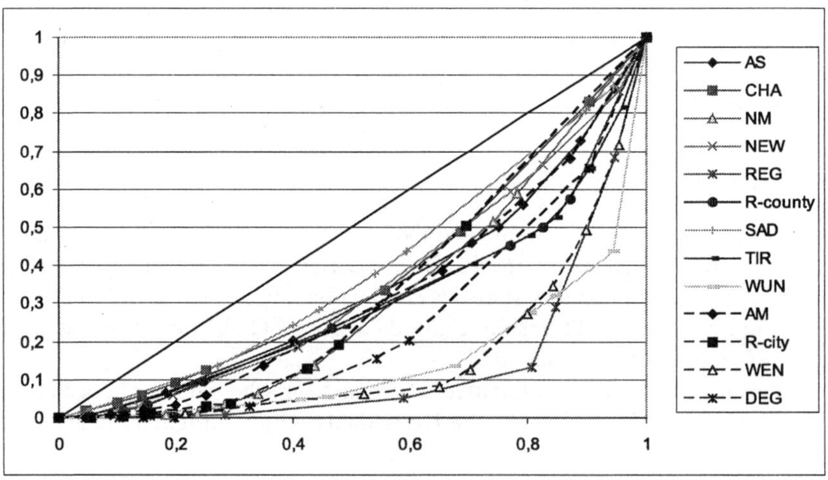

Source: CORIS data, firms weighted by number of employees

Figure 8.4: Lorenz curves of regional specialisation for 13 counties in Eastern Bavaria using the nine value chains

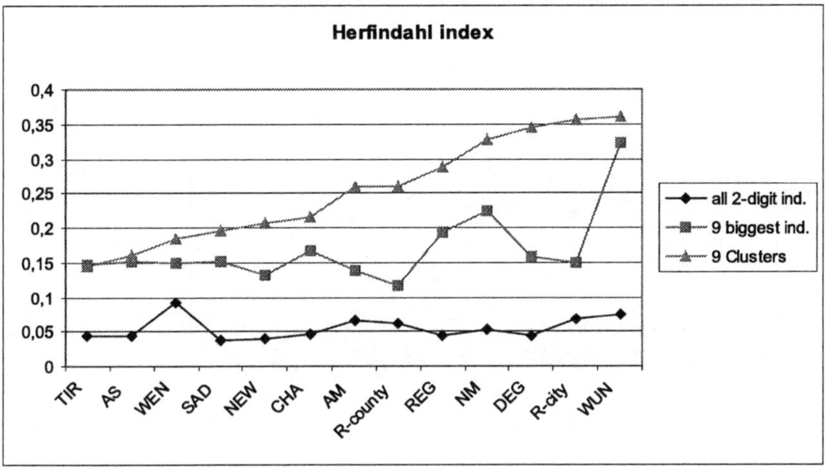

Figure 8.5: The Herfindahl indices of regional specialisation, using official statistics (all 2-digit industries and the nine biggest industries in the region) and the cluster-based CORIS data.

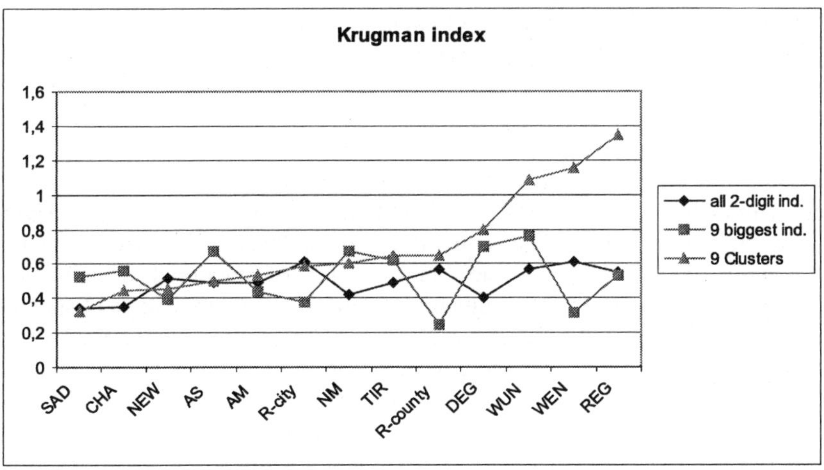

Figure 8.6: The Krugman indices of regional specialisation, using official statistics (all 2-digit industries and the nine biggest industries in the region) and the cluster-based CORIS data.

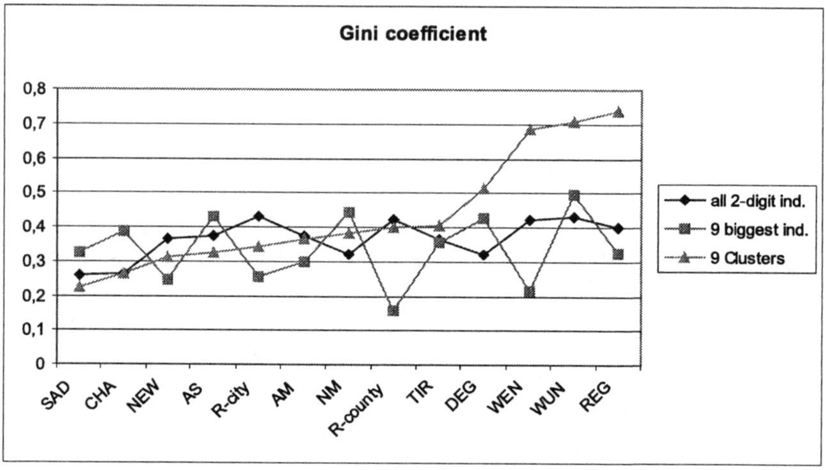

Figure 8.7: The Gini coefficients of regional specialisation, using official statistics (all 2-digit industries and the nine biggest industries in the region) and the cluster-based CORIS data.

Figures 8.3 and 8.4 show that the Lorenz curves for regional specialisation vary considerably between the NUTS3 regions in Eastern Bavaria. Independent of firm size we observe a high level of specialisation for example in the Regen county, a small region in the Bavarian Forest heavily specialised in glass industry. Other regions, like Cham or Schwandorf, are much more diversified across value chains or clusters.

Second, the degree of observed specialisation differs markedly between the concepts of official industry and cluster affiliation.

Third, the variance in regional specialisation is much higher for the cluster-based concept. Three regions (REG, WUN and WEN) show a considerably higher degree of specialisation than the others. The results indicate that these regions exhibit an industrial structure dominated by few value chains or forms of functional specialisation.

A systematic overview of the results for the three different indicators of specialisation is given in Table 8.2, whereas Figures 8.5–8.7 depict the patterns of the individual indices. For the Herfindahl index the cluster-based approach nets higher values than the conventional industry measurement in all counties but one. In the case of the Krugman index this is true for seven out of 13 counties. The Gini coefficient is higher using the cluster-based approach in only five of the thirteen counties. In all three cases the cluster-based approach yields a larger range of values between counties.

The Krugman index and the Gini coefficient tend to move together and produce a similar ordering of the regions. The results of the Herfindahl index, however, differ markedly from the other two measures. This can be verified by the correlation coefficients between the three different indices shown in Table 8.3. The Krugman index and Gini coefficients for the same underlying data sets are highly correlated with correla-

Region	All 2-digit industries			Nine biggest industries			Nine value chains (Clusters)		
	Herf.	Krugm.	Gini	Herf.	Krugm.	Gini	Herf.	Krugm.	Gini
AS	0.044	0.487	0.373	0.151	0.677	0.432	0.160	0.502	0.327
CHA	0.046	0.347	0.262	0.167	0.562	0.386	0.216	0.449	0.262
DEG	0.044	0.404	0.319	0.158	0.696	0.426	0.344	0.797	0.515
NM	0.052	0.419	0.321	0.225	0.675	0.445	0.327	0.605	0.383
NEW	0.039	0.515	0.366	0.131	0.390	0.247	0.207	0.457	0.311
REG	0.043	0.547	0.402	0.192	0.532	0.325	0.287	1.347	0.738
R-county	0.061	0.570	0.420	0.117	0.244	0.160	0.259	0.647	0.399
SAD	0.037	0.337	0.257	0.152	0.522	0.326	0.196	0.322	0.225
TIR	0.044	0.493	0.365	0.148	0.620	0.358	0.145	0.643	0.405
WUN	0.075	0.572	0.431	0.322	0.764	0.496	0.360	1.085	0.708
AM	0.065	0.489	0.372	0.138	0.433	0.299	0.259	0.535	0.366
R-city	0.068	0.614	0.429	0.150	0.379	0.253	0.356	0.589	0.345
WEN	0.092	0.608	0.422	0.149	0.317	0.216	0.184	1.155	0.687

Table 8.2: Specialisation indices for 13 counties in Eastern Bavaria

tion coefficients exceeding 0.98 in all cases. The Herfindahl index is correlated with the other two indices in the case of the two industry data sets, but not for cluster-based data. Cross correlation between the nine biggest industries data and the other two data measurements is not significant. However, cross-correlation between the 2-digit industry measurement and the cluster measurement is statistically significant in both the Krugman and the Gini indices. Nonetheless the correlation coefficient does not exceed 0.6. We conclude that there are certain – but far from perfect – correspondences between information in a comprehensive industry data set and information based on the cluster approach.

The highest degree of specialisation is found for the regions WEN, WUN and REG. All these counties contain extensive shares of glass and porcelain industries, both forming traditional clusters.

Specialisation by occupations

Further evidence of specialisation can be obtained by analysing information on occupations. For this purpose we use a social security microdata set (IABS). IABS is a 2 per cent random sample of all employees obliged to pay contributions to the German social security system. The scientific use file includes detailed information on 130 occupations and gives regional information. Due to data security conventions, however, some of the counties in the economic space selected for our analysis were aggregated. As a result, the number of regions for our empirical investigation is reduced to ten. The dataset includes observations on 7159 persons employed as of 30 June in 2001, the most recent year for which data are available.

We went through the 130 occupations and ordered them into two groups. The first contains 32 occupations that have an affinity to at least one of the nine clusters identified in the region, while the other 98 occupations are classified as being not cluster-specific. For example, glass makers, porcelain painters, electric engineers

		All 2-digit industries			Nine biggest industries			Nine clusters		
		Herf.	Krugm.	Gini	Herf.	Krugm.	Gini	Herf.	Krugm.	Gini
All 2-digit industries	Herfindahl	1.000								
	Krugman	***0.670***	1.000							
	Gini	***0.649***	**0.984**	1.000						
Nine biggest industries	Herfindahl	0.230	0.065	0.139	1.000					
	Krugman	-0.338	-0.438	-0.332	***0.660***	1.000				
	Gini	-0.261	-0.446	-0.342	**0.704**	**0.985**	1.000			
Nine clusters	Herfindahl	0.245	0.186	0.242	0.537	0.206	0.253	1.000		
	Krugman	0.465	***0.558***	***0.583***	0.453	0.067	0.043	0.312	1.000	
	Gini	0.505	***0.557***	***0.597***	0.517	0.127	0.106	0.339	**0.986**	1.000

Note: Bold (bold italic) figures are significant at the 1 per cent (5 per cent) level.

Table 8.3: Correlation coefficients for industry-based specialisation indices of 10 counties in Eastern Bavaria

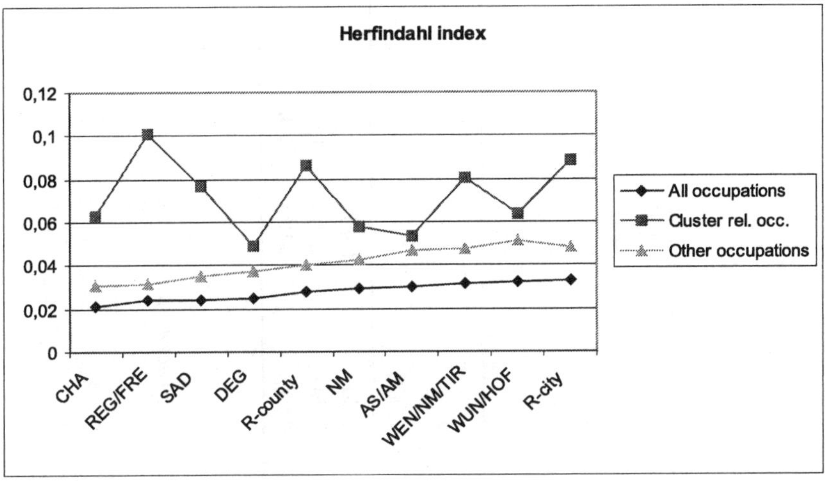

Figure 8.8: Herfindahl indices of regional specialisation by occupation ordered by results for all occupations

and IT experts belong to the first group, secretaries, accountants and salesmen to the second.

Specialisation measures were calculated for the ten regions using all occupations and dividing them by cluster-specific and other occupations. Again, the results in Figures 8.8–8.10 show a high degree of correlation between the Krugman and Gini indices, while the Herfindahl index follows a somewhat different pattern. For the former, the region with the highest number of employees (the city of Regensburg) exhibits the highest degree of specialisation, while smaller regions in northern Upper Palatinate and parts of Upper Franconia show the lowest. It is remarkable that the specialisation rankings for both the Krugman and Gini indices are more or less invariant against changes in the underlying sample of occupations. The correlation matrix in Table 8.4 reveals a high correlation between the Krugman and Gini indices for the same underlying data, but also a high correlation of the results for all occupations and the sub-sample of cluster-specific ones.

It should be stressed that for all cases the indices based on cluster-relevant occupations show the highest values. We conclude that regional specialisation – at least to some extent – is driven by cluster-specific occupations.

8.4.2 Concentration of industries

Measurement concepts

As with indices of regional specialisation, one can also define indices for the measurement of spatial concentration of industries. There is no concentration if the share of an industry in total regional activity is the same across regions. By contrast, the highest

		All occupations			Cluster relevant occupations			Other occupations		
		Herf.	Krugm.	Gini	Herf.	Krugm.	Gini	Herf.	Krugm.	Gini
All occupations	Herfindahl	1.000								
	Krugman	0.035	1.000							
	Gini	-0.005	**0.994**	1.000						
Cluster relevant occupations	Herfindahl	0.040	0.420	0.388	1.000					
	Krugman	-0.010	**0.975**	**0.984**	0.492	1.000				
	Gini	-0.025	**0.960**	**0.975**	0.516	**0.992**	1.000			
Other occupations	Herfindahl	**0.971**	-0.115	-0.157	-0.148	-0.186	-0.201	1.000		
	Krugman	0.078	**0.983**	**0.968**	0.312	**0.921**	**0.901**	-0.045	1.000	
	Gini	0.021	**0.978**	**0.979**	0.235	**0.933**	**0.912**	-0.103	**0.984**	1.000

Note: Bold (bold italic) figures are significant at the 1 per cent (5 per cent) level.

Table 8.4: Correlation coefficients for occupation-based specialisation indices of 10 counties in Eastern Bavaria

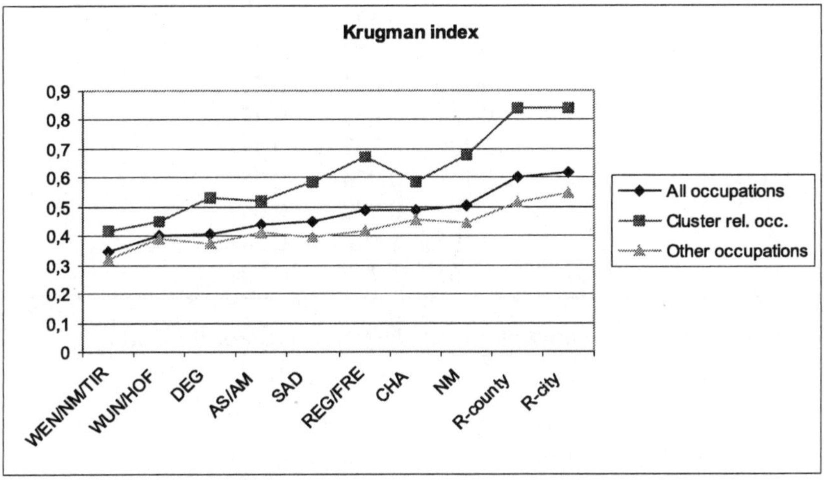

Figure 8.9: Krugman indices of regional specialisation by occupation ordered by results for all occupations

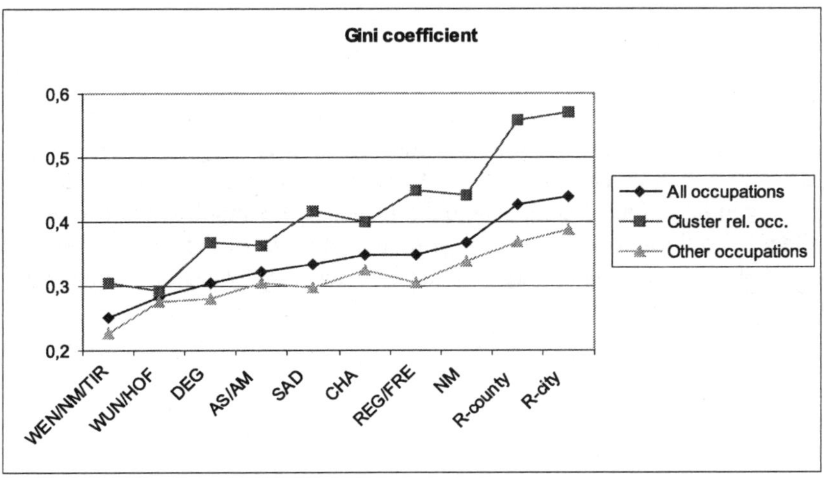

Figure 8.10: Gini coefficients of regional specialisation by occupation ordered by results for all occupations

Clusters	Herf.	Krugm.	Gini
EE	0.215	0.490	0.287
AUT	0.247	0.453	0.290
MAC	0.146	0.611	0.419
IT	0.204	0.667	0.473
PLA	0.120	0.707	0.481
BIO	0.159	0.924	0.585
GLA	0.183	0.970	0.647
LOG	0.196	1.001	0.647
P&C	0.261	1.276	0.769

Table 8.5: Concentration indices for nine clusters in Eastern Bavaria

possible concentration is given if an industry is present in one region only.

The Krugman index as a measure of spatial concentration of industry i is defined as

$$\mathrm{CONC}_i^K = \sum_r |A_{ir} - a_r|, \tag{8.7}$$

while the corresponding Herfindahl measure is

$$\mathrm{CONC}_i^H = \sum_r A_{ir}^2. \tag{8.8}$$

Using the definitions from above, the Gini coefficient as a measure of spatial concentration can be calculated as follows. Starting point is a region's share of total aggregate activity in a given industry A_{ir}. Regions are sorted according to the Balassa index in ascending order. Again, denote the sequence of variables obtained in this way by a tilde. In addition to $\tilde{A}_{ir}$ the corresponding values of $\tilde{a}_r$ are also required, that is, the shares of total regional activity in total aggregate activity. Define cumulated values as

$$\tilde{Z}_{ij} = \sum_{r=1}^{j} \tilde{A}_{ir} \quad \text{and} \quad \tilde{z}_{ij} = \sum_{r=1}^{j} \tilde{a}_r \quad \forall \quad j = 1, \ldots, R. \tag{8.9}$$

The Lorenz curves are obtained if the $\tilde{z}_{ij}$ and $\tilde{Z}_{ij}$ are depicted on the horizontal and vertical axes, respectively. The Gini coefficient can be calculated as:

$$\mathrm{CONC}_i^G = 1 - \sum_{r=1}^{R} (\tilde{Z}_{i,r-1} + \tilde{Z}_{i,r})\tilde{a}_i \quad \text{with} \quad \tilde{Z}_{0,i} = 0. \tag{8.10}$$

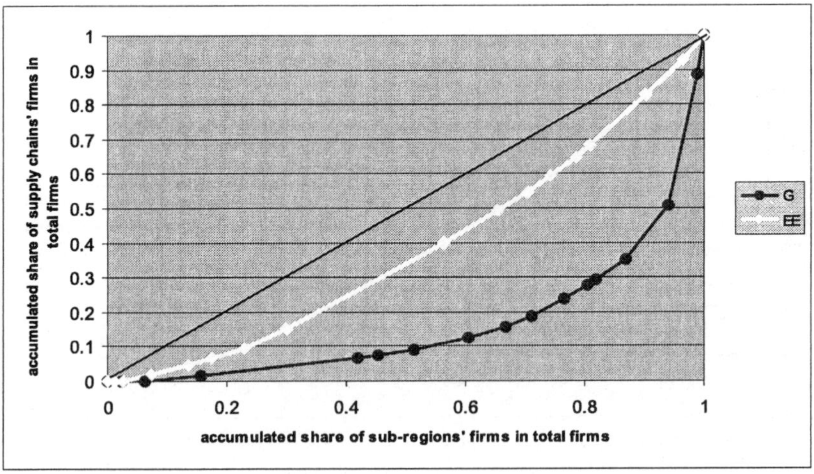

Source: CORIS

Figure 8.11: Lorenz-curves of glass and electronics industries

Concentration by industries

The patterns of supply chains in special fields do not necessarily correlate with population density. For example, the Glass & Glass Processing Industry (G) – one of the traditional specialised industries of the area under consideration – is strongly concentrated in the less populated rural areas of Northern Upper Palatinate and in the Bavarian Forest. Other supply chains – otherwise exhibiting typical attributes of regional specialisation – are either more uniformly distributed in space or are concentrated in urban areas, thereby more or less reflecting the distribution of population.

Applying the measurement concepts defined above to the G and EE data for Eastern Bavaria results in the Lorenz Curves shown in Figure 8.11. The glass supply chain (G) appears to be heavily concentrated, while electronics (EE) is more in line with a uniform distribution. In the glass industry about 50 per cent of firms are located in two sub-regions, representing roughly 6 per cent of total economic activity (as measured by the number of firms). For the EE supply chain we find half of the firms located in sub-regions, representing about one third of total activity.

The three different concentration indices for all clusters are given in Table 8.5 and are visualised in Figure 8.12. The level of concentration varies widely across clusters. The Gini coefficient ranges from 0.287 for EE to 0.769 for P&C. Beside these extreme cases, Automotive Industry (AUT) and Specialised Automation (MAC) tend to show lower concentration than Biotechnology (BIO), Glass Industry (G) and Logistics and Specialised Trade (LOG). These results also suggest that clusters do not occur only in "high tech" value chains, for example information technology, electronics or biotechnology, but are sometimes even more spatially concentrated in so-called "traditional" industries.

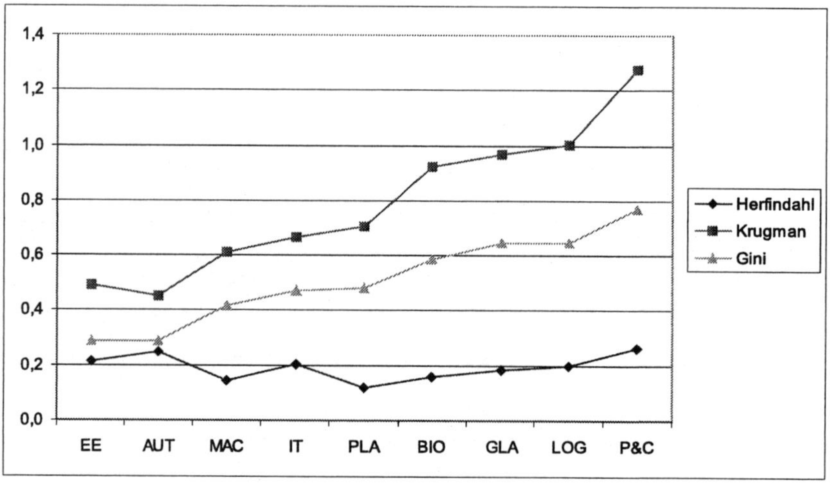

Figure 8.12: Concentration measures for nine clusters

	Herfindahl	Krugman	Gini
Herfindahl	1		
Krugman	0.158	1	
Gini	0.055	**0.986**	1

Note: Bold (bold italic) figures are significant at the 1 per cent (5 per cent) level.

Table 8.6: Correlation coefficients between concentration indices for nine counties in Eastern Bavaria

Again, the correlation between the Krugman and Gini coefficients is striking, while the Herfindahl index gives different information than the other two indices. This is corroborated by the correlation coefficients given in Table 8.6. The correlation coefficient between the Krugman and Gini index exceeds 0.98 and is significant at the 1 per cent level, while both cross-correlations between the Herfindahl and the two other measures are statistically insignificant.

Concentration by occupations

We also considered concentration by occupations using the same methodology as before. The concentration levels of the 130 observations vary widely. Figure 8.13 shows the Gini and Krugman indices of concentration differentiating between cluster-relevant and other occupations. At first glance, the concentration of the 32 cluster-relevant occupations does not deviate markedly from other occupations. Comparing the employment weighted mean of the indices shows that the concentration of cluster-

	N	Herfindahl		Krugman		Gini	
cluster relevant occupations	32	0.187	(0.071)	0.600	(0.215)	0.393	(0.128)
other occupations	98	0.157	(0.071)	0.425	(0.258)	0.275	(0.157)

Table 8.7: Mean and standard errors of concentration indices by industries (employment weights)

relevant occupations is higher for all three measures. The differences, however, are not statistically significant (see Table 8.7).

8.5 CONCLUSIONS

The term "cluster" is widely used and is especially popular in regional economic policy, despite the fact that the concept lacks clear definition. But the existence of clusters is supported by overwhelming and not just anecdotal evidence. A range of typical phenomena for clustering – some of them being very well founded in economic theory - can be observed. For empirical analysis, however, the fuzziness of the concept remains.

The popularity of clusters combined with blurry definitions has led to efforts to track the concept down – among them an urge to dimensionalise clusters and disentangle their various aspects. For some of these dimensions objective measurements exist or can be adapted. The approach in this paper is to look at the differing results of applying traditional industry-based administrative data and data relying on the concept of functional specialisation or clustering.

For obtaining a regional, cluster-oriented, firm-specific database we developed a methodology - so far implemented in Eastern Bavaria – to identify clusters by systematically registering value-chain-oriented structures and functional specialisation in an economic space. In this paper we highlight the two well-known measurement concepts of regional specialisation and spatial concentration of economic activities.

For the number of employees the results show marked differences in the specialisation pattern of the sub-regions and also between the concepts of official industry and cluster affiliation (indications of differences in levels of regional specialisation are much higher when using cluster data). Concerning the indices based on occupations, the cluster-relevant share again yields the highest values.

Also the spatial concentration of value chains varies widely. It is interesting to note that these patterns do not necessarily correlate with population density and are independent of the often invoked distinction between "high tech" and "traditional" industry.

Our results show that economic spaces appear considerably different when examined with cluster-oriented data as opposed to traditional industry classifications.

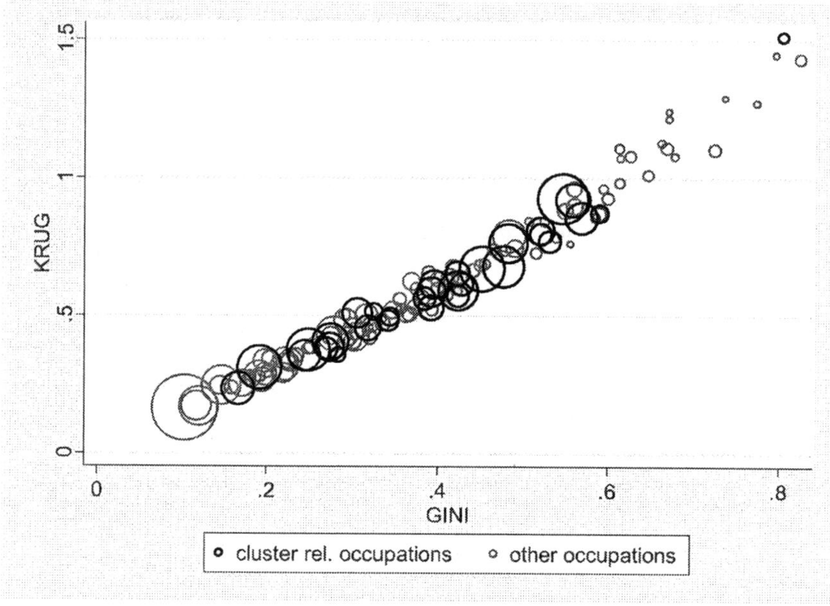

Figure 8.13: Gini and Krugman concentration indices of cluster relevant and other occupations

Profound knowledge about clusters and functional specialisation in a region leads to a new view of regional economic structures and focal points of economic activity. To enable a more systematic approach to cluster-related questions it would be very helpful to create or have access to adequate firm-based and supra-regional information on forward and backward linkages. Then it might be possible to move a step closer to a quantification and operationalisation of some cluster dimensions based on established and sound empirical methods.

REFERENCES

Andersson, Fredrick, Simon Burgess and Julia I. Lane (2004), 'Cities, matching and the productivity gains of agglomeration', *CEP Discussion Paper* **648**, London: Centre for Economic Performance.

Baptista, Rui (2003), 'Productivity and the density of regional clusters', in Johannes Bröcker, Dirk Dohse and Rüdiger Soltwedel (eds) *Innovation Clusters and Interregional Competition*, Berlin, Heidelberg, New York: Springer, 163–181.

Brandenburger, Adam M. and Barry J. Nalebuff (1996), *Co-opetition*, New York: Currency Doubleday.

Combes, Pierre-Philippe and Gilles Duranton (2001), *Labor Pooling, Labor Poaching, and Spatial Clustering*, Centre for Economic Performance, London School of

Economics and Political Science, London.

Dixit, Avinash K. and Joseph E. Stiglitz (1977), 'Monopolistic competition and optimum product diversity', *American Economic Review*, **67**, 297–308.

Duranton, Gilles and Diego Puga (2005), 'From sectoral to functional urban specialisation', *Journal of Urban Economics*, **57**, 343-370.

Duranton, Gilles and Diego Puga (2003), *Micro-foundations of Urban Agglomeration Economies*, Working Paper 9931, National Bureau of Economic Research, Cambridge (MA). Draft of a chapter written for J. Vernon Henderson and Jacques-François Thisse (eds), *Handbook of Urban and Regional Economics*, volume 4, Amsterdam: North Holland.

Enright, Michael J. (2001), *Regional clusters: what we know and what we should know*, Paper prepared for the Kiel Institute International Workshop on Innovation Clusters and Interregional Competition, Kiel, 12–13 November 2001.

Enright, Michael J. (2003), 'Regional clusters: what we know and what we should know', in Johannes Bröcker, Dirk Dohse and Rüdiger Soltwedel (eds), *Innovation Clusters and Interregional Competition*, Berlin, Heidelberg, New York: Springer, 99–129.

Ethier, Wilfred J. (1982), 'National and international returns to scale in the modern theory of international trade', *American Economic Review*, **72** (3), 389–405.

Feenstra, Robert (1998), 'Integration of trade and disintegration of production in the global economy', *Journal of Economic Perspectives*, **12** (4), 31–50.

Feldman, Maryann and David B. Audretsch (1999), 'Innovation in cities: science-based diversity, specialization and localized competition', *European Economic Review*, **43**, 409–429.

Feser, Edward J. and Stewart H. Sweeney (2002), 'Spatially binding linkages in manufacturing product chains', in R. McNaughton and M. Green (eds.), *Global Competition and Local Networks*, New York: Ashgate, 111–129.

Feser, Edward J., Kyojun Koo, Henry C. Renski and Stewart H. Sweeney (2001), 'Incorporating spatial analysis in applied industry cluster studies', prepared for *Economic Development Quarterly*.

Forslid, Rikard and Gianmarco I.PP. Ottaviano (2003), 'An analytically solvable core-periphery model', *Journal of Economic Geography*, **3**, 229–240.

Fosfuri, Andrea and Thomas Rønde (2003), 'High-tech clusters, technology spillovers, and trade secret laws', *Centre for Industrial Economics Discussion Papers* **2003–02**, Copenhagen, University of Copenhagen.

Fujita, Masahisa, Paul Krugman and Anthony J. Venables (1999), *The Spatial Economy*, Cambridge, MA, London, UK: MIT Press.

Fujita, Masahisa and Jacques-François Thisse (2002), *Economics of Agglomeration–Cities, Industrial Location, and Regional Growth*, Cambridge: Cambridge University Press.

Glaeser, Edward L., Hedi Kallal, José A. Scheinkman and Andrei Shleifer (1992), 'Growth in cities', *Journal of Political Economy*, **100**, 1126–1152.

Guinet, Jean (2003), 'Drivers of economic growth: the role of innovative clusters', in Johannes Bröcker, Dirk Dohse and Rüdiger Soltwedel (eds) (2003), *Innovation Clusters and Interregional Competition*, Berlin, Heidelberg, New York:

Springer, 150–162.

Haas, Anette and Jens Südekum (2005), 'Spezialisierung und Branchenkonzentration in Deutschland Regionalanalyse', *IAB Kurzbericht* **01/2005**.

Head, Keith and Thierry Mayer (2004), 'The empirics of agglomeration and trade', in J.Vernon Henderson and Jacques-François Thisse (eds), *Handbook of Urban and Regional Economics*, Volume 4, Amsterdam: North Holland.

Helpman, Elhanan (1998), 'The size of regions', in David Pines, Efraim Sadka und Itzhak Zilcha (eds), *Topics in Public Economics*, Cambridge: Cambridge University Press, 33–54.

Hirschman, Albert O. (1958), *The Strategy of Economic Development*, Newhaven, CT: Yale University Press.

Kim, Sukkoo (1995), 'Expansion of Markets and the Geographic Distribution of Economic Activities: The Trends in U.S. Regional Manufacturing Structure, 1860-1987', *Quarterly Journal of Economics*, **110** (4), 881–908.

Krugman, Paul (1991a), *Geography and Trade*, 2nd ed., Cambridge, MA, London, UK: MIT Press.

Krugman, Paul (1991b), 'Increasing returns and economic geography', *Journal of Political Economy*, **99**, 484–499.

Krugman, Paul and Anthony J. Venables (1995), 'Globalization and the inequality of nations', *Quarterly Journal of Economics*, **110**, 857–880.

Marshall, Alfred (1890), *Principles of Economics*, 8th ed. 1920, London: Macmillan and Co., Ltd.

Martin, Ron and Peter Sunley (2003), 'Deconstructing clusters: chaotic concept or policy panacea?' *Journal of Economic Geography*, **3**, 5–35.

Möller, Joachim and Alexandros Tassinopoulos (2000), 'Zunehmende Spezialisierung oder Strukturkonvergenz? Eine Analyse dersektoralen Beschäftigungsentwicklung auf regionaler Ebene', *Jahrbuch für Regionalwissenschaft*, **20** (1), 1–38.

Ottaviano, Gianmarco I.PP. and Diego Puga (1997), *Agglomeration in the global economy: A survey of the new economic geography*, Centre for Economic Performance, Discussion Paper No. 356.

Porter, Michael E. (2003), 'The economic performance of regions', *Regional Studies*, **37** (6&7), 549–578.

Puga, Diego (1999), 'The rise and fall of regional inequalities', *European Economic Review*, **43**, 303–334.

Rosenthal, Stuart S. and William C. Strange (2003), 'Evidence on the nature and sources of agglomeration economies', paper prepared for J. Vernon Henderson and Jacques-François Thisse (eds.), *Handbook of Urban and Regional Economics*, volume 4, Amsterdam: North Holland.

9. Inter-firm relations and economic clustering in the Dutch Randstad region

Frank G. van Oort*, Martijn J. Burger‡ and Otto Raspe*¶

9.1 INTRODUCTION

The Randstad is known as the western conurbation of the western part of the Netherlands, in which four major cities (Amsterdam, Rotterdam, The Hague and Utrecht) and a number of smaller towns are located within close proximity of each other (see Figure 9.1). This is the geographical definition. In the debate on spatial planning and economic policy in the Netherlands, however, the word 'Randstad' stands for more. The name, including as it does the Dutch word for 'city' (in the singular), suggests that the Randstad is a single, contiguous urban region. Suggestions that the region functions as an integrated economic cluster for basic industries, like manufacturing activities, distribution activities and business services, are numerous (for example, Dieleman and Musterd 1992; VROM 2004). But merely assigning a name such as the Randstad to a collection of towns and cities does not automatically meld them into an economically defined and integrated cluster with urban complementarities. To do so would require the towns to function together as one: to function as an 'urban economic network' for the various types of economic industries. This article examines the question whether the Randstad can indeed be regarded as a single, economic entity in a useful sense. For this, we examine the degree of spatial integration and the degree of locational complementarities of sectoral inter-firm relationships in the Randstad region.

The general contention for different cities within an economic cluster in a region to be complementary to each other requires cities to be specialized in different

* Utrecht University and Netherlands Institute for Spatial Research (RPB), The Hague, The Netherlands.
‡ Department of Applied Economics, Erasmus University Rotterdam, The Netherlands.
¶ We thank Koen Frenken, Bas Karreman, Jan Oosterhaven, Jan Lambooy, Evert Meijers, Piet Rietveld and Jan Ritsema Van Eck for useful comments on an earlier version of this chapter.

industries, while at the same time showing a marked degree of spatial and functional integration (Meijers 2005). Then, not all cities have to be specialized in all possible industries, but they can benefit from specializations elsewhere in the regional network. To date, however, there has been little empirical research into the functional economic cohesion of the Randstad, mainly because of lack of inter-firm relational data. We test the relationship between economic complementarities and spatial integration between all municipalities in the Randstad region (all large and smaller municipalities), relying on newly gathered data that derive from a large scale survey of 1676 businesses, all active in sectors which create added value (the 'basic sectors') in the region[1]. A detailed insight into these companies' economic networks was obtained by asking them to identify their ten most important business relationships with suppliers and other contractors, in terms of physical goods and services as well as information. Using these data, which may be regarded as representative of the entire commercial sector in the Randstad, we can then answer two related questions:

1. To what extent does the Randstad function as a spatially integrated cluster?
2. For basic industries (manufacturing, distribution or business services) do complementarities between municipalities of the Randstad cluster exist?

The remainder of this chapter is organized as follows. Section 9.2 presents a summary of the existing literature on network theory in relation to economic clustering. Here we also conceptualize the key concepts of 'integration', 'specialization' and 'complementarities'. Section 9.3 offers a diagrammatic representation of the network relationships of the surveyed firms. Besides giving a descriptive and structural account of the embeddedness of economic networks in the Randstad cluster, we look at the degree of randomness of the network by determining whether the number of relationships between municipalities displays a significant deviation from the number that is expected from the size of the municipalities concerned. Section 9.4 examines the degree of spatial integration of inter-firm relationships in the Randstad cluster by means of gravity models and Theil-indices. Section 9.5 then looks at the functional complementarities of cities in the Randstad by contrasting the municipal integration measure (Theil-index) with localized specializations in manufacturing, distribution and business services. The final section, 9.6, offers conclusions based on our three research questions.

9.2 CLUSTERS AND URBAN NETWORKS

From the 1960s onwards, the Randstad has internationally been regarded as one of the most important urban networks or functional clusters of economic activities of Europe (Hall 1966). It is a readily accessible network of cities and locations which, given their mutually dependent specializations and their variety, create a favourable setting for economic production. The Randstad forms the heart of the Dutch economy, with some 50 per cent of the gross national product being generated on approximately 25 per cent of the country's total land area (Ritsema van Eck et al. 2006). It is generally

[1] See Ritsema van Eck et al. (2006) for a detailed description of these data.

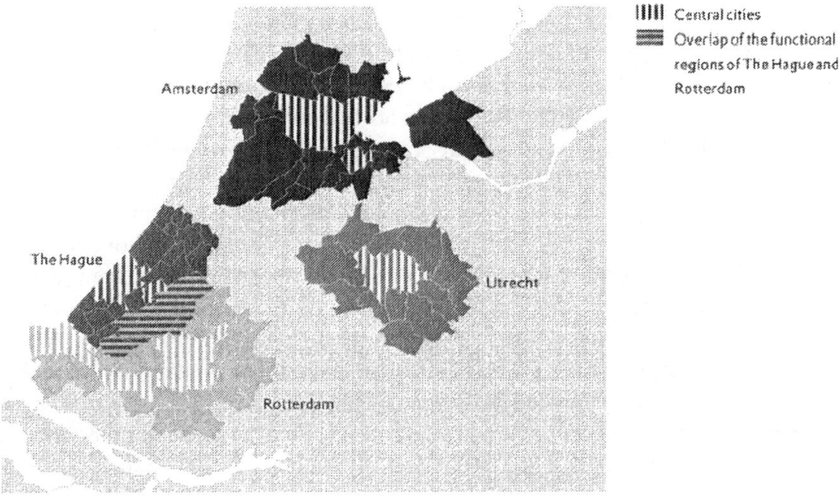

Figure 9.1: The Randstad research area and the 69 municipalities in the survey

assumed in the international literature that such towns and cities complement each other in terms of economic specializations, each being therefore more competitive than it would be in isolation (Batten 1995; Camagni and Capello 2004).

The term 'urban network' is relatively recently introduced as a concept of a 'new' geography, whereby distance and proximity are considered of lesser importance than the position within physical and virtual networks. Castells (1996) describes the emergence of a new dominant structure, driven by the revolution in information technology, worldwide economic restructuring and the growth of societal movements, all with their own dynamic and forms of interaction. He terms this the 'network society'. This network society entails hypothetically a new form of spatial logic, in which flows and positions within networks are of greater importance, and physical presence is no longer a prerequisite of social societal processes. According to Castells (2002), the situation is one of the 'space of places and space of flows', whereby the combination of, and interaction between, places and flows must be seen as crucial. In this, technological and cultural proximity (for example the use of comparable technologies or similarities in work processes) play an important part (Boschma and Lambooy 1998). It is argued that these new types of proximity require less physical proximity. Cooperative relationships between companies and individuals are therefore not predominantly local in nature, but can manifest themselves at any spatial scale (Lambooy 1998).

The concept of the 'network economy' is central to this network society, since especially changes in the structuring of the economy determine the shape and intensity of networks (van Oort et al. 2006). The flexibilization of economic processes and the functional division of tasks between companies create opportunities for a spatial division of labour: different spatial settings or locations become suitable for different economic functions. Economic transitions towards a service economy, particularly the growth in business services and IT activities, strengthen such spatial specialization. The factors that influence the choice of location in differentiated production environments relate to network relations, the (knowledge) infrastructure and logistic location. These factors facilitate the (inter)national and regional flows of people, goods and knowledge. Technological and academic knowledge, for example, tends to circulate in global networks (Ponds and van Oort 2006). Nevertheless, although production networks function on the global level of scale, social reproductions remain confined to the regional, or perhaps even local, scale (Törnqvist 1997). Despite the advances in digital communication, traditional 'face-to-face' contact remains an important condition for the exchange of non-standardized knowledge and products. This 'new' discussion on distances and proximities relates closely to the much older discussion of 'advantages of agglomeration', which are manifest in various ways (Parr 2002). Usually, 'economies of scale' are achieved by locating related activities in industrial districts, readily accessible to each other and by standardizing their production processes. Standardized mass production and the reduction of transport costs serve to reduce the unit cost of any article produced, the reduction being in proportion to the increase in total production. Similarly, 'economies of scope' result from the possibility of diversification. The ease with which knowledge can be exchanged and the mobility of the workforce further enhance opportunities for innovation and growth. 'Economies of expertise' are advantages that companies can derive from using knowledge flows within the networks of which they form part optimally. According to the proponents of the 'new' geography, the economies of expertise are now more important than economies of scale in influencing companies' and individuals' choice of location (Venkatraman and Subramaniam 2002).

Castells (2002) and van der Knaap and Wall (2003) contend that this emphasis on economies of expertise gives rise to a coalescence of towns and urban regions, since the greater opportunities for networking mean that distance becomes less important than accessibility. The argument is that, with concentration and distribution now being seen alongside one another, it becomes possible to take better advantage of the complementarities between towns: specialized locations can focus on their own core activities while also benefiting from those of the other towns in the network. This leads to the emergence of systems of economic complementary urban regions. The notion of a central city on which the population of the surrounding towns is heavily dependent for amenities and employment in this view becomes obsolescent. One location may be regarded as 'central' in terms of one particular function, while other places will be central in terms of another function. As a result, the cities' catchment areas will overlap. The greater urban conurbation then loses some significance as an independently functioning 'daily urban system', instead forming part of an urban network or regionalized economic cluster.

The three key concepts within the theory of urban network and economic regional clusters are 'integration', 'specialization' and 'complementarities'. Integration between the towns of the Randstad results from the improved opportunities for mobility and communication, which facilitate larger transport flows and stronger relationships between the individual urban agglomerations. Specialization and complementarities are both further ingredients to the exploitation of the comparative advantages of the cities and individual (sub)regions (Bailey and Turok 2001). It is frequently assumed that the combination of integration and specialization will result in advantages for the companies in all the urban regions concerned, perhaps in the form of a better standard of amenities or a better functioning economy (Meijers 2005). In our study, we therefore define complementarities as the combination of specialization and integration. Accordingly, complementarities entail that towns will specialize in those activities that arise from their comparative advantages. This offers a more productive (integrated) whole than each individual town or city would be able to offer in isolation.

9.3 INTER-FIRM BUSINESS NETWORKS IN THE RANDSTAD

9.3.1 The Randstad as a closed regional cluster?

To test whether the Randstad does indeed function as such a single economic system or network with complementary sub-economies, as espoused by the literature and government policy, we have examined the spatial dynamics of firms' networks within the region. The network relationships examined concern (sub)contracting, purchasing and selling of products, services and knowledge. In our analyses, we aggregate the relationship flows by town or city (as defined by municipal authority area of which there are 67, see Figure 9.1) since it is at this level of scale that the effects of spatial policy are most manifest. Aspects that are specific to a certain company, such as its structure and organization, are indeed relevant to the company concerned but of less importance to our current research, questions that are predominantly concerned with the spatial planning dimension. Nevertheless, we have taken account of specific firm characteristics by stratifying the population to which the questionnaire was sent according to economic sector and the size of firms (see Ritsema Van Eck 2006). Two in principle contradicting hypotheses on the spatial reach of firms' economic relations exist. Within the network economy, companies increasingly organize themselves into worldwide, extremely specialized, clusters and knowledge networks. At the same time, as we noticed in section 9.2, the immediate surroundings remain important. This is usually labelled the 'global-local paradox'. The regional economic and social climate remains important in the network economy. After all, companies generally seek out the business partners essential to their critical business processes in the immediate vicinity. In this section, we examine the spatial networking patterns of companies in the Randstad.

First, we analyse to what extent the Randstad functions as a closed economic relational system when compared to relations that spill over to regions outside the Randstad. The embeddedness of inter-firm relations in the four agglomerations and the Randstad area can be expressed in an index of the degree of 'openness'. This index divides the number of relationships in the economic network within the region by the number of relationships beyond the region. A value higher than 1 indicates relative closure: the number of internal relationships is larger than that of the external relationships. A value that is lower than 1 indicates relative openness. This index provides us with a benchmark for the economic embeddedness of inter-firm relations in the Randstad region. Table 9.1 presents the degree of openness for purchasing relationships,

	Total	Purchases	Sales	Industry	Distribution	Producer Services
Amsterdam	0.71	0.68	0.75	0.56	0.35	1.16
Rotterdam	0.53	0.46	0.63	0.54	0.36	0.67
The Hague	0.71	0.77	0.65	0.71	0.32	0.98
Utrecht	0.39	0.39	0.40	0.43	0.20	0.52
Randstad	1.34	1.18	1.54	1.22	0.68	1.50

Table 9.1: Degree of openness by urban region and sector

sales relationships, the total number of relationships, and relationships classified by economic sector (industry, wholesale, and producer services). The sales function is more regional in nature, while purchasing is more likely to be conducted beyond the regional boundaries. Table 9.1 shows that 57 per cent of all inter-firm flows is embedded within the Randstad area. There are however some notable sectoral differences. Producer services generally serve the regional production (61 per cent remains within the Randstad), while distribution activities have relatively few internal ties (only 40 per cent of the total). Local specialization in certain sectors gives rise to marked regional differences in the degree of local embeddedness displayed by the business networks. From this, it can be concluded that the Randstad does not function as an equal homogenous system for all sectors.

9.3.2 Visualization of inter-firm network patterns in the Randstad

Figure 9.2 shows the network of inter-company relationships for the complete Randstad. Here, the respondent population is not classified by sector or size.[2] The dots indicate the extent of relationships within one and the same town or city, for example companies in The Hague which maintain a business relationship with other companies in The Hague. The lines indicate the relationships between companies in different towns or cities. A large number of relationships can be seen within the four major cities, but there are also flows between these main centres. Moreover, we see a significant number of criss-cross relationships, that is relationships between companies that are located outside the central cities. In absolute networking terms, the four major cities function as the centres of the web. Not only do companies there maintain the largest number of relationships with others in the same city, but they also are involved in a large number of flows within the larger network. This is particularly true in the case of Amsterdam, which occupies a key position in the Randstad's overall network. Amsterdam is clearly a 'hub' for the whole region.

[2]In the interests of parsimonious presentation, the smallest categories of relationships within and between towns have been omitted from the figure. Moreover, only those relationships that stay entirely within the Randstad are shown. About 43 per cent of all relationships are conducted with companies outside the Randstad (either in the rest of the Netherlands or internationally).

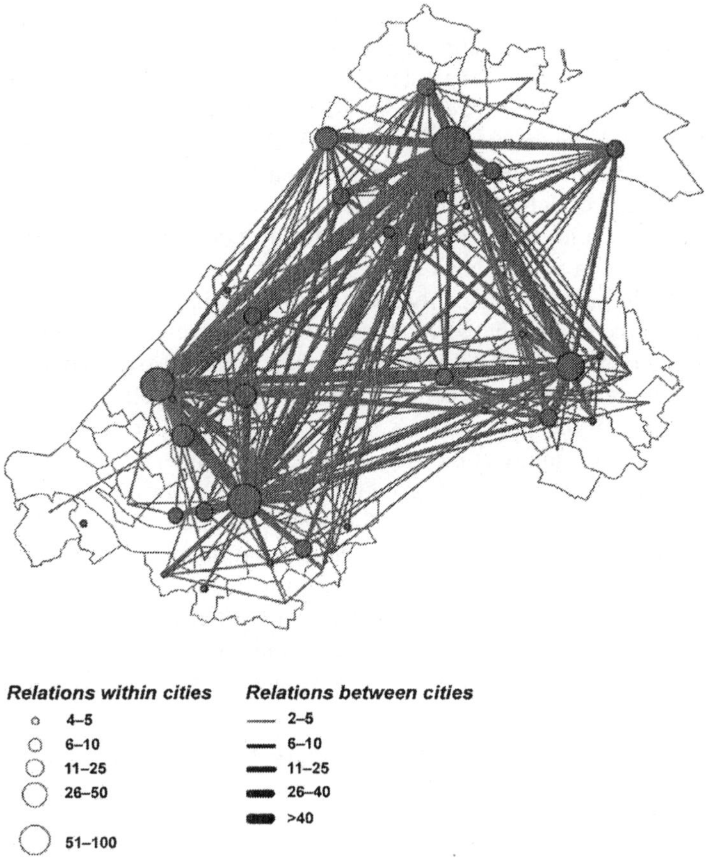

Figure 9.2: The network of inter-firm relationships in the Randstad

9.3.3 Randomness of the network: actual versus expected relations

Figure 9.2 gives a descriptive account of the embeddedness of economic networks in the Randstad cluster. However, one criticism of this is that it focuses on the number of relationships without taking into account the differences in the absolute sizes of the municipalities involved. Accordingly, it remains possible to explain the significant number of relationships conducted entirely within the central city in terms of the size of the city compared to that of the (immediate) surrounding area. In other words, the likelihood of being able to maintain a relationship with (a firm in) a large city is larger than that of maintaining a relationship with a smaller municipality. It is therefore useful to determine what the degree of randomness of the network is by analysing whether the number of relationships between municipalities displays a significant deviation from the number that is expected from the size of the municipalities concerned.

Figure 9.3 shows the same map as Figure 9.2; however allowance is now made for the number of expected relationships based on the size of the originating and destination municipalities. In order to statistically compare the observed versus the expected interaction intensity between cities in the Randstad region, we made use of the likelihood ratio chi-square statistic (Agresti 2002). Where the number of actual relationships is significantly larger than the expected figure, this is shown in dark grey. Where the number of actual relationships is significantly smaller than the expected figure, this is shown in light grey. Non-significant relations are shown in black. The figure demonstrates a predominant pattern, whereby inter-firm relationships of firms located within the same municipality are always larger in number than would be projected based on the size of that town. The relationships between the central cities and their local hinterland are generally also larger than would be expected. The criss-cross relationships entirely outside the central cities are small in absolute numbers, but – corrected for the size of the municipalities involved – also smaller in number than would be expected. Looking solely at the size of the municipalities involved, we would expect a larger number of relationships between them. Inter-firm relations between the four central cities are less than expected as well. The central cities appear to exert a 'magnetic force', attracting many relationships from the regional cluster. Therefore, the Randstad can be regarded as a non-random network (there are significant deviations from the expected interactions). The next section will more closely examine what determines the network structure of the Randstad cluster, using a more formal, econometric model to test and linking this to the question of spatial integration.

9.4 SPATIAL INTEGRATION OF THE RANDSTAD CLUSTER

9.4.1 Modeling spatial integration

The name 'Randstad' suggests that we deal with a cluster that functions as a single city. In this section we will formally test whether the Randstad region can be signified as a spatially integrated (economic) urban system. We econometrically model the degree of spatial integration in the Randstad region in terms of inter-firm linkages. In general we speak of spatial integration when there is no effect of spatial context on inter-firm network intensities, other than the economic mass of sending and receiving localities and the physical distance between them. If the Randstad functions as a spatially integrated cluster (from an economic point of view), the regional network structure of inter-firm relations should be solely determined by these variables. Three adjacent conditions for spatial integration therefore are:

1. Intra-urban interdependency (intradependency) should not be stronger than interdependencies between cities within the Randstad cluster,
2. Interdependencies between cities within one of the urban (sub)regions in the Randstad should not be stronger than interdependencies between cities across these (sub)regions.
3. No observable hierarchy in the different types of inter-municipal interdependencies should be present.

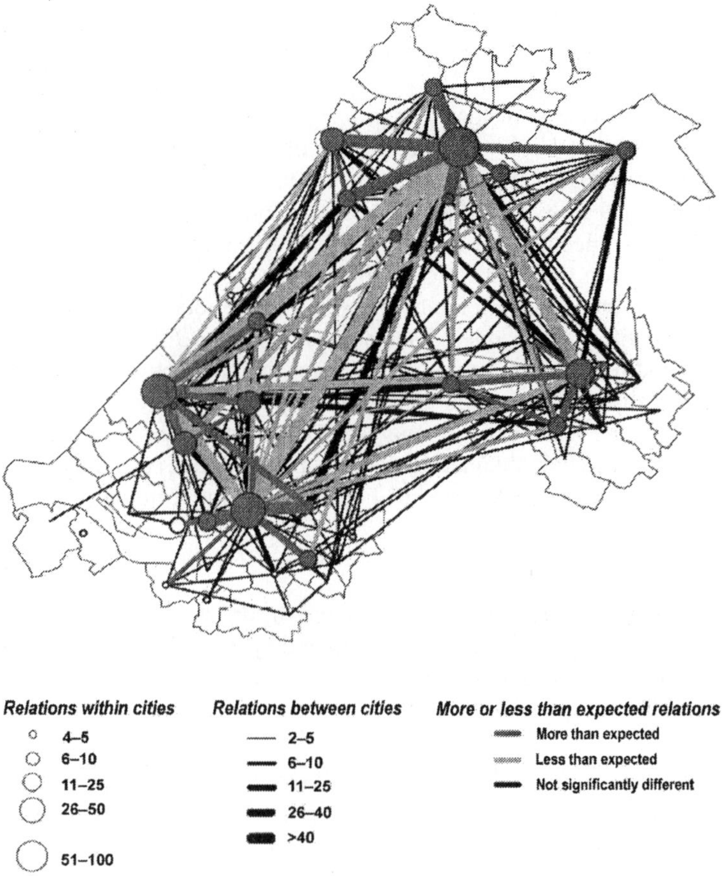

Figure 9.3: The network of inter-firm relationships in the Randstad with more or less than expected relations

To test these conditions we use gravity modeling. Spatial interaction patterns, including inter-firm flows, can be predicted and elucidated based on analogy with Newton's law of universal gravitation (Ullman 1954; Haynes and Forthingham 1984; Sen and Smith, 1995). The gravity model assumes that the gravitational force between two objects (in our study, the interaction between companies, aggregated at the level of the municipality) is dependent on the mass of the objects and the physical distance between them. More specifically, the interaction intensity between two municipalities (the origination and destination) is here hypothesized to be directly correlated with the masses of the municipalities and inversely correlated with the physical distance between the two municipalities. This can be expressed by the formula (9.1):

$$I_{ij} = K\frac{M_i M_j}{d_{ij}^b} \tag{9.1}$$

where I_{ij} is the gravitational force, or in our case the interaction intensity between municipality i and j expressed by the number of linkages, K a proportionality constant, M_i the mass of the municipality of origin, M_j the mass of the municipality of destination, d_{ij} the physical distance between the two municipalities, and b is an impedance factor reflecting the rate of increase of the friction of physical distance (Cliff et al., 1974). In our study, the b parameter is set at 1. The mass of the municipality of destination and origin are here defined as the total number of relationships of each municipality, as embedded in the network. As inter-firm relationships are considered to be undirected in this study, there is no clear distinction between the municipality of destination and the municipality of origin. For this reason, M_i and M_j are taken together as one variable in our analysis. Data on distances (as the crow flies) between municipalities were obtained by linking a weight matrix to the respective files. Intra-municipal distances were calculated by means of the formula (9.2):

$$d_{ij} = \frac{2}{3}\sqrt{A_i \pi} \tag{9.2}$$

in which the intra-municipal distance d_{ii} is two thirds of the radius of the presumed circular area A_i (see Bröcker (1989) and Frost and Spence (1995) for the exact derivation and overview of considerations of this). Formula (9.1) can be resolved to give the following testable comparison (9.3):

$$\ln I_{ij} = K' + \beta_1 \ln(M_i M_j) + \beta_2 \ln d_{ij} + \epsilon \tag{9.3}$$

Logarithmic transformations are applied to adjust for the non-normal statistical distribution of the dependent and independent variables, but provide only a partial solution to this problem. Spatial interaction data should be handled as count data as they 'count' the number of times that something has happened, in our case flow frequencies (expressed as interaction intensity) between and within municipalities. Although these data are often treated as though they are continuous, the application of the linear regression model here can lead to '*inefficient, inconsistent, and biased estimates*' (Long 1997) as many of the underlying assumptions (normal distribution, homoscedasticity) are often not satisfied. For this reason, the use of alternative regression techniques would be more appropriate. Probably the most common regression model applied to count data is the Poisson regression, which is estimated by means of maximum likelihood estimation techniques. In this log-linear model, the observed interaction intensity between municipality i and j has a Poisson distribution with a conditional mean μ that is a function of the independent variables (9.4). In our case,

$$\Pr[I_{ij}] = \frac{\exp(-\mu_{ij})\mu_{ij}^{I_{ij}}}{I_{ij}!}, \text{ where } \mu_{ij} = \exp(K' + \beta_1 \ln(M_i M_j) + \beta_2 \ln d_{ij}) \tag{9.4}$$

In order to correct for overdispersion (conditional variance is larger than the conditional mean) and an excessive amount of zero counts in our data set (the incidence of zero counts is greater than would be expected for the Poisson distribution), we make use of the zero-inflated negative binomial regression, which can be perceived as an extension of the Poisson model.[3] Not correcting for the overdispersion and excess zero problem normally results in incorrect and biased estimates. The zero-inflated negative binomial model considers the existence of two (latent) groups within the population: a group having strictly zero counts and a group having a non-zero probability of counts different than zero. Correspondingly, its estimation process consists of two parts. The first part contains a logit regression of the predictor variables on the probability that there is no interaction between two given municipalities at all. The second part contains a negative binomial regression on the probability of each count for the group that has a non-zero probability of count different than zero. A good technical discussion of the zero-inflated negative binomial model is provided by Long (1997).

In order to test the specified conditions for spatial integration using zero-inflated negative binomial regression, we introduce dummy variables in our model that express the spatial-functional context of the economic interactions between types of localities (regimes). These regimes build up the degree of spatial integration in the Randstad region. We introduce the following six types of urban interdependencies that convey the spatial context of flows between municipalities:

A. Economic relations within municipalities:

1. Intra-nodal relationships that remain entirely with a particular municipality (this can be either the central city or a suburban location). This is also referred to as the intradependency of municipalities.

B. Economic relations within urban (sub)regions of the Randstad:

2. Core-periphery interdependencies between the central cities and one their 'own' suburban municipalities.

3. Inter-periphery or criss-cross interdependencies between the suburbs within a given urban (sub)region.

C. Economic relations between urban (sub)regions:

4. Inter-core interdependencies between the central cities of Amsterdam, Rotterdam, The Hague and Utrecht.

---

[3]An important condition of Poisson regression is that it assumes equidispersion, meaning that the conditional variance of the dependent variable should be equal to the conditional mean. Often the conditional variance is higher than the conditional mean (as in our study), which means that the dependent variable is overdispersed. Not correcting for overdispersion (by means of a negative binomial estimation) would normally result in an incorrect and biased estimation of the dependent variable. The same problem holds for excessive zero counts in the data, meaning that the incidence of zero counts is greater than would be expected for the Poisson (or negative binomial) distribution. In our model, about $3/4$ of the counts are zero as there is little to no economic interaction between many small localities. A zero-inflated model would in this case be appropriate as it allows for the possibility that not all pairs of municipalities are at risk to interact because for example critical mass is lacking. A likelihood ratio test of overdispersion and the Vuong statistic provide tests to examine whether there is significant evidence for respectively overdispersion and excessive zero counts.

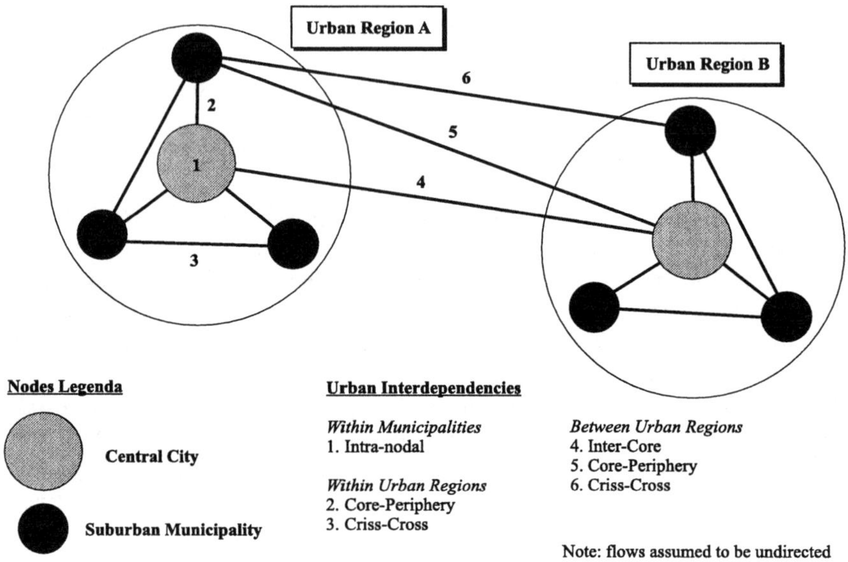

Figure 9.4: Classification of different types of urban interdependencies

5. Core–periphery interdependencies between the central cities and one of the non–'own' suburban municipalities.
6. Inter-periphery or criss-cross interdependencies between suburban municipalities that are not situated in the same urban region.

The different types of urban interdependencies are also displayed in Figure 9.4. Recall that if the Randstad can be characterized as a spatially integrated cluster (from an economic point of view), the regional network structure of inter-firm relations is solely determined by the masses of the municipalities and the physical distances between them; spatial context does not play any role and there is no difference in the relative strength of the different types of interdependencies. More formally, we will test the three conditions for spatial integration as specified above.

9.4.2 Empirical results: general findings

Table 9.2 presents the estimates from the zero-inflated negative binomial regression model for interaction intensity between municipalities in the Randstad region. Overall, the likelihood ratio test of overdispersion (α) and the Vuong-statistic indicate that the zero-inflated negative binomial model fits the data best, which justifies the choice of this model.[4] As indicated above, the zero-inflated negative binomial model consists

[4]The likelihood ratio test of overdispersion (α) indicates that there is significant evidence for overdispersion in all four models. For this reason, the negative binomial estimation is preferred to the Poisson estimation. The significant positive value of the Vuong-statistic supports the superiority of the zero-inflated

of two parts. The negative binomial part corresponds to the estimates for those pairs of municipalities with non-strictly zero counts. The zero-inflated or binary part relates to the logit regression predicting whether an observation belongs to the 'always zero' or 'not always zero' group. Examining the zero-inflated part of the model, it can be observed that in three of the four models presented only a low joint mass significantly increases the probability of belonging to the 'always zero' group. On average, an increase in the joint mass of the two municipalities by 1 per cent decreases the odds of belonging to the non-strictly zero group by 0.60 per cent, holding all other variables constant. This is in line with the finding that the largest share of non-interaction is between many small localities, where critical mass to interact is lacking. The remainder of this section provides a discussion of the negative binomial part of the regression model.

Model 1 represents the null or baseline model and only includes variables of the joint mass of the originating and destination municipalities and the physical distance between them. Recall that if the Randstad can be characterized as functioning as one cluster or urban network, the interaction intensity between municipalities in the Randstad is solely determined by their joint mass and the physical distance between them, while the type of other spatial interdependency should not play any role. As expected, mass has a marked direct correlation with the total number of interactions between the municipalities, while distance has a marked inverse correlation. These values can be interpreted as elasticities: when physical distance increases by 1 per cent, the interaction intensity of firm relations is predicted to decrease by 0.85 per cent. Similarly, an increase in the joint mass of the two municipalities by 1 per cent increases the predicted interaction intensity of firm relations by 0.91 per cent.

Model 2 tests the first condition for spatial integration, which states that the intranodal interdependency should not be stronger than interdependencies between municipalities within the Randstad cluster. In other words, the degree of spatial interaction between firms within municipalities should not exceed the degree of interaction between municipalities. Controlling for mass and physical distance between municipalities in our model, it appears however that this condition is not met. The intra-urban interdependency (intradependency) is significantly stronger than (1) interdependencies between municipalities situated in the same region and (2) interdependencies between municipalities. More specifically, the predicted interaction intensity within municipalities is about 80 per cent higher than between municipalities within the same region. Likewise, concerning interdependencies between municipalities not situated in the same region, this figure is approximately 110 per cent.

In Model 3, the second condition for spatial integration is tested, which states that the interdependencies between cities within one of the urban (sub)regions in the Randstad should not be stronger than interdependencies between cities across these (sub)regions. This condition also is not met. The interaction intensity between municipalities within the same region is predicted to be significantly higher than the interaction intensity between municipalities across urban (sub)region. Holding mass and physical distance constant, the predicted flow between municipalities within the same

negative binomial model over the negative binomial model in most instances; for model 1 there is only a weak preference for using a zero-inflated estimation (Vuong=1.45, p=.070).

urban region is over 30 per cent larger compared to the inter-municipal flows that exceed the level of the urban region.

In Model 4, we tested the third condition for spatial integration, which stated that there should be no observable hierarchy in the different types of inter-municipal interdependencies present. Taking inter-regional criss-cross interdependencies as a reference category (as it is conceptually the weakest type of urban interdependency), we were able to compare the relative strength of the different types of the urban interdependencies, controlling for mass and distance. We looked at whether the interaction intensity significantly differed between the different types by testing for the equality of coefficients by means of a Wald test. This way, we were able to compile a ranking list, in which the different types of urban interdependencies were ranked on the basis of relative strength. From this analysis, it could be inferred that the third condition for spatial integration is not met.

Inter-core interdependencies between the four largest cities (Amsterdam, Rotterdam, The Hague, Utrecht) are the strongest types of urban interdependencies, followed by regional core–periphery interdependencies. Interregional core–periphery and criss-cross interdependencies are the weakest types of relationships. In general, core–periphery relationships weakly prevail over criss-cross relationships at the different spatial levels

From this it can be concluded that the Randstad does not (yet) function as a spatially integrated cluster as none of the three conditions for spatial integration was met. Firm-relations appear to be both regionalized within the agglomeration level of the four (sub)regions, and inter-regionalized between the four larger cities. We can therefore speak of a combination of four (sub)regional core–periphery models and a network model on a higher level ('upscaling') that describes firm interactions within the Randstad cluster most accurately.

9.4.3 Spatial integration by municipality

In the foregoing, we have examined the degree of spatial integration in the Randstad at a system-level, in this section we analyse the extent to which individual municipalities deviate from this global level of integration. This is meaningful for knowing the contributions of municipalities in the integration process, but will also later be used to analyse the degree of complementarities between cities within the Randstad cluster. The degree of spatial integration of each municipality (T_i) in the Randstad cluster can be computed by means of the 'T-index' (Theil 1967; Theil 1972), which derives from the discipline of information theory (Leydesdorff 1991; Frenken 2002). The starting point here is the computation of the degree of spatial integration for each pair of municipalities in the Randstad. The level of integration between municipality i and j in the Randstad system (T_{ij}) can be measured as the natural logarithm of the division of the observed frequency (F_{ij}) and the expected frequency of the interaction (f_{ij}) (9.5). In other words, T_{ij}-values are here expressed as the deviation from the expected frequency of relationships.[5]

[5]Note here the resemblance to the likelihood ratio chi square statistic used in Section 9.3.3.

	Model 1	Model 2	Model 3	Model 4
	Negative Binomial Part			
Intercept	-4.86 (22.2)**	-4.66 (21.6)**	-6.18 (23.8)**	-5.79 (14.1)**
Mass (ln)	0.91 (36.0)**	0.88 (37.2)**	1.02 (41.7)**	0.94 (23.6)**
Distance (ln)	-0.85 (23.5)**	-0.63(9.66)**	-0.58 (9.23)**	-0.58 (8.67)**
Intra-municipal		...	-	-
Other within Region		-0.58 (4.35)**	...	
- Core-Periphery				0.46 (2.88)**
- Criss-Cross				0.24 (1.48)
Between Regions		-0.75 (3.81)**	-0.28 (2.72)**	
- Inter-Core				0.52 (2.47)**
- Core-Periphery				0.13 (0.91)
- Criss-Cross				...
Overdispersion (a)	0.142 (7.95)**	0.114 (8.48)**	0.055 (6.31)**	0.050 (6.38)**
	Zero Inflated Part			
Intercept	-0.54 (0.34)	-11.6 (0.02)	-10.6 (0.03)	2.59 (1.32)
Mass (ln)	-0.62 (4.25)**	-0.67 (5.42)**	-0.61 (4.21)**	-0.55 (2.83)**
Distance (ln)	1.03 (2.70)**	0.70 (0.19)	0.16 (0.36)	0.17 (0.42)
Intra-Municipal		...	-	-
Other within Region		11.8 (0.02)	...	
- Core-Periphery				-15.2 (0.02)
- Criss-Cross				-2.31 (1.19)
Between Regions		15.6 (0.02)	13.2 (0.04)	
- Inter-Core				-31.0 (0.00)
- Core-Periphery				-0.62 (0.76)
- Criss-Cross				...
Vuong-statistic	1.45#	2.39**	1.98*	1.83*
Log Likelihood	-1575	-1556	-1400	-1394
McFadden's Adj. R^2	.360	.366	.349	.349
AIC	1.310	1.297	1.201	1.201
N	2415	2415	2346	2346

** $p<0.01$, * $p<0.05$, # $p<0.10$, absolute z-values between brackets. ... = reference category

Table 9.2: Zero-inflated negative binomial regression on interaction intensity of inter-firm linkages in the Randstad region

$$T_{ij} = \ln\left(\frac{F_{ij}}{f_{ij}}\right) \tag{9.5}$$

In this formula, the expected frequency of interaction is predicted and derived from our null-model (Model 1, Table 9.2), thus taking into account the size of the origin and destination municipality and the physical distance between municipalities. Note that the T_{ij} index can be perceived as a measure of bias: its value will be positive if municipality i would collaborate with municipality j to a larger degree than expected. Similarly, its value will be negative if municipality i interacted with municipality j less than would be predicted on the basis of our null-model. The use of a logarithm renders the measure symmetrical where there is x times as much collaboration or x times less collaboration between the countries. For example, if two municipalities interact with

Rank	Most Integrated Municipalities	T_i	Rank	Least Integrated Municipalities	T_i
1.	The Hague	0.01	69.	Westvoorne	2.80
2.	Rotterdam	0.05	68.	Brielle	2.63
3.	Amsterdam	0.07	67.	Moordrecht	2.53
	Leidschendam-Voorburg	0.07	66.	Nederlek	2.50
5.	Delft	0.08	65.	Vianen	2.20
6	Schiedam	0.09	64.	Rozenburg	2.11
7.	Rijswijk	0.13	63.	Oegstgeest	2.03
	Zoetermeer	0.13		Wormerland	1.90
9.	Utrecht	0.15	61.	Rijnsburg	1.90
10.	Leiden	0.16	60	Binnenmaas	1.89
Rank	**Other Important Municipalities**	T_i			
13.	Haarlem	0.38			
18.	Schiphol	0.53			
29.	Almere	0.70			

Table 9.3: Degree of spatial economic integration (T_i) by municipalities in the Randstad region

each other twice as much as had been expected, the value of T_{ij} will be $\ln 2 = 0.693$. If the level of collaboration had been half of the expected number, the value of T_{ij} will be $ln1/2 = -0.693$. This value is computed for each possible relationship in the Randstad region, resulting in 2415 T_{ij} values (with 69 municipalities). With the summation of non-overlapping subsets of the 2415 T_{ij} values and subsequent division by the individual share of municipalities (F_i/n), it becomes possible to determine the degree of integration (T_i) of a particular city in the Randstad region (see Frenken 2002; Formula 9.6).

$$T_i = \frac{1}{F_i/n} \sum_{j=1}^{n} F_{ij} \ln\left(\frac{F_{ij}}{f_{ij}}\right) \tag{9.6}$$

The interpretation of T_i is that the lower the resulting value, the larger the degree of integration of municipalities within a regional network, allowing for their size. A T_i value zero indicates perfect spatial integration for the respective city. Table 9.3 presents the degree of spatial integration (T_i) for municipalities, presenting the most as well as the least integrated municipalities in the Randstad cluster of economic relationships. Overall, the three largest cities (Amsterdam, Rotterdam and The Hague) and the medium-sized cities situated near those larger cities (Leidschendam-Voorburg, Delft, Schiedam, Rijswijk, Zoetermeer and Leiden) are characterized as the most integrated municipalities in the Randstad region. The small municipalities situated outside the region's core infrastructure of accessible and larger cities have low scores of integration.

9.5 COMPLEMENTARITIES WITHIN THE RANDSTAD CLUSTER

According to the foregoing, it would not be appropriate (yet) to speak of a fully integrated urban system or economic cluster within the Randstad. However, a second often cited form of interdependence between economically specialized cities concerns complementarities. In section 9.2, we defined complementarities as the actual or potential relationship of two places or regions within a cluster that each produce different goods or services for which the other has an effective demand, resulting in an exchange between the locales. In terms of inter-firm network relationships, it is specifically a question of the extent to which a region specializes in activities in industry, trade or business-to-business services, in combination with the degree of integration in the cluster, that is, the extent to which a regional system is characterized by relatively high interaction between its sub-regions. One example is the specialized cluster of business services in the Amsterdam region. In theory, such specialization should lead to a large number of companies in other regions making use of these services, not least because the services are then under-represented in the immediate region. The companies are then able to specialize in another type of activity, which will then attract trading relationships from yet other regions. In this scenario, the regions benefit from each other's specialization, and will still have marked interaction with each other.

In our analysis we look at specializations in the sectors manufacturing, trade and distribution and business services, compared to the level of integration. Specialization has been measured using location quotients (9.7).

$$\mathrm{LQ}_i = \frac{E_{i,j} / \sum_j E_{i,j}}{\sum_i E_{i,j} / \sum_{i,j} E_{i,j}} \tag{9.7}$$

where E represents employment opportunity in region i and sector j. A score larger than 1 indicates that the sector is relatively over-represented in the region, compared to the average for the Randstad as a whole. A score lower than 1 indicates relative under-representation. The degree of spatial integration for each municipality in the Randstad is derived from the earlier introduced T_i-index (see the previous section) Since T_i measures the absence of integration, a negative correlation between LQ and T would therefore indicate a degree of complementarities. As Figure 9.5 shows, only the specialization in business services demonstrates such a negative correlation. Business services are in absolute terms the main specialization of the Randstad region. No such negative correlation is present for any industrial activities or the trade and distribution sector, indicating a lack of complementarities in these sectors. We can conclude that, at present, complementarities are a dominant force behind the emergence of an integrated system of inter-company relationships within the Randstad only for the business services cluster.

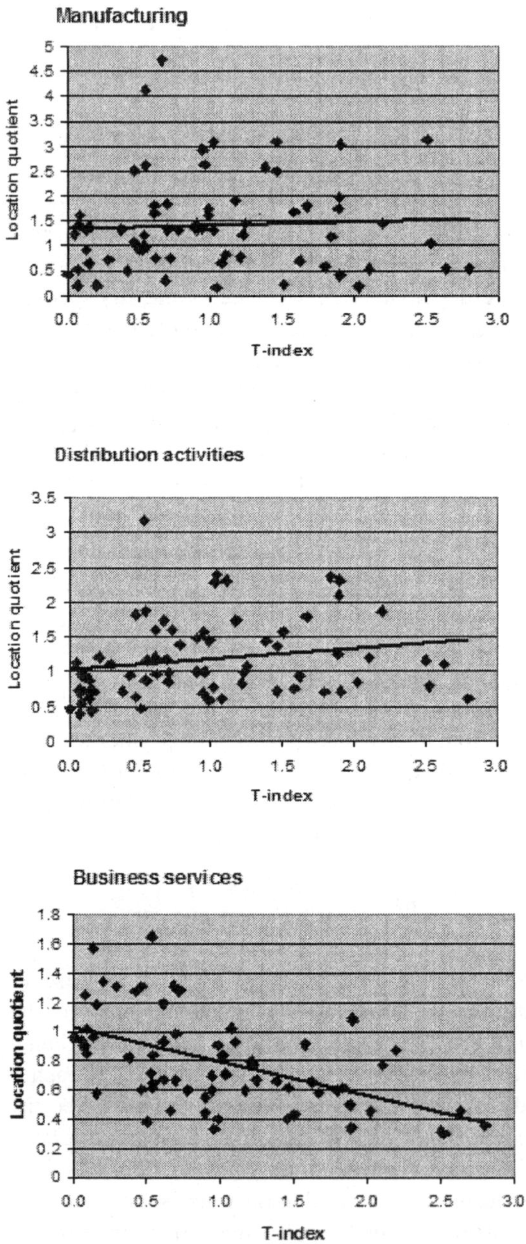

Figure 9.5: The degree of complementarities between municipalities in the Randstad region for three basic industries

9.6 CONCLUSIONS

This paper focuses on the often stated hypothesis that networks of relationships between firms will contribute to the existence of a unified regional economic cluster, consisting of localized and economically specialized sub centres. 'Spatial integration' and 'economic complementarities' are keywords in this debate. In spatial planning terminology, the literature speaks of 'urban economic networks', more or less meaning the same (but extending the debate to other than economic functions as well, like commuting and shopping spatial interactions). We test for spatial economic integration and the existence of economic complementarities for the Randstad region. In this region, business services, distribution activities and high-tech manufacturing activities cluster in what is often called the key economic region of the Netherlands.

This article has examined two interrelated key questions on the clustering of economic activities in the Dutch Randstad region:

1. To what extent does the Randstad function as a spatially integrated cluster?
2. For basic industries (manufacturing, distribution or business services) do complementarities between municipalities of the Randstad cluster exist?

Concerning the first question, we defined spatial integration as a situation when there is no effect of spatial context on inter-firm network intensities within the Randstad cluster, other than the economic mass of sending and receiving localities and the physical distance between them. If the Randstad functions as a spatially integrated economic cluster, the regional network structure of inter-firm relations should be solely determined by these variables. Using *zero-inflated negative binomial regression modeling* we tested three adjacent conditions for spatial integration. None of these conditions was met. Firstly, the intradependency of municipalities is much stronger than the interdependency between municipalities: spatial interaction between firms within municipalities exceeds interactions between municipalities in the Randstad cluster. Secondly, we found that firm-level interdependencies between municipalities within one of the four agglomerations (central cities with their suburban surrounding municipalities) in the Randstad are stronger than interdependencies between municipalities across these (sub)regions. Thirdly, instead of the condition of no observable hierarchy in the different types of inter-municipal interdependencies, we found a hierarchy in which relations between the four largest cities and core–periphery interdependencies within the agglomerations are significantly stronger than other types of urban interdependencies. Criss-cross relations between municipalities apart from the four central cities are overall very weak. Firm-relations can thus both be characterized as regionalized within the agglomeration level of the four (sub)regions, and inter-regionalized between the four larger cities. We can therefore speak of a combination of four (sub)regional core–periphery models and a network model on a higher level ('upscaling') that describes firm interactions within the Randstad cluster most accurately.

Concerning the second question, on complementarities within the system of the cluster, we found that individual municipalities differ in terms of specialization, but that these specializations only coincide with a larger integration of the complete cluster in the case of the business services sector. In the other sectors examined (manufacturing and distribution activities) complementarities are not coinciding with the development of an integrated system of economic relationships.

The Randstad region thus does not function as an optimally integrated economic network or regionalized cluster. Our study seems to indicate a central location model at the regional level, and a network model at the national and international level concerning regional *economic* networks or regionalized economic clusters. This questions policy initiatives that are related to exploiting urban network externalities at the level of the Randstad region. Obviously, these externalities have to be found on other levels of analyses. Because our analysis did not include other patterns of social network relationships (for example commuting or shopping expeditions) it is not possible to make any firm statement with regard to the use of the concept of urban networks as a planning concept. Further research will be directed towards modelling these interactions.

REFERENCES

Agresti, A. (2002), *Categorical Data Analysis*, New Jersey: John Wiley & Sons.

Bailey, N. and I. Turok (2001), 'Central Scotland as a polycentric urban region: useful planning concept or chimera?', *Urban Studies*, **38**, 697–715.

Batten, D. (1995), 'Network cities: creative urban agglomerations for the 21st century', *Urban Studies*, **32**, 313–327.

Boschma, R.A. and J.G. Lambooy (1998), *Economic evolution and the adjustment of the spatial matrix of regions*, in J. van Dijk and F. Boekema (eds.), *Innovatie in Bedrijf en Regio*, Assen: Van Gorcum.

Bröcker, J. (1989), 'How to eliminate certain defects of the potential formula', *Environment and Planning A*, **21**, 817–830.

Camagni, R. and R. Capello (2004), *The city network paradigm: theory and empirical evidence*, in R. Capello and P. Nijkamp (eds), *Urban dynamics and growth*, Amsterdam: Elsevier, 495–529.

Castells, M. (1996), *The Rise of the Network Society*, Oxford: Blackwell Publishers.

Castells, M. (2002), 'Local and global: cities in the network society', *Tijdschrift voor Economische en Sociale Geografie*, **93**, 548–558.

Cliff, A.D., R.L. Martin and J.K. Ord (1974), 'Evaluating the friction of distance parameter in gravity models', *Regional Studies*, **8**, 281–286.

Dieleman, F.M. and S. Musterd (1992), *The Randstad: A Research and Policy Laboratory*, Dordrecht: Kluwer.

Frenken, K. (2002), 'A new indicator of European integration and an application to collaboration in scientific research', *Economic Systems Research*, **14**, 345–361.

Friedmann, J. (1978), 'The urban field as human habitat', in L.S. Bourne and J.W. Simmons (eds), *Systems of Cities: Reading on Structure, Growth and Policy*, Oxford: Oxford University Press, 42–52.

Frost, M.E. and N.A. Spence (1995), 'The rediscovery of accessibility and economic potential: the critical issue of self-potential', *Environment and Planning A*, **27**, 1833–1848.

Hall, P. (1966), *The World Cities*, London: Weidenfeld and Nicolson.

Haynes, K.E. and A.S. Fortheringham (1984), *Gravity and Spatial Interaction Models*, London: Sage.

Van der Knaap, G.A. and R.S. Wall (2003), 'Linking scales and urban network development', in H. van Dijk (ed.), *The European Metropolis 1920-2000*, e-books, Erasmus University Rotterdam.

Lambooy, J.G. (1998), 'Polynucleation and economic development: the Randstad', *European Planning Studies*, **6**, 457–467.

Leydesdorff, L. (1991), 'The static and dynamic analysis of network data using information theory', *Social Networks*, **13**, 301–345.

Long, J.S. (1997), *Regression Models for Categorical and Limited Dependent Variables*, Thousand Oaks: Sage.

Meijers, E. (2005), 'Polycentric urban regions and the quest for synergy: is a network of cities more than the sum of the parts?', *Urban Studies*, **42**, 765–781.

Van Oort, F.G., J. van Brussel, O. Raspe, M.J. Burger, J. van Dinteren and G.A. van der Knaap (2006), *Economic Networks in the Region*, The Hague: Netherlands Institute for Spatial Planning (RPB) and NAi-Publishers (in Dutch).

Parr, J. (2002), 'Agglomeration economies: ambiguities and confusions', *Environment and Planning A*, **34**, 717–731.

Ponds, R.F. and F.G. van Oort (2006), *Knowledge hubs in the Netherlands. Spatial patterns of research cooperation*, The Hague: Netherlands Institute for Spatial Planning (RPB) and NAi-Publishers (in Dutch).

Ritsema van Eck, J., F.G. van Oort, O. Raspe and F. Daalhuizen (2006), *The Randstad as a Network City*, The Hague: Netherlands Institute for Spatial Planning (RPB) and NAi-Publishers (in Dutch).

Sen, A. and T.E. Smith (1995), *Gravity Models of Spatial Interaction Behaviour*, Heidelberg: Springer.

Theil, H. (1967), *Economics and Information Theory,* Amsterdam: North-Holland.

Theil, H. (1972), *Statistical Decomposition Analysis*, Amsterdam: North-Holland.

Törnqvist, G. (1997), 'Territories and networks in Europe: in search of a spatial order', in C. Capineri and P. Rietveld (eds.), *Networks in Transport and Communications*, Ashworth: Ashgate, 85–109.

Ullman, E.L. (1954), 'The role of transportation and the bases for interaction', in W.L. Thomas jr. (ed.), *Man's Role in Changing the Face of the Earth*, Chicago: University of Chicago Press, 862–880.

Venkatraman, N. and M. Subramaniam (2002), 'Theorizing the future of strategy: questions for shaping strategy research in the knowledge economy', in A. Pettigrew, H. Thomas and R. Whittington (eds), *The Handbook of Strategy and Management*, London: Sage, 461–474.

VROM (2004), *Document on Spatial Planning in the Netherlands 2005-2015*, The Hague: Ministry of Housing, Spatial Planning and the Environment (in Dutch).

10. The contribution of new and young firms to the economic development of clusters in Germany: comparative analysis of a growing, a mature and a declining cluster

Anne Otto* **and Stefan Köhler**‡

10.1 MUTUAL RELATIONSHIP BETWEEN START-UPS AND CLUSTERS

The promotion of industrial clusters has become a key element of regional politics since the mid 1990s. Cluster strategies rely on the presumption that start-ups play a crucial role in the development of regional economies. New firms are often highly innovative and follow a dynamic growth path. Thus, regional policies promote the formation of new firms in order to sustain the economic performance of clusters.

Several recent studies have investigated the relationship between regional clusters and start-ups. Sternberg and Litzenberger (2004) and Rocha and Sternberg (2005) both found that German regions with industrial clusters had more entrepreneurial activities than regions without clusters. These two studies confirm Dubini's (1989) hypothesis that clusters are fertile ground for entrepreneurial activity due to the presence of local incubators, for example parent firms and universities. Rocha and Sternberg (2005) suppose that clusters provide new firms with more favourable local environments – for example, availability of venture capital, qualified workforce, and access to regional networks – than do regions without clusters. On the other hand, entrepreneurial activity can diminish in aging and shrinking clusters due to the deterioration of the business climate. For instance, lock-in effects caused by strong relationships between established firms are considered as an important reason for the weak start-up activities in the old-industrialized "Ruhrgebiet" area (Grabher 1993; Brixy and Grotz 2006).

* Institute of Employment Research, Saarbrücken, Germany
‡ Ministry of Economics and Science, Saarbrücken, Germany

Menzel and Fornahl (2005) distinguish between *quantitative and qualitative effects* with respect to the mutual relationship between start-ups and clusters. Several studies find that the spin-off activities of local parent firms crucially aid the emergence of clusters (for example, Bünstorf, Klepper 2005; Garnsey, Heffernan 2005; Boschma, Wenting 2004). A large population of start-ups with good survival prospects and dynamic employment growth are seen as prerequisites for the growth and performance of industrial clusters. In contrast, high firm density and exhausted resources may cause more intense competition among firms within mature and aging clusters. It is assumed that new firms compete mainly with other young firms as a consequence of established cluster firms' dominant market position. Hence, new firms will not last long in mature and declining clusters. In contrast to growing clusters, the *quantitative effects of new business creation* should be rather negligible in ageing clusters.

New skills, competences and products are introduced primarily by new firms. Entrepreneurial activities thereby contribute to the enlargement of the cluster's knowledge and resource pools. The injection of innovations from start-ups is also essential for ensuring the cluster's ability to adapt to changing market conditions and local environments. Feldman, Francis and Bercovitz (2005) suppose that entrepreneurs are 'structural change agents', capable of creating and attracting the necessary resources and institutions to promote their businesses. They take advantage of local resources to start their firms, but in turn they also add new resources to the local environment. Hence, entrepreneurs are able to interact with and positively shape their local environments (*qualitative effect of start-ups*). The majority of start-ups within a cluster are born as spin-offs from local parent firms (*quantitative effect of clusters*). These parent firms are specialized in areas which represent the cluster's technological competencies. Since most entrepreneurial spin-offs continue to operate in the same field as the parent firm, the activities of start-ups remain concentrated within the cluster's existent technological boundaries (*qualitative effect of clusters*) (Menzel and Forndahl 2006).

The objective of this paper is to analyse the quantitative effects of new business creation on the evolution of clusters. These effects are measured using several indicators of entrepreneurship such as market entry and exit rates, new firm survival, firm growth, and aggregated employment effects of start-up cohorts. The data comes from the 'Establishment File' of the German Social Insurance Statistics, which includes information on entrepreneurial activity in West Germany from 1984 to 2002. The downside of this data is that a 19-year study period is rather short in light of clusters' long-term evolutionary processes.

We examine the quantitative impact of entrepreneurial activities on the economic development of three industrial clusters in West Germany. Each of these three clusters is in a different development stage. The region of Munich is a growing cluster specializing in medical technology. The mature cluster around Tuttlingen specializes in the production of surgical instruments. Finally, the shrinking textile and clothing industry cluster in the region of Neckar-Alb is in the midst of a long term process of decline.

These three cases were selected on the basis of criteria that seek to deal with the conceptual fuzziness and other problems involved in the identification of clusters (Martin and Sunley 2003; Steiner 1998). The first criterion that the cluster should exhibit is a high degree of industrial agglomeration. Regional concentrations of single industries are measured by location quotients[1] based on employment data. The values of the location quotients in the selected clusters must be above the average location quotients over all counties in Western Germany during the period of analysis (1984–2002). However, the identification of growing clusters is not bound to this criterion. Other main features of clusters are the presence of inter-firm and inter-organizational networks and local institutional settings (for example, chambers of commerce, educational institutions, universities, research institutes) (Enright 2000, 2002; Steiner 1998). Several studies (for example, for Munich: BMBF 2005; for Tuttlingen: Binder, Sautter 2005; for Neckar-Alb: Haas et al. 1983, Staber 2001) show that the three clusters selected for our study meet these three key criteria.

The chapter is structured as follows. We first describe the data and the indicators of entrepreneurship (section 10.2). The empirical analysis – sections 10.3–10.5 – consists of the three cluster case studies. Here, the quantitative effects of entrepreneurial activities on cluster evolution are examined for each cluster during the period 1984–2002. The last section compares the results of the case studies and discusses implications for regional cluster policy.

10.2 DATABASE AND INDICATORS OF ENTREPRENEURIAL ACTIVITIES

The 'IAB Establishment Register' – also sometimes known as the 'German Social Insurance Statistics' – provides data on the number of start-ups and firm closures, and on the development paths and employment effects of new firms. The characteristics of this database are documented by Fritsch and Brixy (2004). It includes all enterprises employing at least one person covered by German Social Insurance. Therefore, small start-ups without any employees are not included. New businesses with more than 20 employees are also excluded. It is assumed that such larger start-ups emerge as a consequence of outsourcing and reorganization activities rather than as a result of entrepreneurship. Hence, these large spin-offs are not considered original start-ups. The 'Establishment File' includes longitudinal data on the number of employees in each firm. Thus, it is possible to study both survival and employment growth of new firms. The period of analysis in our study extends from 1984 to 2002. The quantitative effects of start-ups are assessed using several indicators of regional entrepreneurial activities (Table 10.1). Established firms are defined as businesses which were already in existence at the beginning of the study period.

Net market entry measures the balance of market entries and exits. A positive value indicates an increase in the firm stock within the cluster. Meanwhile, turbulence (sum of market entries and exits) represents the intensity of entrepreneurial activities. The share of net market entries in the overall turbulence value indicates the effectiveness of entrepreneurship. For instance, low values of effectiveness are likely to result from intraregional displacement within the cluster. The survival rates of new firms and their employment growth reflect the development paths of start-ups and their prospects in

[1] The location quotient is defined as the ratio of an industry's share in the local economy to the industry's share in the national economy.

the cluster. The contribution of entrepreneurship to employment growth is analysed by cumulatively summing the employment effects of start-up cohorts.

10.3 THE MUNICH REGION – A GROWING MEDICAL TECHNOLOGY CLUSTER

High-tech medical firms offer highly specialized products and services due to product differentiation and weak market pressure. Medical technology is a cross-sectional field. Innovative activities require competence in multiple technological areas (for example software technologies and life sciences). The industry exhibits a high degree of geographical concentration. The Munich Region, a metropolitan area in South Germany, supports a growing cluster around medical technology. The region contains some of the best high-tech infrastructure in Europe. There are concentrations of technological competencies in fields related to medical technologies (for example, semiconductor industry, software technology, life sciences and nanotechnology), as well as in traditional export-oriented industries (for example, automotive, aerospace and mechanical engineering). Their presence creates a seedbed for potential spin-offs into medical technology. Most of the cluster-firms are knowledge-intensive small- and medium-sized enterprises, which operate mainly in diagnostic systems, medical software, and in therapeutic and surgical instruments. Many of these firms are also engaged in bilateral business and research agreements with other firms and research institutions. For instance, the Central Institute of Medical Technology (CIMT) and the Innovation Centre for Therapeutic Medicine (ITEM) are both devoted to promoting medical technologies and business networks in Munich. Furthermore, medical technology firms have access to a pool of qualified workers, and venture capital is available from over 35 financial institutions. Product certification agencies represent another institutional element within the cluster (for example, TÜV Product Services Company) (BMBF 2005, Landeshauptstadt München 2004).

Munich's medical technology cluster experienced dynamic growth during the period of analysis. The number of medical technology-based firms increased by 42.7 per cent (1984: 431 firms; 2002: 615 firms) and the number of employees increased by 66.6 per cent (1984: 4,600; 2002: 7,700). This rate of employment growth is far above the national average (West Germany: 19.2 per cent). Growth also accelerated during the study period. Between 1984 and 1989, 31.8 new medical technology-based firms were formed each year. Between 1990 and 1996 the average increased to 40.0, and it then further increased to 41.8 between 1997 and 2001 (Table 10.2, Figure 10.1). During these three periods the average annual firm closure figures were 19.0, 25.4, and 35.6 respectively. The increase in the number of start-ups and firm closures caused more intense turbulence (sum of start-ups and market exits). Net market entry (balance of market entries and exits) and entrepreneurial effectiveness (net entry's share of turbulence) both declined after 1993, owing to an increase in the number of firm closures. This means that a small number of new firm formations shaped the firm stock of this cluster significantly, especially in the 1980s and in the first years of the 1990s. The businesses formed during these early years make up the majority of Munich's

***Entry rate*:** number of start-ups per 10,000 employees

***Exit rate*:** number of firm closures per 10,000 employees

***Survival rate*:** the share of new firms that survived up to a certain year after the new businesses started.

***Net market entry*:** the difference between the number of start-ups and firm closures.

A positive (negative) net market entry indicates an increase (decline) in the number of firms in a region (of the stock of firms in a region).

***Turbulence*:** the sum of the number of start-ups and firm closures.

High (low) values of turbulence indicate that the region experiences intense (weak) entrepreneurial activities during a certain period of time.

***Effectiveness of entrepreneurial activity*:** quotient of net market entry and turbulence.

The effectiveness shows high (low) values if the stock of firms changed as a result of a small (large) number of start-ups and firm closures. High positive values for the effectiveness indicator imply an attractive market for new firms. In this case the risk of failure for start-ups is low as a consequence of weak competition between new businesses and established firms. Low positive values suggest that new firms could not survive without facing the competition with established firms (for example in respect to local market shares). Negative effectiveness values indicate that new firms would only be able to survive if established businesses exit the market (high-density displacement effects) (Fritsch, Niese 2004).

***Employment growth*:** The employment growth of start-up cohorts is measured by calculating the average number of persons employed in all surviving firms of each start-up cohort.

***Gross direct employment effect of start-up cohorts*:** the share of employment of the surviving firms of start-up cohorts in total employment at the end of the period of analysis.

Sources: Fritsch, Niese (2004); Fritsch, Müller, Weyh (2005).

Table 10.1: Indicators for measuring the quantitative direct effects of new and young firms

current pool of medical technology-based firms. Probably more intense competition among cluster-firms resulted from increased firm density during the 1990s, thereby lessening the impact of entrepreneurial activity on cluster growth.

On average over 70 per cent of all new firms from the 1984–92 cohorts survived the first five years on the market (Table 10.3). These survival rates are extraordinarily high compared to the 50 per cent average rate amongst start-ups in Western Germany (Brixy and Grotz 2006). The unusually high survival rates suggest that Munich's medical technology cluster provides a favourable business climate for new firms, though the effect is also probably attributable to the overall growth of the health-care sector during the 1990s. Only members of the youngest cohorts (1996–97) display a lower survival rate. This increased risk of failure amongst the newest firms might point to growing local competition within the cluster, as suggested by the low effectiveness values. All existent medical technology companies in 1984 (first year of observation period) are treated as 'old' and 'established' firms. About half of these established firms (47.4 per cent) survived until 2002. Their long-term durability is remarkably high, especially considering the low survival rates of new firms.

The average firm size of a start-up cohort is defined as the average number of persons employed in the surviving firms. The employment growth of the start-up cohorts is measured by change in the average firm size. For purpose of summary, cohorts are aggregated into groups of three or four (Figure 10.2). All of the cohorts exhibit long-term growth. In their fifth year of existence, the surviving medical technology-based start-ups employ an average of five to six persons. By their tenth year this average has increased to between six and eight. The surviving established firms experienced high rates of employment growth between their first and thirteenth years of existence. However, the growth rates later diminished, which is possibly due to the general deterioration of the business climate in Germany after 2001.

The gross direct employment effect of start-ups is defined as the 1984–99 start-up cohort's collective share of total employment in 2002. All together, the 1984–99 cohorts employed 2,300 persons in 2002. This represents 29.4 per cent of Munich's total medical technology employment (Table 10.4). The surviving established firms employed 3,300 persons in 2002, that is, 42.8 per cent of all employees in Munich's medical technology industry. The remaining 27.8 per cent of the cluster's workforce is located in large spin-off firms. Recall that these large start-ups (> 20 employees) were excluded from the analysis since their formation tends to reflect reorganization of larger existent firms rather than entrepreneurial activity.

Theses results confirm rather clearly that the quantitative effects of new business creation played a decisive role in enlarging the stock of firms and employees in Munich's medical technology cluster during the period of analysis. These positive quantitative effects result from a combination of strong entrepreneurial activities, high survival rates and high rates of employment growth amongst start-ups in medical technology. Established organizations, large spin-offs, and relocations contributed substantially to the employment growth of this cluster as well.

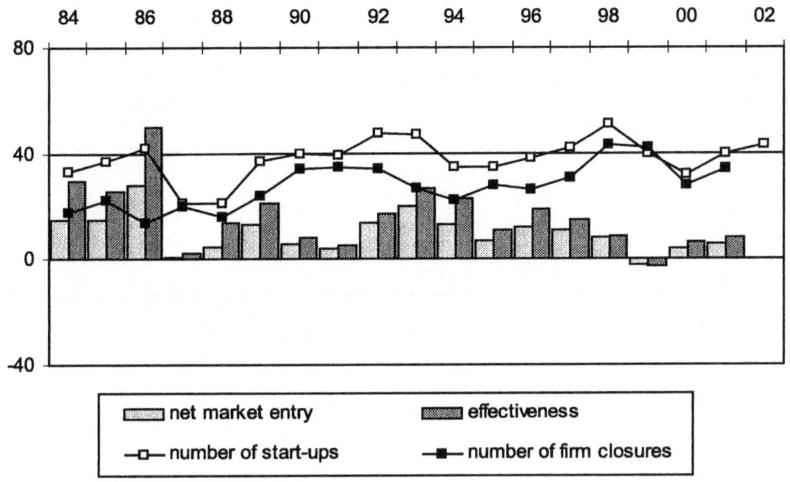

Figure 10.1: Entrepreneurship activities in the Munich region 1984–2002

Indicators	Munich Region			Tuttlingen			Neckar-Alb		
	84–89	90–96	97–01	84–89	90–96	97–01	84–89	90–96	97–01
Average Number of start-ups	31.8	40.3	41.0	18.7	16.3	12.6	67.3	49.7	28.2
Average Number of firm closures	19.0	29.4	35.6	14.0	22.6	20.4	96.1	111.3	80.6
Net Market Entry	12.8	10.9	5.4	4.7	-6.3	-7.8	-28.9	-61.7	-52.4
Turbulence	50.8	69.7	76.6	32.7	38.9	33.0	163	161	109
Effectiveness	25.2	15.6	7.0	14.3	-16.2	-23.6	-18	-38	-48
Entry rate (Average)	0.33	0.39	0.38	4.3	3.4	2.7	3.1	2.2	1.3
Exit rate (Average)	0.20	0.28	0.27	3.2	4.8	4.3	4.5	5.0	3.7

Table 10.2: Entrepreneurship indicators in the three industrial clusters

Start-up cohorts	Munich Region	Tuttlingen	Neckar-Alb Region
1984–86	73.9	69.4	53.7
1987–89	72.2	53.8	52.9
1990–92	72.1	64.8	40.1
1993–95	82.9	40.5	33.3
1996–97	60.5	50.0	29.1

Table 10.3: Average five year survival rates of start-ups in %

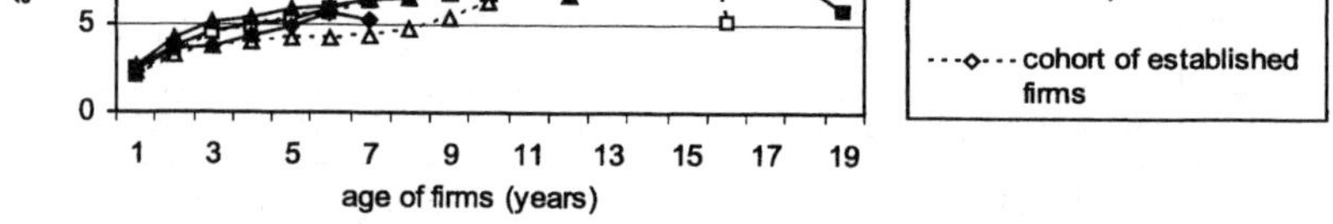

Figure 10.2: Average firm size of surviving start-ups and established firms – Munich region

	Munich Region		Tuttlingen		Neckar-Alb Region	
start-up cohorts	abs.	rel.	abs.	rel.	abs.	rel.
1984–86	482	6.2	230	3.2	235	2.1
1987–89	311	4.0	77	1.1	203	1.8
1990–92	528	6.8	190	2.6	179	1.6
1993–95	433	5.6	111	1.5	120	1.1
1996–97	517	6.7	79	1.1	159	1.4
Sum	2.271	29.4	687	9.5	896	7.9
cohort of established firms	3.307	42.8	6.185	85.1	9.521	84.5
larger spin-offs, branch plants	2.152	27.8	393	13.6	854	7.6
Total	7.730	100.0	7.265	100.0	11.271	100.0

Table 10.4: Cumulated gross employment effect of cohorts in 2002

10.4 TUTTLINGEN – A MATURE SURGICAL INSTRUMENTS CLUSTER

Tuttlingen is a traditional and unique cluster for the manufacture of surgical instruments. Most of the cluster-firms are located in the county of Tuttlingen, which is situated in Southern Germany (Baden-Württemberg). This cluster emerged during the second half of the 19th century. The first manufacturer of surgical instruments was set up in 1866 and has since become one of the best-known manufacturers of medical technology products world-wide (Aesculap Corporation). The cluster developed into a "world centre of medical technology" in the first half of the 20th century, and the cluster-firms then succeeded in regaining and maintaining their leading positions on the world market after World War II. At present, Tuttlingen contains about 500 small- and medium-sized firms engaged in the production and trade of surgical products, as well as about 200 suppliers and subcontractors. A few large-scale enterprises act as hubs within the cluster (Binder, Sautter 2005; BMBF 2005). Its singularity is evidenced by the following indicators. The location quotient of medical technology in the county of Tuttlingen amounted to the extraordinarily high value of 22.6 as of 2002. Entry rates of new medical technology-based firms clearly exceed the average for all West German counties in the 1980s and 1990s.

Since the early 1970s the medical technology cluster in Tuttlingen has been affected by structural change as a result of intense competition from low-cost manufacturers. The cluster-firms in Tuttlingen moved standardized and labour-intensive production units to developing countries with low production costs in order to maintain their competitiveness. Surgical instruments produced in low-cost countries are then re-imported and finished primarily by local small crafts enterprises (for example, polishing and grinding of the instruments). Afterwards, these refined products are re-exported by distributors (see Halder 2005). Thus, the number of suppliers and distributors increased, as the cluster became progressively integrated into global value chains and trading networks.

Most of these suppliers are very small craft firms which produce and refine surgical instruments for a few large-scale producers. The latter have bound the suppliers by contracts in order to sustain their firm-specific competitive advantages. Networks are characterized by close and dense social relations between producers and suppliers (Binder, Sautter 2005; Sautter 2005). The Competence Centre of Minimal Invasive Medicine and Technology acts as an interface between regional research institutions and enterprises. However, the cluster's supporting infrastructure for start-ups is rather insufficient compared to other regional centres of medical technology production in Germany, for example Munich (BMBF 2005).

The Tuttlingen cluster experienced a process of concentration during the period of analysis. The number of firms fell by 14 per cent from 327 in 1984 to 282 in 2002. At the same time the number of employees rose by 57 per cent from 4,600 in 1984 to 7,300 in 2002. This rate of employment growth greatly exceeds the national average (West Germany).

The balance of start-ups and shut-downs (net market entry) remained positive between 1984 and 1992, except for the years 1985 and 1987 (Figure 10.3, Table 10.2). These results indicate that new business creation contributed to an increase in the number of cluster-firms during this period. However, the trend is quite different during the following years (1993–2002). With the exception of 2001, the cluster exhibited negative net entry values, which was driven by an increase in the number of firm closures and a decline in the number of start-ups. Thus, the total number of medical technology cluster-firms dropped from 389 in 1993 to 282 in 2002. The negative values for the effectiveness of entrepreneurial activities might indicate that competition among cluster-firms became more intense, leading to intraregional displacement effects. This could be a reason for the declining survival rates, too. On average, only 40.5 per cent of all new medical technology-based firms in the 1993–95 cohort survived the first five years on the market, and only 50.0 per cent of the 1996–97 cohort (Table 10.3). In contrast, the five-year survival rates of the older start-up cohorts were much higher with the exception of the 1987–89 cohort.

Sautter (2005) gives several explanations for the decrease in the number of start-ups during the period 1993–2002. He assumes that new manufacturing firms could only succeed on the market by introducing highly innovative products. The close and dense social networks between producers, suppliers and distributors might prevent external firms from gaining access to this cluster. Furthermore, the introduction of new regulations for medical technology products at the end of the 1990s increased the costs of product certification. These increased production costs could have heightened the risk of failure for new firms.

Whereas Munich's start-ups are highly innovative and knowledge-intensive, most of the new businesses in Tuttlingen are small suppliers and specialized crafts enterprises. Such start-ups require less venture and risk capital for specific investments in human capital (BMBF 2005). Hence, market entry and exit barriers for new firms are lower in Tuttlingen than in the Munich Region. This difference can be seen as an important reason for the higher entry-rates and shorter survival prospects of new establishments in Tuttlingen.

In contrast, the old and established firms have great survival prospects in both of the two clusters. As with Munich, over half (50.9 per cent) of Tuttlingen's existent firms in 1984 survived through 2002.

Most of the cohorts experienced similar growth patterns during the first six years (Figure 10.4). The average firm size in each cohort hovered between four and five employees by the sixth year. Thereafter the developmental paths of the cohorts diverge: firm growth in the 1987–89 and 1990–92 cohorts stagnated, while the 1993–95 and 1996–99 cohorts continued to grow until the ninth and seventh year, respectively. The average firm size of the oldest start-up cohorts (1984–86) grew from the sixth to the nineteenth year by a factor of 5.0. The established cluster-firms experienced dynamic growth as well. Their average size rose by a factor of 2.7 from 16.7 in 1984 to 44.5 in 2002. Additionally, the total number of persons employed in surviving established businesses grew from 4,600 in 1984 to 6,100 in 2002. Therefore, the vast majority of employees (85.0 per cent) within Tuttlingen's medical technology cluster worked in established enterprises in 2002 (Table 10.4). This means that the old firms succeeded in sustaining and expanding their market position within the cluster. Only 9.5 per cent (687 persons) of the workforce in Tuttlingen's medical technology cluster were employed in surviving start-ups by 2002. The residual 5 per cent of employees are located in the large spin-off firms which were excluded from the analysis.

In Tuttlingen the 1990s saw the number of start-ups decline, survival prospects deteriorate, and the growth of new businesses (small supplier firms) stagnate. These results indicate that – like other mature clusters – Tuttlingen suffers from high density effects, which imply intense competition and strong displacement effects among firms. Although entrepreneurial activities were declining, the rates of start-up activity remained extraordinarily high within the cluster during the 1990s. Low entry barriers can be seen as the major reason for these high entry rates. One could conclude that the quantitative effects of new business creation were crucial for sustaining the cluster's firm stock, particularly in the 1980s. However, it was the expansion of the established firms that contributed most substantially to employment growth within the cluster. The employment effects of new firms were rather negligible, especially during the 1990s. Thus the cluster's hub and spoke structure became even more pronounced.

The future prospects of the producers and suppliers in Tuttlingen's surgical instruments cluster depend on the following factors: the changes in the national healthcare system, the international market demand for surgical instruments, and the ability to avoid the lock-in effects that often result from dense social networks between producers and suppliers.

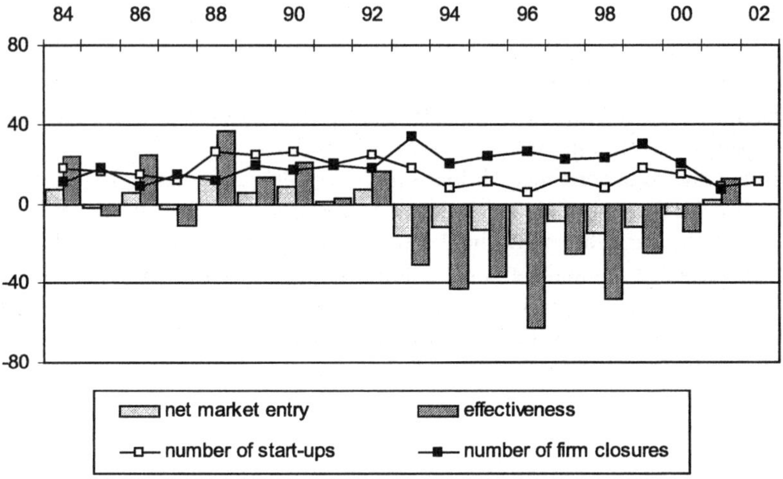

Figure 10.3: Entrepreneurship activities in Tuttlingen 1984–2002

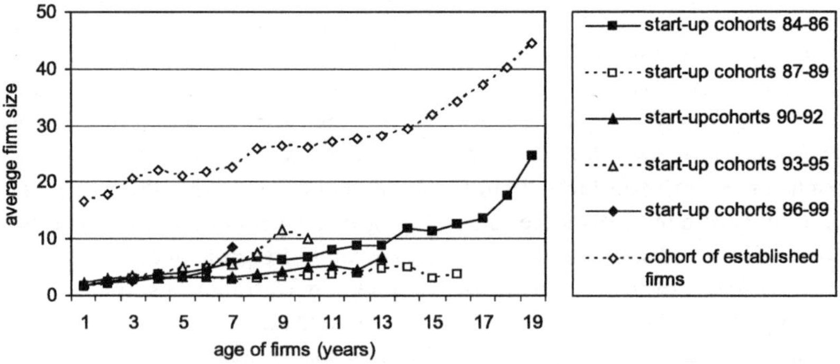

Figure 10.4: Average firm size of surviving start-ups and established firms – Tuttlingen

10.5 NECKAR-ALB – A DECLINING TEXTILE AND CLOTHING INDUSTRY CLUSTER

The Neckar-Alb region is situated in the Southwest of Germany (Baden-Württemberg) and consists of three counties: Reutlingen, Zollernalb and Tübingen. The historical origins of this traditional textile and clothing (t&c) industry center go back to the 19th century. For instance, the world's first technical college of textiles was set up in Reutlingen in 1800. It continues to be one of the world's most popular textile universities today. The previous success of this cluster was based on the spatial concentration of small t&c businesses, which were deeply embedded in social networks and engaged in cooperative partnerships. The small size of most firms is the outcome of long-term inheritance processes within the owners' families (Haas et al. 1983; Haas and Zademach 2005; Staber 1997, 2001). During the past several decades the t&c cluster in Neckar-Alb has experienced long-term regional restructuring due to industrial decline.

International competition sharply increased on the world market beginning in the early 1960s. The local t&c firms were thus obliged to shift production units (for example refining activities) to low-cost-countries in order to sustain competitive advantages. Meanwhile, most of the cluster-firms became integrated into global value chains. The activities that remain in Neckar-Alb mainly consist of organization and management tasks, as well as design, distribution and sales of textile and clothing products (Haas and Zademach 2005). The absence of production activities causes the cluster's value chain to be rather fragmented at the local level.

Nevertheless, some cluster-firms succeeded in maintaining their competitive position by specializing in the production of technical textiles. The customers for these innovative products are highly concentrated in Neckar-Alb and surrounding areas, for example the automotive and healthcare industry. A further regional advantage for these cluster-firms is their proximity to specialized research institutes, suppliers of chemical textiles, and textile machinery producers. Technical textile refining firms act as bridging entrepreneurs within the local production and innovation networks. However, the competitiveness of these firms is threatened by the recent rise in energy prices, since their production processes are highly energy-intensive (Industrie- und Handelskammer Reutlingen 2005).

The Neckar-Alb cluster has suffered from major industrial decline. Between 1984 and 2002 the number of jobs in the t&c industry decreased by 69 per cent from 36,300 to 11,200. Thus, the industry's share of regional employment dropped from 17.9 per cent to 5 per cent. Despite this decline, the German t&c industry is still highly concentrated in the Neckar-Alb region: the location quotient of the t&c industry in Neckar-Alb amounted to 6.94 in 2002. The location quotient in the county of Zollernalb (22.6) is the highest amongst all counties in West Germany for this industry.

Between 1984 and 1989 an average of 67.3 new t&c firms were opened in Neckar-Alb annually (Table 10.2). In contrast, only 49.7 and 28.2 start-ups were set up annually in the periods 1990–96 and 1997–2001 respectively. During these three periods the average number of annual firm closures was 69.1, 111.3 and 80.6 respectively. Hence, the negative values for net market entry and entrepreneurial effectiveness increased whereas the values of the turbulence declined, particularly during the 1990s

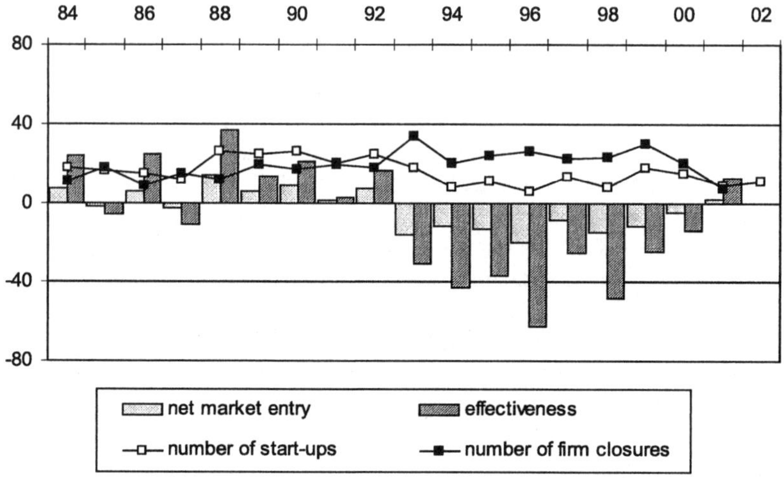

Figure 10.5: Entrepreneurship activities in Neckar-Alb 1984–2002

(Figure 10.5). The total number of cluster-firms dropped 63 per cent from 821 in 1984 to 304 in 2002 on account of decreasing entrepreneurial activities. Furthermore, the survival prospects of new firms diminished: only 33 per cent and 39 per cent of the start-ups from the 1993–95 and 1996–97 cohorts survived the first five years on the market (Table 10.3). In addition, only 22 per cent of all established firms in 1984 remained in the market through 2002.

All start-up cohorts and the group of established firms show only slight employment growth (Figure 10.6). A closer look reveals that the average firm size of the established cluster-firms actually declined between the 9th and 12th year, probably as a result of intra-organizational restructuring. The surviving established cluster-firms are the most important employers within the t&c industry in Neckar-Alb. They accounted for 84.5 per cent of the cluster's total employment in 2002 (Table 10.4). In contrast, the employment shares of start-ups and large spin-offs are rather small, amounting to only 7.9 per cent and 7.6 per cent respectively.

This case study shows rather clearly that the quantitative effects of new business creation are negligible during the aging and shrinking stage of a cluster's development. The decline of entrepreneurial activities and the increasing risk of failure for new firms point to the deterioration of the entrepreneurial climate within the Neckar-Alb cluster, particularly during the 1990s. The established organizations experienced slight employment growth, and survival rates were lower than those in Munich's and Tuttlingen's clusters. These results suggest that the decline of the t&c industry affects all firms, irrespective of their age. However, the established firms are of major significance for the local labour market.

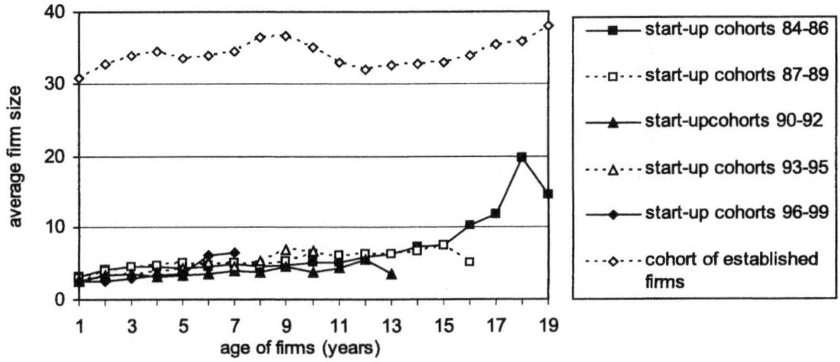

Figure 10.6: Average firm size of surviving start-ups and established firms – Neckar-Alb

10.6 CONCLUSIONS

The empirical results of the three cluster case studies reveal that the role of new firm formation in the development of clusters varies across different developmental phases. Furthermore, the results confirm that the quantitative effects of start-ups were especially important in boosting the number of firms and employees during the growth phase in Munich's medical technology cluster. The positive quantitative effects of start-up activities derive from a combination of positive balances of market entries and exits, high survival rates and dynamic employment growth of new firms in this cluster. These results suggest that growing clusters provide favourable local environments for the formation and growth of new firms.

New firms play less of a role in clusters that have reached later stages of development. Although the contribution of new business creation helped to sustain Tuttlingen's firm stock during the 1980s, thereafter the number of start-ups declined, the survival prospects diminished, and firm growth stagnated. This led to strong intraregional displacement effects. Therefore, entrepreneurial activities did not contribute significantly to the rise in the number of employees within this cluster during the 1990s. Tuttlingen's dynamic growth was instead the result of strong economic performance by the surviving established firms.

The decline of the t&c cluster in Neckar-Alb is evidenced by decreasing entry rates, survival rates and growth rates for start-ups. These results can be seen as proof of an unfavourable business climate within this shrinking cluster.

The study's empirical findings imply that different policy measures might be more effective at supporting new firms depending upon the cluster's phase of development. For instance, new firms might have great demand for venture and risk capital in order to invest in human capital and research activities during the growth stage of a cluster. Ensuring an adequate supply of capital could help firms to better exploit market opportunities and to benefit from favourable market conditions during this phase.

The values of the entry rates in both mature clusters, Tuttlingen and Neckar-Alb, were extraordinarily high and exceeded the rates of all other counties in Western Germany by far. These findings were surprising and might indicate that mature and shrinking clusters still possess great potential for spin-off-activities, even though the survival prospects of new firms were rather short. Other studies find similar results, for example Sorenson and Audia's (2000) of entrepreneurial activities in shoe industry clusters in the United States. The contradictory combination of high entry rates and low survival rates in the clusters of Tuttlingen and Neckar-Alb could be labeled as the ambivalence of entrepreneurship in industrial clusters. Social network theory and organizational ecology provide an explanation for this contradiction. Entrepreneurs tend to open new firms in their existent location. On the one hand, it is assumed that these actors are tightly bound to regional social networks and already have many contacts with constituents (for example, customers, suppliers) within the cluster. The extra resources embedded in these local social networks, which are otherwise not available, help the entrepreneurs to overcome the liabilities of newness and smallness (Aldrich and Zimmer 1986; Westlund and Bolton 2003). Thus, the propensity of entrepreneurs to start a new business should be higher in regions with clusters than in regions without clusters. Studies by Sternberg and Litzenberger (2004) and Rocha and Sternberg (2005) support this hypothesis. On the other hand, organizational ecology assumes that intense competition among new firms reduces their survival rates, especially given the combination of high firm density and exhausted resources in mature and shrinking clusters. The intensity of the competitive effect depends on the degree to which demand for resources among the cluster-firms overlaps. Thus, the risk of failure increases in specialized clusters (Staber 2001; Hannan and Freeman 1988).

The analysis of the established firms revealed two additional unexpected results. First, the two case studies of the medical technology clusters in Munich and Tuttlingen showed that the long-term survival rates of the established cluster-firms were extraordinarily high. Second, the surviving established firms remain the most important employers within the clusters of Tuttlingen and Neckar-Alb as of 2002. The established organizations contributed decisively to the overall employment growth of medical technology in Tuttlingen whereas the old t&c firms in Neckar-Alb showed only slight growth. These findings might point to the need for policy support for established firms in mature and declining clusters. This would represent a divergence from most cluster policies, which tend to concentrate support upon new firms.

Sorenson and Audia (2000) argue that these old organizations appear to be less vulnerable to local competition within industrial agglomerations. They give three explanations for this conjecture. (1) Access to local resources is particularly critical for the success of firms when they are young. Established businesses embedded in local networks can access resources through routinized relations. (2) Vulnerability might be an effect of firm size. Large enterprises do not face as intense competition as small firms. (3) Established firms have more experience responding to structural changes and competitive threats. It is possible that these strategic experiences enable them to reduce their future risk of failure. One reason for the lower survival rates of the old t&c-firms in Neckar-Alb – in comparison to the old cluster-firms in Tuttlingen and Munich – could be their structural inertia. These firms were probably not able to respond successfully to structural changes and cost pressure on the world textile market.

This study represents a first step in understanding the quantitative effects of entrepreneurship on the evolution of clusters. Comparing the development paths and survival prospects of cluster- and non-cluster firms might reveal further systematic results. Moreover, analysing the role of established firms in the evolution of clusters could be a promising future issue for entrepreneurship and cluster research.

REFERENCES

Aldrich, H. E. and C. Zimmer (1986), 'Entrepreneurship through social networks', in D. Sexton, S. Raymond (eds), *The Art and Science of Entrepreneurship*. Cambridge Mass.: Ballinger P.C., 3–23.

Binder, R. and B. Sautter (2005), 'Entrepreneurship in cluster - the surgical instrument cluster of Tuttlingen, Germany', in M. Fritsch, J. Schmude (eds), *Entrepreneurship in the region*. Heidelberg: Phyisca, 143–169.

Boschma, R.A. and R. Wenting (2004), 'The spatial evolution of the British automobile industry', *Papers in Evolutionary Economic Geography*, **5**.

Brixy, U. and R. Grotz (2006), 'Regional patterns of new firm formation and survival in Western Germany', *IAB-Discussion-Paper Nr. 5/2006*.

Bundesministerium für Bildung und Forschung (BMBF) (2005), *Situation der Medizintechnik in Deutschland im internationalen Vergleich*, Bonn/Berlin.

Bünstorf, G. and S. Klepper (2005), 'Heritage and agglomeration: the Akron tire cluster revisited', *Papers on Economics and Evolution*, **8**.

Dubini, P. (1989), 'The influence of motivations and environment on business startups: some hints for public policies', *Journal of Business Venturing*, **4**, 11–26.

Enright, M.J. (2000), *Survey on the characterization of regional clusters: initial results*. Working Paper, Institute of Economic Policy and Business Strategy, Competitiveness Program, University of Hong Kong.

Enright, M.J. (2002), 'Regional clusters: what we know and what we should know', in J. Bröcker, J. Dohse, R. Soltwedel (eds), *Innovation Clusters and Interregional Competition*, Berlin, Heidelberg, New York: Springer, 99–129.

Feldman, M., J. Francis and J. Bercovitz (2005), 'Creating a cluster while building a firm: entrepreneurs and the formation of industrial clusters', *Regional Studies*, **39**, 129–141.

Fritsch, M. and U. Brixy (2004), 'The establishment file of the German social insurance statistics', *Schmollers Jahrbuch/Journal of Applied Social Science Studies*, **124**, 183–190.

Fritsch, M. and M. Niese (2004), 'Alternative Indikatoren des Gründungsgeschehens', in M. Fritsch, R. Grotz (eds), *Empirische Analysen des Gründungsgeschehens in Deutschland*, Heidelberg: Physica, 5–17.

Fritsch, M., P. Müller and A. Weyh (2005), 'Direct and indirect effects of new business formation on regional employment', *Applied Economic Letters*, **12**, 545–548.

Garnsey, E. and P. Heffernan (2005), 'High-technology Clustering through Spin-out and Attraction: The Cambridge Case', *Regional Studies*, **39**, 1127–1144.

Grabher, G. (1993), *The Embedded Firm*, London: Routledge.

Haas, H.-D., W. Hess and G. Scherm (1983), 'Industrielle Monostrukturen an Mikrostandorten. Ansätze zur Arbeitsplatzsicherung im Rahmen der Stadtentwicklungsplanung dargestell am Beispiel Albstadt', *Münchener Studien zur Sozial- und Wirtschaftsgeographie*, **24**.

Haas, H.-D. and H.-M. Zademach (2005), 'Internationalisierung im Textil- und Bekleidungsgewerbe', *Geographische Rundschau*, **57**, 30–38.

Halder, G. (2005), 'Chirurgische Instrumente aus Tuttlingen und Sialkot/Tuttlingen: Lokale Produktion für den Weltmarkt', *Geographische Rundschau*, **57**, 12–20.

Hannan, M. T. and J. Freeman (1988), 'Density Dependence in the Growth of Organizational Populations', in Glenn, Carroll R. (ed.), *Ecological Models of Organizations*. Cambridge, Massachusetts: Ballinger P.C., 7–31.

Industrie- und Handelskammer Reutlingen (2005), *Perspektiven der Textilregion Neckar-Alb*.

Landeshauptstadt München (ed.) (2004), *Wachstumsmarkt Medizintechnik. Eine Standortbestimmung für den Wirtschaftsraum München*.

Martin, R. and P. Sunley (2003), 'Deconstructing Clusters: Chaotic Concept or Policy Panacea?', *Journal of Economic Geography*, **3**, 5–35.

Menzel, M.-P. and D. Fornahl (2005), 'Der Zusammenhang zwischen Unternehmensgründungen und der Entwicklung regionaler Cluster', *Zeitschrift für Wirtschaftsgeographie*, **49**, 131–149.

Rocha, H. and R. Sternberg (2005), 'Entrepreneurship: The Role of Clusters. Theoretical Perspectives and Empirical Evidence from Germany', *Small Business Economics*, **24**, 267–292.

Sautter, B. (2005), 'Einfluss auf die Gründungsaktivität im Cluster. Eine Längsschnitt-Analyse des Tuttlinger Medizintechnik-Clusters 1870-2002', *Wirtschaftsgeographie*, **31**, Münster: Lit.

Sorenson, O. and P. Audia (2000), 'The social structure of entrepreneurial activity: Geographic concentration of footwear production in the US, 1940-1989', *American Journal of Sociology*, **106**, 424–462.

Staber, U. (1997), 'Specialization in a Declining Industrial District', *Growth and Change*, **28**, 475–495.

Staber, U. (2001), 'Spatial proximity and firm survival in a declining industrial district: the case of knitwear firms in Baden-Württemberg', *Regional Studies*, **35**, 329–341.

Steiner, M. (1998), 'The discreet charm of clusters: an introduction', in Steiner, M. (ed.), *Clusters and Regional Specialisation On Geography, Technology and Networks*. London, 1–17.

Sternberg, R. and T. Litzenberger (2004), 'Regional clusters in Germany their geography and their relevance for entrepreneurial activities', *European Planning Studies*, **12**, 767–791.

Westlund, H. and R. Bolton (2003), 'Local social capital and entrepreneurship', *Small Business Economics*, **21**, 77–113.

11. On building clusters versus leveraging synergies in the design of innovation policy for developing economies

Edward Feser*

11.1 INTRODUCTION

The design and implementation of innovation policy is a major concern in both developed and developing countries. In Europe and the United States, exploitation of the innovation capabilities embedded in human capital and advanced infrastructure are viewed as an essential source of global competitive advantage as standardized, labor intensive activities migrate to least cost locations in Asia, Latin America, and Africa. Addressing the needs of industry clusters is viewed in many quarters as a necessary element of innovation strategies:

> *'Clusters of Innovation', the title of a project on regional clusters in the United States, has become a particularly popular term among private and public sector leaders. This reflects increasing pressure many U.S. and European companies and locations face to compete on innovation rather than productivity alone. Clusters turn out to provide particularly fertile ground for innovations because they are well aligned with modern innovation processes* (Ketels 2004, p. 1).

Europe and the US are not alone. Many developing economies, motivated by clear instances of technology-oriented development success in India, China, Brazil and elsewhere, are also beginning to use cluster concepts to both motivate and inform innovation policy making (Melo 2001a, 2001b; Mani and Romijn 2003; Feser 2005). This reflects a rejection of "implicit stages" views of development, which assign less developed countries the role of satellite production centers for knowledge-based, highly industrialized economies. The literature identifying technology-based clusters in developing economies is growing rapidly, along with policy applications designed to

* University of Illinois at Urbana-Champaign

foster cluster growth (Quandt 1997; Voyer 1997a, 1997b; Altenburg and Meyer-Stamer 1999; Quandt 1999; Bortagaray and Tiffin 2000). In the midst of all this activity, however, there remains considerable uncertainty about what cluster oriented innovation strategies involve, what kinds interventions are likely to be most effective, and how such policies should be evaluated (Benneworth et al. 2003; Boekholt and McKibbin 2003).

There is certainly substantial writing on innovation and technology policy, most of which pre-dates the modern fascination with clusters. The innovation policy literature is chiefly concerned with evaluating a wide range of interventions designed to boost basic and applied innovation and ultimately growth in incomes. The influence of regulation, standards setting, infrastructure investments, research subsidies, risk financing, technology transfer, and public sector procurement on the rate of business innovation have all been subject to considerable research (Justman and Teubal 1986; Markusen 1993; Simons 1993; Malecki 1997; Shapira et al. 2001). More recently, innovation policy discussions, particularly the concept of National Innovation Systems (NIS), have come to be dominated by perspectives in neo-Schumpeterian evolutionary economics. NIS emphasizes the non-linear process of innovation, including feedback effects between stages of innovation and various innovation actors, as well as between the public policies and noncommercial institutions that constitute the framework in which innovation and learning occur. The Regional Innovation Systems (RIS) concept, or "reduced-NIS" as described by Hertog et al. (2001), asserts that a decentralized regional approach to innovation policy is likely to be more effective than a centralized national model (Asheim and Isaksen 1997; Cooke et al. 1997; Cooke and Morgan 1998; Moulaert and Sekia 1999; Morgan 2004). It is fair enough to ask what unique policy insights the concepts of industry clusters and clustering bring to this already rich innovation debate.

This paper argues that there are chiefly two. The first is that businesses in regional clusters are likely to innovate more, and therefore enjoy higher levels of productivity and sustained growth, than firms in peripheral locations. At the core of most cluster theories is the thesis that businesses compete not as isolated units but rather within complex webs of interdependence that include both market and non-market institutions, and that there are certain advantages when those interdependencies are localized. It is fairly widely accepted that clusters are groups of interdependent firms and related institutions (such as universities, labs, and industry associations) and that regional clusters are geographic concentrations of such groups (Boekholt and Thuriaux 1997; Rosenfeld 2002). Porter (2002) has argued quite explicitly that regional clusters are the principal engines of innovation in an economy. The implication is that governments should actively concentrate public science and technology investments, as well as other innovation programs, both by sector and location where possible. This is what I call a *regional innovation cluster building* view. Note that I include under the rubric "building" what some authors describe as "activating." For example, Ketels (2004) argues that lacking sound analyses of cluster composition and characteristics, policy officials will be tempted to "create" clusters where they do not exist:

> *Cluster development, however, should not aim to create clusters, but to activate them. Activating an existing base of companies and institutions to jointly upgrade their cluster is much more effective than investing huge sums in the risky business of creating clusters from scratch* (p. 4).

Whether one describes this perspective as cluster building or activating is irrelevant for my purposes. The key feature is the conceptual linkage between clusters as entities and macroeconomic outcomes such as innovation, productivity and growth. The Council on Competitiveness in the United States perhaps characterizes this connection most clearly when it links national economic performance to regional cluster formation and growth: "Future US competitiveness will hinge not just on policies and investments at the national level, but on the capacity to foster clusters of innovation in regions across the country."[1]

The second fundamental implication of clusters is that an understanding of business interdependence should be embedded into the design and implementation of innovation programs, as well as most other kinds of economic development interventions, to improve their impact and success. This more nuanced perspective is what I call a synergy leveraging view, where the target outcome is not any particular cluster's expansion and competitive performance, but rather the greater efficacy of programs or policies which are themselves motivated by clearly identified sources of market failure and, therefore, theoretically sound connections to regional macroeconomic welfare. Re-designing policies to leverage clustering synergies removes cluster policy from the realm of traditional industrial policy – that is, the use of public resources to promote selected industrial strengths – while still taking advantage of the most persuasive insights in the microeconomic theories of Porter and his adherents. It also emphasizes that clusters are less informative about what we should do in regional economic development than about how we should do it. This view has been expressed already by several scholars in one fashion or another, but the insight has tended to get lost in the face of the seemingly powerful intuitive logic of cluster building (Nauwelaers 2001; Raines 2001; Benneworth et al. 2003).

Note that both the cluster building and synergy leveraging perspectives are essentially hypotheses that deserve serious empirical investigation. While they need not be mutually exclusive, they may occasionally contradict one another, such as when efforts to boost inter-firm synergies and collective learning can be best achieved by strengthening linkages with distant partners rather than regionally based firms. Such contradictions are likely to be more common in developing and transitioning economies than highly developed ones.

While both approaches could be used in tandem, this paper argues that attempts to build discrete regional technology clusters as a means to promote innovation economy-wide are likely to meet with very limited success in the context of most developing and transitioning economies. The fact that some industries and/or innovations cluster – either in abstract space as described by DeBresson (1989) or in geographic space as in Porter (1990) – is not a sufficient guide for policy, the vast descriptive

[1] Council on Competitiveness website (www.compete.org/nri/clusters_innovation.asp), accessed 1 May 2005.

literature notwithstanding. The case for exploiting interdependencies to improve the effectiveness of innovation programs and policies is much stronger conceptually, and regional technology-based clusters may very well emerge naturally as a result. It follows that policy makers in less developed countries and the eastern European transition economies should not view clusters as offering a distinct model of technology-based economic development, but rather as providing a set of useful insights and analytical frameworks for improving the design and implementation of a wide variety of innovation strategies. The distinction is not a trivial one, especially for less favored regions where existing innovation clusters are nonexistent or very shallow and the potential for wasting scarce resources is great.

11.2 BUILDING CLUSTERS VERSUS LEVERAGING CLUSTER SYNERGIES

The cluster building view holds that an important route to raising rates of innovation is to nurture the expansion of discrete spatial agglomerations of technology-related activity, including formally and informally linked businesses, university research competencies, government laboratories, colleges and technology training institutes, and private sector contract R&D houses. This is accomplished with the application of a broad portfolio of policy interventions, some of which aim to build the science base, some of which enhance the general framework conditions in which firms operate, and some of which seek to expand the technology sector directly via recruitment or entrepreneurship programs. Examples of such interventions are listed in Table 11.1, which was derived from several well-cited papers offering practical guidance to policy makers. The process usually involves conducting an analysis to identify strengths and weaknesses among a set of related businesses (industry cluster analysis), together with an assessment of the regional science and technology base, the results from which drive the selection of focus clusters and the prescription strategies for cluster growth.

The perspective differs from the synergy leveraging view in that its explicit aim is to develop a discrete technology-based specialization that can capture increasing returns to scale and foster collective learning and innovation. Conversely, the perspective implicitly asserts that a broad-based S&T strategy (for example, one that is largely sector-, technology-, or location-neutral) will generate less net innovation overall than one that is focused on building specific, localized S&T competencies. Its most persuasive theoretical logic derives from theories of spatial externalities and knowledge spillovers, the basic principles of which are documented extensively elsewhere and need not be recounted here. However, it is Michael Porter's *The Competitive Advantage of Nations* (1990), subsequent writings (Porter 1998, 2000, 2002), and prolific international consulting practice that have exerted by far the greatest influence on the application of clusters to development policy. Therefore, understanding how cluster concepts are being used in policy making requires careful consideration of Porter's ideas and how they have been absorbed and applied.

There are two ways that Porter's work might be interpreted: first, as a treatise on clusters as geographically localized concentrations of industrial activity; and, second,

Supply-side interventions	Objectives
Identity	Creation of cluster industry association or similar private sector organization to serve as catalyst and key stakeholder for cluster interests.
Location incentives, recruitment	Attract inward investment by directly reducing business costs through tax and non-tax incentives. Cluster analysis used to identify gaps in supply chains as possible recruitment targets, with the objective being to increase business locations per unit of recruitment effort or resources. Cluster analysis may also be used to identify labor skill requirements of related industries in order to "sell" local labor pools to relocating firms.
Business networks	Establishment of forums for information sharing and joint problem solving of firms in selected sectors. Encourage cooperation in areas of marketing, training, sourcing, sales.
Business development services	Identification and articulation of demand of local firms for business development services (development of BDS markets); encouragement of closer alignment between services supplied and firm needs (development of BDS supply). Closely related to provision of industrial extension.
University research competencies	Investment in specific research disciplines that reflect unique strengths of existing faculty or desirable strengths.
Non-university labs, research "catalysts"	Creation or funding of intermediary agencies designed to conduct independent research and/or foster collaboration between university and industry researchers (a brokering or catalyst function); may also seek to leverage national government sources of research funding.
R&D incentives, subsidies, awards	Provision of incentives to increase R&D activity of industry, usually small firms or firms located in peripheral regions.
Regulatory assistance	Guidance with regulatory compliance issues. Designed to free up engineering and research staff in industry to focus on R&D and innovation activities.
Incubators	Development of facilities to provide subsidized space and services to high tech start-ups.
Industrial extension	Provision of technical and business development services to smaller firms, usually through regional network of extension offices and sometimes based in engineering universities and colleges.
Training	Skill upgrading of workers in identified cluster firms by focused training programs, delivered on demand or available through community colleges. Professional certificate programs for industry specializations (e.g., information technology, networking).
Basic education	Improvement of primary and secondary education as long-term labor pool upgrading strategy.
Lab space, buildings, parks	Provision of specialized facilities and space (e.g., wet labs in biotechnology) via grants, low cost loans, and other inducements.
Risk-based financing	Attraction of venture capital through creation of venture capital pools (via public sector investing power) and marketing of area firms/industry to traditional venture capital sources.

Table 11.1: Common cluster building interventions

Demand-side interventions	Objectives
Procurement	Targeting of public sector purchasing to local firms or firms in target development regions.
Regulation and regulatory enforcement	Recognition in regulatory design and enforcement of impacts on markets, particularly in sectors such as environmental controls, electronics, information technology, and media.
Supply chain development	Foster purchasing linkages among firms in product or value chains, via supplier fairs and assistance (BDS or extension) to suppliers with meeting technical or standards requirements of customers, usually larger firms. Help with meeting international standards (e.g. ISO).

Basic categories of interventions are from Enright (2001), Rosenfeld (2001) and De Vol (2000).

Table 11.1: Common cluster building interventions – Cont.

as an explanation of clustering (Clancy et al. 2001). Although Porter's most useful contributions in *The Competitive Advantage of Nations* relate to hypotheses about business interdependence (or clustering irrespective of geography), particularly the roles of cooperative competition and non-market institutions (Cooke et al. 1997), his empirical approach has encouraged a heavy focus on localized clusters as geographic phenomena. With regard to innovation, Porter is explicit that regional clusters – not just clustering dynamics – are the key: "Strong and competitive clusters are a critical component of a good business environment and are the driving force behind regional innovation and rising productivity" (Porter 2002, p. 9). A result is that devising recipes for building clusters according to ideal-types – the process of singling out for special policy attention those localized groups of industries in a country or region that appear to conform to pre-set criteria – has become a multi-million dollar consulting business.

The Competitive Advantage of Nations (Porter 1990) seeks to explain, ex post, the source of competitiveness of leading export-oriented industries in selected industrialized countries. Failed industries are not part of the study. The methodology therefore includes no serious evaluation of competing hypotheses. But more fundamentally, the inductively derived diamond model of competitiveness, perhaps the most well-known and applied concept in the book, is static. What works for globally competitive, export-oriented industries today – or in the late 1980s, as the case may be – may not be what accounted for their initial rise. The fact that the present sources of competitiveness of Silicon Valley's information technology industry conform to the diamond framework does not constitute sufficient evidence of the adequacy of the model as an explanation of how Silicon Valley got to be the way it is. Yet clearly for many policy makers, the most compelling message in *The Competitive Advantage of Nations* is that one can use the diamond, or some other similar descriptive model, to devise strategies to replicate the current conditions of globally competitive industrial complexes in advanced economies.

Unfortunately, the Porter diamond offers few realistic policy handles for less developed nations and lagging regions in developed ones. How exactly does a government build sophisticated home demand or a culture of competition that exemplifies just the right balance of rivalry and cooperation in a place with limited economic activity to begin with? Porter (1990, pp. 675–76) does offer some guidance for developing nations: "To progress, the developing nation faces the daunting task of upgrading all four parts of the national 'diamond' sufficiently to reach the threshold necessary to compete in advanced countries." He suggests the first step is to improve education, information, technology, and modern infrastructure. But he remains confident that clusters are central: "As a starting point, a nation must identify those industries where its factor advantages today provide some competitive advantage but where other determinants of national advantage are also actually, or potentially, present" (p. 677).

At issue here is not the messenger but the method. The new industrial districts and related literature on flexible specialization also spawned a considerable amount of reasoning and policy prescription by ideal-type (for example, the ideal Italianate district), probably not the intention of Piore and Sabel (1984) and other early contributors such as Brusco (1982) and Bellandi (1989; see also Goglio 2002). Arguments about what is and is not truly a cluster, as well as the proliferation of typologies of clusters and industrial districts (for example, Courlet and Pecqueur 1991; Markusen 1996; Rosenfeld 1997; Capello 1999; McCormick 1999; Enright 2000), reflect efforts by subsequent researchers to acknowledge the variety of territorial production systems that operate quite competitively. Note that the fundamental thesis that business interdependence is an important element of competitiveness is not disputed by these typologies. Rather, the concern is the form – both functional and spatial – that that interdependence takes at a given point in an industry's life cycle and a region's development trajectory.

Unresolved even as differing types of "Porterian" and "Italianate" clusters are identified and documented are absolutely fundamental questions related to direction of causality, the relative significance of various competitiveness factors in different development contexts, and the feasibility of alternative policy interventions. Reliance on ideal-types limits serious consideration of such issues and as a result may generate lessons that are not grounded in a careful analysis of the history of leading clusters, even if that is the basic intention. For instance, UNIDO's Cluster Development Program aims to draw lessons "from the experience of successful clusters and [implement] them through technical cooperation projects in various developing countries" (Russo et al. 2000, p. 2). One specific objective is to help cluster actors "develop a consensus-based vision of the cluster as a whole" (p. 6). Yet we have no evidence whatsoever that such a consensus was instrumental in establishing the most successful technology clusters in the world today. Consider Intel co-founder Gordon Moore's view of the semiconductors business in Silicon Valley:

> *What 'works' right now in this dynamic, regional, high-technology economy tells us little of how precisely Silicon Valley came to be just such a place, or how any such place comes into being. The potential disaster lies in the fact that these static, descriptive efforts culminate in policy recommendations that resemble recipes or magic potions* (Moore and Davis 2001, p. 3).

One might argue that working to establish a collective vision among firms and related institutions in a set of industries cannot hurt, ceterus paribus. But in the world of development policy, ceterus paribus never applies. Every intervention exacts an opportunity cost in human, financial, and political capital. Porter's model does not constitute an explanation of causes of localization, grounded in any theory of industry location or externalities. It is at heart an empirical observation of a tendency toward spatial co-location of competitive, exporting firms. This observation has proven highly convincing to policy makers and many analysts, so that building regional clusters – as opposed to raising productivity, boosting innovation, redressing market failures, or other objectives directly related to regional welfare – has become a common goal of development policy. Regional welfare improvements are viewed as a natural outcome of cluster building efforts.

A synergy leveraging view of clusters, in contrast, holds that innovation policies should aim to nurture and exploit innovative synergies between interdependent firms and institutions, regardless of whether a discrete spatial cluster emerges as a result. The difference in perspectives therefore hinges largely on the nature of the policy objective: in the building view, it is the cluster itself; in the leveraging view, it is the synergies that presumably drive clustering. Existing theory and empirical research on clusters emphasizes that businesses operate not in isolation, as postulated by the standard neoclassical model of competition, but rather as part of larger formal and informal networks (Best 1990). Those networks jointly constrain and offer opportunities to enhance businesses' competitive positions. They also influence processes of joint learning and innovation. The process of clustering, whether viewed from the perspective of strategic management (Porter), industrial districts (Marshall), new growth theory, or NIS/RIS, suggests industrial policy can be made more effective by exploiting networking dynamics. With regard to technology policy, this implies that cluster linkages – whether they are regional, national, or global in scope – are the conduits through which innovative impulses flow.

As an example of what is meant by leveraging synergies, consider a typical innovation strategy: attempts by government to increase the rate of advanced technology adoption among small firms. One possible mechanism for increasing adoption rates is the provision of publicly subsidized industrial extension programs targeted toward small and medium sized enterprises in specific sectors and regions identified as existing or potential clusters (Shapira 2001). Alternatively, a synergy leveraging approach to industrial extension might attempt to exploit pressures within extended buyer–supplier chains, which most likely span a wide range of sectors and locations, to maximize limited extension program resources. Technology surveys indicate that among the most important influences on firm adoption behavior are the production systems of end-market customers that require close integration with supplier systems (Bergman and Feser 2001). Thus, industrial extension programs might begin by encouraging or aiding the adoption of best-practice technologies among major buyers within extended supply chains, many of which will be large firms, coupled with assistance to local SME suppliers as pressures for upgrading begin to build. Ultimately, the issue is the means by which the same basic strategy – industrial extension – is implemented.

Tendler and Amorim (1996) describe a similar approach with respect to government procurement in Brazil, where a key feature of the program was not just the injection of demand via public spending in specific regions, but also the establishment of appropriate incentives for the local business support agency to provide the right kinds of assistance to local producers; that is, the way in which demand was injected. One result was a competitive regional furniture cluster comprised mostly of small and medium sized enterprises (SMEs). More important was the job creation in a less favored region that the carefully designed procurement strategy produced. In the case of synergy leveraging, the focus shifts from the cluster itself to the effective design of institutions and strategies of policy implementation given a model of economy-wide interdependent competition.

A third useful example is the provision of business development services (BDS) for SMEs in peripheral European regions, as described by Lagendijk (2000). BDS programs have had a history of limited effectiveness. Support agencies often have difficulty attracting clients, probably because they have been too focused on technical rather than organizational and managerial deficits facing client companies. Whatever the reason, BDS programs often suffer from a mismatch between the kinds of services supplied and those in greatest demand. Lagendijk argues that the problem can be corrected by understanding how businesses operate in a relational or associational economy. Clusters are an important mechanism for interactive learning among and between businesses, public agencies, and other key regional institutions: "To improve the way business support can contribute to regional development, policies need to adopt new perspectives that are especially geared to improving relational assets in the region" (Lagendijk 2000, p. 173). Instead of technical problem solving:

> *linear and unfocused forms of business support need to be complemented, if not replaced, by more interactive forms of support framed within a strategic context. Interaction here refers to the role of brokering . . . it may also included focused 'intelligence gathering' that provides firms with new strategic insights and improves the articulation of business needs. These processes can be focused, framed and facilitated . . . by adopting a cluster perspective* (Lagendijk 2000, p. 189).

The key here is that the focus is on using a theoretical and empirical understanding of business clustering to better implement BDS programs and policies. This is consistent with Nauwelaers' (2001) thesis that cluster strategy does not entail new development instruments but rather a new "mode of intervention of the public actor" (p. 100). Development organizations may reorient strategies away from a top-down model focused on provision of basic inputs and infrastructure to a more facilitative role where the goal is to involve private sector actors in the formation of regional policy. With respect to evaluation and impact, the target outcome is not growth of a cluster, but rather a better fit between the needs of SMEs and the kinds of programs offered by BDS support agencies. The value of the cluster concept is then evidenced by whether programs are more efficacious when informed by cluster ideas, not whether a specific cluster emerges or grows in a given region.

11.3 AVAILABLE EVIDENCE

These two perspectives – building clusters versus leveraging synergies – are not necessarily mutually exclusive, though they may occasionally contradict one another in certain respects. It is possible to imagine both approaches informing innovation policy in significant ways. However, there may be empirical and conceptual arguments that suggest that one approach or the other is likely to be more efficacious in the long run from the point of view of effective knowledge-based economic development, particularly in developing or transitioning economies where deep, localized clusters of technology-oriented firms are rare. This section considers the question of empirical work, focusing on research relevant to the innovation question.

First, there have been a number of attempts to explain the causes of localized clustering itself (Dumais et al. 1997; Ellison and Glaeser 1997; Sweeney and Feser 1998; Feser and Sweeney 2000; Sweeney and Nagle 2004). If knowledge spillovers explain why enterprises seek proximate locations, that would lend some support to the cluster building view as well as verify an important consequence of firm interdependence. The challenge for any empirical work on co-location, however, is that most economic activity is localized given the generally concentrated pattern of human settlement. Spillovers are only one reason that businesses might cluster. Others include access to markets, labor, infrastructure, suppliers, natural resources, historical lock-in, and even chance. In developing countries, businesses often concentrate near administrative centers because the public sector accounts for a high share of demand and because government bureaucracies often heavily influence the mix and distribution of business opportunities (Lall et al. 2001). Existing studies are hampered by very weak measures of spillovers (for example, patents), a dearth of appropriate methodologies for controlling for competing location factors, and a lack of suitable time series for addressing questions of causality. It is fair to say that the empirical study of the co-location of innovative businesses is still fairly rudimentary.

Second, there is a body of work that finds some evidence that innovations, as opposed to firms, tend to cluster geographically and that knowledge spillovers are often localized (Jaffe 1986; Griliches 1992; Jaffe et al. 1993; Feldman 1994; Adams and Jaffe 1996; Breschi 1999; Feldman 1999; Lall et al. 2001; Wallsten 2001; Koo 2002). While findings vary, collectively the research offers modest evidence of the spatial clustering of innovations, at least as measured mainly by patents and patent citations. We might therefore draw the tentative conclusion that an active strategy of developing high tech specializations in particular regions would yield higher rates of innovation. However, we cannot be sure because few of the studies consider whether the specific mix of S&T resources, industrial activity, and other basic factors such as infrastructure and basic education are critical to the result. It is also important to note that all of the research on knowledge spillovers is confined to the developed country context and much of it considers innovation trends in a fairly narrow group of sectors. A related literature finds that rates of innovation and productivity tend to be higher among businesses that are proximate to research universities (Jaffe 1989; Acs et al. 1992, 1994; Anselin et al. 1997; Anselin et al. 2000). Aside from firms, the role of universities in technology clusters has received the most attention. But again, analysis of the developing country context is limited.

Third, there is a small but expanding literature that examines the relationship between clusters and economic performance using quasi-experimental rather than case study methods.[2] For example, Baptista and Swann (1998) use a database of innovations in the UK to examine whether companies proximate to other enterprises tend to innovate at higher rates. They find evidence that those in the same lines of business do: "Using regional employment as a measure of a cluster's strength, it was found that a firm is more likely to innovate if located in a region where the presence of firms in its own industry is strong. The effects of the proximity of firms in other industries do not appear to be significant . . ." (Baptista and Swann 1998, p. 538). In related work, Bapista (2001) finds that technology adoption rates are higher in clusters, mainly because proximity helps to reduce the uncertainty of technology upgrading and increases information about the availability and utility of new technologies, a conventional diffusion effect.[3] Porter (2002) conducted a six-city analysis in the US that claims to demonstrate, among other things, that clusters of technology-related activity generate higher rates of innovation, entrepreneurship, and growth. However, since the study considered only successful technology agglomerations, it cannot speak to the relative advantages of clustered versus unclustered industrial development.

Finally, there is an enormous case study literature, the review of which could easily consume another paper or two. The richest of such studies investigate clustering dynamics using industrial districts and flexible specialization concepts. In a recent review of the literature pertaining to Latin America, Altenburg and Meyer-Stamer (1999) drew the following conclusions: (1) while clustering is widespread in Latin America, clusters in the region are rarely propelled by competitive small and medium sized firms (SMEs), as is common in Europe; (2) addressing the weakness of SMEs must therefore be a major focus of LAC cluster strategies, particularly the establishment of connections between transnational corporations and small firms; (3) because most clusters in Latin America are centered on the production of standardized commodities, innovation policy will have the most success by encouraging the diffusion of technologies from TNCs to local firms, rather than attempting to grow an indigenous R&D presence; 4) because there is a decided lack of cooperation among firms in LAC clusters, the promotion of networking via the use of brokers and other incentives is critical to encouraging interfirm synergies.

---

[2]Here I ignore the large empirical literature on agglomeration economies since most of it explores the relationships between geography, linkages, and productivity using only very crude measures of clustering (urban and city size as proxies for urbanization and localization economies). Similarly, Glaeser et al. (1992) and Glaeser et al. (1995) use only aggregate measures of concentration to study the links between localization, specialization, and urban growth.

[3]"Interpersonal connections and networking play an important role in knowledge transfer, and supply-side factors are often significant in determining diffusion paths. This leads to the need for policy to consider the role of supplier-user relationships, professional and trade associations, academic and public-funded R&D, and organisations manufacturing complementary assets and technologies. The significance of these institutional relationships becomes larger as their geographical scope becomes smaller" (2001, p. 44). Other studies have also found evidence of a relationship between agglomeration (either co-location of similar businesses or location in a highly urbanized area) and technology adoption. Examples are Harrison et al. 1996b; 1996a) and Kelley and Helper (1999). The pattern of causality is unclear in many technology adoption studies, however, due to the heavy use of cross-sectional rather than time series data.

Some of these conclusions echo the findings of Schmitz and Musyck (1994), who review the general industrial district literature in Europe to derive lessons for developing countries. They argue that the European experience shows the value of an industrial policy that is decentralized to the local and regional level and is implemented by both governmental and non-governmental units. They also conclude that the "emergence of the industrial districts does not result from consciously pursued local or regional industrial strategy" (p. 904). Indeed, in the cases they reviewed, they found that growth first occurred spontaneously and then was enhanced by local institutional support structures (including development policy). An important trend in the industrial districts literature is a shift from a focus on purely local connections between businesses to a more sophisticated consideration of inter-firm innovation dynamics within global commodity chains (Humphrey and Schmitz 2000; Schmitz 2000). The shift is motivated by recognition that full-scale clusters of the Italianate or Porterian variety are rarely found in developing countries and that external linkages are often more important to the competitiveness of developing country firms than internal ones.

One particular piece of case study work warrants special mention. Swann et al. (1998) attempt to identify the specific conditions – in terms of size, diversity, linkages between agents, and so forth – under which biotechnology and information technology clusters begin to attract new entrants and generate increasing returns and spillovers. They also focus on clustering over time, finding that the "forces that influence the growth and entry of firms in clusters are not simply related to the stage of each technology: they depend also on the stage of the cluster in its own life cycle" (p. 2). Clusters eventually become "congested" and cease growing. They may even fail to regenerate themselves as their underlying technology strengths wane. This theme of cluster sustainability has received little attention in the literature (though see Bergman 2002 and Pouder and St. John 1996), largely because so many definitions of clusters are normative in character (for example, "a cluster is a concentrated agglomeration of highly competitive firms"). In the view of Swann et al. (1998, p. 306), policy makers should "consider the creation of powerful and visible magnets for industrial location." They find that universities and laboratories are among the most important institutions driving the success of innovation clusters. Thus government should promote "promising points of intersection" between technology industries and university research competencies as a way to boost innovation rates. Swann (1999) finds that clusters are competitive only when they have a high level of internal sectoral diversity, a serious implication for the more narrow and underdeveloped innovation clusters in less favored regions.

Given this diverse empirical literature, what can be said about the relative value of clusters as an innovation policy focus, whether from the point of view of building clusters or leveraging innovative synergies? Clearly S&T agglomerations are common in highly industrialized countries, there is mounting evidence that knowledge spillovers tend to be localized and are therefore a source of regional scale economies, and a deep case study literature argues that there are significant innovation effects derived from formal and informal networking among local firms and support agents (labs, universities, government agencies, business development services). The literature on the relationship between presence in a cluster and economic performance is relatively weak, but based on what we know now, developing and transition economy governments should clearly consider the role of clusters and clustering in the design of innovation policy. But what is the right approach: to aggressively attempt to build specific regional innovation clusters or to adopt the more conservative strategy of using clusters as a way to redesign conventional innovation policy? Or, put differently, is aiming to build innovation clusters among specific businesses in selected locations as a strategic policy objective the best way to harness the benefits of clustering? There are several reasons to suggest that it may not be, especially in less favored regions.

First, it is widely accepted in the literature that the public sector's capacity to build innovation clusters from scratch (or even "catalyze" them, to employ a common euphemism) is severely limited, even in highly industrialized economies. Obviously the problem is of particular significance in the developing country context, where innovation activity is often modest to nonexistent. Ironically, it is not uncommon in the literature to find detailed recipes for cluster promotion juxtaposed with cautious pronouncements that innovation clusters cannot be created from nothing and that policy accounts for only a small part of most competitive clusters' success. Making "policy flexibility" an ingredient in the recipe is the usual tack for finessing the contradiction. But the real problem is in making the notion of a spatial cluster – rather than innovation, income, growth or other direct economic outcome – the relevant objective.

Second, researchers have shown convincingly that there is no single model of a competitive localized cluster. This does not imply that more typologies of innovation clusters with attendant guides for growth need to be developed, but rather that the objective of strategically growing a full-scale regional cluster with a host of coordinated interventions is probably too broad to be useful in any practical sense. Clusters are groups of businesses and related support institutions such as universities, colleges, government laboratories, and development agencies linked in various ways and at various levels of geography: local, regional, national, international, global, or combinations thereof.[4] The linkage, which may be formal or informal (traded or untraded), might derive from buyer–supplier ties, shared labor pools, codified transfer of knowledge or technologies, tacit transfer of knowledge, shared social and cultural norms, and the like. Theoretically, there are a great many dimensions on which businesses might be related, and each dimension may manifest itself at different spatial scales, such as labor pools at the regional level, shared knowledge at the global level, and so on. A single firm may be a member of one cluster defined as an industrial district and another cluster defined as a global trading network or value chain. Focusing policy on only the local or regional dimension of business linkages necessarily leaves out key dimensions of interdependence that have real implications for innovation and competitiveness.

Third, cluster building is full of political risks. It may overstate the public sector's capacity to develop coordinated, multifaceted development strategies, given the size of the challenge in developing countries as well as political and ethical pressures to

[4] Some authors have argued for additional dimensions. Enright (2001) outlines a total of eleven, two of which relate to geography. Others are density, breadth, depth, activity base, strength of competitive position, stage of development, technological activities, innovative capacity, and ownership structures. In any case, there is no single best typology of clusters.

diffuse resources across sectors, institutions, and regions. Publicly laying out a goal to nurture a regional biotechnology, information technology, automotive or other cluster is also a highly visible act that will be judged, several years hence, at its face value: that is, did the professed innovation cluster materialize? There is an appreciable risk of unmet expectations that have real costs in terms of garnering political, financial, and leadership capital for subsequent development initiatives. Few would dispute that the size of the risk is inversely related to the existing size of the S&T base at the start of the intervention.

Fourth, cluster building often focuses attention away from basic needs and toward interventions that promise immediate impacts on the size and scope of the innovation cluster itself. Those include investments in research competencies in the universities, the development and placement of government laboratories, the supply of venture capital financing, the provision of R&D and other incentives to existing firms, and the recruitment of high technology enterprises. Such strategies may make sense in developed economies where the advanced infrastructure and institutional capacity are already in place. However, in developing economies many basic needs remain to be fulfilled, including the provision of good roads, airports, public transportation, schools, basic telecommunications, and accountable and efficient government. Most such needs benefit multiple sectors, not just those in target clusters.

Finally, highly specialized cluster building initiatives could unintentionally help lock a region into an industrial specialization or innovation competency that will eventually face decline. As Pouder and St. John (1996) note, "Once a super nova for state-of-the-art innovation, the hot spot quickly becomes an industry black hole." Analysts typically caution against "picking winners", but that concern usually references the possibility of inadvertently targeting a low growth or declining sector. The more significant but less appreciated problem is a kind of policy lock-in effect; that as active cluster building efforts reorient economic policy from the basic approach of providing and maintaining a level playing field to one of tailoring institutional structures to particular industrial specializations, the public sector's ability to adapt to changing economic circumstances declines. The very process of carrying out the objectives of funding selected research competencies rather than meritorious research in general, encouraging specialized venture capital sources, building dedicated rather than general incubators, developing targeted business incentives, and so on effectively specializes public sector government and administrative competencies just as it aims to specialize the industrial base. An economic policy regime with a narrow set of competencies is less nimble when economic and technological conditions change, as they inevitably do.

Given these problems, the more conservative approach of viewing cluster concepts as a tool for leveraging innovative synergies among businesses to improve the implementation of innovation policy has distinct advantages. First and foremost, the leveraging view shifts attention away from generalized cluster building, an impractical strategy where the existing S&T base is modest. Second, it is more agnostic with respect to the level of geography in which business linkages manifest themselves. Rather, it allows that key formal and informal linkages occur at all spatial scales and between different kinds of firms (large and small, branch manufacturers and headquarters, buyers and suppliers, and so on). The goal is to look for ways to strengthen and use those linkages to increase innovation and growth rates. Third, it can help inform a wide range of interventions which themselves can be legitimated using conventional and theoretically sound policy analytic tools such as concepts of public goods and market failure. Fourth, it places emphasis on the most important insights of the cluster literature – the notions of cooperative competition and collective efficiency – without biasing policy away from strategies that are not aimed at immediate growth and expansion of a selected group of industries. Fifth, it reduces the burden on applied cluster analysis, which due to a variety of data and methodological limitations, can realistically offer only a general impression of overlapping science, technology, and industry strengths in most regions (Feser and Luger 2002). Finally, it probably most closely matches current policy practice in most places, where clusters are being used to inform existing policies rather than as separately conceived development strategies implemented with substantial targeted investments.

11.4 SUMMARY AND GUIDES

The tendency of economic activity in general, and innovative and knowledge-intensive activity in particular, to concentrate functionally and geographically suggests to policy makers that an effective S&T strategy might be to target groups of related high technology sectors in specific regions for development attention. The goal is to replicate elements of successful innovation clusters from around the world. As a result of that interest, various typologies of clusters and associated guides for how to expand them have been developed. The implication is a model of policy design, implementation, and evaluation that involves identifying or "mapping" groups of sectors that qualify as clusters by some definition (whether Porterian, Italianate, and so on); assesses strengths, weaknesses, or impediments to growth in said clusters; prescribes and implements policies to rectify weaknesses, maximize strengths, and spur growth in the clusters; and evaluates policies for overall impact on subsequent cluster expansion and performance (Ketels 2004). The view has led naturally to the question: what policies are most effective for generating and sustaining innovation clusters as engines of regional growth?

This paper argues that policy makers in developing and transitioning economies would be better off viewing cluster concepts and cluster analysis as offering insights on how to improve the design and implementation of conventional innovation policies. This shifts the policy objective from building clusters per se to increasing rates of innovation by implementing development strategies in ways that leverage interfirm synergies and connections to nonmarket institutions, even when firms are not part of concentrated regional agglomerations. It also shifts the perspective of policy evaluation from cluster expansion as an outcome to innovation as an outcome. The following are a series of specific policy guides that follow from this view.

National, regional, and local development agencies in developing and transitioning economies should still include applied cluster analysis in their suite of analytical tools. To acknowledge the limited prospects of a government-led "cluster building" effort in developing economies is not an argument against the value of applied regional cluster analysis. Cluster analysis is the process of systematically analysing strengths, weaknesses, opportunities, and threats facing a set of interrelated existing or potential regional industries (Bergman and Feser 1999). It aims to document key linkages to non-market institutions such as universities and laboratories, identify areas of joint research and industrial strength where possible, evaluate competitive advantages on a global basis, and solicit corporate views of the need for various policy interventions. In highly developed economies, it relies heavily on extensive secondary data on industry linkages (for example, input–output), innovation (for example, OECD innovation surveys and matrices), employment, and output. In developing and transition economies where timely secondary data are much more limited, particularly at the subnational level, cluster analysis must utilize primary data collection techniques to a much greater extent. Recently, the collection of data via surveys and focus groups has become more common and a number of model survey instruments and focus group protocols are available. In general, cluster analysis has substantially improved the richness of applied economic studies at the regional scale.

Applied cluster analyses must be flexible in approach and avoid methods based on ideal types that reinforce a solely "cluster finding" mentality. The way that most agencies are using the results of cluster analyses indicates that the general capability of cluster analysis for exposing co-dependencies among businesses, local support agencies, universities and colleges, and so forth is more useful than its potential for selecting specific sets of specializations for development policy focus. Analyses are most flexible when they utilize a variety of cluster definitions, data sources, and analytical methods and result in indicators and data series that are updated and consulted regularly. Cluster analysis should be viewed not as a one-time exercise but as an ongoing tool for exploring a wide variety of economic questions that formerly were explored using a sector-based logic.

Cluster analyses should be part of broader strategic planning processes that incorporate substantial private sector involvement and public opinion. Another very common use of cluster analysis is as a means of motivating and facilitating public–private discussions about development challenges and goals, both for existing firms as well as potential growth industries. Cluster analysis methods should be designed to maximize corporate and public involvement in the generation and interpretation of results. The formation of corporate steering groups, the organization of public meetings to review and discuss findings, and the utilization of focus groups to collect qualitative information on strengths and weaknesses in the local business environment all help lay the groundwork for subsequent policy initiatives by including the views and motivating the support of the eventual stakeholders of those policies.

S&T policy should remain as sector-, technology-, and location-neutral as is reasonable, letting market imperatives and research competencies drive public resource flows. In both developing and transition economies, interest in clusters should not derail efforts to improve the necessary basic framework conditions for innovation and entrepreneurship. Those conditions are largely sector- and location-neutral and reward scientific and innovative activity on their merits rather than on the basis of their fit with pre-determined industrial specializations. Issues such as support for basic university research, technical training and education, intellectual property protections, and anti-trust law are more critical for long-run growth than near term clusters or clustering.

Any efforts to target specific technology sectors or S&T competencies for growth (cluster building) should be demand-driven and circumscribed in extent. Most research indicates that the public sector has played a very modest role in influencing the establishment of the leading innovation clusters around the world and only a slightly stronger one in their subsequent competitive success. In less developed economies where the incidence of market failure is greater, government might be expected to successfully exert greater influence on cluster formation and growth. However, cluster building can exact a significant opportunity cost in that it often diverts resources from other general policy initiatives such as the provision of infrastructure and improved basic education. The low risk, low cost approach to cluster building puts local businesses in the driver's seat by organizing a forum for firms to express joint concerns, engage in collective problem-solving on issues of common concern, and make collective requests for services or policy changes. Porter (2002, p. xvi) argues that major anchor companies in local clusters play a key role in organizing neighboring firms for joint action. Above all, development agencies should avoid pursuing unrealistic objectives, such as creating entirely new industrial or research strengths in the current fashionable industries (for example, biotechnology). In many developing economies, the clustering of innovation is likely to be tied to more traditional industries.

S&T investments should be measured for impact on overall innovation rates, not innovation in targeted clusters. Perhaps the largest pitfall in economic policy making related to clusters is confusion over means and ends. Clusters and clustering are a means to competitive success, not an end in themselves. Ultimately, attempts to build and support clusters or to leverage synergies among firms are only a route to boosting overall rates of innovation and growth. If a cluster strategy results in a rapid rate of expansion of a narrow segment of busineses and industries but overall net decline in innovation and growth at the macro level (either the nation or region, depending on the level of intervention), it must be regarded as a failure. It is still unclear whether cluster strategies will have an appreciable net positive impact on overall innovation and growth rates in developing countries. Indeed, we should not forget that the relationship between overall innovation rates and the prevalence of regional industry clusters is still unproven in highly developed countries.

Policy evaluations should be undertaken that compare the impact of cluster-informed interventions with the impact of conventionally designed policies. Important proof of the value of the cluster concept is in whether policies and programs designed to exploit cluster dynamics are actually more effective than those that essentially use a traditional, sector-based logic. Conventional policy prescriptions implemented based on a model of clustering must therefore be evaluated against non-cluster-based implementations of the same policy. For example, a number of states in the US have sought to make a very common development strategy – the attraction of inward investment through marketing and incentives – more effective by targeting potential supplier firms to existing local end-market producers. Suppliers and end-market producers are identified via analyses of business linkages, a kind of cluster analysis. What makes marketing and recruitment cluster-based strategies in this case are not the initiatives themselves, but rather the way in which those initiatives are implemented. It follows that we should evaluate whether the level of inward investment generated by cluster-targeted programs is higher than the level for broad-based or untargeted programs, a question that is rarely asked. The focus is typically on whether cluster-targeted recruitment programs have demonstrated success in filling out local supply chains, an outcome that could occur just as easily with an untargeted strategy as a targeted one. Without comparing different approaches to implementation, it is impossible to gauge if acknowledging this particular version of interdependence – the co-location of firms in value chains – really improved development policy efficacy.

REFERENCES

Acs, Zoltan J., David B. Audretsch and Maryann P. Feldman (1992), 'Real effects of academic research: Comment', *American Economic Review*, **82**, 363–367.

Acs, Zoltan J., David B. Audretsch and Maryann P. Feldman (1994), 'R&D spillovers and recipient firm size', *Review of Economics and Statistics*, **76**, 336–340.

Adams, James D. and Adam B. Jaffe (1996), 'Bounding the effects of R&D: An investigation using matched establishment-firm data', *RAND Journal of Economics*, **27**, 700–721.

Altenburg, Tilman and Jorg Meyer-Stamer (1999), 'How to promote clusters: Policy experiences from Latin America', *World Development*, **27**, 1693–1713.

Anselin, Luc, Attila Varga and Zoltan J. Acs (2000), 'Geographic spillovers and university research: a spatial econometric perspective', *Growth and Change*, **31**, 501–515.

Anselin, Luc, Attila Varga and Zoltan J. Acs (1997), 'Local geographic spillovers between university research and high technology innovations', *Journal of Urban Economics*, **42**, 422–448.

Asheim, Bjørn T. and A. Isaksen (1997), 'Location, agglomeration and innovation: towards regional innovation systems in Norway?', *European Planning Studies*, **5**, 299–330.

Baptista, Rui (2001), 'Geographical clusters and innovation diffusion', *Technological Forecasting and Social Change*, **66**, 31–46.

Baptista, Rui and Peter Swann (1998), 'Do firms in clusters innovate more?', *Research Policy*, **27**, 525–540.

Bellandi, Marco (1989), 'The industrial district in Marshall', in E. Goodman, J. Bamford and P. Saynor, *Small Firms and Industrial Districts in Italy*, London: Routledge, 136–152.

Benneworth, Paul, Mike Danson, Phil Raines and Geoff Whittam (2003), 'Confusing clusters? Making sense of the cluster approach in theory and practice', *European Planning Studies*, **11**, 511–520.

Bergman, Edward M. (2002), *Sustainability of clusters: toward dialogue*, Vienna, Austria, Vienna University of Economics and Business Administration, 20.

Bergman, Edward M. and Edward J. Feser (1999), *Industrial and Regional Clusters: Concepts and Comparative Applications*, Morganton, WV: Regional Research

Institute, West Virginia University.

Bergman, Edward M. and Edward J. Feser (2001), 'Innovation system effects on technological adoption in a regional value chain', *European Planning Studies*, **9**, 629–648.

Best, M.H. (1990), *The New Competition*, Cambridge, MA: Polity Press.

Boekholt, Patries and Shonie McKibbin (2003), *European Trend Chart on Innovation Thematic Report: Cluster Policies*, Brussels: European Commission Enterprise Directorate-General.

Boekholt, Patries and Ben Thuriaux (1997), 'Public policies to facilitate clusters: Background, rationale and policy practices in international perspective', in T.J.A. Roelandt and P. d. Hertog (eds), *Boosting Innovation: The Cluster Approach*, Paris: OECD.

Bortagaray, Isabel and Scott Tiffin (2000), *Innovation clusters in Latin America*, 4th International Conference on Technology Policy and Innovation, Curitiba, Brazil.

Breschi, Stefano (1999), 'Spatial patterns of innovation: Evidence from patent data', in A. Gambardella and F. Malerba (eds), *The Organization of Economic Innovation in Europe*, Cambridge, UK: Cambridge University Press, 71–102.

Brusco, Sebastiano (1982), 'The Emilian model: Productive decentralisation and social integration', *Cambridge Journal of Economics*, **6**, 167–184.

Capello, Roberta (1999), 'Spatial transfer of knowledge in high technology milieux: Learning versus collective learning processes', *Regional Studies*, **33**, 353–365.

Clancy, Paula, Eoin O'Malley, Larry O'Connell and Chris Van Egeraat (2001), 'Industry clusters in Ireland: an application of Porter's model of national competitive advantage to three sectors', *European Planning Studies*, **9**, 7–28.

Cooke, P. and K. Morgan (1998), *The Associational Economy: Firms, Regions and Innovation*, Oxford: Oxford University Press.

Cooke, Philip, Mikel Gomez Uranga and Goio Etxebarria (1997), 'Regional innovation systems: Institutional and organisational dimensions', *Research Policy*, **26**, 475–491.

Courlet, C. and B. Pecqueur (1991), 'Local industrial systems and externalities: an essay in typology', *Entrepreneurship and Regional Development*, **3**, 305–315.

DeBresson, Chris (1989), 'Breeding innovation clusters: a source of dynamic development', *World Development*, **17**: 1–16.

DeVol, Ross C. (2000), *Blueprint for a High-Tech Cluster: The Case of the Microsystems Industry in the Southwest*, Santa Monica, CA: Milken Institute.

Dumais, Guy, Glenn Ellison and Edward L Glaeser (1997), *Geographic concentration as a dynamic process*, Cambridge, MA: National Bureau of Economic Research.

Ellison, Glenn and Edward L Glaeser (1997), 'Geographic concentration in U.S. manufacturing industries: a dartboard approach', *Journal of Political Economy*, **105**, 889–927.

Enright, Michael J. (2000), 'The globalization of competition and the localization of competitive advantage: policies toward regional clustering', in N. Hood and S. Young (eds), *The Globalization of Multinational Enterprise Activity and Economic Development*, London: Macmillan, 303–331.

Enright, Michael J. (2001), *Regional clusters: what we know and what we should know*, Kiel Institute International Workshop on Innovation Clusters and Interregional Competition, Kiel, Germany.

Feldman, Maryann P. (1994), *The Geography of Innovation*, Dordrecht: Kluwer.

Feldman, Maryann P. (1999), 'The new economics of innovation, spillovers and agglomeration: A review of empirical studies', *Economics of Innovation and New Technology*, **8**, 5–25.

Feser, Edward J. (2005), 'Industry cluster concepts in innovation policy: a comparison of U.S. and Latin American experience', in G. Maier and S. Sedlacek, *Spillovers and Innovations: Space, Environment and the Economy*, Vienna: Springer.

Feser, Edward J. and Michael Luger (2002), 'Cluster analysis as a mode of inquiry: Its use in science and technology policymaking in North Carolina', *European Planning Studies*, **11**, 11–24.

Feser, Edward J. and Stuart H. Sweeney (2000), 'A test for the coincident economic and spatial clustering of business enterprises', *Journal of Geographical Systems*, **2**, 349–373.

Glaeser, Edward L., Hedi D. Kallal, José Scheinkman and Andrei Scleifer (1992), 'Growth in cities', *Journal of Political Economy*, **100**, 1126–1152.

Glaeser, Edward L., José A. Scheinkman and Andrei Shleifer (1995), 'Economic growth in a cross-section of cities', *Journal of Monetary Economics*, **36**, 117–143.

Goglio, Silvio (2002), 'Introduction: The industrial district as a proving ground', *European Planning Studies*, **10**, 421–424.

Griliches, Zvi (1992), 'The search for R&D spillovers', *Scandanavian Journal of Economics*, **94**, 29–47.

Harrison, B., M.R. Kelley and J. Gant (1996a), 'Innovative firm behavior and the local milieu: exploring the intersection of agglomeration, firm effects, and technological change', *Economic Geography* **72**, 233–258.

Harrison, B., M.R. Kelley and J. Gant (1996b), 'Specialization versus diversity in local economies: the implications for innovative private-sector behavior', *Cityscape*, **2**, 61–93.

Hertog, Pim den, Edward M. Bergman and David Charles (2001), 'Creating and sustaining innovative clusters: Towards a synthesis', in P. d. Hertog, E.M. Bergman and D. Charles (eds), *Innovative Clusters: Drivers of National Innovation Systems*, Paris: OECD, 405–419.

Humphrey, John and Hubert Schmitz (2000), *Governance and upgrading: Linking industrial cluster and global value chain research*, Sussex, UK, Institute of Development Studies, University of Sussex.

Jaffe, Adam B. (1986), 'Technological opportunity and spillovers of R&D: Evidence from firms' patents, profits, and market value', *American Economic Review*, **76**, 984–1001.

Jaffe, Adam B. (1989), 'Real effects of academic research', *American Economic Review*, **79**, 957–970.

Jaffe, Adam B., Manuel Trajtenberg and Rebecca Henderson (1993), 'Geographic localization of knowledge spillovers as evidenced by patent citations', *Quarterly Journal of Economics*, **108**, 577–598.

Justman, Moshe and Morris Teubal (1986), 'Innovation policy in an open economy: A normative framework for strategic and tactical issues', *Research Policy*, **15**, 121–138.

Kelley, M.R. and S. Helper (1999), 'Firm size and capabilities, regional agglomeration, and the adoption of new technology', *Economics of Innovation and New Technology*, **8**, 79–103.

Ketels, Christian (2004), 'European clusters', *Structural Change in Europe*, **3**, 1–5, Bollschweil, Germany: Habarth Publications.

Koo, Jun (2002), *Agglomeration and spillovers in a simultaneous framework*, Chapel Hill, Department of City and Regional Planning, University of North Carolina at Chapel Hill: **24**.

Lagendijk, Arnoud (2000), 'Learning in non-core regions: Towards "intelligent clusters" Addressing business and regional needs', in F. Boekema, K. Morgan, S. Bakkers and R. Rutten (eds), *Knowledge, Innovation and Economic Growth: The Theory and Practice of Learning Regions*, Cheltenham, UK: Edward Elgar, 165–191.

Lall, Somik V., Zmarak Shalizi and Uwe Deichmann (2001), *Agglomeration economies and productivity in Indian industry*, Washington, DC, World Bank: 27.

Malecki, Edward J. (1997), *Technology and Economic Development*, Harlow, Essex: Longman.

Mani, Sunil and Henny Romijn (2003), *Innovation, Learning and Technological Dynamism of Developing Countries*, New York: United Nations University Press.

Markusen, Ann (1993), *Can technology policy serve as industrial policy?*, Conference on Strengthening U.S. Industrial Competitiveness in the 1990s, South Bend, Indiana.

Markusen, Ann (1996), 'Sticky places in slippery space: A typology of industrial districts', *Economic Geography*, **72**, 293–313.

McCormick, Dorothy (1999), 'African enterprise clusters and industrialization: theory and reality', *World Development*, **27**, 1531–1551.

Melo, Alberto (2001a), *Industrial policy in Latin America and the Caribbean at the turn of the century*, Washington, DC, Research Department, Inter-American Development Bank: 59.

Melo, Alberto (2001b), *The innovation systems of Latin America and the Caribbean*, Washington, DC, Research Department, Inter-American Development Bank: 75.

Moore, Gordon and Kevin Davis (2001), *Learning the Silicon Valley way*, Stanford, CA, Stanford Institute for Economic Policy Research, Stanford University: 31.

Morgan, Kevin (2004), 'Sustainable regions: governance, innovation and scale', *European Planning Studies*, **12**, 871–889.

Moulaert, Frank and Farid Sekia (1999), *Innovative region, social region? An alternative view of regional innovation*, European Meeting on Applied Evolutionary Economics. Grenoble, France.

Nauwelaers, Claire (2001), 'Path-dependency and the role of institutions in cluster policy formation', in Å. Mariussen (ed.), *Cluster Policies-Cluster Development?*, Stockholm: Nordregio, 93–107.

Piore, Michael J. and Charles F. Sabel (1984), *The Second Industrial Divide*, New

York: Basic Books.

Porter, Michael E. (1990), *The Competitive Advantage of Nations*, New York: Free Press.

Porter, Michael E. (1998) 'Clusters and the new economics of competition', *Harvard Business Review*, **77–90**.

Porter, Michael E. (2000), 'Location, competition, and economic development: Local clusters in a global economy', *Economic Development Quarterly*, **14**, 15–34.

Porter, Michael E. (2002), *Clusters of Innovation: Regional Foundations of U.S. Competitiveness*, Washington, DC: Council on Competitiveness.

Pouder, Richard and Caron H. St. John (1996), 'Hot spots and blind spots: geographical clusters of firms and innovation', *Academy of Management Review*, **21**, 1192–1225.

Quandt, Carlos (1997), 'The emerging high-technology cluster of Campinas, Brazil', *Technopolis*, **97**, Ottawa, Canada.

Quandt, Carlos (1999), *The concept of virtual technopoles and the feasibility of incubating technology-intensive clusters in Latin America and the Caribbean*, Ottawa, Canada: International Development Research Centre.

Raines, Philip (2001), *Local or national competitive advantage? The tensions in cluster development policy*, Glasgow, UK, European Policies Research Center, University of Strathclyde: 31.

Rosenfeld, Stuart A. (1997), 'Bringing business clusters into the mainstream of economic development', *European Planning Studies*, **5**, 3–23.

Rosenfeld, Stuart A. (2001), *Backing into clusters: Retrofitting public policies*, Symposium on Strategic Responses to Integration Pressures: Lessons from Around the World. JFK School of Government, Harvard University.

Rosenfeld, Stuart A. (2002), *A Governor's Guide to Cluster-Based Economic Development*, Washington, DC: National Governors Association.

Russo, Fabio, Michele Clara and Mukesh Gulati (2000), *Cluster development and promotion of business development services (BDS): UNIDO's experience in India.* Vienna, PSD Technical Working Papers Series, United Nations Industrial Development Organization: 33.

Schmitz, Hubert (2000), *Local upgrading in global chains*, Rio de Janeiro, Instituto de Economia da Universidade Federal do Rio de Janeiro–IE/UFRJ: 16.

Schmitz, Hubert and Bernard Musyck (1994), 'Industrial districts in Europe: policy lessons for developing countries?', *World Development*, **22**, 889–910.

Shapira, Philip (2001), 'US manufacturing extension partnerships: technology policy reinvented?', *Research Policy*, **30**, 977–992.

Shapira, Philip, Hans Klein and Stefan Kuhlmann (2001), 'Editorial: Innovations in European and US innovation policy', *Research Policy*, **30**, 869–872.

Simons, Gene R. (1993), 'Industrial extension and innovation', in L. M. Branscomb (ed.), *Empowering Technology: Implementing a U.S. Strategy*, Cambridge: MIT Press, 167–201.

Swann, G.M. Peter (1999), 'Innovation and the size of industrial clusters in Europe', in A. Gambardella and F. Malerba (eds), *The Organization of Economic Innovation in Europe*, Cambridge, UK: Cambridge University Press, 103–124.

Swann, G.M. Peter, Martha Prevezer and David Stout (eds) (1998), *The Dynamics of Industrial Clustering*, Oxford, UK: Oxford University Press.

Sweeney, Stuart H. and Edward J. Feser (1998), 'Plant size and clustering of manufacturing activity', *Geographical Analysis*, **30**, 45–64.

Sweeney, Stuart and Nick Nagle (2004), *Space-time analysis of industry clustering*, Working paper, Department of Geography, University of California at Santa Barbara.

Tendler, Judith and Mônica Alves Amorim (1996), 'Small firms and their helpers: Lessons on demand', *World Development*, **24**, 407–426.

Voyer, Roger (1997a), *Emerging high-technology industrial clusters in Brazil, India, Malaysia and South Africa*, Ottawa, Canada, International Development Research Centre: 24.

Voyer, Roger (1997b), *Knowledge-based industrial clustering: International comparisons*, Montreal, Canada, Nordicity Group Ltd.: 31.

Wallsten, Scott (2001), 'An empirical test of geographic knowledge spillovers using geographic information systems and firm-level data', *Regional Science and Urban Economics*, **31**, 571–599.

12. Geographic concentration of sectors in the German economy: some unpleasant macroeconomic evidence for regional cluster policy

Björn Alecke*, **Christoph Alsleben**‡, **Frank Scharr**§, **Gerhard Untiedt**¶

12.1 INTRODUCTION

With the emergence of the New Economic Geography pioneered by Paul Krugman (1991a,b) the issue of spatial concentration of industries has found renewed interest among economists. The theoretical work of this approach has added to the longstanding insights of trade models of natural advantage and models of technological external economies of scale (Fuijita and Thisse, 2002) to significantly deepen our understanding of how pecuniary externalities may induce firms belonging to the same industry or industry group to cluster together. Nevertheless, most authors of this line of research acknowledge that there is still a lack of empirical evidence regarding the actual significance and determinants of geographical concentration of industries, as well as its relevance for economic policy.

Notwithstanding the paucity of empirical evidence, actors inspired by the less formal work of Michael Porter (1990) have been calling for Germany to abandon the traditional regional policy of granting investment subsidies to the least developed regions in favour of concentrating aid to specific industries in specific regions. Indeed, such policy proposals demanding a more active stance in regional policy and suggesting fostering firms only in alleged clusters have found ever more supporters. Ironically, however, the actual practical implementation of a cluster-oriented regional policy has

*GEFRA Gesellschaft für Finanz- und Regionalanalysen, Ludgeristr. 56, 48143 Münster, Germany

‡Graduiertenkolleg "Allokationstheorie, Wirtschaftspolitik und kollektive Entscheidungen", University of Dortmund, Germany

§Hegelstr. 36, 39104 Magdeburg, Germany

¶GEFRA Gesellschaft für Finanz- und Regionalanalysen, Ludgeristr. 56, 48143 Münster, Germany failed so far because there is no consensus amongst politicians about which regions and which industries in Germany could be deemed clusters.

This lack of consensus could be seen as a direct consequence of the lack of empirical efforts to test in a rigorous and systematic manner for the existence of clusters. Although the empirical delineation of clusters is seriously hampered by the vague and indeterminate definition of the cluster-concept per se,[1] in our view the geographic concentration of a sector or group of sectors should be one among other constitutive elements of any cluster definition. Thus, it seems obvious that sound empirical evidence of how much sectors are actually concentrated and whether there are differences across sectors or groups of sectors would be of great interest in the current cluster debate.[2] However, to the best or our knowledge there are only two existent studies assessing the degree of localization across German industries: Lau (1996) and Keilbach (2002). Both authors present mixed results with some sectors displaying a significant degree of geographic concentration and others showing no geographic concentration at all.

The empirical findings of Lau and Keilbach are of limited use for guiding current regional "cluster" policy. One set of problems concerns their dataset. Both authors use twenty year old manufacturing employment data, which lacks a detailed level of sectoral and regional disaggregation and which is organized according to an outdated industrial classification scheme. The second issue – and for the purposes of this paper more important – is the fact that both authors apply the spatial Gini coefficient for measuring geographic concentration. As stressed in a seminal paper by Ellison and Glaeser (1997), the Gini coefficient has the severe disadvantage of not being able to discriminate between concentration due to internal economies of scale, that is, geographical concentration registered simply because employment is concentrated within one firm, and those due to external economies of scale, that is, geographical concentration registered because the locational decisions of different firms are correlated. It is only this latter cause of geographical concentration on which both the new economic geography and the cluster approach of Porter focus. In order to disentangle internal and external economies of scale as a source of geographic concentration, Ellison and Glaser proposed a new concentration measure which is explicitly based on a location decision model. Their so-called EG index could best be grasped as a measure of geographical concentration purged of that part which is due to internal economies of scale. High values of the EG index point to a significant degree of geographic concentration which is caused by an actual correlation in the location decisions of different plants.

[1]This line of criticism is most forcefully put forward in a recent paper by Martin and Sunley (2003) who argue that the whole cluster-concept is thinly theorized and plagued by the lack of any agreed method for empirically identifying and mapping clusters. In their view cluster advocates could always counter any disappointing empirical findings by insisting that the sectoral and geographical boundaries of clusters have been incorrectly and inappropriately specified and measured.

[2]Of course, even if one finds substantial geographic concentration this result alone does not provide insight into the nature and strength of its causes such as knowledge spillovers, local inter-firm linkages, pooled local labour markets or social networks which are commonly seen as the distinctive features of clusters. But, as admitted by Martin and Sunley, the results of a top-down approach could be interpreted as some kind of a necessary condition. If one finds a significant degree of geographic concentration for sectors this evidence at least suggests the existence and location of possible clusters. Further work has then to be done based on more detailed bottom-up methods to supplement this finding and to verify the existence of a cluster in a particular region. This second step could then be interpreted as examining a sufficient condition.

The aim of this paper is to analyse the degree of geographic concentration in the German economy using the EG index. Our work differs from the previous research undertaken by Lau (1996) and Keilbach (2002) both because we use the EG instead of the Gini index to measure geographic concentration, but also because we utilize more recent, more detailed and more comprehensive data. We thereby contribute to a growing empirical literature that has applied the EG index already to other countries such as the US (Ellison and Glaeser, 1997), the UK (Devereux et al., 1999), France (Maurel and Sédillot, 1999), Italy (Lafourcade and Mion, 2004) or Belgium, Portugal, and Ireland (Barrios et al., 2003). What distinguishes this paper from that work (including our own (Alecke el al., 2006)) is that our present study is not confined only to manufacturing industries but - to our knowledge for the first time - encompasses agricultural and service sectors as well. Thus, we are able to give a very complete picture of the degree of geographic concentration of economic sectors in Germany.

The remainder of the paper is structured as follows. Section 12.2 introduces the EG index as a measure for geographic concentration, and discusses its advantages against more traditional measures such as the widely used Gini index. Furthermore, a short description of the database is given. In section 12.3 we present our results. Considering employment at the plant-level we first describe the concentration pattern of 3-digit NACE groups using the EG index. Then we turn to the question of whether the degree of geographic concentration changes when measured at a more aggregated sectoral level, that is, at the 2-digit level of NACE divisions. Since the concept of the EG index can be extended to measure the co-agglomeration of sectors we also investigate if concentration of 2-digit divisions is due merely to the concentration of its 3-digit (sub)groups ("within"-concentration) or if there is a common effect on all the 3-digit groups within a certain 2-digit division ("between"-concentration). Finally, we examine whether plants in technology related industries and knowledge intensive service sectors tend to co-locate close to one another. The last section concludes and gives some policy recommendations.

12.2 MEASURING GEOGRAPHIC CONCENTRATION BY THE ELLISON-GLAESER INDEX

A widely used measure of geographic concentration (Brülhart and Torstensson (1996), Audretsch and Feldman (1996), Amiti (1999)) is the spatial variant of the Gini coefficient proposed by Krugman (1991a).[3] However, it has the severe disadvantage that it measures concentration of economic activity deriving from both internal economies of scale, that is, the "concentration" within a firm, and from natural advantages or external economies of scale, that is, concentration resulting from the colocation of firms (or plants). In order to distinguish between these two causes of concentration, we instead use a measure of agglomeration recently proposed by Ellison and Glaeser (1997, in the following EG).

This so-called EG index of agglomeration is derived from an explicit location decision model. The point of departure is the "raw concentration" of an industry defined

[3]For a survey see, for example, Devereux et al. (1999).

as $G := \sum_i s_i - x_i$ where s_i is the portion of the industry's employment located in region i and x_i is the percentage of total employment in that region. G measures concentration relative to total employment; as long as an industry mimics the pattern of aggregate employment it is not considered as being concentrated. Ellison and Glaeser assume that firms choose their locations to maximize profit and that there exists an allocation process which yields the observed distribution of total employment in expectation. They then go on to show that – given their model of firms' location decision – $E(G) = (1 - \sum_i x_1^2)(\gamma + (1-\gamma)H)$ where H is the plant Herfindahl index defined as the sum of squared plant employment shares of the respective industry and γ is a combined measure of the strength of natural advantages and externalities between plants in a broad sense. However, in an empirical application values for γ are not directly observable. Thus, as long as values for s_i, x_i und H are available, γ becomes the measure of interest and could be computed by rearranging the above expression for $E(G)$:

$$\gamma = \frac{G - (1 - \sum_i x_i^2)H}{(1 - \sum_i X_i^2)(1 - H)} \tag{12.1}$$

The most important advantage of the EG index of agglomeration is that it measures geographic concentration "purged" from the influences of industrial concentration due to internal economies of scale. That is, an industry which is highly localized due to the presence of a single large plant in a particular region, will show a lower value for γ than an industry with the same size but which is geographically concentrated due to a number of smaller, unrelated plants in a region. A Gini index, for instance, is not able to distinguish between these two cases.

A second advantage of the EG index of agglomeration that it is based on a probabilistic model of plants location choices which allows one to test an observation against the unique null hypothesis that there is no agglomeration, that is, plants choose their location in a pure random manner as if darts were thrown at a dartboard independently from each other. In that case one would have $\gamma = 0$ and consequently $E(G) = (1 - \sum_i x_i^2)H$. As the variance of γ could be computed under the null, this allows one to make inferences about the significance of estimates.

Another advantage of the EG index is that it allows meaningful comparisons across industries in which the size distribution of plants differ. It is also comparable regardless of differences in the level of geographic aggregation at which employment data for the respective industries are available.

Unfortunately, the EG agglomeration index cannot provide hints as to the various causes for geographic concentration. Ellison and Glaeser establish as a result of their location model that the effects of natural advantages and spillovers are observationally equivalent and, thus, γ could only be estimated as a linear combination of two parameters corresponding to different sources, that is, natural advantages and spillovers, of concentration levels. Of course, this shortcoming is in no way specific to the EG agglomeration index but is true for all other indices of geographic concentration as well.

The empirical analysis presented below uses plant level data, which provides the 1998 distribution of employment at the plant level across 213 3-digit NACE groups. In order to account for the fact that administrative boundaries are not necessarily economically relevant, we calculate geographic concentration at the regional level of the 97 planning regions (PR, Raumordnungsregionen). These regions represent functional, economically self-contained units of space with regard to commuting and trade patterns. Two things are important to note here. First, our data cover all existing plants with at least one employee. Second, the employment data are not classified and contain precise figures for each plant regardless of its size. Therefore, no further alteration of the data is necessary and we compute the Herfindahl indices directly from it.

12.3 GEOGRAPHIC CONCENTRATION OF ECONOMIC SECTORS IN GERMANY

12.3.1 To what extent are 3-digit NACE groups agglomerated?

Despite the common belief that the geographic concentration of economic activities is widespread, in reality not much is known about the degree of agglomeration of German sectors. In fact, as stressed by EG, by computing their proposed index we are able to present for the first time a formal test that the extent of localization in Germany is greater than what would be expected to arise randomly. If plants' location decisions are independent we would expect that the index of raw concentration G should equal $(1 - \sum_i x_i^2)H =: G_0$. As a first step, we thus test whether $E(G)$ is significantly different from G_0. The mean values of G and G_0 across all 3-digit economic sectors (so-called groups) are 0.050 and 0.026, respectively, with their difference being highly significant.[4] More precisely, 175 out of the 213 groups are significantly more (or less) geographically concentrated than what one would expect if there is no correlation between plants' location decisions.[5] Accordingly, for 38 sectors the hypothesis of a pure random location decision cannot be rejected.

Figure 12.1 shows the distribution of gamma at the 3-digit-sector level. In the figure, each bar gives the number of groups for which gamma lies in an interval of width 0.05. A first observation is that the degree of localization varies greatly from sector to sector. The minimum value of gamma is -0.222, the maximum is 0.568. A second result is that the distribution of gamma is quite skewed, with a mean of 0,025 and a median of 0,008. Most strikingly, however, is the large number of sectors (102 groups) lying in the interval between 0.00 and 0.01. Thus, nearly half of the sectors have a gamma value which points only to a slight positive agglomeration. In total, most groups (74 per cent) have a gamma lower than 0.02 which – as argued in Ellison and Glaeser – should be regarded as a low degree of geographic concentration.[6] We find that only 14 per cent of all sectors have a gamma greater than 0.05 (all of which are highly significant), which, according to EG, is the upper benchmark value for high geographic concentration.

---

[4]The difference is more than three times larger than the average standard deviation of G.

[5]For these industries the difference between G and G_0 is larger than 1.96 times its standard deviation. From the 175 sectors with a significant difference only 2 display a negative difference. Since a positive or negative difference between G and G_0 means simultaneously a positive or negative value of γ, these results mean that only in two economic sectors dispersion forces dominate clustering forces.

[6]See Ellison and Glaeser (1997), p. 903.

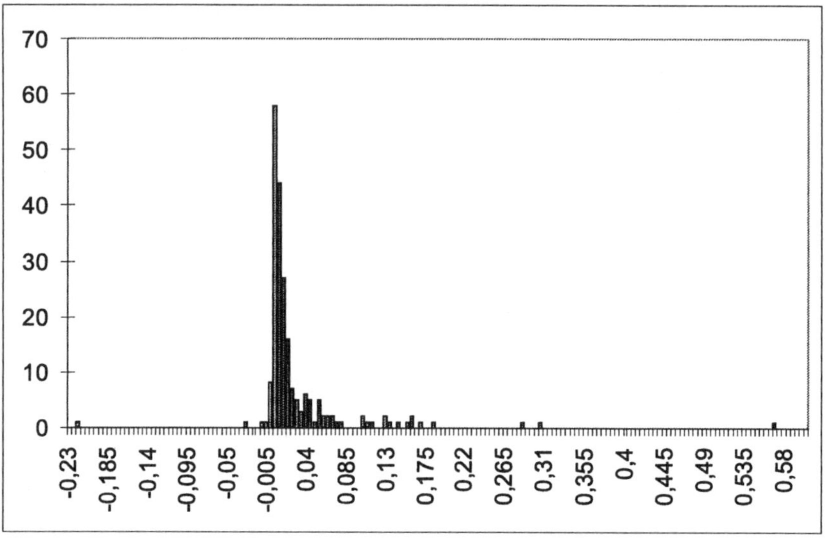

Figure 12.1: Histogram of gamma

Taken together, our results show that in about 80 per cent of all German economic sectors plants' location decisions could be regarded as significantly positively correlated. For only two sectors do we find a significant negative correlation, indicating that these plants are widely scattered. However, in most cases with a positive value of gamma the resulting geographic concentration could be regarded as very weak. The localization of economic activity which has received so much attention in the recent literature on clusters seems only to be of empirical relevance for a minority of sectors in Germany. Obviously, for economic policy makers this raises the question, which sectors are geographically concentrated and which are not?

12.3.2 Patterns of concentration across sectors (3-digit NACE groups)

Table 12.1 evidences patterns of concentration by showing the 30 most concentrated economic sectors as measured by gamma. While a full explanation of varying concentration levels across industries is beyond the scope of this paper, the presumable causes of certain patterns are apparent. For instance, it is not surprising that resource extractive sectors dominate the top group. Nine out of the first seventeen sectors with the highest values of gamma belong to the NACE section C "Mining and Quarrying". A strong dependence on natural resources is also presumably the reason for the high gamma values of sectors like Manufacture of coke oven products (23.1), Processing and preserving of fish and fish products (15.2), Sea and coastal water transport (61.1), Manufacture of ceramic tiles and flags (26.3), Manufacture of refined petroleum products (23.2) and Fishing, fish farming and related service activities (05.0).

Rank Gamma	NACE	Group	Gamma
1	23.1	Manufacture of coke oven products	0.5685
2	11.2	Service activities incidental to oil and gas extraction, excluding surveying	0.3030
3	33.5	Manufacture of watches and clocks	0.2825
4	10.1	Mining and agglomeration of hard coal	0.1839
5	36.2	Manufacture of jewelery and related articles	0.1683
6	15.2	Processing and preserving of fish and fish products	0.1587
7	67.1	Activities auxiliary to financial intermediation, except insurance and pension funding	0.1581
8	61.1	Sea and coastal water transport	0.1501
9	11.1	Extraction of crude petroleum and natural gas	0.1440
10	13.1	Mining of iron ores	0.1345
11	14.3	Mining of chemical and fertilizer minerals	0.1288
12	10.2	Mining and agglomeration of lignite	0.1282
13	14.4	Production of salt	0.1107
14	63.2	Other supporting transport activities	0.1073
15	17.6	Manufacture of knitted and crocheted fabrics	0.1032
16	10.3	Extraction and agglomeration of peat	0.1020
17	13.2	Mining of non-ferrous metal ores, except uranium and thorium ores	0.0768
18	92.1	Motion picture and video activities	0.0702
19	26.3	Manufacture of ceramic tiles and flags	0.0690
20	23.2	Manufacture of refined petroleum products	0.0675
21	17.2	Textile weaving	0.0631
22	28.6	Manufacture of cutlery, tools and general hardware	0.0625
23	29.6	Manufacture of weapons and ammunition	0.0593
24	19.3	Manufacture of footwear	0.0587
25	62.2	Non-scheduled air transport	0.0539
26	28.4	Forging, pressing, stamping and roll forming of metal; powder metallurgy	0.0530
27	26.2	Manufacture of non-refractory ceramic goods other than for construction purposes; manufacture of refractory ceramic products	0.0529
28	65.2	Other financial intermediation	0.0515
29	20.2	Manufacture of veneer sheets; manufacture of plywood, laminboard, particle board, fibre board and other panels and boards	0.0502
30	05.0	Fishing, fish farming and related service activities	0.0455

Table 12.1: The 30 most concentrated 3-digit NACE groups

Meanwhile, a more striking result is that high and medium technology industries are not among the most concentrated sectors.[7] These industries lie in the middle of the field or even at the lower end of the ranking as Table 12.5 in the appendix demonstrates. The only exception is the group Manufacture of weapons and ammunition (29.6), which according to the common classification developed by Grupp et al. (2000) belongs to the high technology sector. Rather than hi-tech producers, the most concentrated manufacturing industries appear to be more mature or traditional industries such as Manufacture of watches and clocks (33.5), Manufacture of jewellery and related articles (36.2), Manufacture of knitted and crocheted fabrics (17.6), Textile weaving (17.2), Manufacture of cutlery, tools and general hardware (28.6), Manufacture of footwear (19.3), Forging, pressing, stamping and roll forming of metal; powder metallurgy (28.4), Manufacture of non-refractory ceramic goods other than for construction purposes; manufacture of refractory ceramic products (26.2), and Manufacture of veneer sheets; manufacture of plywood, laminboard, particle board, fibre board and other panels and boards (20.2). As stressed by Barrios et al. (2003) this finding may point to history as a major explanation for today's location patterns of economic activity for traditional sectors. In general, our results for the manufacturing industry are much in line with those found in the literature already cited.

Table 12.2 displays the 30 least concentrated sectors in terms of gamma. Similar to the case for the most agglomerated sectors, an intuitively plausible explanation also exists for the great majority of the most dispersed sectors. For instance, 9 sectors belong to the NACE section G "Wholesale and retail trade; repair of motor vehicles, motorcycles and personal and household goods trade; Maintenance and repair of motor vehicles and consumer durables". For these service sectors the need to be close to final demand should naturally be of overriding importance. The same reasoning should be valid for other service sectors such as Restaurants (55.3), Telecommunications (64.2), Post and courier activities (64.1), Higher education (80.3), Human health activities (85.1), Social work activities (85.3), Sewage and refuse disposal, sanitation and similar activities (90.0), Activities of other membership organizations (91.3), Other service activities (93.0), parts of the section F "Construction" (Building installation (45.3) and Building completion (45.4)) and parts of the section E "Electricity, gas and water supply" (Production and distribution of electricity (40.1) and Manufacture of gas; distribution of gaseous fuels through mains (40.2)).

Contrary to what one would expect, a number of manufacturing industries are among the most dispersed industries, such as Manufacture of bodies (coachwork) for motor vehicles; manufacture of trailers and semi-trailers (34.2), Manufacture of wooden containers (20.4), Manufacture of television and radio transmitters and apparatus for line telephony and line telegraphy (32.2), and Manufacture of pesticides and other agro-chemical products (24.2). Interestingly, the latter two industries are typically characterized as high-tech industries (see Grupp et al. (2000)).

[7] We use a common classification developed by Grupp et al. (2000).

Rank Gamma	NACE	Group	Gamma
184	45.3	Building installation	0.0017
185	45.4	Building completion	0.0016
186	51.5	Wholesale of non-agricultural intermediate products, waste and scrap	0.0015
187	34.2	Manufacture of bodies (coachwork) for motor vehicles; manufacture of trailers and semi-trailers	0.0015
188	91.3	Activities of other membership organizations	0.0014
189	50.5	Retail sale of automotive fuel	0.0012
190	55.3	Restaurants	0.0011
191	60.2	Other land transport	0.0011
192	50.4	Sale, maintenance and repair of motorcycles and related parts and accessories	0.0011
193	50.3	Sale of motor vehicle parts and accessories	0.0011
194	52.7	Repair of personal and household goods	0.0010
195	93.0	Other service activities	0.0007
196	15.8	Manufacture of other food products	0.0006
197	85.3	Social work activities	0.0005
198	52.4	Other retail sale of new goods in specialized stores	0.0002
199	85.1	Human health activities	0.0001
200	52.3	Retail sale of pharmaceutical and medical goods, cosmetic and toilet articles	0.0001
201	52.1	Retail sale in non-specialized stores	0.0001
202	90.0	Sewage and refuse disposal, sanitation and similar activities	-0.0003
203	64.2	Telecommunications	-0.0005
204	52.6	Retail sale not in stores	-0.0009
205	20.4	Manufacture of wooden containers	-0.0011
206	64.1	Post and courier activities	-0.0015
207	40.1	Production and distribution of electricity	-0.0016
208	32.2	Manufacture of television and radio transmitters and apparatus for line telephony and line telegraphy	-0.0019
209	40.2	Manufacture of gas; distribution of gaseous fuels through mains	-0.0028
210	80.3	Higher education	-0.0053
211	72.4	Database activities	-0.0124
212	24.2	Manufacture of pesticides and other agro-chemical products	-0.0329
213	62.3	Space transport	-0.2217

Table 12.2: The 30 least concentrated 3-digit NACE groups

12.3.3 The agglomeration of 2-digit NACE divisions and co-agglomeration

As we find a significant but only moderate degree of concentration for most of the sectors on the level of the 3-digit NACE groups an interesting question is whether we can detect a higher concentration of economic activity at a more aggregated sectoral level, that is, at the 2-digit level of NACE divisions. When dealing with empirical classification systems for economic activities such as ISIC, SIC or NACE it is often unclear which level of aggregation best encapsulates "related fields of economic activities". In fact, it might be possible that the 3-digit level of NACE defines sectors too narrowly in order to capture the full benefits accruing to plants when locating near other plants of the same sector and, thus, might fail to delineate "localization" effects between these plants. In order to explore this issue further we calculate the degree of concentration at the 2-digit level for 57 NACE divisions.

As a further extension we also make use of the fact that, as shown by Ellison-Glaeser, it is always possible to express the value of gamma for any combination of sectors as the weighted average of the gammas of the individual sectors and some combination-specific component which they called "co-agglomeration". For measuring the degree to which a combination of sectors is co-agglomerated, EG propose an index γ^c defined by:

$$\gamma^c = \frac{[G/(1-\sum_{i=1}^{n} x_i^2)] - H - \sum_{j=1}^{r} \gamma_j w_j^2 (1-H_j)}{1 - \sum j = 1^r w_j^2} \tag{12.2}$$

with $G = \sum_{i=1}^{m} (s_i^{\text{comb}} - x_i)^2$, s_i^{comb} $(i = 1, \ldots, M)$ = share of the combination of sectors' employment located in region i, x_i $(i = 1, \ldots, M)$ = share of total employment in region i, r = number of sectors in the combination of sectors, $H_j (r = 1, \ldots, K)$ = sector j's plant Herfindahl index, $H = \sum_{j=1}^{r} w_j^2 H_j$ = the plant Herfindahl index of the combination of sectors, w_j = employment share of the j-th sector in the combination of sectors employment, γ_j = calculated value of the agglomeration index γ for the j-th sector.

It reflects how much the location decisions of firms that belong to an arbitrary combination of sectors are correlated; $\gamma^c = 0$ would indicate that there is no correlation across sectors and hence no more agglomeration in the combination of sectors than that simply resulting from the concentration of the sectors itself. From equation (12.1) and (12.2) it follows that

$$\gamma = \frac{\sum_{j=1}^{r} \gamma_j w_j^2 (1-H_j)}{1 - \sum_{j=1}^{r} w_j^2 H_j} + \frac{\gamma^c (1 - \sum_{j=1}^{r} w_j^2)(}{1 - \sum_{j=1}^{r} w_j^2 H_j} \tag{12.3}$$

Equation (12.3) allows us a meaningful decomposition of the agglomeration index of the combination of sectors. The first term on the RHS of the equation gives a weighted average of the agglomeration indices for each of the r sectors and may be interpreted as a measure of importance of the intra-industry concentration component. The second term on the RHS is a weighted expression of the co-agglomeration index for the combination of sectors and measures the degree of geographic concentration due to the inter-industry component. Thus, by computing γ^c for every combination of sectors according to the aggregation rules from the 3-digit NACE groups to the 2-digit NACE division we are able to determine whether the concentration of divisions is due merely to the concentration of its (sub)groups – which would imply that localization advantages are group-specific ("within"-concentration) – or if there is a common effect on all the groups within a certain division ("between"-concentration).

Table 12.3 lists the values of γ (column 1) and γ^c (column 5) for all 56 NACE 2-digit divisions sorted by the order of magnitude of γ. Column 2 of the table displays the number of 3-digit groups within each 2-digit division, and columns three through five list the fraction of groups within a division that fall in the not very concentrated (<0.02), intermediate, and very concentrated (>0.05) ranges respectively. Column six shows the fraction of inter-industry-concentration according to equation (12.3).

Turning first to the "simple" gamma of the 2-digit divisions, the order of magnitude is lower than in the 3-digit case. The mean value of gamma is now 0.015 compared to 0.025, the median 0.007 compared to 0.008. Also, the distribution of gamma at the higher level of aggregation has shifted to the left. Now 84 per cent of the gammas are below 0.02, and only 7 per cent are above 0.05. Thus, we conclude that geographic concentration at the two-digit industry level is weaker than at the three-digit level.

However, with regard to the concentration pattern our previous results remain nearly unchanged. The ten most concentrated sectors are those in which the access to natural resources or infrastructural conditions is necessary (that is, the divisions of the section A "Mining and quarrying" (10, 11, 13), Water transport (61), Manufacture of coke, refined petroleum products and nuclear fuel (23), Fishing, fish farming and related service activities (5), Air transport (62)) or which could be regarded as traditional industries (Manufacture of tobacco products (16), Tanning and dressing of leather; manufacture of luggage, handbags, saddlery, harness and footwear (19) or Manufacture of textiles (17)). The 10 least concentrated sectors are with one exception (Manufacture of food products and beverages (15)) consumer oriented service sectors (Hotels and restaurants (55), Sale, maintenance and repair of motor vehicles and motorcycles; retail sale of automotive fuel (50), and Retail trade, except of motor vehicles and motorcycles; repair of personal and household goods (52)) or other service sectors making available basic supply (Activities of membership organizations n.e.c. (91), Other service activities (93), Health and social work (85), Sewage and refuse disposal, sanitation and similar activities (90), Post and telecommunications (64), and Electricity, gas, steam and hot water supply (40)).

Once again, technologically oriented industries are not among the most concentrated sectors but lie instead in the middle of the field or even at the bottom of the ranking (Manufacture of office machinery and computers (30), Manufacture of motor vehicles, trailers and semi-trailers (34), Manufacture of other transport equipment (35), Manufacture of chemicals and chemical products (24), Manufacture of machinery and equipment n.e.c. (29), Manufacture of medical, precision and optical instruments, watches and clocks (33), Manufacture of electrical machinery and apparatus n.e.c. (31), Manufacture of radio, television and communication equipment and apparatus (32)). The same is true for knowledge intensive service sectors although these appear to be slightly more concentrated than high- or medium-tech industries (Insurance and pension funding, except compulsory social security (66), Computer and related

Rank	gamma	NACE	Division	# three digit	<0.02	[0.02, 0.05]	>0.05	Sum of $w_j\gamma(j)$	Coaggl gamma	Rank	Between Industry	Rank
1	0.1301	11	Extraction of crude petroleum and natural gas; service activities incidental to oil and gas extraction, excluding surveying	2	0.0%	0.0%	100.0%	0.2021	0.0940	1	34.8%	32
2	0.0897	10	Mining of coal and lignite; extraction of peat	3	0.0%	0.0%	100.0%	0.1671	-0.0115	48	-5.6%	46
3	0.0791	61	Water transport	2	0.0%	50.0%	50.0%	0.1136	0.0158	6	8.7%	41
4	0.0643	23	Manufacture of coke, refined petroleum products and nuclear fuel	3	33.3%	0.0%	66.7%	0.0945	0.0680	3	18.0%	39
5	0.0478	62	Air transport	3	33.3%	33.3%	33.3%	0.0127	0.0866	2	45.7%	26
6	0.0443	5	Fishing, fish farming and related service activities	1	0.0%	100.0%	0.0%					
7	0.0435	13	Mining of metal ores	2	0.0%	0.0%	100.0%	0.0824	-0.0085	47	-4.1%	45
8	0.0286	16	Manufacture of tobacco products	1	0.0%	100.0%	0.0%					
9	0.0249	19	Tanning and dressing of leather; manufacture of luggage, handbags, saddlery, harness and footwear	3	0.0%	66.7%	33.3%	0.0493	0.0019	36	4.3%	43
10	0.0248	17	Manufacture of textiles	7	28.6%	42.9%	28.6%	0.0431	0.0215	5	72.5%	2
11	0.0180	66	Insurance and pension funding, except compulsory social security	1	100.0%	0.0%	0.0%					
12	0.0177	30	Manufacture of office machinery and computers	1	100.0%	0.0%	0.0%					
13	0.0153	27	Manufacture of basic metals	5	80.0%	20.0%	0.0%	0.0227	0.0121	9	60.6%	15
14	0.0152	18	Manufacture of wearing apparel; dressing and dyeing of fur	3	100.0%	0.0%	0.0%	0.0159	0.0062	18	4.0%	44
15	0.0138	2	Forestry, logging and related service activities	1	100.0%	0.0%	0.0%					
16	0.0129	1	Agriculture, hunting and related service activities	5	60.0%	40.0%	0.0%	0.0164	0.0116	10	55.5%	19
17	0.0127	72	Computer and related activities	6	83.3%	16.7%	0.0%	0.0135	0.0113	11	45.5%	27
18	0.0123	36	Manufacture of furniture; manufacturing n.e.c.	6	66.7%	16.7%	16.7%	0.0269	0.0042	23	15.3%	40
19	0.0116	34	Manufacture of motor vehicles, trailers and semi-trailers	3	100.0%	0.0%	0.0%	0.0141	0.0077	15	33.6%	34
20	0.0112	35	Manufacture of other transport equipment	5	60.0%	40.0%	0.0%	0.0284	0.0046	22	31.1%	35

Table 12.3: Agglomeration and Co-Agglomeration in 2-digit NACE divisions

Rank	gamma	NACE	Division	# three digit	<0.02	[0.02, 0.05]	>0.05	Sum of $w_j\gamma(j)$	Coaggl gamma	Rank	Between Industry	Rank
21	0.0110	73	Research and development	2	50.0%	50.0%	0.0%	0.0117	0.0226	4	27.1%	37
22	0.0105	70	Real estate activities	3	66.7%	33.3%	0.0%	0.0126	0.0092	12	50.2%	20
23	0.0102	67	Activities auxiliary to financial intermediation	2	50.0%	0.0%	50.0%	0.0288	0.0138	7	37.2%	31
24	0.0100	20	Manufacture of wood and of products of wood and cork, except furniture; manufacture of articles of straw and plaiting materials	5	80.0%	0.0%	20.0%	0.0154	0.0091	13	64.0%	10
25	0.0095	92	Recreational, cultural and sporting activities	7	57.1%	28.6%	14.3%	0.0181	0.0085	14	70.0%	3
26	0.0092	14	Other mining and quarrying	5	60.0%	0.0%	40.0%	0.0302	0.0057	20	43.5%	28
27	0.0080	26	Manufacture of other non-metallic mineral products	8	62.5%	12.5%	25.0%	0.0169	0.0064	17	63.8%	11
28	0.0075	41	Collection, purification and distribution of water	1	100.0%	0.0%	0.0%					
29	0.0071	28	Manufacture of fabricated metal products, except machinery and equipment	7	71.4%	0.0%	28.6%	0.0179	0.0052	21	57.4%	17
30	0.0062	21	Manufacture of pulp, paper and paper products	2	100.0%	0.0%	0.0%	0.0068	0.0061	19	48.5%	22
31	0.0055	37	Recycling	2	100.0%	0.0%	0.0%	0.0051	0.0071	16	45.9%	24
32	0.0049	24	Manufacture of chemicals and chemical products	7	100.0%	0.0%	0.0%	0.0090	0.0040	24	62.6%	13
33	0.0049	29	Manufacture of machinery and equipment n.e.c.	7	85.7%	0.0%	14.3%	0.0093	0.0039	25	64.2%	9
34	0.0043	63	Supporting and auxiliary transport activities; activities of travel agencies	4	75.0%	0.0%	25.0%	0.0171	0.0029	28	38.0%	30
35	0.0040	71	Renting of machinery and equipment without operator and of personal and household goods	4	100.0%	0.0%	0.0%	0.0057	0.0034	27	60.8%	14
36	0.0039	25	Manufacture of rubber and plastic products	2	100.0%	0.0%	0.0%	0.0056	0.0007	42	5.9%	42
37	0.0038	65	Financial intermediation, except insurance and pension funding	2	50.0%	0.0%	50.0%	0.0046	0.0127	8	18.9%	38
38	0.0035	33	Manufacture of medical, precision and optical instruments, watches and clocks	5	60.0%	20.0%	20.0%	0.0104	0.0028	29	48.4%	23

Table 12.3: Agglomeration and Co-Agglomeration in 2-digit NACE divisions – cont.

Rank	gamma	NACE	Division	# three digit	<0.02	[0.02, 0.05]	>0.05	Sum of $w_j\gamma(j)$	Coaggl gamma	Rank	Between Industry	Rank
39	0.0033	31	Manufacture of electrical machinery and apparatus n.e.c.	6	66.7%	33.3%	0.0%	0.0118	0.0012	39	27.6%	36
40	0.0027	22	Publishing, printing and reproduction of recorded media	3	100.0%	0.0%	0.0%	0.0040	0.0019	37	34.2%	33
41	0.0026	60	Land transport; transport via pipelines	3	100.0%	0.0%	0.0%	0.0029	0.0036	26	56.7%	18
42	0.0026	32	Manufacture of radio, television and communication equipment and apparatus	3	100.0%	0.0%	0.0%	0.0027	0.0027	30	68.0%	6
43	0.0025	51	Wholesale trade and commission trade, except of motor vehicles and motorcycles	7	85.7%	14.3%	0.0%	0.0060	0.0020	34	64.8%	8
44	0.0023	74	Other business activities	8	100.0%	0.0%	0.0%	0.0039	0.0021	32	74.3%	1
45	0.0023	45	Construction	5	100.0%	0.0%	0.0%	0.0026	0.0021	31	57.9%	16
46	0.0023	80	Education	4	100.0%	0.0%	0.0%	0.0022	0.0021	33	69.9%	4
47	0.0020	15	Manufacture of food products and beverages	9	66.7%	22.2%	11.1%	0.0064	0.0019	35	66.8%	7
48	0.0018	91	Activities of membership organizations n.e.c.	3	100.0%	0.0%	0.0%	0.0026	0.0019	38	38.3%	29
49	0.0013	55	Hotels and restaurants	5	100.0%	0.0%	0.0%	0.0031	0.0009	41	45.8%	25
50	0.0007	93	Other service activities	1	100.0%	0.0%	0.0%					
51	0.0004	50	Sale, maintenance and repair of motor vehicles and motorcycles; retail sale of automotive fuel	5	100.0%	0.0%	0.0%	0.0020	-0.0006	45	-89.5%	47
52	0.0004	85	Health and social work	3	100.0%	0.0%	0.0%	0.0003	0.0006	43	69.8%	5
53	0.0002	52	Retail trade, except of motor vehicles and motorcycles; repair of personal and household goods	7	100.0%	0.0%	0.0%	0.0004	0.0001	44	62.6%	12
54	-0.0003	90	Sewage and refuse disposal, sanitation and similar activities	1	100.0%	0.0%	0.0%					
55	-0.0003	64	Post and telecommunications	2	100.0%	0.0%	0.0%	-0.0012	0.0011	40	-126.8%	48
56	-0.0021	40	Electricity, gas, steam and hot water supply	3	100.0%	0.0%	0.0%	-0.0015	-0.0034	46	49.4%	21

Table 12.3: Agglomeration and Co-Agglomeration in 2-digit NACE divisions – cont.

activities (72), Research and development (73), Recreational, cultural and sporting activities (92), Financial intermediation, except insurance and pension funding (65), Other business activities (74)). But note, however, when judged by the absolute value of gamma both technology oriented industries and knowledge intensive services are only slightly concentrated (all of the values are below the suggested threshold by EG of 0.02).

As is apparent from columns three to five in table 12.3, the most or least concentrated divisions generally encompass the most or least concentrated groups, respectively. Indeed, with a correlation coefficient of 0.96 there is a close relationship between the value of gamma at the 2-digit sector level and the weighted average of the gammas of the respective 3-digit subsectors. This finding suggests that the degree of concentration at the more aggregated level is due mainly to the degree of concentration of its components. But clearly, this finding does not rule out the possibility that the effects of intra-industry concentration are reinforced or reversed by even stronger effects due to inter-industry concentration. To account for this latter effect, column six lists the values of the index of co-agglomeration c proposed by EG for the 48 two-digit divisions that contain more than one 3-digit group. The magnitude of the co-agglomeration index can be interpreted in the same way as the "simple" agglomeration index, such that values below 0.02 indicate low co-agglomeration and values above 0.05 indicate high co-agglomeration. As is evident from the table, the evidence for co-agglomeration is rather weak, since the value of c is below 0.02 in 90 per cent of the divisions. In only three 2-digit sectors could co-agglomeration amongst 3-digit subsectors be considered substantial. We find values of c above 0.05 in the following divisions: Extraction of crude petroleum and natural gas; service activities incidental to oil and gas extraction, excluding surveying (11), Manufacture of coke, refined petroleum products and nuclear fuel (23) and Air transport (62).

Column seven in table 12.3 allows one to compare the relative importance of intra- versus inter-industry concentration as a source of observe concentration at the 2-digit level as a whole. In the column results for the computation of the second term of equation (12.3) are given according to which one can express inter-industry agglomeration as a fraction of the division's total agglomeration. A fraction of intra-industry concentration greater than 50 per cent corresponds to a stronger effect of co-agglomeration on the degree of concentration of the 2-digit division than the weighted average of concentration of its 3-digit subgroups. Negative values, which we find in only four divisions, indicate that the effects can go in the opposite direction as well. In more than half of the cases the fraction falls into the range of 33 per cent to 67 per cent, which we interpret as indicating that the intra- versus inter-industry components are of roughly the same order of magnitude. We observe that in only six divisions is the ratio above 67 per cent, with a maximum value of 74 per cent. Thus, only in a small subset of sectors do co-agglomeration forces dominate the group-specific agglomeration effects. However, by looking at the absolute value of agglomeration of the respective divisions, it appears that this effect is of significance only for the division Manufacture of textiles (17). On the other side, a notable divergence of the intra- versus inter-industry concentration effects exists in cases where the division exhibits an agglomeration index above 0.02, such as Mining of coal and lignite; extraction of peat (10) and Mining of metal ores (13). In these cases high values for the weighted averages of the agglomeration indices of the groups and subgroups coincide with slight negative values for the co-agglomeration indices. These results seem plausible since the location decisions of plants in these divisions should be determined mainly by the availability of natural resources. Thus, as long as the natural resources that are specific to the groups within the divisions, that is, coal, lignite and peat on the hand and iron and non-ferrous metal ores on the other hand, itself are not localized in the same regions the negative values of c should come as no surprise.

To sum up, we could not find a significant relationship between the degree of co-agglomeration (c) and its magnitude relative to the weighted average of the agglomeration of groups within a division (j); the spearman rank correlation is 0.05 and the standard correlation is 0.07. Although two fifths of all 2-digit divisions are more concentrated than the (weighted) average of their 3-digit subgroups in absolute terms, these divisions are only very slightly concentrated. An implication of this is that by judging the importance of intra- versus inter-industry concentration in relative terms on a more aggregate sectoral level, one should always keep the absolute degree of concentration in mind.

12.3.4 The agglomeration of technology oriented industries and knowledge intensive services and co-agglomeration

Despite the lack of evidence of high-tech agglomeration in Germany, one could object that the NACE typologies do not capture technological fields of economic activity. For instance, common definitions of "the" information and communication technologies (ICT) sector encompass a variety of different 2-digit NACE divisions or 3-digit NACE groups. In order to test whether the potentially inappropriate NACE definitions hide existing concentration, we conduct further examinations using hand-compiled categories of "high-technology", "medium-technology" and "knowledge intensive" service sectors. These definitions conform to the classification scheme used by the yearly "Reports on Germany's Technological Performance". In addition, following a usual classification of the ZEW we also build a broad ICT sector which consists of a number of different 3-digit NACE groups. We then compute the values of the agglomeration and co-agglomeration indices proposed by EG for these four comprehensive technology sectors.

Results are given in Table 12.4. Our findings are still in contrast to what common wisdom about geographic concentration in technology related industries or knowledge intensive services suggests: all broad sectors do have a gamma close to zero. In addition they all also have a c close to zero, which indicates that the correlation in the location decisions of plants operating in different technological fields is very low.

12.4 DISCUSSION AND CONCLUSION

The aim of this paper is to explore the geographic concentration of economic sectors in Germany with the help of Ellison and Glaeser's (1997) concentration index. We thereby add to previous empirical work measuring geographic concentration in other

Group	Gamma	Co-Agglo-meration
High technology industries	0.0026	0.0012
Medium technology industries	0.0030	0.0020
Knowledge intensive services	0.0030	0.0028
Information and communication technology sector	0.0033	0.0027

Table 12.4: Agglomeration and co-agglomeration in high- and medium-tech industries, knowledge intensive services and the ICT sector

countries using the EG index and plant level employment data. However, whereas the existing empirical evidence is confined to agglomeration in manufacturing industries, our data encompasses agricultural and service sectors as well. Thus, we are able to give a much more complete picture of the degree of geographic concentration in the overall economy. The questions we ask are (I) are location decisions of plants in the same sector really correlated? or, in other words, is their extent of geographic concentration greater than what would be expected to arise randomly? and (II) what magnitude and what patterns of geographic concentration do sectors reveal?

Concerning the first question at the most disaggregated sectoral level of the 3-digit NACE groups, we find that in about 80 per cent of all German economic sectors plants' location decisions are significantly positively correlated. However, in most cases the resulting geographic concentration could be regarded as weak. Only 14 per cent of all sectors are very concentrated. Thus, the localization of economic activity that has received so much attention in the recent literature on clusters appears to be empirically relevant for only a small minority of sectors in Germany.

To answer the second question, we show the 30 most and 30 least concentrated economic sectors as measured by the EG agglomeration index. Not surprisingly, the top 30 group is dominated by resource extractive sectors belonging to the NACE section "Mining and Quarrying" or by other sectors with a strong dependence on natural resources such as "Manufacture of coke oven products" or "Sea and coastal water transport". What is striking is that high and medium technology industries are not among the most concentrated sectors. Rather, these industries lie in the middle field or even at the lower end of the ranking. Instead, the most concentrated manufacturing industries appear to be more mature or traditional industries belonging for instance to the textile and leather industry. Thus, our findings point to history as a major explanation for today's concentration pattern. Our results for the manufacturing industry are much in line with those already found in the literature. With regard to the least concentrated sectors, it is also possible to offer intuitively plausible explanations for our findings. For instance, since the need to be close to final demand is of overriding importance in the service industries, the fact that the great majority of the most dispersed sectors are customer related services such as "Retail sale of automotive fuel" or "Restaurants" comes as no surprise.

To account for the possibility that the 3-digit level of NACE groups defines sectors too narrowly in order to grasp "localization" effects between plants in these sectors, we also calculate the EG agglomeration index at the 2-digit level of NACE divisions. Although the degree of geographic concentration generally decreases slightly and the distribution of the EG index shifts to the left, the overall concentration pattern does not change much when measured at the more aggregated sectoral level. Still, the most concentrated sectors are those in which access to natural resources is necessary and the least concentrated sectors remain consumer oriented service sectors. Technology oriented industries and knowledge intensive services are not among the most concentrated sectors and their degree of geographic concentration is generally very weak. Since the concept of the EG index can be extended to measure the co-agglomeration of sectors we also look for the tendency of plants in technology related industries and knowledge intensive service sectors to co-locate close to others. Our findings indicate that the correlation in the location decisions of plants operating in different technological fields is very low.

We conclude that economizing in transportation costs plays the most significant role for plants in the same sector to cluster together or not to cluster at all – at least for those geographic concentrations which are measurable by a macroeconomic yardstick. Contrary to conventional wisdom, our analysis reveals no unambiguous positive relationship between the degree of geographic concentration of sectors and the intensity with which these sectors use knowledge as a production factor. In other words, the possibility of knowledge spillovers does not naturally cause a positive correlation in the location decisions of plants in the same sector. Instead our findings give some support to the results of a recent study by Orlando (2002), who finds that knowledge spillovers between firms in the same sector do not attenuate by distance. If this is true there is simply no need for plants in technology related industries and knowledge intensive service sectors to co-locate in order to benefit from knowledge spillovers. As Germany is a relatively small country with every major city within one-day travel distance, spatial proximity may actually be a poor proxy for the importance of personal contact, trust, and so on. The policy implications of our results are clear-cut: if pecuniary but not technological externalities are the main driving force for agglomeration processes, then firms and workers should be able to reap the benefits of localization economies. Regarding cluster policy, besides the long-established methods of classical R&D-policy there seems to be little economic justification for an additional cluster policy on a regional level.

REFERENCES

Alecke, B., C. Alsleben, F. Scharr and G. Untiedt (2006), 'Are there really high-tech clusters? The geografic concentration of German manufacturing industries and its determinants', *The Annals of Regional Science*, **40**, 19–42.

Amiti, M. (1999), 'Specialisation patterns in Europe', *Weltwirschaftliches Archiv*, **134** (4), 573-593.

Arrow, K. J. (1962), 'Economic welfare and the allocation of resources for invention', in R.R. Nelson *The Rate and Direction of Inventive Activity*, Princeton University Press, 609–626.

Audretsch, D.B. and M.P. Feldman (1996), 'R&D spillovers and the geography of innovation and production', *American Economic Review*, **86** (3), 630–640.

Barrios, S., L. Bertinelli, E. Strobl and A. C. Teixeira (2003), 'Agglomeration economies and the location of industries: a comparison of three small European countries', *CORE Discussion Paper*, 2003-**67**.

Brülhart, M. and J. Torstensson (1996), 'Regional integration, scale economies and industrial economies', *Center for Economic Policy Research Discussion Paper*, **1435**.

Devereux, M.P., R. Griffith and H. Simpson (1999), 'The geographic distribution of production activity in the UK', *The Institute for Fiscal Studies, Working Paper* **26/99**.

Dumais, G., G. Ellison and E. Glaeser (1997), 'Geographic concentration as a dynamic process', *NBER Working Paper*.

Duranton, G. and H.G. Overman (2002), 'Testing for localisation using micro-geographic data', *CEPR Discussion Paper*, **3379**.

Ellison, G. and E.L. Glaeser (1997), 'Geographic concentration in U.S. manufacturing industries: a dartboard approach', *Journal of Political Economy*, **105** (5), 879–927.

Fujita, M. and J.-F. Thisse (2002), *Economics of Agglomeration – Cities, Industrial Location, and Regional Growth*, Cambridge: Cambridge University Press.

Grupp, H., H. Legler, A. Jungmittag and U. Schmoch (2000), *Hochtechnologie 2000 - Neudefinition der Hochtechnologie für die Berichterstattung zur technologischen Leistungsfähigkeit Deutschlands*, Bericht des FhG-ISI und des NIW im Auftrag des Bundesministeriums für Bildung und Forschung.

Helsley, R. and W. Strange (1990), 'Matching and agglomeration economies in a system of cities', *Regional Science and Urban Economics*, **20**, 189–212

Jaffe, A.B., M. Trajtenberg and R.M. Henderson (1993), 'Geographic localization of knowledge spillovers as evidenced by patent citations', *Quarterly Journal of Economics*, **108** (3), 577–598.

Keilbach, M. (2002), 'Determinanten der räumlichen Konzentration von Industrie und Dienstleistungsbranchen. Eine empirische Analyse für Westdeutschland', *Jahrbuch für Regionalwissenschaft*, **22**, 61–79.

Krugman, P. (1991a), *Geography and Trade*, Cambridge, Mass.: MIT Press.

Krugman, P. (1991b), 'Increasing returns and economic geography', *Journal of Political Economy*, **99** (3), 483–499.

Lafourcade, M. and G. Mion (2004), 'Concentration, spatial clustering and the size of plants: disentagling the sources of co-location externalities', *PSE Working Papers*, 2005-**42**.

Lau, D. (1996) 'Local concentration and international competitiveness: some empirical evidence for manufacturing sectors in selected European countries', *Konjunkturpolitik*, **42**, 181–205.

Marshall, A. (1920), *Principles of Economics*, London: MacMillan.

Martin, R. and P. Sunley (2003), 'Deconstructing clusters: chaotic concept or policy

panacea?' *Journal of Economic Geography*, **3**, 5–35.
Maurel, F. and B. Sédillot (1999), 'A measure of the geographic concentration in French manufacturing industries', *Regional Science and Urban Economics*, **29**, 575–604.
Orlando, M.J. (2002), *Measuring R&D spillovers: on the importance of geographic and technological proximity*, Kansas City: Federal Reserve Bank of Kansas City.
Porter, M. (1990), *The Competitive Advantage of Nations*, New York: Free Press.

APPENDIX

Rank Gamma	NACE	Group	Gamma
1	23.1	Manufacture of coke oven products	0.5685
2	11.2	Service activities incidental to oil and gas extraction, excluding surveying	0.3030
3	33.5	Manufacture of watches and clocks	0.2825
4	10.1	Mining and agglomeration of hard coal	0.1839
5	36.2	Manufacture of jewellery and related articles	0.1683
6	15.2	Processing and preserving of fish and fish products	0.1587
7	67.1	Activities auxiliary to financial intermediation, except insurance and pension funding	0.1581
8	61.1	Sea and coastal water transport	0.1501
9	11.1	Extraction of crude petroleum and natural gas	0.1440
10	13.1	Mining of iron ores	0.1345
11	14.3	Mining of chemical and fertilizer minerals	0.1288
12	10.2	Mining and agglomeration of lignite	0.1282
13	14.4	Production of salt	0.1107
14	63.2	Other supporting transport activities	0.1073
15	17:6	Manufacture of knitted and crocheted fabrics	0.1032
16	10.3	Extraction and agglomeration of peat	0.1020
17	13.2	Mining of non-ferrous metal ores, except uranium and thorium ores	0.0768
18	92.1	Activities of business, employers and professional organizations	0.0702
19	26.3	Manufacture of ceramic tiles and flags	0.0690
20	23.2	Manufacture of refined petroleum products	0.0675
21	17.2	Textile weaving	0.0631
22	28.6	Manufacture of cutlery, tools and general hardware	0.0625
23	29.6	Manufacture of weapons and ammunition	0.0593
24	19.3	Manufacture of footwear	0.0587
25	62.2	Non-scheduled air transport	0.0539
26	28.4	Forging, pressing, stamping and roll forming of metal; powder metallurgy	0.0530
27	26.2	Manufacture of non-refractory ceramic goods other than for construction purposes; manufacture of refractory ceramic products	0.0529
28	65.2	Other financial intermediation	0.0515
29	20.2	Manufacture of veneer sheets; manufacture of plywood, laminboard, particle board, fibre board and other panels and boards	0.0502
30	05.0	Fishing, fish farming and related service activities	0.0455
31	15.7	Manufacture of prepared animal feeds	0.0447
32	73.2	Research and experimental development on social sciences and humanities	0.0444
33	35.1	Building and repairing of ships and boats	0.0439
34	35.3	Manufacture of aircraft and spacecraft	0.0425
35	27.1	Manufacture of basic iron and steel and of ferro-alloys	0.0405
36	31.5	Manufacture of lighting equipment and electric lamps	0.0395
37	62.1	Scheduled air transport	0.0391
38	17.3	Finishing of textiles	0.0377
39	36.5	Manufacture of games and toys	0.0373
40	92.4	Motion picture and video activities	0.0369

Table 12.5: Degree of concentration in 3-digit NACE groups (ranking according to the EG-Index)

Rank Gamma	NACE	Group	Gamma
41	19.2	Manufacture of luggage, handbags and the like, saddlery and harness	0.0360
42	61.2	Inland water transport	0.0342
43	19.1	Tanning and dressing of leather	0.0338
44	16.0	Manufacture of tobacco products	0.0332
45	17.1	Preparation and spinning of textile fibres	0.0294
46	92.2	Activities of trade unions	0.0285
47	72.6	Other computer related activities	0.0282
48	51.7	Other wholesale	0.0265
49	01.3	Growing of crops combined with farming of animals (mixed farming)	0.0257
50	15.4	Manufacture of vegetable and animal oils and fats	0.0239
51	17.5	Manufacture of other textiles	0.0234
52	01.2	Farming of animals	0.0224
53	70.2	Letting of own property	0.0219
54	31.4	Manufacture of accumulators, primary cells and primary batteries	0.0215
55	33.4	Manufacture of optical instruments and photographic equipment	0.0204
56	26.5	Manufacture of cement, lime and plaster	0.0203
57	24.5	Manufacture of soap and detergents, cleaning and polishing preparations, perfumes and toilet preparations	0.0197
58	72.1	Hardware consultancy	0.0191
59	30.0	Manufacture of office machinery and computers	0.0189
60	33.3	Manufacture of industrial process control equipment	0.0187
61	34.1	Manufacture of motor vehicles	0.0187
62	66.0	Insurance and pension funding, except compulsory social security	0.0182
63	36.1	Manufacture of furniture	0.0182
64	15.5	Manufacture of dairy products	0.0181
65	27.3	Other first processing of iron and steel	0.0177
66	17.4	Manufacture of made-up textile articles, except apparel	0.0176
67	72.5	Maintenance and repair of office, accounting and computing machinery	0.0175
68	60.3	Transport via pipelines	0.0170
69	20.5	Manufacture of other products of wood; manufacture of articles of cork, straw and plaiting materials	0.0168
70	74.4	Advertising	0.0167
71	18.2	Manufacture of other wearing apparel and accessories	0.0163
72	35.5	Manufacture of other transport equipment n.e.c.	0.0160
73	29.4	Manufacture of machinetools	0.0150
74	72.2	Software consultancy and supply	0.0150
75	26.1	Manufacture of glass and glass products	0.0146
76	28.7	Manufacture of other fabricated metal products	0.0144
77	02.0	Forestry, logging and related service activities	0.0138
78	36.3	Manufacture of musical instruments	0.0137
79	55.2	Camping sites and other provision of short-stay accommodation	0.0136
80	27.5	Casting of metals	0.0135
81	18.1	Manufacture of leather clothes	0.0133
82	27.4	Manufacture of basic precious and non-ferrous metals	0.0132
83	55.4	Bars	0.0126
84	20.1	Sawmilling and planing of wood; impregnation of wood	0.0126

Table 12.5: Degree of concentration in 3-digit NACE groups (ranking according to the EG-Index) – cont.

Rank Gamma	NACE	Group	Gamma
85	52.5	Retail sale of second-hand goods in stores	0.0125
86	91.2	Social work activities	0.0122
87	29.1	Manufacture of machinery for the production and use of mechanical power, except aircraft, vehicle and cycle engines	0.0121
88	31.2	Manufacture of electricity distribution and control apparatus	0.0119
89	29.3	Manufacture of agricultural and forestry machinery	0.0119
90	31.1	Manufacture of electric motors, generators and transformers	0.0118
91	24.7	Manufacture of man-made fibres	0.0117
92	14.1	Quarrying of stone	0.0117
93	24.6	Manufacture of other chemical products	0.0110
94	45.5	Renting of construction or demolition equipment with operator	0.0109
95	21.1	Manufacture of pulp, paper and paperboard	0.0108
96	70.3	Real estate activities on a fee or contract basis	0.0105
97	17.7	Manufacture of knitted and crocheted articles	0.0104
98	45.1	Site preparation	0.0102
99	35.2	Manufacture of railway and tramway locomotives and rolling stock	0.0101
100	71.2	Renting of other transport equipment	0.0095
101	20.3	Manufacture of builders carpentry and joinery	0.0094
102	73.1	Research and experimental development on natural sciences and engineering	0.0092
103	24.1	Manufacture of basic chemicals	0.0085
104	63.1	Cargo handling and storage	0.0082
105	36.4	Manufacture of sports goods	0.0081
106	27.2	Manufacture of tubes	0.0081
107	36.6	Miscellaneous manufacturing n.e.c.	0.0080
108	92.5	Radio and television activities	0.0079
109	63.3	Activities of travel agencies and tour operators; tourist assistance activities n.e.c.	0.0078
110	37.1	Recycling of metal waste and scrap	0.0077
111	41.0	Collection, purification and distribution of water	0.0076
112	71.1	Renting of automobiles	0.0075
113	28.2	Manufacture of tanks, reservoirs and containers of metal; manufacture of central heating radiators and boilers	0.0073
114	74.6	Investigation and security activities	0.0072
115	14.2	Quarrying of sand and clay	0.0071
116	51.1	Wholesale on a fee or contract basis	0.0070
117	60.1	Transport via railways	0.0070
118	51.2	Wholesale of agricultural raw materials and live animals	0.0070
119	22.1	Publishing	0.0067
120	24.3	Manufacture of paints, varnishes and similar coatings, printing ink and mastics	0.0066
121	29.5	Manufacture of other special purpose machinery	0.0066
122	26.4	Manufacture of bricks, tiles and construction products, in baked clay	0.0066
123	01.1	Growing of crops; market gardening; horticulture	0.0065
124	32.1	Manufacture of electronic valves and tubes and other electronic components	0.0064
125	34.3	Manufacture of parts and accessories for motor vehicles and their engines	0.0064
126	25.1	Manufacture of rubber products	0.0062
127	72.3	Data processing	0.0059
128	91.1	Veterinary activities	0.0059
129	74.8	Miscellaneous business activities n.e.c.	0.0058

Table 12.5: Degree of concentration in 3-digit NACE groups (ranking according to the EG-Index) – cont.

Rank Gamma	NACE	Group	Gamma
130	26.7	Cutting, shaping and finishing of ornamental and building stone	0.0058
131	51.4	Wholesale of household goods	0.0058
132	71.4	Renting of personal and household goods n.e.c.	0.0058
133	28.5	Treatment and coating of metals; general mechanical engineering	0.0057
134	15.1	Production, processing and preserving of meat and meat products	0.0056
135	24.4	Manufacture of pharmaceuticals, medicinal chemicals and botanical products	0.0056
136	32.3	Manufacture of television and radio receivers, sound or video recording or reproducing apparatus and associated goods	0.0056
137	26.6	Manufacture of articles of concrete, plaster and cement	0.0055
138	25.2	Manufacture of plastic products	0.0054
139	22.3	Reproduction of recorded media	0.0052
140	80.2	Provision of services to the community as a whole	0.0052
141	51.6	Wholesale of machinery, equipment and supplies	0.0052
142	80.4	Primary education	0.0051
143	35.4	Manufacture of motorcycles and bicycles	0.0050
144	29.7	Manufacture of domestic appliances n.e.c.	0.0048
145	28.3	Manufacture of steam generators, except central heating hot water boilers	0.0048
146	15.3	Processing and preserving of fruit and vegetables	0.0047
147	15.6	Manufacture of grain mill products, starches and starch products	0.0046
148	33.2	Manufacture of instruments and appliances for measuring, checking, testing, navigating and other purposes, except industrial process control equipment	0.0045
149	37.2	Recycling of non-metal waste and scrap	0.0044
150	28.1	Manufacture of structural metal products	0.0042
151	31.3	Manufacture of insulated wire and cable	0.0040
152	92.7	News agency activities	0.0039
153	55.5	Canteens and catering	0.0037
154	29.2	Manufacture of other general purpose machinery	0.0036
155	74.3	Technical testing and analysis	0.0036
156	55.1	Hotels	0.0034
157	71.3	Renting of other machinery and equipment	0.0034
158	33.1	Manufacture of medical and surgical equipment and orthopaedic appliances	0.0034
159	21.2	Manufacture of articles of paper and paperboard	0.0034
160	14.5	Other mining and quarrying n.e.c.	0.0033
161	40.3	Steam and hot water supply	0.0033
162	65.1	Monetary intermediation	0.0032
163	74.1	Legal, accounting, book-keeping and auditing activities; tax consultancy; market research and public opinion polling; business and management consultancy; holdings	0.0032
164	67.2	Activities auxiliary to insurance and pension funding	0.0032
165	50.1	Sale of motor vehicles	0.0031
166	45.2	Building of complete constructions or parts thereof; civil engineering	0.0031
167	74.7	Industrial cleaning	0.0030
168	92.3	Activities of other membership organizations	0.0029
169	70.1	Real estate activities with own property	0.0026
170	52.2	Retail sale of food, beverages and tobacco in specialized stores	0.0025
171	15.9	Manufacture of beverages	0.0023
172	26.8	Manufacture of other non-metallic mineral products	0.0023

Table 12.5: Degree of concentration in 3-digit NACE groups (ranking according to the EG-Index) – cont.

Rank Gamma	NACE	Group	Gamma
173	80.1	Administration of the State and the economic and social policy of the community	0.0022
174	74.2	Architectural and engineering activities and related technical consultancy	0.0022
175	74.5	Labour recruitment and provision of personnel	0.0021
176	22.2	Printing and service activities related to printing	0.0020
177	18.3	Dressing and dyeing of fur; manufacture of articles of fur	0.0020
178	63.4	Activities of other transport agencies	0.0019
179	85.2	Higher education	0.0019
180	51.3	Wholesale of food, beverages and tobacco	0.0019
181	31.6	Manufacture of electrical equipment n.e.c.	0.0018
182	50.2	Maintenance and repair of motor vehicles	0.0017
183	23.3	Processing of nuclear fuel	0.0017
184	45.3	Building installation	0.0017
185	45.4	Building completion	0.0016
186	51.5	Wholesale of non-agricultural intermediate products, waste and scrap	0.0015
187	34.2	Manufacture of bodies (coachwork) for motor vehicles; manufacture of trailers and semi-trailers	0.0015
188	91.3	Sewage and refuse disposal, sanitation and similar activities	0.0014
189	50.5	Retail sale of automotive fuel	0.0012
190	55.3	Restaurants	0.0011
191	60.2	Other land transport	0.0011
192	50.4	Sale, maintenance and repair of motorcycles and related parts and accessories	0.0011
193	50.3	Sale of motor vehicle parts and accessories	0.0011
194	52.7	Repair of personal and household goods	0.0010
195	93.0	Library, archives, museums and other cultural activities	0.0007
196	15.8	Manufacture of other food products	0.0006
197	85.3	Adult and other education	0.0005
198	52.4	Other retail sale of new goods in specialized stores	0.0002
199	85.1	Secondary education	0.0001
200	52.3	Retail sale of pharmaceutical and medical goods, cosmetic and toilet articles	0.0001
201	52.1	Retail sale in non-specialized stores	0.0001
202	90.0	Human health activities	-0.0003
203	64.2	Telecommunications	-0.0005
204	52.6	Retail sale not in stores	-0.0009
205	20.4	Manufacture of wooden containers	-0.0011
206	64.1	Post and courier activities	-0.0015
207	40.1	Production and distribution of electricity	-0.0016
208	32.2	Manufacture of television and radio transmitters and apparatus for line telephony and line telegraphy	-0.0019
209	40.2	Manufacture of gas; distribution of gaseous fuels through mains	-0.0028
210	80.3	Compulsory social security activities	-0.0053
211	72.4	Database activities	-0.0124
212	24.2	Manufacture of pesticides and other agro-chemical products	-0.0329
213	62.3	Space transport	-0.2217

Table 12.5: Degree of concentration in 3-digit NACE groups (ranking according to the EG-Index) – cont.

13. Clusters and networks . . . their spell has by no means been broken!

Martin Wrobel*

13.1 INTRODUCTION

The attraction that clusters and networks[1] have held for public institutions and private enterprises for more than a decade now remains undiminished despite increasing criticism of the way that the concept has been used in practice (for example, Hellmer 2004; Rehfeld 2005). The normally slow transfer of research findings into policy practice has progressed rapidly in the case of "clusters and networks". Hardly any other research approach from regional economics has been embraced with such enthusiasm during the past 10–15 years by both the public institutions responsible for regional structural development and by private sector firms (Sternberg et al. 2004, 164). Indeed, the term cluster has come to be seen as synonymous with economic growth, jobs, innovations and synergies – in other words with competitiveness and prosperity. These positive associations are fostered by the hype surrounding specific clusters such as Silicon Valley and Route 128 (Saxenian 1994), and Wolfsburg and Jena in Germany (Hendry et al. 2000). Their reputation in the field of regional policy as "engines of structural development" became known world-wide in a very short time. The rapid dissemination of the cluster and network concept was also encouraged by a ubiquitous, constantly growing pressure on regional policy makers and private enterprise to assert themselves in the increasingly tough national and international competition for jobs, funding, quality production conditions, and the largest market shares.

*The author is a member of the regional research network of the Institute for Employment Research (Institut für Arbeitsmarkt- und Berufsforschung (IAB)) at the Hannover location. Many thanks to Uwe Blien, Gerhard Bahrenberg, Anne Otto and Frank Bauer for their helpful comments regarding earlier versions of this paper.

[1] An extensive definition and exact differentiation of the terms cluster and network can be found in section 13.4.3 of this chapter.

13.2 CLUSTERS: AT THE TOP OF THE WISH LIST – BACKGROUND

The economic, social and political order changes globally ever more rapidly and more profoundly leading to increasing competitive pressure. Structural change associated with the transition from Fordism to post-Fordism during the late 20th century fundamentally reorganized the structures underlying political, economic and social processes. This happened within only a few decades. Beginning in the 1970s, the Fordist mass production according to Taylorist principles was superseded by made-to-order production that was increasingly geared towards a growing variety of market demands (bespoke production) (Schachtschneider 2002, 132; Maier/Tödtling 2002, 157 ff.; Cappellin 1998, 60; Piore/Sabel 1985). The growing focus on productivity diminished the importance of enterprise size (economies of scale) and access to production factors – aspects which had until then been most important in strategic planning. As international competitive pressure increased, productivity became the decisive factor in the industrial production of the industrial nations (Porter 2000, 19; Porter 1998b, 80). Process sequences that were no longer up-to-date – and therefore no longer competitive – were radically restructured by means of standardisation, automation, concentration and rationalisation processes. Meanwhile, renewed attention to issues of optimal location amongst corporate planners raised the spectre of firm relocation (Porter 1998b, 78), which intensified competition between regions seeking to win and retain these firms.

Although the changes were global, differing initial conditions caused some regions to be affected more adversely. In the industrial nations for instance the negative effects of the radical changes were worst felt in regions characterised by old industries, particularly those whose economic structure was defined by one or two leading industries. Deindustrialisation processes frequently signalled the start of the decline of these leading industries, as well as industries that were closely linked with them on either side of the supply chain. Examples of such regions in Germany include the Ruhr area, with its coal and steel industries, and Bremen with its shipbuilding industry. Many regions were unable to compensate for the economic and social consequences (increased unemployment, higher social costs and so on), which often meant a definite reduction in their ability to act independently. It is especially these regions which now urgently seek a regional-policy "rescue concept" that can help halt the slide and enhance the region's competitiveness. Cluster and network concepts offer just such an allure: the concepts currently appear to be an extremely popular planning instrument in regional structural development (Berwert et al. 2004, 8). This is particularly so because cluster formations have the inherent potential to eventually sustain and perpetuate structural development by means of self-reinforcing processes within the cluster – in other words, without intervention from outside (Porter 1998b, 84; Rehfeld 2005, 3). Enthusiasm has also spread to regions facing problems other than deindustrialisation (for example, those in a geographical-political peripheral location). Even many economically healthy regions have increasingly embraced cluster strategies in order to boost the existing strengths in their economic structure.

By implementing cluster strategies in their own structural development policy, the regions are clearly orienting themselves towards Germany's "new" regional planning and structural policy guidelines. In addition, they are also adapting to the increasingly cluster-oriented allocation of EU funds under the Objective 2 and Objective 3 programmes, which are important for German regions (Rehfeld 2005, 3). The main aim of the regional structural policy pursued in Germany until the mid-1980s was to balance out regional disparities in a show of solidarity. This has been replaced by a policy that appears to follow the maxim "strengthening strengths", and which attempts to distinguish regions by emphasising existing differences (Sedlacek 1994, 98 ff.; Iwer et al. 2002, 24 ff.; Stuchtey 2002, 51). Increasingly scarce fiscal resources in the budgets of the federal, regional and local governments prevent for reasons of economic efficiency and sustainability the continuation of previously extensive distribution programs. For this reason, the attention of regional policymakers is being directed more than ever before at particular industries and sectors in the regional economy. Industries are selected on the basis of their potential to excel and thereby enhance the overall regional economy. This latter prospect forms the justification for granting special assistance to these industries (Stuchtey 2002, 51). One important aspect is that such industry emphases are a necessary precondition for initiating clusters. They form the foundation upon which future cluster initiatives can build and the fertile ground on which the cluster itself can thereafter develop (Cooke 2003, 48; Porter 2002, 23). A cluster cannot emerge from "nothing". Bruch-Krumbein and Hochmuth (2000, 15) sum this up with the following observation: "... if it is not possible to build on existing economic structure conditions, it is not possible to induce a cluster". An industry emphasis in a regional economy is defined here as a nationally, if not an internationally competitive competence, that is, an outstanding sectoral concentration of actors, institutions and know-how (Rehfeld 2005, 4). Owing to the fact that it only requires allocating assistance to a single industry (as opposed to all branches of the economy) the cluster concept of regional development coheres perfectly with the newly reorganised regional policy paradigm.

13.3 WHAT ARE CLUSTERS AND NETWORKS AND WHAT CONSTITUTES THEIR APPEAL?

In recent debates regarding the regional economy, clusters have generally been understood to mean (in the broadest sense) briefly "... an organisation form of industries that generate higher productivity and more innovations than structures that are spread out across a greater space" (Porter 2002, 21). The underlying idea of the cluster from the business perspective – achieving competitive advantages by means of the geographical concentration of firms in a value chain – is by no means new.

Although the topic is still subject to a great deal of academic controversy, there are essentially three different factors to explain why enterprises in a value chain would concentrate geographically (Schamp 2000, 150 ff.):

1. factors associated with the theory of transaction costs,
2. access to knowledge-sharing networks and institutions,
3. factors associated with dynamic urban agglomeration advantages.

The first approach assumes that spatial proximity facilitates reciprocal interactions, thereby lowering actors' transaction costs. This reduction applies to costs of the mutual interaction (for example, searching for and procuring information) and those incurred by the division of labour across large distances (Schamp 2000, 151; Krätke 1995, 68 f.; Storper/Walker 1989; Scott 1988).

The focal point of the second reason is the growing importance of knowledge and information as factors in corporate development. In addition to a better overview of the market and the competitors, under certain conditions players concentrated in one geographical area also gain access to special "pools of knowledge", which are formed and shared through frequent face-to-face contacts. These pools comprise above all non-codified/non-codifiable knowledge. Such tacit knowledge is generally tied to specific people or groups of people, and is therefore neither ubiquitous nor fully transferable to other regional contexts (Kujath 2002, 184). Only those who play a part in the local context can gain access to such knowledge because participation is contingent upon building up personal relationships of trust and reciprocity through ongoing interaction with the "knowing" local players. This then often leads to an exchange of experience in the course of a transfer of knowledge (via learning by doing, . . . by using, . . . by interaction) (Schamp 2000, 118). Especially in knowledge-intensive and innovative business segments such as research and development (which is a key area for strategic corporate development in many firms), tacit knowledge plays an important role and has a direct effect on the capacity for innovation and learning and thereby on productivity (Rallet/Torre 1998, 41 f.).

The third reason for geographical concentration is based on the factor of "uncertainty". Constantly and rapidly changing market conditions demand flexibility and instantaneous adjustment to newly arising requirements. For firms this results in increased uncertainty due to a lack of continuity and ability to plan ahead. They attempt to reduce this uncertainty by choosing a location that minimises the risks (Wrobel 2004, 159). Cluster can potentially do just that. For example, it is comparatively easier for enterprises that belong to a cluster to raise their competitiveness by concentrating on their own core competences. Whereas growth strategy of vertical integration often proved to be inefficient during the course of increasingly global economic integration (Stuchtey 2000, 2), the outsourcing of non-core segments is made easier by a comparatively high spatial density of specialists. In the best possible scenario, local specialists will cover all stages of the value added process in the value chain. Such outsourcing lowers firms' search, organisation and transaction costs, and simultaneously raises their (planning) certainty since such transactions tend to be permanent and contractual (Porter 1998, 81; Tichy 1998, 227). Moreover, "short distances" in the cluster function to reduce the response time when complications arise. Such complications tend to arise more frequently as the number of interfaces in the value added process grows along with the increase in the amount of organisation required.

Whilst the concentration of enterprises makes the individual cluster members more resistant to price fluctuations and increases their flexibility and response speed due to the integrated capacities, it is above all the possibility of knowledge transfer that distinguishes the cluster as a particularly advantageous organisational form.[2] Knowledge transfers enhance both firms' competitiveness and their innovative capacity (Porter 2000, 21). For instance, the knowledge spillovers that occur when employees switch between enterprises in the cluster function to regularly upgrade know-how within the enterprises (Mirbach 1998, 17 ff). The presence of a pool of specialised and experienced labour in a cluster region represents another advantage for enterprises. Owing to the large number of potential employers, the cluster location offers the worker an increased chance of being offered a new job in the event of losing a job, thus providing relative security. For the enterprises the costs of searching for specialised workers are reduced, which can also gradually relieve them of some of the burden of workforce training. In addition to this, workers will often independently extend and expand their qualification level via formal and informal contacts with other local specialists (Tichy 1998, 226). Firms' costs are also reduced by public subsidies to cluster organisations and related institutions such as universities, research centres, training programmes, infrastructure development schemes, relocation incentives, and so on. These programs are often specifically intended to promote clusters, and hence tailored directly to the needs of member firms (Porter 1998b, 83). Utilisation of such publicly funded resources not only reduces costs for firms, but also encourages communication amongst relevant actors.

Close spatial proximity allows enterprises to observe the local competition continuously and to measure themselves against it. Such benchmarking processes have a motivating effect, which provides an incentive for firms to increase their performance, consequently strengthening the cluster as well as the overall regional economy (Jonas 2005, 273 f.). Ideally, a cluster in the specific economic segment enables the region to develop into an economic powerhouse of national or even international importance (Iwer et al. 2002, 19). This process occurs as enhanced visibility draws further (cluster-specific) enterprises, new capital and additional workers into the region, which can in turn stimulate and accelerate the development of the cluster. The hope is that this will culminate in a "self-reinforcing cycle" (Porter 1998b, 83).

13.3.1 Not everything clusters, and certainly not everywhere...

As the discussion so far has shown, a cluster provides many advantages for a region, and cluster participation provides many advantages for individual enterprises. It is easy to see why regions – especially those suffering from structural deficits and underdevelopment – would want to set up their own Silicon Valley. Yet if the cluster concept is examined more closely it should come as little surprise that most attempts to implement it fail to meet expectations. Theoretically, the cluster concept begins from the premise that industry emphases in a region are already competitive at the national or even international level. But such regional centres of excellence are the exception rather than the rule, which implies that cluster and network concepts of regional struc-

[2] Remarks on the definition of clusters and networks that appear later in this paper will show that it is no longer possible here to speak clearly of a factor that promotes the development of a cluster, as above all the active transfer of knowledge must be regarded as a constituent element of networks (in the sense of strategic cooperation relationships).

tural development should not be understood as policy blueprints. Attempts to utilise the concept this way will likely fail (Sternberg et al. 2004, 178; Rehfeld 2005, 4). Unfortunately, many regional policy actors still fail to comprehend the very limited applicability of cluster-building strategies. A critical, theory-based examination of the concept on the part of the policy-makers, which would lead to more clarity and a better ability to assess the workability of the concept in their own region-specific context, has so far not materialised (cf. Berwert et al. 2004, 8).

13.4 THE EXAMPLE OF BREMEN

The German state of Bremen represents a typical old industrial region that is now fervently searching for strategies to overcome its inherited structural deficits. Shipbuilding had been one of Bremen's leading industries and a supporting pillar of the local economic structure. However, the worldwide reorganisation of the shipbuilding industry during the 1980s caused a rapid collapse of Bremen's economic base within only a few years. Such structural change presents particularly acute challenges insofar as Bremen is an urban city state. Associated suburbanisation processes tend to further disadvantage the core city, but in the case of Bremen this entails out-migration to other states. This trend is reflected in falling population figures (in particular due to changes of residence) and a steady outflow of jobs. The population fell from 681,665 to 660,225 (-3.1 per cent) in the decade from 1990 to 2000, and the number of employees covered by social security declined from 302,282 to 283,576 (-6.2 per cent) during the same period. About one third of the job losses were attributable to suburbanisation processes, while the remaining two thirds were the result of the population-related drop in demand (Wrobel 2004, 54 ff.). There is little reason to believe that current suburbanisation trends in Germany will cease or be surpassed by other forms of spatial development in the near future. On the contrary, evidence suggests the trend will continue with approximately the same dynamics (Brake et al. 2001, 273 ff.).

Given these developments and future outlook, action is needed in order to alter Bremen's course. In this context, economic planners and policy-makers in the state of Bremen have also begun to embrace the cluster and network concept as a promising instrument for regional structural development. Hopes and desires have been aroused, particularly insofar as the concept promises (as many successful examples have shown – for example Porter 1998b, 79) to release endogenously available potentials which would otherwise remain underutilised. In this respect Meyer-Stamer (2000) cites as the central strength of the cluster concept the fact that "it opens up a different view of the existing reality and therefore reveals potentials that would otherwise remain hidden . . ." (p. 21).

A starting point for the use of cluster and network strategies was the logistics sector, which is considered by the political and economic players to be one of the outstanding sectors on which to pin the state's economic development hopes. This choice was based not only on increasing turnover figures amongst Bremen's logistics firms, but also the development prospects of logistics in the overall economy: on account of increasing spatial and functional fragmentation of value chains (increase in the number of interfaces). One indicator of this development is the declining share of value added generated within individual enterprises. In the period from 1990 to 1997/98 for example it fell from 56 per cent to 33 per cent in the Ford group and from 64 per cent to 50 per cent in the Daimler-Benz group (now Daimler). In the period from 1993 to 1997/98 it fell by 5 percentage points to 38 per cent in the Bayer group and by 8 percentage points to 34 per cent at Degussa (McKinsey & Company 2000, 10). In the course of fragmentation and technological development, logistics has been transformed from a function oriented solely toward physical processes to an integral element in planning, organisation and optimisation of all transactions within and between firms (Wrobel 2004, 63 ff.). In 2002, Bremen was sufficiently convinced of the sector's endogenous development potentials to make it a centerpiece of the policy document "InnoVision 2010", which presented a plan to expand Bremen's logistics sector into a modern, nationally leading centre of excellence by 2010.

Expectations that cluster-building projects in the logistics sector would stimulate the overall regional labour market have so far failed to materialise. As early as 2004, a study was released showing the unlikelihood of cluster policy success in Bremen (Wrobel 2004). Conducted between 2001 and 2003, the study utilised modern sociological network analysis methods to examine Bremen's logistics sector and the feasibility of activating latent employment potentials across the short- and medium-term time horizons. The study first tested the hypothesis that the logistics sector in the state of Bremen is an (industry) emphasis of importance at the national level due to the traditional structures of the location as a port and handling centre, which should therefore be given particular support. The study then tested the plausibility of using cluster strategies to overcome deficits in Bremen's economic structure, to activate the suspected development potentials, and to induce an urgently needed employment stimulus by means of targeted private and public investment.

13.4.1 The logistics sector as an emphasis in the regional economy

The logistics sector is a typical cross-sectional sector according to its spectrum of responsibility and the associated extent of interconnections with other industries. It does not emerge as such from either the official statistics on industries or from output-based calculation of GDP by sector in the national accounts. Before it was possible to conduct an analysis of the logistics sector, it was therefore necessary to more accurately operationalise the sector. This was achieved through a two-step procedure. Briefly: in the first step special data matrices were generated by combining statistics on industrial activity and occupational titles. These matrices portrayed the potential of logistics. Taking this potential as a starting point, in the second step collected expert knowledge was incorporated into the matrices and then a matrix optimisation procedure was used to eliminate any imbalances. In this way it was possible to determine the "genuine" logistics shares in the cells. Considering only the initial statistics would have greatly exaggerated the size of the sector (Wrobel 2004, 84 ff.).

Formulating a precise definition of the logistics sector permitted initial insights regarding the size of the sector, its development in the decade 1990–2000, its status

Employees covered by social security	30.06.1990	Survey date 30.06.1995	30.06.2000	Change (1990–2000)
		State of Bremen		
total	302,282	293,465	283,566	-18,716
in logistics	25,515	23,283	22,477	-3,038
Share of logistics (%)	8.4	7.9	7.9	-0.5[b]
total employment trend[a]	100.0	97.0	93.8	-6.2
employment trend in logistics[a]	100.0	91.3	88.1	-11.9
		Western Germany		
total	22,368,078	22,597,347	22,846,530	478,452
in logistics	1,434,861	1,378,119	1,366,099	-68,762
Share of logistics (%)	6.4	6.1	6.0	-0.4[b]
total employment trend[a]	100.0	101.0	102.1	2.1
employment trend in logistics[a]	100.0	96.1	95.2	-4.8

[a]: 1990 = 100

[b]: Figures in percentage points

Source: Wrobel 2004, 99.

Table 13.1: Benchmark figures for the logistics sector

within Bremen's economy, and its development potentials (Table 13.1). Corresponding figures for Western Germany are included for comparison.

In Western Germany the total number of employees covered by social security[3] rose by about 2.1 per cent to 22.846 million persons from 1990 to 2000. During this same period the figure fell by 4.8 per cent in the logistics sector. In the year 2000 some 1.366 million workers covered by social security were employed in the logistics sector, 68,000 fewer than in 1990. The share of employees in logistics as a percentage of overall employment in Western Germany was therefore 6.0 per cent in the year 2000.

The situation in the state of Bremen clearly differs from the overall trends amongst the other West German states. For instance, during the decade 1990–2000 Bremen suffered severe job cuts at macroeconomic level: the number of employees covered by social security fell by 6.2 per cent from 302,282 to 283,566 workers. The logistics sector was not immune to this development; employment there declined by 11.9 per cent to 22,477. Although the magnitude of logistics job losses was considerably greater in

[3]In Germany most employment is covered by compulsory social security schemes. Only people below a certain (low) income threshold, civil servants and self employed are exempted. The figures given in Tables 13.1 and 13.2 and mentioned in the text refer to the Employment Statistics which cover all people included in this social security system.

		Growth		Total
		positive	negative	
Stock	high	6,498 [28.9%]	8,231 [36.6%]	14,729 [65.5%]
	low	1,681 [7.5%]	6,068 [27.0%]	7,749 [34.5%]
Total		8,179 [36.4%]	14,299 [63.6%]	22,478 [100%]

Source: Wrobel 2004, 106.

Table 13.2: 4-field matrix of employment in Bremen's logistics sector

Bremen than in Western Germany as a whole, the sector continued to account for a greater proportion of total employment in Bremen than in Western Germany overall (7.9 per cent versus 6.0 per cent). Whereas the decline at the national level is presumably attributable to rationalisation and automation processes typical of structural change, the severity of the decline in Bremen suggests that relocation and suburbanisation processes may have additionally contributed at the local level. These processes are caused by negative agglomeration effects such as lack of space (bottlenecks in commercial space), excessive land prices and rents, high traffic density, and so on. The disproportionately large reduction in logistics employment in Bremen (-11.9 per cent) compared with the country as a whole (-4.8 per cent) suggests that other factors besides structural change have played a role in the city state. Nevertheless, structural change in the state of Bremen has also proceeded much more rapidly than in the country as a whole. For instance, in many "old", declining sub-sectors of logistics, job losses were clearly more pronounced in Bremen than in Germany's western states. The logistics sector therefore seems to have remained more traditional in its structures in the territorial states than in the city states.

Despite its recent woes, the logistics sector in Bremen can still be classified as a high-stock sector since the share of logistics as a percentage of overall employment in the city state is greater than in Western Germany. This concentration can be regarded as an indication of an existing cluster, or at least a conductive environment for initiating one.

A more in-depth examination of the structures of the sector in the form of a 4-field matrix provides a more complete picture (Table 13.2): just under two thirds of all employees in logistics-related activities in the state of Bremen are working in logistics sub-sectors that are concentrated in Bremen (high-stock row).

However, over half of these employees in high-stock areas are working in sub-sectors in which the number of jobs shrank during the period from 1990 to 2000. A further 27 per cent are working in declining low-stock logistics-relevant industries. Just under 6,500 of the employees in the Bremen logistics sector are working in growing high-stock sectors, that is, sectors that are concentrated in Bremen and exhibit positive growth. Correlation analysis was unable to show a statistically significant relationship between stock and growth.

Given Bremen's strength in logistics and the sector's growing importance in the economy as a whole (Baumgarten/Walter 2000), it is possible to partly confirm that the logistics sector in the state of Bremen is indeed a regional economic emphasis worth promoting. In addition to an existing industry-specific core of enterprises in the region (critical mass), a significant amount of historically evolved institutional support infrastructure is already present. Examples include educational institutions such as the course in logistics at the Bremerhaven University of Applied Sciences, the special research field of logistics at the University of Bremen, the German Academy of Foreign Trade and Transport, and the Institute of Shipping Economics and Logistics. There is also a good supply of transport infrastructure including the ports, the goods distribution centre, and the airport.

13.4.2 Disproportionate decline in spite of good starting conditions – why?

If the logistics sector is a growing power of the state of Bremen and of national importance, how can the disproportionate job losses of the 1990s be explained? Can they really be attributed solely to the impact of negative agglomeration effects? A shift-share analysis provides insights into these questions.

Shift-share analysis makes it possible to compare the development of Bremen's logistics sector with that of Western Germany by relating the growth rates to each other, and then to explain any observed differences in terms of "structure" (Tengler 1989, 43; Krätke/Scheuplein 2001, 47 f.). This allows one to distinguish whether the observed differences in growth are attributable to the sectoral economic structure (that is, the mix of industries), or to regional location conditions (for example, the region type, the geographical location, the quality of the facilities and so on).

The analysis shows that location conditions are primarily responsible for the above average job losses in Bremen's logistics sector. The negative impact of these basic conditions on employment in the logistics sector is so pronounced (-12.0 per cent) that it entirely cancels out positive impulses from the sectoral economic structure (+4.8 per cent). Sub-sectors whose employment growth is affected positively by the regional location conditions are the exception in Bremen. Particularly troubling is the fact that sub-sectors that are experiencing substantial growth in the overall economy are not doing so in Bremen. Sub-optimal location factors have hampered the city-state's ability to reap gains in these potentially high-growth areas. A good example can be found in the sub-sector "haulage, storage, cold-storage". In the period from 1990 to 2000, the number of employees in this field rose by 37.8 per cent to 184,684 in Western Germany, whereas in Bremen the number of employees grew by only 310 or 6.0 per cent. On the basis of the structural conditions it should have been possible to create approximately 1,953 additional jobs in this sub-sector during the 1990s, but unfavourable location conditions reduced the actual number to a mere 310 positions.

Apart from a few exceptions, locational factors fail to boost either the old (traditional) or the new (modern) logistics sub-sectors in Bremen. This indicates that the existing location factors, which decisively helped to shape Bremen's current sectoral economic structure, have either deteriorated more quickly in Bremen compared to the rest of the country or have been superseded in importance by "new" location factors (cf. Wrobel 2004, 144 ff.; Maier/Tödtling 2001, 43). How else can it be explained that factors which once strongly encouraged growth now have exactly the opposite effect: they clearly hinder growth. Since there are no signs of an above-average level of deterioration in the existing location conditions in Bremen (infrastructure and so on), it must be assumed that other factors have become more important. These new location conditions appear to shape the structure of contemporary logistics quite seriously, and they also increasingly affect the older, traditional industries. In Bremen this is especially noticeable in the field of maritime industries. The diminishing importance of the old location factors is evident in the results attained for the logistics-related industries, which are highly concentrated in the state of Bremen. If the old location advantages still had the same weight as they formerly did, then the previous structural development would have continued. In contrast, Bremen's locational factors appear just barely suited to meet the requirements of modern logistics.

But what are these "new" location factors? Examination of the ongoing debate surrounding firms' location decision criteria can provide clues. In the course of the intensifying location competition between regions for job-creating firms, it is often no longer enough to provide just the so-called hard location factors (wage level and costs, land prices and rent levels, taxes, infrastructure and so on) and soft location factors (quality of life, image, consultation and transfer institutions and so on) in adequate quantity and quality (Heidenreich 1997, 502 ff.). A third category has been added: that of network factors. This category includes region-specific possibilities for specialisation and cooperation, reduction of risk and uncertainty, easier product diversification, knowledge transfer rates conducive to innovation, and the self-reinforcing effects of cooperation advantages (Kujath 1998, 19 ff.). Clusters and networks can claim to offer all of these factors.

13.4.3 Cluster and network – a central definition

The results of the study so far have made three things clear: firstly, the data indicate that Bremen's logistics sector qualifies as a regional emphasis worth promoting; secondly, however, the sector is gradually losing strength and competitiveness; and thirdly, evidence suggests that the sector's decline can be attributed not simply to the effects of structural change but above all to a relative lack of "new" location factors, the so-called network factors. Network analysis can help provide answers to the question of whether cluster and network structures have been able to evolve at all in Bremen's logistics sector, and if so, how likely it is that these structures can induce the urgently needed employment boost by activating latent potentials.

As mentioned above, clusters and networks are based on interactive relationships between players who are generally concentrated in one region. The quantity and quality of these relationships provides information about the quality and efficiency of a cluster/network formation. Attributes of these interaction relationships also form the basis of the network analysis. In order to compile these data for the purpose of analysing the network structures in Bremen's logistics sector, a written survey of enterprise was conducted using a standardised questionnaire.

Firms were asked to identify their five most important trading relationships at the functional transaction level, as well as their five most important relationships in terms of strategic cooperation and communication. This differentiation between the two relationship categories reflects the distinction between clusters and networks that is used in this paper. Given the proliferation of definitions and typologies, there exists no uniform set of agreed upon definitions of the concept or view of the precise relationship between them. Nonetheless, this paper utilises a definition whereby the network represents a further development of the cluster. Its basis is the mutual trust gained through continuous interaction at the functional level (Harrison 1992; Bathelt/Glückler 2000, 171). The basic idea underlying this definition derives from Gelsing, who had already analysed the difference between a "trade network" and a "knowledge network" in the early 1990s (Gelsing 1992, 117). Other authors subsequently took up such considerations and in some cases further developed the concept within the context of rediscovered cluster strategies (Grabher 1993; Schamp 2000; Elsner 2000). The definition of clusters and networks used for the study of the Bremen logistics sector follows Elsner (2000):

> "*We define (regional) clusters as (regional concentrated) groups of firms which are functionally interconnected (vertically as well as horizontally), including manufacturing and services, plus related ("hard" and "soft") infrastructures and public, semi-public, and social agents financing and/or running them.* The crucial point here is the functional relationships which are determined through the market either as vertical supplier relationships or, in the horizontal case, as specific substitutional or complementary relations among the products of participating firms (including in this way, what is often called technological "network externalities"). The network in contrast, shall be understood as strategic, as distinct from "functional". Thus, a network normally is based on a cluster. The functional interdependence in clusters may result in strategic interaction in networks. *We define (regional) networks, therefore, as (regional) clusters which develop an intensive, lasting and comprehensive multilateral cooperation, which utilize specific infrastructures and which, therefore, cooperate with relevant public, semi-public and social agents.*" (Elsner 2000, 413 ff. italics added)

13.4.4 Is there a cluster and a network?

The sampling method was complicated by the fact that it was not possible to generate a "pure logistics" database for the state of Bremen due to the lack of a clear delimitation of the sector. This is mainly the result of the positioning of logistics functions within manufacturing enterprises. It was therefore necessary to do without a precise determination of the population size as defined by the number of operating units. A sample of 500 Bremen enterprises were "manually" selected as targets for the survey instrument. These enterprises were selected according to specific criteria such as size, location, and sub-sector in order to obtain the most representative cross-section of the sector possible. Attention was also paid, however, to ensuring that all of the most important players in Bremen's logistics sector were included.

With an (unadjusted) response rate of 11.2 per cent, the dataset covers enterprises that account for over 30 per cent of the employees working in the Bremen logistics sector, including most of the large firms. Although the final dataset does not map the sector in its entirety, it is reasonably representative of the overall regional network structure for purposes of analysis.

Network analysis can be used to ascertain the existence and the quality of a regional cluster and accompanying network formations on the basis of the relational data obtained from the survey. Network analysis, which was rarely used for economic analysis until a few years ago, allows one to examine not only the structure of large groups, but also the position, that is, the degree of integration, of each individual within the group (Schnegg/Lang 2002, 47; Jansen 1999; Pappi 1987; Freeman 1979). Whilst network analysis derives from graph theory, many classical procedures from empirical social research also continue to play a role. These include the concept of homophily and multiplexity (Schnegg/Lang 2002, 47).

Since the conventional social-sciences statistics programmes do not provide software for network analysis, it is necessary to use programmes developed especially for this, such as UCINET for Windows (Borgatti et al. 2002). UCINET stands out in particular due to its simple handling and its broad spectrum of analysis modules (Jansen 1999, 263 ff.). It was therefore chosen for the analysis of the Bremen data. The results of the analysis confirm the existence of a cluster in the region's logistic sector, albeit an incomplete one (Figure 13.1).

The most important quality criterion for a cluster formation is the density of its internal network of relationships, that is, the degree of connectivity amongst all the members. The theoretically highest possible density of 100 per cent would attain in a formation where all members were in mutual contact with all the other members. In reality, however, such a high density cannot generally be achieved due to scarce time resources and simply lack of necessity for a network that completely incorporates all of the enterprises. According to Jansen (1999, 89), the realistic density of a formation is somewhere between 0 and 0.4, that is, between 0 and 40 per cent. Important factors influencing the density are the size of the formation and the firm-level interests underlying the relationship. For example, the maximum achievable density decreases as the network of relationships grows.

In the case of cluster formation recorded by the enterprise survey, which comprises 78 actors (without external relationships), the maximum theoretical number of connections is 3003 [$= (N+(N-1))/2$] (Jansen 1999, 88). If this value was reached, it would mean that each enterprise was in contact with every other recorded enterprise – 100 per cent network density. In actuality, however, only 84 relationships were observed within the partial network, which means a general (standardised) density value of 2.8 per cent for the business-motivated cluster (without taking into account external relationships). Compared directly with other clusters such as the film industry cluster in Potsdam-Babelsberg (13 per cent) or the timber industry cluster in Brandenburg (0.3 per cent) (Krätke/Scheuplein 2001, 122 and 172), Bremen's density can be classified as average. This implies that there is still potential for a further increase in the

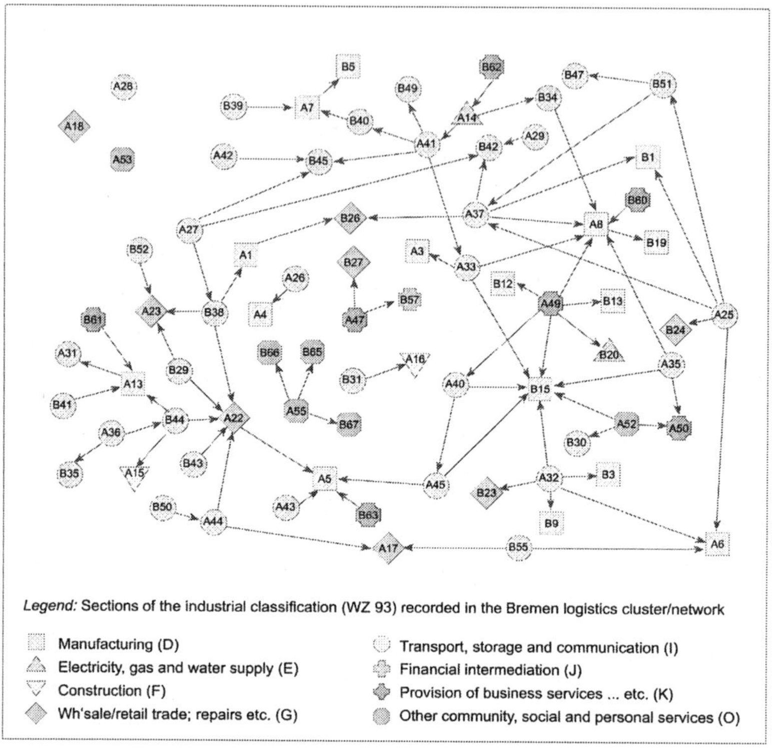

[a]External relationships are excluded. In the coding of the enterprises, an A indicates an enterprise that participated in the survey, a B indicates an enterprise captured during the survey. The arrows show the supply direction in the relationship – in the sense of the value chain (relationships at functional level).

Source: Wrobel 2004, 191.

Figure 13.1: The internal network of relationships[a] in Bremen's logistics cluster

density of cluster relationships within the region.

The visual density of the observed cluster formation is also relatively high overall. The figure shows only a small number of enterprises that are not linked to the cluster at all (A18, A28 and A53), or confined to insular sub-networks of 2 to 4 enterprises (A4-A26, B31-A16 and so on). However an exceptionally large number of peripheral firms (37) inhabit the network, that is, firms that are only connected to the cluster by a single relationship. This is one main reason that the cluster exhibits a network density of "only" 2.8 per cent. These peripheral firms cause the network structure to appear increasingly "frayed" or "fuzzy" towards the edges. These peripheral actors, of whom there are many in the cluster, are connected by a small group of enterprises that occupy conspicuously central positions in the network and thus form so-called hubs in the network structure (for example, A8, A22, A37 or B15). The firms in central positions are mainly either manufacturing enterprises that represent the most important industries in Bremen as far as employment is concerned, or enterprises from the field of transport, storage and communication. This latter group is engaged in logistics services.

External relationships exist at regional, national, and international levels. Nonetheless, the majority of the cluster enterprises only maintain regional transaction relationships – the external interconnections are not particularly pronounced and do not significantly increase the density of the cluster structures. The core of the (recorded) cluster remains regional.

The picture of the network, that is, the strategic cooperation relationships in the logistics sector clearly differs from that of the functional relationships (Figure 13.2).

The density of 2.0 per cent calculated for the partial[4] network is consistent with the theoretical expectations regarding the emergence of a network. Strategic networks generally only develop on the basis of established cluster structures. Therefore the consequent network structures cannot be expected to be more extensive than the underlying transactional structures.

Overall, this network represents little more than a fragmented ensemble of firm relationships. Seventeen insular sub-networks were observed, which vary in size between two and eight participants. Only seven of the seventeen sub-networks consist of more than three partners. Moreover, three enterprises in the Bremen logistics sector (A17, A32 and A48) maintain no regional cooperative relationships at all. This fragmented structure can hardly serve to connect Bremen's logistics sector in the form of a sectoral network. Also, the enterprises of the individual sub-networks are typically sparsely linked. In the case of the larger sub-networks, a single firm often forms the hub of the formation (hub & spoke structure – cf. Markusen 1999). As with the cluster, external relationships do not contribute significantly to the network structure's density.

One interesting aspect is the extent to which strategic network structures mirror functional cluster relations. For example, the interlinking of the enterprises A15-B44-A13-A31 is identical in the cluster structure, where the group is linked to the formation via the relationship between the enterprises B44 and A22. The correspondence of links across the two analysical levels can be seen as a reflection of the fact that strategic relationships between enterprises develop more rapidly and more easily when the enterprises have prior mutual business connections.

On the other hand, according to cluster theory the insularity of the sub-networks indicates sub-optimal use of the potentials inherent in the existing regional concentration of logistics know-how. On this basis it seems unlikely that innovation-based economic growth dynamism will emerge from such fragmentary inter-firm network structures. This calls into question the hope that innovation in the logistics sector can potentially spur significant regional employment growth in the short- to medium-term.

Calculating centrality indicators can further deepen our understanding of the dynamics of Bremen's logistics cluster. Centrality indicators express the visibility of firms within the network.

---

[4]Without taking into consideration external relationships. The density of 2 per cent results from 50 observable relationships out of a possible maximum of 2,485.

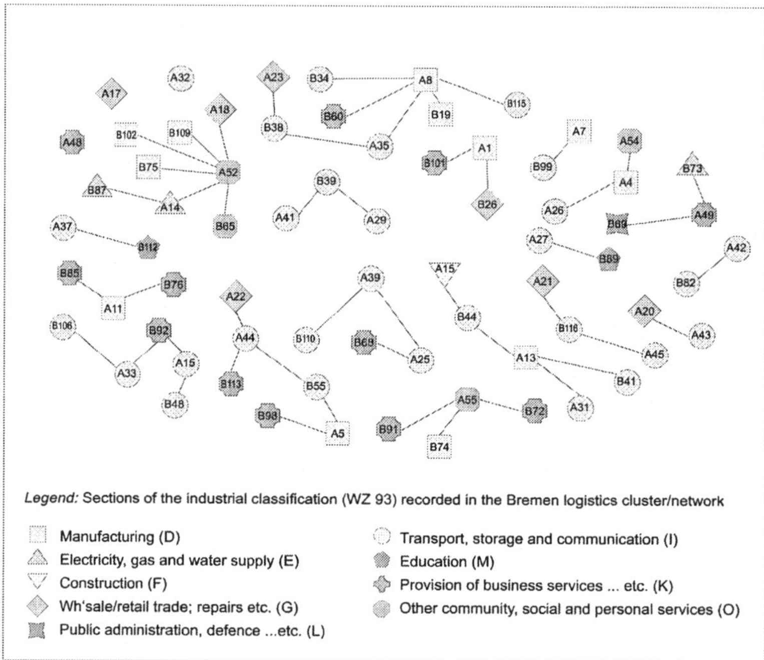

[a]External relationships are excluded. In the coding of the enterprises, an A indicates an enterprise that participated in the survey, a B indicates an enterprise captured during the survey. Due to the reciprocal interactions in strategic cooperation relationships, the links are shown as non-directional.
Source: Wrobel 2004, 218.

Figure 13.2: The internal network of relationships[a] in Bremen's logistics network

> "Concepts of the centrality of actors assume that the actor who is involved in many relationships in the network and is therefore 'visible' is prominent in the network." (Jansen 1999, 121 according to Knoke/Burt 1983).

Furthermore, the more prominent an actor is within a network, the wider is his scope of action vis-à-vis access to network resources, information, and power (Jansen 1999, 121). The relevant concepts are:

- degree-based centrality,
- closeness-based centrality and
- betweenness-based centrality.

The degree-based concept of centrality (as a measure of possible communication activity) attempts to capture the integration of an actor into the network. An actor is more central the greater number of direct connections he has (Jansen 1999, 125 ff.). A high level of centrality is to be equated with far-reaching access to resources within the cluster or network (infrastructure facilities, production capacities, knowledge specific to the cluster/network and so on) (cf. Krätke/Scheuplein 2001, 135 f.).

The closeness-based concept of centrality can be regarded as an expansion of the degree-based concept, since it takes into account indirect relationships in addition to direct ones. "In a closeness-based measure of centrality the actor who is separated from all others by only short paths is central" (Jansen 1999, 125 ff.). This expresses how often an actor has to rely on third parties in order to obtain information or other resources. The fewer intermediary actors that are involved in the transmission, the faster, more reliable and less adulterated is the transfer (Jansen 1999).

The betweenness-based concept of centrality measures an actor's network power. It indicates how often the actor is located on the shortest connecting path between two other actors in the network, that is, how often he has to act as an intermediary within the network (Jansen 1999, 125 ff.). This presumably gauges an actor's relative power position in the network, because he controls the flow of resources and information between other actors (Krätke/Scheuplein 2001, 136).

When interpreting the calculated centrality indicators it is important to note that only the results for respondents can be analysed. The full scope of relationships for those firms that were indirectly captured remains unknown. Including these enterprises in the calculations would have led to biased results.

Centrality indicators: cluster

As a cluster enterprise grows in size, it gains contacts, independence and power in the cluster. In this respect a clear jump is apparent between the enterprise size categories of 20–99 and 100–499 employees (logistics staff[5]) (Table 13.3).

When the analysis is expanded to include other firm characteristics such as age, turnover (Table 13.4), and the development of turnover (Table 13.5), it becomes clear that the nodes in the network (that is, the central positions) are occupied above all by well established enterprises with large workforces, and high, stable levels of turnover in logistics. These enterprises exhibit a high degree of integration, relative independence and a high level of control power in the cluster.

This central group is mainly comprised of enterprises in the manufacturing industry – or rather their logistics departments. In relation to the enterprise as a whole, logistics is probably seldom one of the core competences in these enterprises (competences upon which many enterprises focused increasingly as competition was growing). It can be reasonably presumed that the majority of their turnover is made in or through more central segments of the enterprise. In many cases logistics work may already have been outsourced or assigned to specialised logistics service firms. Moreover, these enterprises tend to possess a stable turnover and customer base, which rarely expands considerably.

[5] In the analysis of the logistics sector and its cluster and network structures, only the employees who pursue logistics-relevant activities are of interest, in other words those who can be classed as logistics staff. This delimitation is of importance in particular with regard to the industrial enterprises interviewed in the survey, in which the number of logistics staff often makes up only a relatively small share of the entire workforce.

Logistics staff, size classes[b]		Measure of possible communication activity (degree)	Measure of relative independence (closeness)	Measure of communication control (betweenness)
(1) < 20	(n = 8)[c]	2.60	4.48	1.66
(2) 20–99	(n = 11)	2.83	4.79	3.92
(3) 100–499	(n = 13)	5.00	5.35	8.03
(4) 500–999	(n = 2)	6.49	5.79	8.37
(5) 1.000+	(n = 0)	–	–	–
Overall	(n = 34)	3.82	4.99	5.22

[a]: as of 01.01.2001.

[b]: Calculation is based on the results of the enterprise survey conducted in the course of the project.

[c]: It was only possible to evaluate those firms that provided information about both their interconnections at the functional level and about the size of their logistics workforce.

Source: Wrobel 2004, 197.

Table 13.3: Cluster positions (means) by firm size category (logistics staff[a])

Turnover, size classes[b]		Measure of possible communication activity (degree)	Measure of relative independence (closeness)	Measure of communication control (betweenness)
(1) < € 2.5 m.	(n = 7)[c]	2.60	3.67	1.09
(2) € 2.5 – 10 m.	(n = 7)	5.75	5.14	8.82
(3) > € 10 m.	(n = 14)	3.80	5.65	6.38
Overall	(n = 28)	3.99	5.03	5.67

[a]: annual turnover (as of 2000).

[b]: Calculation is based on the results of the enterprise survey conducted in the course of the project.

[c]: It was only possible to evaluate those firms that provided information about both their interconnections at the functional level and about the size of their turnover.

Source: Wrobel 2004, 198.

Table 13.4: Cluster positions (means) by turnover size categories (in logistics[a])

Turnover development[b]		Measure of possible communication activity (degree)	Measure of relative independence (closeness)	Measure of communication control (betweenness)
(1) increasing	(n = 22)[c]	3.48	5.02	4.96
(2) stagnating	(n = 4)	3.90	4.67	6.58
(3) falling	(n = 3)	4.76	5.64	5.41
(4) fluctuating without a trend	(n = 3)	4.33	5.66	6.47
Overall	(n = 32)	3.73	5.10	5.34

[a]: Development in the period 1995 to 2000.

[b]: Calculation is based on the results of the enterprise survey conducted in the course of the project.

[c]: It was only possible to evaluate those firms that provided information about both their interconnections at the functional level and about the size of their turnover development.

Source: Wrobel 2004, 199.

Table 13.5: Cluster positions (means) by turnover development categories (in logistics[a])

In contrast, the peripheral positions are occupied primarily by small and very small enterprises with comparatively low but growing turnover levels. One might assume that many of these firms are young enterprises whose business connections have yet to be fully developed. In fact, this is not the case: only 9.3 per cent of the enterprises interviewed were younger than 10 years old.

On the basis of these results, the overall picture that emerges is that of a clearly defined cluster formation dominated by large enterprises in the fields of manufacturing and logistics services, particularly service providers in the economic class of transport, storage and communication. The majority of the small and very small enterprises occupy decentralised, peripheral positions with a low level of integration in the formation. The fact that a small number of large, well-established firms occupy such dominant positions suggests that dynamic, developing firms will continue to be relegated to peripheral positions within the cluster. These findings suggest sclerotic (firmly established) structures and a comparatively old network, factors which may prevent the cluster from developing further or at least may slow down the process considerably (Wrobel 2004, 197 ff.; Friedrichs 1993, 911 ff.). In this sense, traditional is synonymous with a late phase in the life cycle of the cluster, in which it ceases to grow further or even begins to decline (Wrobel 2004, 172 ff.).

> "The older a cluster the more inward-looking it becomes, the more it secludes itself against outside influences, the more it develops 'laager-mentality'" (Tichy 1998, 230)

Logistics staff, size classes[b]		Measure of possible communication activity (degree)	Measure of relative independence (closeness)	Measure of communication control (betweenness)
(1) < 20	(n = 6)[c]	2.14	1.50	0.06
(2) 20–99	(n = 11)	1.69	1.45	0.03
(3) 100–499	(n = 9)	3.02	1.48	0.15
(4) 500–999	(n = 2)	5.00	1.56	0.58
(5) 1.000+	(n = 0)	–	–	–
Overall	(n = 28)	2.45	1.48	0.11

[a]: as of 01.01.2001.
[b]: Calculation is based on the results of the enterprise survey conducted in the course of the project.
[c]: It was only possible to evaluate those enterprises which gave information about both their network relationships (in the sense of strategic cooperation) and about the size of their logistics workforce.
Source: Wrobel 2004, 221.

Table 13.6: Network positions (means) according to the size classes of logistics staff[a]

In other words, old routines can become so deeply engrained that the cluster inadvertently shelters itself from potentially beneficial external influences, including those from its own periphery. Such a situation is aptly characterised by the slogan "Learning new skills is easy, unlearning old habits is tough" (Tichy 1998, 229 following Ichniowski/Shaw 1995). There is a danger that the cluster formation will lose competitiveness in the long term as a result of this type of "deep-seated" behaviour, as insularity deprives the cluster of many opportunities to build trust and cooperative relationships. The latter are, however, an essential element in the cluster's capacity for innovation (and innovation competition) and hence in its long-term survival prospects.

Centrality indicators: network

The centrality indicators calculated for the strategic network are universally lower than those for the functional cluster. Low values with only marginal differences between units confirm the image of a highly fragmented network structure, a fact which was already evident in the two-dimensional representation (Figure 13.2). This fragmented structure does not permit precise differentiation of rank ordering of the participants on the basis of their respective network positions (Table 13.6).

The closeness and betweenness values clearly indicate that a network of strategic cooperation relationships is practically non-existent in the Bremen logistics sector. The structures are so fragmented and incomplete that it is impossible to meaningfully analyse the positions of the individual actors on the basis of network path distances. This effectively also rules out significant results on the closeness and betweenness indicators because they are based on the path distances in the network. It is important to note that indicators smaller than 1 characterise a network in which no actor occupies a central position (Krätke/Scheuplein 2001, 181). The centrality indicators calculated on the basis of turnover and the development of turnover also provide hardly any new or more extensive insights.

It seems very surprising that cooperative networks would be of absolutely no importance in the Bremen logistics sector, which raises the question of why the results portray such a fragmentary network. There appear to be several likely reasons. A lack of awareness among (regional) actors of the potential gains to be made through cooperation may have inhibited the development of denser network structures. A lack of potential cooperation partners in the immediate geographical vicinity or perhaps a lower relevance of strategic cooperations – as compared with other industries – also may have functioned to block to a considerable extent the formation of networks in the region.

13.4.5 Insights from the examination of Bremen's logistics sector

Examination of the Bremen logistics cluster has shown that the sector does indeed represent an emphasis in the regional economy with latent (employment generating) growth potentials. This determination is based on the fact that it was possible to identify logistics sub-sectors which developed dynamically by domestic standards during the period from 1990 to 2000. However, these (growth) potentials were often inadequately utilised in the state of Bremen (Wrobel 2004, 133 ff.). At the same time, the findings of the study also make it clear that the conditions for successful business locations have changed considerably as hard and soft location factors have been joined by the new so-called network factors. Especially as far as the network factors are concerned, the state of Bremen appears to exhibit considerable deficits in areas of importance for modern logistics. This is evident above all in the very insular, fragmentary structure of cooperative networks in the region. This deficit of cooperative relationships suggests an under-developed innovation infrastructure, which may even be deteriorating further (Sternberg/Arndt 2001, 375). As explained earlier, this poorly developed level of interaction can ultimately be seen as a consequence of the sclerotic structures of the cluster formation itself. Strategic cooperation relationships represent a valuable form of knowledge exchange, which operates most productively when there exists sufficient spatial proximity[6] for frequent face-to-face contacts (cf. Jonas 2005, 276 ff.). In this sense it appears that many actors in the Bremen logistics cluster are neglecting a potent and available development resource. This is to the detriment of the cluster and thus ultimately of the region. Lack of cooperative interaction primarily hampers the development of innovations, which are necessary in the long term in order to maintain competitiveness, counteract ageing processes of the product life-cycle, and generate new jobs for the region. Given the current lack of network development,

[6]The concept of proximity has promoted considerable debate in academic circles, especially insofar as it relates to innovation and learning. Many scholars approach the concept of proximity in a multidimensional way. Not only geographical but also cognitive, organisational, social and institutional proximity are regarded as important in learning and innovation processes. In addition, there are also issues regarding the ideal degree of proximity. Such considerations generally lead to the conclusion that both too great a proximity and too large a distance have a detrimental effect on learning and innovation processes (cf., for example, Boschma 2005; Torre/Gilly 2000; Oinas 2000).

it appears unlikely that cluster-oriented regional development policies will succeed in turning the sector's growth potential into actual job gains during the near future.

Despite the cost and time required for the formulation and implementation of any cluster policy, the underlying basis for Bremen's logistics cluster policy was fundamentally sound insofar as the sector possesses potential for further development. However, the hopes attached to the policy by local actors were rather unrealistic, especially given the short time horizons during which employment gains were expected to occur. Such unjustified exuberance is largely driven by the myth of the cluster as a "panacea" which lulls regional actors into believing that cluster-promoting policies will cure every economic ill.

13.5 CLUSTER – A EUPHORIA OF HOPES AND ERRORS

Why is it then that more and more regional actors are increasingly waging their public monies on clusters and networks as regional structural development instruments despite the considerable risks involved? First and foremost is a genuine belief that cluster policies will bring about improvements in the region's structural situation, hopes which are rendered plausible by a considerable amount of hype and the presence of many success stories. However, this strategic reorientation in regional policy is also frequently plagued by a lack of understanding of the concept, which leads to the assumption that clusters and networks can be successfully installed anywhere. Many actors do not possess a clear sense of what clusters and networks actually entail. This is not surprising in the light of the diversity of different definitions of clusters and networks that appear in the literature (Genosko 2002, 53; Berwert et al. 2004, 8). This conceptual fuzziness is already apparent in Porter's definition of a cluster. Although Porter's *The Competitive Advantage of Nations* is largely responsible for the renewed interest in clusters and networks, the book relies on a deliberately vague and generalised definition in order to address the broadest array of actors and make the concept palatable to actors in the private sector. The definition also managed to claim universal validity by referring to general, fundamental business activities such as formulating a business strategy, forming the company organisation, and strategically interacting with other actors and enterprises (Martin/Sunley 2003, 9). The central problem inherent in Porter's cluster definition (and also in many subsequent definitions) is its lack of a clear, functional, sectoral and spatial delimitation (Martin/Sunley 2003, 10).

> "The very definitional incompleteness of the cluster concept has been an important reason for its popularity (Perry, 1999): clusters have 'the discrete charm of obscure objects of desire' (Steiner 1998, 1)".

Martin and Sunley conclude from such considerations that the elasticity of the cluster concept, which affords a wide-ranging scope of interpretation, should be regarded more as a weakness than a strength (cf. Martin/Sunley 2003, 9 f.). Given the widespread misapplication of the cluster concept in regional policy and its proliferation as a supposed "panacea" (Tichy 2001, 184), analysts must heed Martin and Sunley's injunction if cluster concepts hope to retain any scientific validity. In accordance with this, Hellmer aptly summarises the results of a study of the German track vehicle industry (Dybe and Kujath, 2000) with the words "[...] regional clusters [in general] constitute more of an exception in the geographical economic landscape. [...] more realism is called for as regards the practicability of the approach in regional policy" (Hellmer 2004, 35). Other authors also call for more realism and prudence (for example, Rehfeld 2005, 1 ff.; Berwert et al. 2004, 8 ff.; Bergman/Feser 1999). But, until there is a consensus definition of the cluster and network concept, that is, a definition that is generally acknowledged by experts and used uniformly, the muddled policy debates will most likely continue.

Just how difficult it will be to convey such a demand for more realism, however, can be seen in the scientific debate regarding the dangers of cluster and network strategies as regional development concepts. For instance, one important danger of cluster development is the increasing degree of specialisation in the region, and the consequent development of an economic monostructure that is less adaptable and more vulnerable to downturns. The view that "prosperity and success are [clusters' and networks'] worst enemies" (Tichy 2001, 196) has long been generally accepted in most research circles. The more successfully a cluster/network formation works over time – and a key factor for success is sufficient specialisation within the cluster – the greater is the danger of it concentrating entirely on preserving the existing (successful) structures and routines. In the process, the cluster can gradually cut itself off from the outside world (Tichy 1998, 228 ff., Tichy 2001, 194). The result of this separation is that the cluster no longer benefits from knowledge or innovations originating outside of the cluster. Such stimuli are, however, generally necessary in order to maintain the capacity for innovation and thereby guarantee the cluster's long-term viability (for example, Porter 1998b; Fritsch 2000; Meyer 2002). Alienation from the wider market can hinder firms' ability to perceptively respond to changing market conditions. Such an inward-focused view also gradually undermines the innovation-promoting local competitiveness which leads to the emergence of a kind of "collective sluggishness". The initial effect of this dynamic is to halt the cluster's development at the current stage for a certain time. Eventually, however, an absence of innovations in the fields of the products, production methods and organisation forms will lead to rapid ageing and possibly even disintegration of the formation (Porter 1998b, 85). In this context Grabher speaks of an "evolutionary dead end" (Grabher 1994, 79 ff.). Furthermore, monostructures of any kind are in principle more vulnerable to external change than more diversified structures; this too is an old insight.

For these reasons some experts are now advising regions to set up and promote not one cluster but rather several clusters simultaneously (Tichy 2001, 194 ff.). Certain metropolitan regions are even said to possess multiple cluster potentials (so-called "super-clusters") (Krätke 2004, 157 following Scott 2001), which would make them suitable candidates on account of their preexistent structures. The fact that this "understanding" is – as has already been shown – diametrically opposed to other findings from cluster and network research is willfully ignored by many states and communities due to existent constraints. Thus, regional (private and public) actors wishing to set up a cluster find themselves confronted by substantial preliminary costs for which no return can be guaranteed. Of course it is impossible to ensure that a cluster initiative will actually result in a functioning cluster (Semlinger 2003, 63 f.). Nor will clusters emerge solely by means of political measures carried out by public institutions. Although such measures are generally beneficial in spurring cluster development, they constitute neither a necessary nor an adequate condition. The role of public institutions in cluster initiatives is generally that of influencing regional conditions in such a way as to increase decisively the probability of a cluster being successfully initiated and established (Cappellin 2003; Brenner/Fornahl 2001; Porter 1998a). In addition to the uncertainty of whether an initiative will ultimately succeed, there is also the fact that it can take a cluster several decades to develop to the point that its growth is reflected in labour market data (Sternberg et al. 2004, 179; Ballmann 2002, 116 f.). During this time, actors must continue to devote considerable financial and personal resources, but hopefully with decreasing intensity as the cluster gains independence.

13.6 SUMMARY

In summary, it can be stated that the cluster and network concept is frequently misunderstood in policy practice, and it is generally overrated with regard to its capabilities (especially in the short term). Contrary to much popular opinion, clusters and networks do not represent a "miracle cure for regional policy". Misconceptions have arisen as the cluster concept and its underlying theoretical constructs have migrated from the academic to the public sphere. In the process clusters have metamorphosed from a sound (albeit imperfect) economic development instrument taken seriously in scientific terms (Cumbers/MacKinnon 2004, 959 ff.) into a mere buzzword for regional structural policy. Although it is supposedly "on the pulse of the times", the cluster fad is largely bereft of content and frequently misused in a populist way. It is not possible to predict whether or how this development can be reversed in the near future. If it is not possible to break the spell of the cluster and to endow it with a greater degree of credibility, reliability (of success) and sustainability, the concept could soon suffer a fate mapped out by Martin and Sunley:

> "Like many fashion labels which are not accompanied by a high-quality product, the cluster approach could go out of fashion as quickly as its popularity has mushroomed." (Martin/Sunley 2003, 28)

REFERENCES

Ballmann, M. (2002), 'Himmelhoch jauchzend – zu Tode betrübt', in McKinsey & Company (ed.), *Cluster*, Hamburg: McK Wissen, **01** (1), 116–117.

Bathelt, H. and J. Glückler (2000), 'Netzwerke, Lernen und evolutionäre Regionalentwicklung', *Zeitschrift für Wirtschaftsgeographie*, **44** (3/4), 167–182.

Baumgarten, H. and S. Walter (2000), *Trends und Strategien in der Logistik 2000+. Eine Untersuchung der Logistik-Dienstleistung und anderer Dienstleistungsunternehmen*, Berlin: Technische Universität Berlin,

Bergman, E.M. and E.J. Feser (1999), *Industrial and Regional Cluster: Concepts and*

Comparative Applications, WebBook, http://www.rri.wvu.edu/WebBook/Bergman-Feser/contents.htm, (2002).

Berwert, A., P. Vock and M. Tiri (2004), *Cluster der schweizerischen Volkswirtschaft. Kombination von Wertschöpfungsketten mit Wissens- und Innovationsdaten*. Kurzversion: Zentrum für Wissenschafts- und Technologiestudien (CEST). Bern: CEST 2004/8a. http://www.cest.ch/Publikationen/2004/CEST_2004_8a.pdf.

Borgattii, S.P., M.G. Everett and L.C. Freeman (2002), *UCINET 6 for Windows. Software for Social Network Analysis*, Natick Analytic Technologies.

Boschma, R.A. (2005), 'Proximity and innovation: a critical assessment', *Regional Studies*, **39** (1), 61–74.

Brake, K., J. Dangschat and G. Herfert (eds) (2001), *Suburbanisierung in Deutschland. Aktuelle Tendenzen*, Opladen: Leske + Budrich.

Brenner, T. and D. Fornahl (2001): *Politische Möglichkeiten und Maßnahmen zur Erzeugung lokaler branchenspezifischer Cluster*, Jena: Max-Planck-Institut zur Erforschung von Wirtschaftssystemen.

Bruch-Krumbein, W. and E. Hochmuth (2000), *Cluster und Clusterpolitik. Begriffliche Grundlagen und empirische Fallbeispiele aus Ostdeutschland*, Marburg: Schüren.

Cappellin, R. (1998), 'The transformation of local production systems: international networking and territorial competitiveness', in M. Steiner (ed.) *Clusters and Regional Specialisation – On Geography, Technology and Networks*, European Research in Regional Science No. 8, London: Pion, 57–80.

Cappellin, R. (2003), 'Networks and technological change in regional clusters', in J. Bröcker, D. Dohse, R. Soltwedel (eds) *Innovation Clusters and Interregional Competition*, Berlin: Springer, 52–78.

Cooke, P. (2003), 'Regional innovation and learning systems, clusters and local and global value chains', in J. Bröcker, D. Dohse, R. Soltwedel (eds), *Innovation Clusters and Interregional Competition*, Berlin: Springer, 28–51.

Cumbers, A. and D. MacKinnon (2004), 'Introduction: clusters in urban and regional development', *Urban Studies*, **41** (5/6), 959–969.

Dybe, G. and H.J. Kujath (2000), *Hoffnungsträger Wirtschaftscluster. Unternehmensnetzwerke und regionale Innovationssysteme: Das Beispiel der deutschen Schienenfahrzeugindustrie*, Berlin: Edition Sigma.

Elsner, W. (2000), 'An industrial policy agenda 2000 and beyond – experience, theory and policy', in W. Elsner, J. Groenewegen (eds), *Industrial Policy After 2000*, Boston/Dordrecht/London: Kluwer, 411–486.

Freeman, L.C. (1979), 'Centrality in social networks. conceptual clarification', *Social Networks*, **1**, 215–239.

Friedrichs, J. (1993), 'A theory of urban decline: economy, demography and political elites', *Urban Studies*, **30**, 907–917.

Fritsch, M. (2000), 'Ansatzpunkte und Möglichkeiten zur Verbesserung regionaler Innovationsbedingungen – Ein Überblick über den Stand der Forschung', in H. Hirsch-Kreinsen and A. Schulte (eds) *Standortbindungen – Unternehmen zwischen Globalisierung und Regionalisierung*, Berlin: Edition Sigma, 103–128.

Gelsing, L. (1992), 'Innovation and the development of industrial networks', in B.A.

Lundvall (ed.), *National Systems of Innovation. Towards a Theory of Innovation and Interactive Learning*, London: Printer, 116–128.

Genosko, J. (2002), 'Regionale Netzwerke und regionaler Arbeitsmarkt: Kumulative Prozesse zirkulärer Verursachung?', in J. Fischer, S. Gensior (eds), *Sprungbrett Region? Strukturen und Vorraussetzungen vernetzter Geschäftsbeziehungen*, Berlin: Edition Sigma, 53–70.

Grabher, G. (1993), 'Rediscovering the social in the economics of interfirm relations', in G. Grabher (ed.), *The Embedded Firm. On the Socioeconomics of Industrial Networks*. London: Routledge, 1–31.

Grabher, G. (1994), *Lob der Verschwendung. Redundanzen in der Regionalentwicklung: Ein sozioökonomisches Plädoyer*, Berlin: Edition Sigma.

Harrison, B. (1992), 'Industrial districts: old wine in new bottles?', *Regional Studies*, **26**, 469–483.

Heidenreich, M. (1997), 'Wirtschaftsregionen im weltweiten Wettbewerb', *Kölner Zeitschrift für Soziologie und Sozialpsychologie*, **49** (3), 500–527.

Hellmer, F. (2004), 'Wirtschaftscluster', *Geographische Revue* **1/2004**, 27–37.

Hendry, C., J. Brown and R. Delfilippi (2000), 'Regional clustering of high technology-based firms: opto-electronics in three countries', *Regional Studies*, **34**, 129–144.

Ichniowski, C. and K. Shaw (1995), 'Old dogs and new tricks: determinants of the adoption of productivity-enhancing work practices', in *Brookings Papers on Economic Activity: Microeconomics*, Washington DC: The Brookings Institution, 1–65.

Iwer, F., J. Dispan, R. Grammel and S. Stieler (2002), *Strukturwandel und regionale Kooperation. Arbeitsorientierte Strukturpolitik in der Region Stuttgart*, Marburg: Schüren.

Jansen, D. (1999), *Einführung in die Netzwerkanalyse. Grundlagen, Methoden, Anwendungen*, Leske + Budrich.

Jonas, M. (2005), 'Brücken zur regionalen Clusterforschung. Soziologische Annäherung an ein ökonomisches Erklärungskonzept', *Zeitschrift für Soziologie*, **34** (4), 270–287.

Knoke, D. and R.S. Burt (1983), 'Prominence', in R. S. Burt, M. J. Minor (eds), *Applied Network Analysis*. Beverly Hills: Sage, 195–224.

Krätke, S. (1995), *Stadt - Raum - Ökonomie: Eine Einführung in aktuelle Problemfelder der Stadtökonomie und Wirtschaftsgeographie*, Basel: Birkhäuser.

Krätke, S. (2004), 'Urbane Ökonomien in Deutschland. Clusterpotenziale und globale Vernetzungen', *Zeitschrift für Wirtschaftsgeographie*, **48** (3–4), 146–163.

Krätke, S. and C. Scheuplein (2001), *Produktionscluster in Ostdeutschland. Methoden der Identifizierung und Analyse*, Hamburg: VSA.

Kujath, H.J. (1998), 'Zwischen Marginalisierung und Aufstieg. Regionen unter dem Einfluss technologischen Wandels und industrieller Restrukturierung', in H.J. Kujath (ed.), *Strategien der regionalen Stabilisierung. Wirtschaftliche und politische Antworten auf die Internationalisierung des Raums*, Berlin: Edition Sigma, 83–107.

Kujath, H.J. (2002), 'Organisatorische und räumliche Dynamik "reifer" Industriesysteme. Das Netzwerk der deutschen Schienenfahrzeugbauindustrie als Beispiel', in J. Fischer, S. Gensior (eds), *Sprungbrett Region? Strukturen und Voraussetzungen vernetzter Geschäftsbeziehungen*, Berlin: Edition Sigma, 179–202.

Maier, G. and F. Tödtling (2001), *Regional- und Stadtökonomie 1. Standorttheorie und Raumstruktur*. Wien/New York: Springer.

Maier, G. and F. Tödtling (2002), *Regional- und Stadtökonomie 2. Regionalentwicklung und Regionalpolitik*. Wien/New York: Springer.

Markusen, A. (1999), 'Sticky places in slippery spaces: a typology of industrial districts', in *Routledge Studies in the Modern World Economy*, **22**, 98–124.

Martin, R. and P. Sunley (2003), 'Deconstructing clusters: chaotic concept or policy panacea?', *Journal of Economic Geography*, **3**, 5–35.

McKinsey & Company (2000), *Synergetic Growth. How Cooperations can Capture the Benefits of Regional Clusters*, Düsseldorf.

Meyer, S. (2002), *Strukturerneuerung und Regionalentwicklung durch Kooperationen und Netzwerke. Strukturwandel und Strukturpolitik*, Band 5. Frankfurt am Main: Lang.

Meyer-Stamer, J. (2000), *Clusterförderung als Element lokaler und regionaler Standortpolitik: optionen, Hindernisse und Grenzen - Perspektiven für NRW*, http://-www.uni-duisburg.de/Institute/INEF/Intra/debate_meyer.pdf, 8.8.2001.

Mirbach, M. (1998), *Regionales Beschäftigungswachstum und dynamische Agglomerationseffekte. Eine empirische Untersuchung der Bedingungen regionalen Strukturwandels. Volkswirtschaftliche Forschung und Entwicklung*, Band 90, München: tuduv.

Oinas, P. (2000), 'Distance and learning: does proximity matter?', in F. Boekeman, K. Morgan, S. Bakkers, R. Rutten (eds), *Knowledge, Innovation and Economic Growth. The Theory and Practice of Learning Regions*, Cheltenham, UK and Northampton, MA, USA: Edward Elgar, 57–69.

Pappi, F.U. (1987), *Methoden der Netzwerkanalyse*, München: Oldenbourg.

Perry, M. (1999), 'Clusters last stand', *Planning Practice and Research* **14** (2), 149–152.

Piore, M.J. and C.F. Sabel (1985), *Das Ende der Massenproduktion. Studie über die Requalifizierung der Arbeit und die Rückkehr der Ökonomie in der Gesellschaft*, Berlin: Wagenbach.

Porter, M.E. (1990), *The Competitive Advantage of Nations*, London: Macmillian.

Porter, M.E. (1998a), 'The Adam Smith Address: location, clusters, and the "new" microeconomics of competition', *Business Economics*, **33** (1), 7–14.

Porter, M.E. (1998b), 'Clusters and the new economics of competition', *Harvard Business Review*, **6**, 77–90.

Porter, M.E. (2000), 'Location, competition, and economic development: local clusters in a global economy', *Economic Development Quarterly*, **14** (1), 15–34.

Porter, M.E. (2002), 'Mehr Kunst als Wissenschaft', in McKinsey & Company (ed.), *Cluster*, McK Wissen, **01** (1), 116–117.

Rallet, A. and A. Torre (1998), 'On geography and technology: proximity relations in localised innovation networks', in M. Steiner (ed.), *Clusters and Regional Specialisation - On Geography, Technology and Networks. European Research*

in Regional Science, No. 8. London: Pion, 41–56.
Rehfeld, D. (2005), 'Perspektiven des Clusteransatzes. Zur Neujustierung der Strukturpolitik zwischen Wachstum und Ausgleich', Gelsenkirchen: *IAT-Report*, Nr. 2005–06.
Saxenian, A.L. (1994), *Regional Advantage: Culture and Competition in Silicon Valley and Route 128*, Cambridge, MA: Harvard University Press.
Schachtschneider, U. (2002), *Empirische Nachhaltigkeitsansätze im Lichte von Theorien der Entwicklung der modernen Gesellschaft*, Universität Oldenburg, http://-docserver.bis.uni-oldenburg.de/publikationen/dissertation/2003/schemp02/ inhalt.-html, 3.11.2005
Schamp, E.W. (2000), *Vernetzte Produktion. Industriegeographie aus institutioneller Perspektive*. Darmstadt: Wissenschaftliche Buchgesellschaft.
Schnegg, M. and H. Lang (2002), 'Netzwerkanalyse - eine praxisorientierte Einführung', *Methoden der Ethnographie*, **1**, NWA 1.3., http://www.methoden-der-ethnographie.de/heft1/Netzwerkanalyse.pdf, 4.11.2005.
Scott, A.J. (1988), *New Industrial Spaces. Flexible Production Organization and Regional Development in North America and Western Europe*, London: Pion.
Scott, A.J. (2001), *Global City-Regions: Trends, Theory, Policy*, Oxford: Univ. Press.
Sedlacek, P. (1994), *Wirtschaftsgeographie - Eine Einführung*, Darmstadt: Wissenschaftliche Buchgesellschaft.
Semlinger, K. (2003), 'Vertrauen als Kooperationshemmnis – Kooperationsprobleme von kleinen und mittleren Unternehmen und Auswege aus der Vertrauensfalle', in H. Hirsch-Kreinsen, M. Wannöffel (eds), *Netzwerke kleiner Unternehmen*, Berlin. 61–88.
Steiner, M. (1998), 'The discrete charm of clusters: an introduction', in M. Steiner (ed.), *Clusters and Regional Specialisation - On Geography, Technology and Networks*, European Research in Regional Science No. 8, London: Pion, 1–17.
Sternberg, R. and O. Arndt (2001), 'The firm or the region: what determines the innovation behaviour of European firms?', *Economic Geography*, **77** (4), 364–382.
Sternberg, R., M. Kiese and L. Schätzl (2004), 'Clusteransätze in der regionalen Wirtschaftsförderung. Theoretische Überlegungen und empirische Beispiele aus Wolfsburg und Hannover', *Zeitschrift für Wirtschaftsgeographie*, **48** (3–4), 164–181.
Storper, M. and R. Walker (1989), *The Capitalist Imperative. Territory, Technology, and Industrial Growth*, Oxford: Basil Blackwell.
Stuchtey, M. (2000), *Titanische Aufgaben*, http://www.brandeins.de/home/inhalt_detail.asp?id=935&MenuID=130&MagID=31&sid=su6468821427392006, Sept. 30, 2005
Stuchtey, M. (2002), 'Zurück zu den Wurzeln', in McKinsey & Company (ed.), *Cluster*, McK Wissen, **01** (1), 48–51.
Tengler, H. (1989), 'Die Shift-Analyse als Instrument der Regionalforschung', *Schriften zur Regionalforschung* **28** NF. Stuttgart: Poeschel.
Tichy, G. (1998), 'Less dispensable and more risky than ever', in M. Steiner (ed.), *Clusters and Regional Specialisation - On Geography, Technology and Networks*, European Research in Regional Science No. 8. London: Pion, 226–237.
Tichy, G. (2001), 'Regionale Kompetenzzyklen – Zur Bedeutung von Produktlebens-

zyklus- und Clusteransätzen im regionalen Kontext', *Zeitschrift für Wirtschaftsgeographie*, **45** (3–4), 181–201.

Torre, A. and J. P. Gilly (2000), 'On the analytical dimension of proximity dynamics', *Regional Studies*, **34** (2), 169–180.

Wrobel, M. (2004), 'Die Logistik als Motor regionaler Strukturentwicklung. Sektorale Clusterstrukturen und Netzwerkpotentiale am Beispiel Bremen und Hamburg'. *Strukturwandel und Strukturpolitik*, (8), Frankfurt am Main: Lang.

14. Cluster approaches to local economic development: conceptual remarks and case studies from Lower Saxony, Germany

Matthias Kiese[*‡]

14.1 REGIONAL CLUSTER RESEARCH

Since the 1990s, the cluster concept has become highly fashionable among regional scientists and policy-makers alike. In the academic realm, the rising interest in clusters has triggered the rise of regional cluster research, an interdisciplinary field of research devoted to the emergence, evolution and governance of clusters. These main tasks may serve to subdivide regional cluster research into three broad strands. While cluster theory includes all efforts to explain the existence and development of clusters, empirical cluster research focuses on their identification and measurement, including their performance vis-à-vis other more dispersed or diversified spatial configurations. Finally, cluster policy research serves to apply cluster concepts to economic development, but it should also analyse the political processes involved in the governance of clusters. While it makes sense to distinguish these three strands analytically, they are nevertheless intrinsically interwoven: all of them are indispensable for our understanding of the complex cluster reality around us.

The origins of the cluster concept are commonly traced back to the work of Marshall (1890) who found dense networks of small handicraft firms in the cutlery industry of Sheffield and the German towns of Solingen and Remscheid, and in the Lancashire cotton industry which are now commonly referred to as Marshallian indus-

* University of Hannover, Institute of Economic and Cultural Geography

‡ An earlier draft of this chapter was presented to the Summer Seminar of the Gesellschaft für Regionalforschung and the Institut für Arbeitsmarkt- und Berufsforschung in Weimar on 24 June, 2005. The author gratefully acknowledges constructive comments from several participants. The paper especially benefited from fruitful discussions with Edward J. Feser during his appearance in the 15th International Seminar in Economic Geography at the University of Hannover in January, 2006. Useful comments by Esther Schricke and Dennis Stockinger helped to further improve the manuscript. The usual disclaimer applies.

trial districts. For reasons elaborated on further below, Porter's work on the sources of initially national and later regional competitive advantage kicked off a popular rediscovery of the concept rarely witnessed in regional science before (Porter 1990, 1998). Porter (1998: 197–8) defines clusters as "geographic concentrations of interconnected companies, specialized suppliers, service providers, firms in related industries, and associated institutions (for example, universities, standards agencies, and trade associations) in particular fields that compete but also cooperate." Though rather vague, this broad definition has so far been the most widely used and comes closest to a common denominator amongst the many alternative suggestions (cf. Martin, Sunley 2003: 12). One may argue that there is at least one definition of a cluster for each scholar laying hands on the concept. However, our revived interest in clusters cannot ignore Porter's work as a starting point. Another influential intervention came from the OECD working group on clusters, which shifted our focus towards the mutual dependency and interaction among actors linked by value chains based on trade and innovation linkages, knowledge flows, a common knowledge base or common factor conditions (Roelandt, Hertog 1999: 13). However, this focus on value chains captures only part of a fully developed cluster structure. We suggest viewing an ideal cluster as a value system of which the value chain forms the backbone. Besides this vertical dimension, horizontal and diagonal linkages also need to be taken into account (cf. Rupprecht-Däullary 1994: 20; Fontanari 1996: 45). Horizontally, firms operating on the same stage of the value chain may only rarely engage in full-scale co-operation, but they often do interact in various other ways. All remaining actors neither connected via the value chain nor competing directly constitute the diagonal, or lateral, dimension. These include knowledge-intensive business services, universities, other institutions of research and education, financial services such as banks and venture capitalists, professional associations, institutionalised networks, industry-specific infrastructure, and so on. The territorial boundary of such a cluster rarely conforms to administrative areas, but is rather defined by a more or less steep drop in the intensity of interaction among actors. The distinction between cluster insiders and outsiders may be aided by distinguishing between dominant modes of communication, as proposed by Bathelt, Malmberg, Maskell (2004): inside the cluster, learning processes take place among actors just by being there through local "buzz". Meanwhile, interaction with agents located outside the local milieu requires prior investment in building channels of communication, or "pipelines", to add an external dimension to the cluster. Hence, we may conceptualise clusters as localised value systems with elements and linkages in vertical, horizontal, diagonal and external dimensions. The model depicted in figure 14.1 does not suggest a cluster is a fully localised value system. Instead, all parts of the value chain, as well as competitors, and other organisations and institutions outside the cluster's territorial confines are subsumed in the external dimension.

At present, there is no universal theory of regional clusters. Instead, different academic disciplines nurture our theoretical understanding of how clusters emerge and evolve – most notably economics, regional economics and economic geography, and social and political sciences (cf. Porter 1998: 207). Hence, you may call clusters an eclectic concept, a theoretical bastard, or "a complex amalgamation of 'old' development theories" (Feser 1998: 23), but they certainly do not exist in a theoretical vacuum

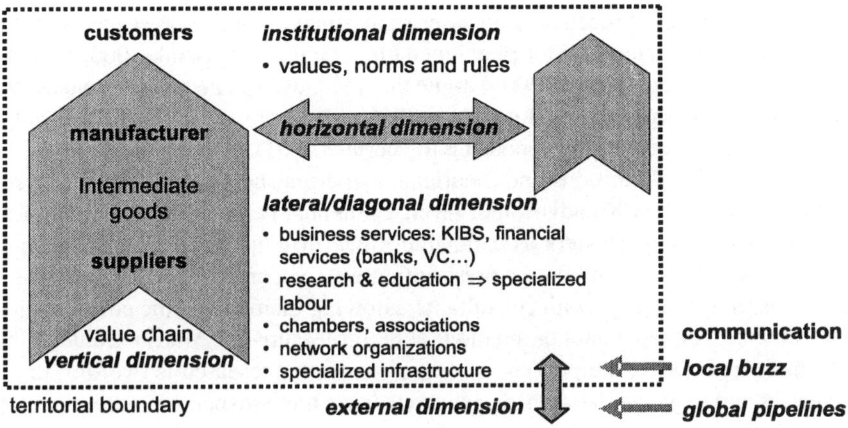

Note: Based on Rupprecht-Däullary 1994: 20; Fontanari 1996: 45; OECD 1999: 13; Bathelt, Glückler 2002: 212f.; Bathelt, Malmberg, Maskell 2004

Figure 14.1: The cluster as a localised value system

Economics	Regional Economics Economic Geography	Social and Political Science
Evolutionary Economics (New) Institutional Economics Transaction Cost Theory Endogenous Growth Theory Economics of Knowledge, Innovation, and Learning	Agglomeration Economics Polarisation Theory (sectoral/regional) Endogenous Regional Development Geographical Economics	Network Theory Embeddedness Approach Social Capital Governance

Table 14.1: Building blocks of a cluster theory

as is occasionally claimed. Although the different building blocks of a cluster theory compiled in table 14.1 have not yet been integrated to form a general cluster theory, some convergence of partial approaches can already be observed, as evident from the knowledge-based theory of spatial clustering, which combines insights from agglomeration economics, the economics of knowledge and learning, and evolutionary thinking (Maskell 2001; Malmberg, Maskell 2002; Bathelt 2005).

With many competing definitions and theoretical perspectives, the absence of a general theory and resulting difficulties in distinguishing them from related territorial innovation models such as industrial districts, innovative milieus, or learning regions (Moulaert, Sekia 2003), clusters obviously qualify for fuzzy concept status as defined by Markusen (1999). However, in support of clusters we may argue that the broad range of theoretical approaches is an asset rather than a liability as it merely reflects the diversity of empirical cluster phenomena (cf. Grabher, Hassink 2003; Lagendijk 2003). Benneworth and Henry (2004) argue that the cluster concept is a typical exhibit of hermeneutic theorising, which has generally come to replace epistemological theorising in economic geography according to Barnes (2001). Furthermore, competition between alternative definitions and theories may be praised as a discovery procedure as Hayek (1978: 179–190) advocated. From a practical perspective, Feser and Luger (2003) advocate using clusters as a flexible mode of enquiry in regional economic analysis, rather than as a model or prescription as it is commonly used. In any case, fuzziness is most welcome with consultants, allowing them to sell the concept widely, and to truncate, rewrap, adapt or amend it at their pleasure (cf. Martin, Sunley 2003).

As indicated above, the purpose of empirical cluster research is twofold: to identify clusters and to gauge their performance vis-à-vis more dispersed and/or diversified economic structures. On the first account, research has yielded a set of both quantitative and qualitative methods to detect clusters at various spatial scales (cf. Krätke, Scheuplein 2001: ch. 3, or see Sautter 2004 for an overview). At the macro scale, statistical data is used to identify concentrations of industry with location quotients and the like. Input-output analysis or coefficients of association allow us to detect linkages between industries or between regions, and growth differentials can be dissected with shift-share analysis, for instance. At the meso scale, interviewing experts, consulting existing research reports or participatory tools like moderated workshops are the most common means of identifying potential clusters according to Bergman and Feser (1999). In Germany, competitive tendering has become another meso-level means to detect potential clusters: following the success of the BioRegio contest to identify and promote the most promising biotech regions (cf. Dohse 2000; Cooke 2002: 26–33), the Federal Ministry of Education and Research launched similar contests in its attempt to regionalise its innovation policy (cf. Koschatzky 2002). At the micro-level, network analysis has been borrowed from the social sciences to trace the patterns of materials and mainly information flows within the cluster context, with discontinuities pointing to possible cluster boundaries. Finally, value chains or even systems may be subjected to a functional analysis including their degree of localisation, which can again be used to delineate a cluster. Since each of these methods has specific strengths and weaknesses, a proper identification of potential or actual clusters ideally requires a mix of top-down and bottom-up instruments. However, few consultants or policy-makers are willing to commit the resources any solid, comprehensive analysis would require before advising or taking action.

On the second account, there is no clear evidence for the superiority of clusters vis-à-vis dispersed and/or diversified spatial economic structures. Looking at case studies of regional economic development worldwide, you easily come across highly competitive regions without pronounced cluster properties such as Austin, Texas, where high-tech employment increased faster than in any other Metropolitan Statistical Area in the US between 1988 and 1991 (cf. Acs 2002). On the other hand, old industrial areas typically suffer from decline not because of the absence, but due to the presence of previously successful clusters resisting competitive pressures for structural change (cf. Grabher 1993 for the Ruhr area). Hence, the potential of clusters as a model for successful regional development obviously depends on the industry life cycle of the relevant industry (cf. Tichy 2001). Empirical cluster research shows a strong tendency to focus on case studies of particularly successful clusters, trying to find out what makes them so competitive. As the literature review by Malmberg and Maskell (2002) shows, no convincing evidence could be found for local input-output linkages as a source of competitive advantage, a dissatisfaction which has led to a "learning turn", whereby localised learning is assumed to be the key behind successful clusters. However, the evidence is also very patchy beyond some highly selective case studies, thus triggering an "external turn" and refocusing the search for the sources of regional competitive advantage outside the cluster's boundaries. Last, but not least, there is the old argument between specialisation and diversity, or localisation and urbanisation economies. Recent research on spillovers does provide some evidence that knowledge spillovers are indeed bounded in space (see Feldman 2000 for an overview), but the benefits of specialisation vis-à-vis diversity is mixed and tends to favour the latter, if anything (cf. Glaeser, Kallal, Scheinkman 1992; Feldman, Audretsch 1999).

Having outlined the theoretical fuzziness and scanty evidence associated with the cluster approach, the only "fuzzy concept" feature that does not apply to clusters is policy distance (cf. Markusen 1999). Given its serious theoretical and empirical shortcomings, the popularity of utilising cluster approaches for local economic development appears even more surprising. The second part of the paper attempts to define cluster policy and to assess its prevalence in order to understand how clusters as a policy tool have managed to surge so far ahead of our theoretical understanding and empirical evidence. After briefly reviewing the relevance of the supranational and national levels for cluster policy, the main section of the paper deals with cluster policies in the German federal state of Lower Saxony, including five sub-regional case studies and the state government's new structural policy. A comparative evaluation follows. We then conclude by sketching a strategy for regional cluster research to gain policy relevance by spotlighting the institutional structures and political processes governing cluster policy.

14.2 MAKING SENSE OF THE CLUSTER POLICY HYPE

Leaving aside the conceptual fuzziness of clusters, all public efforts to promote the emergence and growth of clusters may be called cluster policy. Hence, cluster policy can be seen as an industrial policy designed to promote the specific assets of regions by growing potential clusters (for example, mere agglomerations of industries, incomplete networks) into working clusters, or by fostering the development of already existing clusters (cf. Bruch-Krumbein and Hochmuth 2000: 69 f.). Fromhold-Eisebith and Eisebith (2005) juxtapose explicit cluster policy conceived and implemented top-down by the state, and implicit cluster policy initiated bottom-up by a group of firms from the same or related industries without any particular political impetus. While the distinction between policy as public action and private initiatives is clearly useful and necessary, equating 'explicit' with top-down policy and 'implicit' with bottom-up business-led initiatives appears troublesome. Public efforts at different spatial scales may promote clusters, or various elements thereof, without the explicit aim of promoting clusters. Conversely, private initiatives may easily pursue the explicit aim of promoting the establishment or growth of clusters. The authors acknowledge the possibility of an explicit reference to clusters in private initiatives, and only implicit cluster orientation in top-down policy. However, they do see a close practical association between the explicit-implicit and public-private dichotomies. They then pose the general question of "whether a reliance on the cluster notion makes a difference at all", as the cluster label is often detached from the underlying concept in the political arena.

For their Global Cluster Initiative Survey (GCIS), Sölvell, Lindqvist, Ketels (2003: 31) use the term cluster initiative to denote "an organised effort to increase the growth and competitiveness of a cluster within a region, involving cluster firms, government and/or the research community". In contrast to state-led cluster policy, the cluster's firms here assume centre stage as cluster promoters with government playing an assisting role, if anything. In a broader sense, cluster initiatives may be seen as a conceptual umbrella encompassing cluster policies defined as some sort of government action. To complete this glossary, cluster policies often involve the establishment of particular cluster organisations to assume responsibility for cluster promotion. Whether private, public or organised as public-private partnerships (PPP), cluster organisations are staffed with one or more cluster manager(s) or clusterpreneurs, a new species of economic development professional who needs to be simultaneously "visionary, facilitative, analytical and excelling in networking" (Andersson, Schwaag-Serger, Sörvik et al. 2004: 100; see also Lagendijk 2000; Benneworth, Danson, Raines et al. 2003). Assembling best practice worldwide, the Cluster Policies Whitebook recommends that the same or another individual(s) take on the role of a cluster engineer, who acts as a broker linking firms, universities, and governmental agencies with members of the cluster organisation on a continuous basis (Andersson, Schwaag-Serger, Sörvik et al. 2004: 101).

Conducted in early 2003, the GCIS was the first study to survey cluster initiatives across all industries world-wide. Of 509 initiatives identified as the total population, 238 or 46.8 per cent participated in an online survey, the findings of which are published in Sölvell, Lindqvist, Ketels (2003). A follow-up survey was done two years later, but the results are not yet available at the time of writing. The GCIS's findings show that cluster initiatives per se are not a completely new phenomenon, but their mass appearance certainly is. Only 9.2 per cent of all responding initiatives were launched before 1995, the first in the sample as early as 1984. The first major rise in cluster promotion occurred in the mid-1990s, with 18.5 per cent of the cluster projects initiated between 1995 and 1998. However, the real boom of cluster initiatives did not begin until 1999; of all the initiatives that existed in early 2003, 72.3 per cent got off the ground in 1999 or later. Although the appearance of cluster initiatives is a global phenomenon, more than half of them (53 per cent) are located in Europe. Western and Northern Europe account for 43 per cent, while Eastern and Southern Europe account for only 10 per cent of all initiatives world-wide. Besides Europe, other "hot spots" of cluster promotion include North America (18 per cent), and Australia and New Zealand (16 per cent). Only 5.7 per cent of all initiatives are in East and South-east Asia, and a further 4.9 per cent in Central and Southern America. From a global viewpoint, cluster promotion is minuscule in South and West Asia at 1.9 per cent, and in South and East Africa at 0.9 per cent.

Reflecting their widespread prevalence across the globe, almost all industries or technologies are subject to cluster promotion somewhere. However, information and telecommunication technology (ICT) is clearly favored by cluster promoters, being the target of one in three initiatives. Although the majority of initiatives promote various high-tech industries including ICT, medical devices, production technology, biopharmaceuticals, aerospace, defense, analytical instruments and control equipment, a significant minority are aimed at less technology-intensive industries. These include construction, metal manufacturing, textiles, apparel, footwear and leather products, food processing and the manufacture of furniture.

To understand the boom of cluster initiatives, it is useful to look at who initiates and funds them, and how this has changed over time. From a static perspective, cluster projects initiated by the business sector (27 per cent) are almost as common as those initiated by government (32 per cent), though 35 per cent of all initiatives are joint public-private efforts. However, when it comes to funding, most of the burden falls on the public purse. For every exclusively privately funded initiative (18 per cent), there are three initiatives which receive public funding only (54 per cent), while another quarter are jointly funded by way of PPP, compared to 35 per cent joint initiation. In some cases, universities also initiate cluster projects (5 per cent), but contribute to their funding in only 1 per cent of all cases. Although negligible overall (2 per cent), international organisations do provide a critical source of funding to some initiatives in developing countries. Switching to a dynamic perspective, an examination of funding sources by age of the initiative highlights a remarkable trend (table 14.2): while those initiatives launched in 1996 or earlier are funded in equal proportion by government, business, or jointly, the level of private engagement declined steadily, again at the expense of public budgets. Almost three quarters of the initiatives begun in 2002 and 2003 are funded by government alone. To a certain extent, this shift in the sources of funding can be attributed to the cyclical downswing that seriously hit the ICT industry after the Y2K gold rush. More profoundly, however, it appears to reflect the diffusion of cluster initiatives in space and time. While the first initiatives mushrooming in regions with promising cluster potential found it relatively easy to mobilise private funding, the cluster fashion spread to locations with less favourable starting conditions over time, shifting the balance from private investment towards public subsidy.

As a consequence, the cluster policy movement risks sinking increasing amounts of public funding into a growing number of policy driven clusters lacking a critical mass of firms or favourable conditions for organic development, or in some cases even "wishful thinking" clusters with no particular source of advantage on which organic development could be founded (cf. Enright 2003: 104). Apart from a critical mass of firms and/or research capacity, starting conditions for cluster promotion should include at least partial localisation of value chains, and the will of local agents such as firms, institutions of research and education, venture capitalists, and politicians to co-operate (cf. Sternberg, Kiese, Schätzl 2004: 165). As a policy concept, the diffusion of the cluster fashion bears striking resemblance to the spread of science parks,

	Before 1996 n = 34	1997-1999 n = 64	2000-2001 n = 85	2002-2003 n = 42
Government	32%	47%	62%	71%
Joint	32%	30%	25%	17%
Business	35%	23%	13%	12%

Source: Global Cluster Initiative Survey (Sölvell, Lindqvist, Ketels 2003: 54)

Table 14.2: Funding of cluster initiatives by year of launch

which started off in the South-East of England during the early 1980s as property investments promising high returns, but evolved into an economic development tool to reverse the decline of old industrial areas as they spread throughout the UK (cf. Massey, Quintas, Wield 1992). Mirroring the UK experience, the simultaneous mushrooming of innovation centres in Germany soon outgrew the spatially uneven potential of the high-tech start-ups they were originally intended to nurture (cf. Sternberg 2004 for a recent overview).

Given that clusters are conceptually fuzzy, and that their benefits lack convincing empirical proof, what explains the popularity of the concept in regional policy and local economic development? Apart from the appeal of fuzziness itself (see above), the changing environment for local economic development can be seen as a causal factor in the sudden re-emergence of what was essentially around since Marshall's days. Most prominently, globalisation intensifies locational competition between space economies at all scales – from the economic battle between Japan, Europe, and America foreseen by Thurow (1992) to a plethora of country, region and place rankings.[1] It is no coincidence that the recent cluster fashion has been accompanied by the emergence of regional competitiveness as a new economic development paradigm. A vast literature has developed around this issue that cannot be reviewed here.[2] Suffice to say that competitiveness is now widely seen as the key precondition for regional prosperity and growth. Just as firms tend to resort to their core competencies in response to intensifying international competition (Pralahad, Hamel 1990), regions try to improve their competitive position by strengthening their strengths – promoting clusters being the most obvious way of doing so. Beyond this dominant globalisation-competitiveness-cluster nexus, other factors driving cluster policy include the transition towards a knowledge-based economy (OECD 1996), the increasing dearth of public funds and the resulting need to focus them, and new ways of thinking about regional development like flexible specialisation (Piore, Sabel 1984),

[1] On the concept of locational competition, see Sheppard 2000; Malecki 2004; and Siebert 2006.

[2] At the core of this topical debate is the question whether territorial entities (that is, places, regions, nations, and even supranational spaces) compete at all, as firms compete in a market, and if so, how they compete. For an overview, see, for example, Krugman 1994 and 1996; Camagni 2002; Boschma 2004; Budd, Hirmis 2004; Kitson, Martin, Tyler 2004; Turok 2004; and Bristow 2005).

endogenous potential (Hahne 1986), or the network paradigm (Cooke, Morgan 1993). In addition to these environmental influences, we should not underestimate the role of consultants accelerating the hype (cf. Martin, Sunley 2003). While Michael Porter pioneered the cluster salesman's profession and presumably holds a sizeable portion of the global market himself, management and policy consultants around the globe have eagerly jumped on the bandwagon. In Germany, management consultancy McKinsey & Co. and one of their spin-offs engage actively in devising cluster concepts for local and regional authorities. They market these concepts with slogans like "Silicon Valley is everywhere" (Stein, Stuchtey 2003), "Do-it-yourself Silicon Valley" (Dodt, Stein, Strack 1999), "the art of leading a region like a firm" (Stuchtey 2003), and a "plan for German job creation", which is a reference to the AutoVision concept in Wolfsburg (Heuser, Kraljic, Stuchtey 2001). The federal government should adopt a "new spatial logic" as the development of new globally attractive clusters was neither alchemy nor chance (Jung, Kluge 2006).

Looking behind this marketing machinery, what is McKinsey's formula for raising a region's competitiveness? McKinsey & Co. (2002) formulate ten success factors which may be grouped as follows:

- a long-term organisation in PPP, in which government or a large firm may take the lead;
- clearly visible leadership by a well-respected local personality and a clear commitment of the partners involved, including permanent communication and consultation within a wider regional context whilst combining a clear top-down vision for long-term growth with concrete and focused bottom-up projects;
- stamina to reach long-term goals and "early wins" to maintain momentum and public support and to keep all stakeholders motivated;
- quantitative targets allowing the installation of a monitoring system to ensure that only viable projects are pursued, using public money for investments rather than subsidies.

What makes an industry prone to cluster in space? Steinle and Schiele (2002) argue that a divisible production process and a transportable product or service are the key preconditions. McKinsey & Co. (2002) define seven criteria that qualify an industry for cluster promotion. Some of them are in line with regional science literature, such as a significant share of local employment indicating the industry's quantitative importance, local employment growth, and the potential for synergy. The remaining criteria are not necessarily needed for spatial clustering, but rather to make a cluster dynamic and competitive, such as high value added per employee, high R&D intensity, low barriers to entry (meaning a strong potential for firm foundations), and a propensity to export (as borrowed from export base theory). McKinsey use these criteria as in input in the design of cluster policies. However, they are likely to be mixed with the client's political desires and the influence of pressure groups, such that the outcome – called a "business plan for the region" constitutes a peculiar mix of economic and political rationality.

14.3 SCALES OF CLUSTER POLICY IN GERMANY: AN OVERVIEW

Four administrative levels are relevant for cluster policies in Germany: the EU, the federal government, the state governments of the 16 Länder, and the municipal level including counties and county-free towns. At the supranational level, the EU's regional policy goals are expected to be amended for the 2007–2013 period to encompass not just cohesion, but also the promotion of a competitive and knowledge-based European economy envisioned by the Lisbon and Gothenburg summits. Under a new goal dubbed "regional competitiveness and employment", structural funds would be available for cluster promotion outside lagging regions. At the national level, the last ten years have witnessed an increasing regionalisation of innovation policy by the Federal Ministry of Education and Research. Since 1995, the BMBF has produced a range of competitive programmes to identify and mobilise the strongest regions' endogenous potential. Implementing industry networks at the regional scale is the main thrust of programmes like BioRegio, InnoRegio, ProInno, EXIST (cf. Koschatzky 2002) or, most recently, kompetenznetze.de for the locational marketing of over 100 networks of competence in 21 fields of innovation and 32 regions (VDI Technologiezentrum GmbH 2004). However, the federal government does not promote cluster explicitly, that is, by making reference to the concept, but implicitly by promoting regional strengths and fostering networks as potential cluster backbones. Since 2004, East Germany's patchy progress in narrowing the income gap vis-à-vis the western federal states has led to public discussion about whether the promotion of "growth cores" or clusters would be a better strategy for catching up than the promotion of the weakest regions (cf. Dohnanyi 2005). Consequently, the federal government has announced it will increase its efforts to promote and strengthen business clusters and networks in the new Länder (Bundesregierung 2004: 15 f.).

Within Germany's multi-level governance structure, the federal states enjoy a significant degree of autonomy. Given the quantity of cluster hype, it is little wonder that virtually all of them have formulated some kind of cluster strategy for their territory. North Rhine-Westphalia, the state most experienced with regionalised structural policy due to the old industrial legacy of the Ruhr area, chose to scale down the cluster concept to promote so-called fields of competence (cf. Grote-Westrick, Rehfeld 2003; Bucksteeg 2005). The high-tech state of Bavaria, on the other hand, selected six high-tech clusters, ten production-oriented clusters and three generic technologies for its "Cluster Offensive" launched in February 2006. The state government earmarked €50 m to establish a cluster platform for each of these 19 fields as an "organised creative network of industry and science" to accelerate the commercialisation of research output (Stoiber 2006, cf. StMWIVT 2006). The State of Lower Saxony occupies a position somewhere between the old industrial and new high-tech centers. It falls within the broad mess of "grey regions", which are chronically underrepresented in cluster research and regional science in general. We therefore use Lower Saxony as a case study to look at cluster policies at the state and municipal level in greater detail.

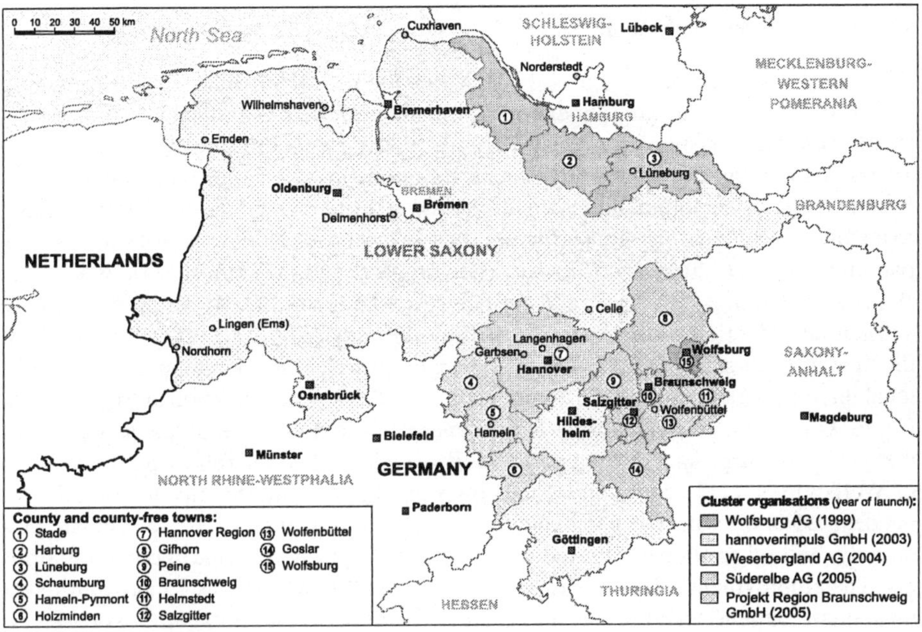

Note: Cartography by Stephan Pohl

Figure 14.2: Cluster policies in Lower Saxony

14.4 CLUSTER POLICIES IN LOWER SAXONY

In the German federal state of Lower Saxony, management consultancy McKinsey & Co. devised cluster-based concepts for local economic development. They began in 1998 when called upon by automobile manufacturer Volkswagen AG (VW) to address serious problems at its company town of Wolfsburg, where VW was founded and is still headquartered. The state government, which holds a blocking minority stake in VW, initially stood back and watched Wolfsburg's AutoVision initiative get off the ground, along with a similar project the consultants conceived for the former coal and steel city of Dortmund, in North Rhine-Westphalia (cf. Ziesemer 2004; Küpper 2005; Küpper, Röllinghoff 2005). In 2002, the state then commissioned McKinsey to work out a blueprint to increase the economic performance of the Hannover region, using the state capital as its pilot project for a new structural policy. Three other regions were due to follow, with the latest initiatives becoming operational in early 2005. The next part of the paper briefly outlines these five case studies and the state's new structural policy. The aim is to conduct some initial comparative evaluations, which will lay the groundwork for more detailed empirical research.

14.4.1 AutoVision Wolfsburg

Wolfsburg is a company town of 122,000 inhabitants as of 2004 (Stadt Wolfsburg 2005). It dates back to the foundation of the automobile plant in 1938.[3] As the VW Beetle became a symbol for West Germany's rapid economic upswing during the 1950s, Wolfsburg emerged as the country's boom town (cf. Herlyn, Tessin 2000). Employment at the dominant VW plant peaked at around 70,000 in the 1980s, leading to a vulnerable economic monostructure. In 1992, the automotive industry and VW in particular slipped into a severe crisis. The company laid off some 15,000 workers at Wolfsburg within a few years, and further downsizing could only be prevented by a substantial reduction of the hours worked by the remaining staff (cf. Pohl 2005). At the time of writing, around 50,000 people are employed at the Wolfsburg plant. When local unemployment climbed to 19 per cent in 1998, VW commissioned McKinsey & Co. to work out a concept for the development of a self-sustaining business environment in Wolfsburg. As a starting point, McKinsey identified the following weaknesses of Wolfsburg's local economy: besides high unemployment, the city was highly dependent on VW, with the car manufacturer accounting for 60 per cent of all jobs directly, and up to 95 per cent indirectly through input-output and income multipliers. The employment relation between suppliers and the OEM was 75 per cent lower than at comparable locations such as Stuttgart, a benchmark region with a dense network of automotive suppliers (cf. Morgan 1999; Strambach, D'Lorio, Steinlein 2001; Fuchs, Wassermann 2005: 235–6). This virtual absence of suppliers in the region is due in part to a relatively high degree of vertical integration in VW's aging Wolfsburg plant, but also because of the company's high-wage policy designed to lure qualified staff to a formerly unattractive place just off the iron curtain. Hence, suppliers in close proximity were once seen as unwelcome competition for labour, but are now in high demand for just-in-time delivery. At its Wolfsburg plant, VW not only integrates an unusually large portion of the value chain by today's standards, but also performs many services in-house. Consequently, the city is a virtual service desert, with the share of employment in services 55 per cent below the German average. High wages and a long tradition of job security also produced an environment less conducive to new firm foundation, which was 30 per cent below the national average in relative terms. Retail in the city centre meanwhile lost between 200 and 300 million Euro each year in purchasing power flowing out to larger cities in the region, while existing attempts to reverse Wolfsburg's economic fortune were deemed insufficient (Wolfsburg AG 2005a).

Informed by this stocktaking, VW and local government jointly founded the Wolfsburg AG in July 1999 to handle a number of cluster-building projects included in McKinsey's AutoVision concept. Targets set were to cut unemployment in half by 2003, to develop a mobility cluster around the car maker, and to link this cluster to other industries in an attempt to broaden the economic base, namely ICT, the leisure industry and healthcare services. Four modules were developed to turn this vision into

[3] Originally, the then National Socialist government named the car Kraft-durch-Freude-Wagen and the associated town Stadt des KdF-Wagens. These names were changed to Volkswagen and Wolfsburg after World War II.

reality.[4] First, the Innovation Campus is an innovation centre designed to increase the rate of new firm foundation with special reference to the ICT industry. Besides some 13,000 m^2 of office space, the Innovation Campus also provides business development, workshops, education, and other services and infrastructure to start-ups, fosters the development of networks among firms to form a business community, and stages an annual business plan competition called "promotion", which is targeted at the four industries chosen for cluster promotion. According to Wolfsburg AG (2005b), the Innovation Campus had led to the creation of 1,688 new jobs in 279 firms by September 2005. Second, Supplier Location Services has been developed to address the dearth of local suppliers, mainly by trying to attract suppliers to Wolfsburg in order to increase the competitiveness of VW's logistics. Furthermore, this module aims at fostering joint R&D between VW and its suppliers at a Simultaneous Engineering Centre, which houses around 385 VW and 280 supplier staff next to the Innovation Campus. The centre hosted Germany's first automotive supplier fair. The cluster organisation attributes 3,940 new jobs in 101 supplier firms to the supplier modules efforts. Third, the most spectacular module attempts to turn a place previously perceived as rather unattractive into a tourist destination. The ErlebnisWelt promotes a new range of leisure and entertainment facilities in order to make Wolfsburg more attractive for its residents and visitors. New attractions and events are oriented around VW's €500 m Autostadt, an automotive theme park showcasing VW's brands (cf. Henn 2001). Located adjacent to the plant, the Autostadt employs around 2,000 staff and attracts around two million visitors to Wolfsburg each year (Schumacher 2005). However, the employment impact of the surrounding activities is still rather meagre. According to the cluster organisation, 177 jobs have been created, mostly temporary positions, with a further 265 attributed to knock-on effects. Fourth, the Personnel Service Agency (PSA) provides personnel services like recruiting, temporary staffing, outplacement, personnel consulting, as well as qualification and training measures, mainly to VW. By renting out temporary staff to VW, the PSA makes the car maker's labour supply more flexible while undercutting VW's wage contract with the trade union. The margin is shared by VW and the Wolfsburg AG, the latter reinvesting it into its other economic development tasks. Due to its close association with VW, the PSA is also represented at all their plants in West Germany. Although the monthly average of temporary staff provided by PSA declined from 3,209 in 2000 to 727 in 2005, the PSA claims to have created 1,989 permanent jobs between 1999 and September 2005 (Wolfsburg AG 2005b).

The AutoVision concept envisages cluster promotion in three phases. Scheduled from 1997 to 2002, the first stage included the establishment of the Wolfsburg AG as the cluster organisation with its four original modules, and the establishment of a new cluster in the automotive/mobility and leisure business. Another five years were tentatively allotted to the further development of the mobility and leisure clusters, as

[4] In April 2003, the Health Project was added with the vision of establishing an independent cluster eventually employing around 700 people. At the same time, a network for sustainability and business was launched to develop projects in environmental research and business (http://www.wolfsburg-ag.com, 2006-01-08). Both modules aim to broaden the local economic base in the long run. They are not dealt with in greater detail here because no data is available yet.

well as diversification into ICT and health services. Beyond this ten-year horizon, the four targeted clusters are intended to integrate and network more closely. To facilitate this, each cluster has been assigned a cluster manager who draws on a total of 217 (2005) Wolfsburg AG staff for cluster services.[5] The first phase of the MobileLife-Campus is scheduled for completion in spring 2006 and will become the physical hub for this synergy-leveraging strategy; it will also house the AutoUni, a corporate university VW founded in 2002. During its more than six years of operation, Wolfsburg AG has made a significant contribution to reversing Wolfsburg's fortunes. Since peaking at an annual average of 17.2 per cent, local unemployment dropped sharply to 8.8 per cent in 2001, and further declined to 7.7 per cent by the end of 2003. However, the next year it increased again to 9.4 per cent, which is slightly above the average for West Germany (Stadt Wolfsburg 2005). Through its modular activities, Wolfsburg AG (2006) claims to have directly created 8,170 new jobs between 1998 and December 2005, of which only 3.6 per cent are temporary. Almost half of them are attributed to supplier location (48 per cent), followed by the Personnel Service Agency at 24 per cent. The Innovation Campus and the ErlebnisWelt account for 21 per cent and 4 per cent of new job creation, respectively. Sternberg, Kiese and Schätzl (2004: 173) argue that the rapid decline in unemployment has been greatly abetted by VW's extensive use of early retirement schemes, instantly removing some 3,000 people from the local labour market. However, there is no denying the fact that total employment in Wolfsburg recovered at an annualised rate of 3.5 per cent from 83,000 in mid-1996 to 105,700 by mid-2003, accompanied by a further rise in the city's commuter surplus (Stadt Wolfsburg 2005). Wolfsburg is boom town once again, reaching 9th place in the 2004 Prognos Future Atlas, which ranks 439 counties and county-free towns in Germany. Wolfsburg even ranks first on certain dynamic growth variables (Prognos AG 2004).

Critics like Sternberg, Kiese and Schätzl (2004: 173) claim that promoting a cluster around the already dominant car maker serves to increase the local economy's dependence on the fate of not only a particular industry, but also of a single company. Strengthening the local value chain by attracting suppliers and service providers may increase the competitiveness of the emerging cluster, but also exposes the economy to the risk of a particular product and business cycle. Hence, Wolfsburg provides yet another example of the archetypal conflict between the goals of growth/competitiveness and stability in regional policy and local economic development (cf. Schätzl 1994: 22 f.). Attempts to diversify either are closely linked to the automotive sector as in the case of ICT with VW as the key customer, or alternatively lack any endogenous resources to feed on, such as health services. The long-term vision of interweaving the four target industries nurtures this concern even further. A critical question in this respect is what would happen if VW should fall prey to a hostile takeover one day – it takes little imagination to guess what an investor might do to a dinosaur assem-

[5] This move has been informed by the Cluster Policies Whitebook (Andersson, Schwaag-Serger, Sörvik et al. 2004). Wolfsburg AG has altered the suggested job titles from clusterpreneur to cluster manager and from cluster engineer to cluster services, respectively. In order to utilize the dispersed competencies of this exceptionally large cluster organisation, the Wolfsburg AG draws on various business units rather than on a handful of designated staff for cluster services (Heinecke, forthcoming).

bly plant with 50,000 workers. On the other hand, without VW there would be no Wolfsburg in the first place, and there appears no viable way to break away from the company town's dependent trajectory. As with everything else in Wolfsburg, the cluster organisation's fate is closely tied to that of VW: when the car plant's demand for temporary staff gradually declined to zero in 2004 and 2005, the Wolfsburg AG started losing money again just after breaking even for the first time in 2003 (Wolfsburg AG 2006). One may also critique the fact that the cluster organisation as a local development agency overtly serves some of VW's corporate goals, such as the establishment of a supplier park to improve just-in-time delivery, or the PSA to supply labour on more flexible terms. However, this peculiar mix of public and private interests follows naturally from a cluster agency conceived as a PPP between a local authority and an exceptionally dominant firm.

Due to its specific setting and history, lessons from the Wolfsburg case may extend only to other towns dominated by a single large company. According to Widuckel (2002: 7), Wolfsburg's sudden reversal of fortune was achieved through an in-depth analysis of local potential and weaknesses, the strengthening of existing approaches for local economic development, as well as the venturing into new businesses compatible with existing structures such as the leisure industry. He regards the close working relationship between VW and local government as a necessary precondition, while McKinsey's consulting expertise was only a tool for acquiring and processing knowledge at the analysis stage.

14.4.2 Hannoverimpuls

With approximately 1.2 million inhbitants, the Hannover Region is a significant urban agglomeration in Germany. In 2000, the state capital of Lower Saxony was home to the international exhibition EXPO 2000, which brought with it substantial public investment in infrastructure and temporarily boosted the local and wider regional economy (cf. Brandt, Klodt, Kramer et al. 2001). Almost simultaneously, the city of Hannover joined forces with the surrounding county to form a new administrative unit in what is still seen as a unique local government reform in Germany (cf. Priebs 2002). Despite these infrastructural and institutional improvements, local policy-makers saw the danger of the region falling behind other national and European city-regions in the locational competition game (cf. McKinsey & Co. 2002: 9–10). The economic hangover following EXPO 2000 and an unemployment rate of 12.4 per cent – around two points above the national average – led the city, regional, and state governments in 2002 to jointly commission McKinsey & Co. to develop a concept for the sustainable improvement of the region's competitiveness. Eagerly aware of the consultants' track record in Dortmund and Wolfsburg, the state government decided to co-fund concept development in Hannover as a pilot project for similar initiatives it was planning for other parts of Lower Saxony.

Without making their methods transparent to the public, McKinsey & Co. (2002) identified in an unpublished report cluster potential in five so-called focus industries. These included automotive, the almost ubiquitous ICT industry, optical technologies, life sciences, and manufacturing technology. In part, the McKinsey report is consistent with Revilla Diez's (2002) findings that the region previously lacked any fully working cluster characterised by intensive cooperative linkages between various actors and consequent gains in regional competitiveness through synergies and higher productivity. Following Enright's classification (2003: 104), Revilla Diez (2002) rates the region's automotive industry grouped around VW's utility vehicle plant and some larger suppliers like Continental AG (tire systems) as a latent cluster, since the weakness of linkages leaves much potential for synergy and interactive learning untapped. Some other industries singled out by McKinsey constitute potential clusters, that is, life sciences and the ICT business, which display only a few elements of working clusters. In life sciences, the region's academic competencies are not sufficiently matched by the business sector. Meanwhile, ICT firms view the nationwide shortage of skilled ICT labour, the insufficient density of supporting industries, and the lack of cooperation with consulting, facilities as serious weaknesses of the local ICT sector (Revilla Diez 2003). In general, McKinsey agreed on improving linkages within and between the focus industries, so they developed the vision of "Hannover 2012 – Crossroads of Technology". Twenty-seven projects were proposed to create a total of 45,000 new jobs within a decade (McKinsey & Co. 2002).

Following McKinsey's analysis, the state and regional governments jointly founded the cluster organisation hannoverimpuls GmbH in April 2003 to successively turn the consultancy's concept into reality. However, McKinsey's twenty-seven proposals were not all implementable. Some of them required further specification or revision, while others had to be abandoned entirely or replaced by alternative projects. This process led to lost time and delays in getting cluster promotion off the ground. During its first three years of operation, Plug & Work has emerged as the organisation's flagship project. An innovative project that does not feature in the consultants' blueprint, Plug & Work stages annual competitions to attract promising start-ups, relocations, and offices of established companies to the EXPO 2000 site south-east of the city centre. Equipped with state-of-the-art infrastructure and modern architecture, the EXPO 2000 site had been set aside for ICT and media industries after the event, but remained largely idle following the downturn in the ICT business cycle (cf. Revilla Diez 2003). During the first four years after the EXPO 2000 event, some public research and educational establishments were relocated to the site, including the ICT and media subsidiary of the region's innovation centre, CampMedia. Other ICT and media firms were reluctant to follow. Assisted by sponsors, hannoverimpuls utilised excess office space to house the winners of the Plug & Work competition free of charge for one year. Hannoverimpuls offered winners additional benefits like telecommunications infrastructure and internet access as well as providing consulting, start-up advice and networking events. In 2004, the first Plug & Work competition attracted 180 applications, of which 40 firms were selected to start operations in the EXPO Park with an initial staff of 105. According to the author's own survey, the majority of these firms were start-ups displaying a favourable relation of opportunity vs. necessity entrepreneurs. At 2.43:1, the overall ratio for Germany is rather unfavourable by international standards (Sternberg, Brixy, Schlapfner 2006: 15). The ratio amongst Plug & Work start-ups is 7:1, indicationg growth potential. When the promotional measures expired after one year, two-thirds of the firms remained in the region and had expanded their employment by 35 per cent. However, the majority of firms and staff left the EXPO 2000 site for better access to urban amenities in the city centre. Those who remained on the EXPO Park were joined by the next generation of Plug & Work winners in September 2005. This time 24 winners were selected from amongst seventy applicants. In 2006, hannoverimpuls expanded the Plug & Work competition to its other four focus industries, providing free office space and other incentives at dedicated sites across the region. Establishing a vibrant and self-sustaining ICT and media community from scratch at the EXPO 2000 site will likely require many additional iterations of the competition,as well as the spark of a major relocation or an upturn in the ICT business cycle.

How can we assess the Hannover experience after just three years of operational cluster promotion? Hannoverimpuls entered the cluster promotion game with no working clusters in the region, and the challenges facing the local economy were much less pressing than in the case of Wolfsburg. The cluster organisation is an entirely public initiative,[6] and local business involvement is by and large confined to project sponsoring, such as for the Plug & Work competition. In the face of political pressures and recurrent electoral campaigns, hannoverimpuls has been constantly forced to communicate successes in order to maintain the legitimacy of its public funding. McKinsey's initial target of creating 45,000 new jobs within a decade was soon abandoned when Brandt (2004) exposed the underlying growth assumptions as unrealistic. At the end of 2005, hannoverimpuls attributes the creation of 1,171 jobs in 596 firms to its activities. These figures rise to 2,569 jobs in 1,435 firms when the efforts of local partner agencies are included. One of the main benefits so far is that hannoverimpuls has focused, streamlined and accelerated the city's and the region's economic development efforts, but some overlapping competencies with pre-existing organisations will still need to be resolved for the cluster organisation to realise its full potential. Nonetheless, the state government of Lower Saxony decided in 2004 to use the Hannover experience as a basis for reorienting its entire structural policy.

14.4.3 The Learning State: Lower Saxony's New Structural Policy

After watching McKinsey & Co. at work in Wolfsburg and Dortmund, and commissioning the consultancy to develop a cluster concept in Hannover as a statewide pilot project, in 2004 the state ministry for labour, transport and the economy introduced a New Structural Policy strongly resembling McKinsey's approach (cf. Natzmer forthcoming). The state government now encourages partnerships of counties and county-free towns to design so-called regional growth concepts characterised by five defining requirements (table 14.3). First, private initiative should be incorporated in PPP fashion. Second, the concept and its projects need to be written in business-plan style to allow for subsequent controlling. Third, the project is to be designed by a project team comprised of staff from business, administration, associations and universities,

[6]The public stakeholders failed to attract private equity into the cluster organisation. The only long-term private commitment they managed to secure is the Belgium-based multinational corporation Interbrew (now InBev) which committed itself to an annual contribution of €500.000 for ten years in a move to soothe their takeover of the traditional Gilde brewery.

Requirements	Instruments		
	Growth Projects	Growth Co-operation	Regional Growth Concepts
Private public partnership	•	•	•
Business plans	•	•	•
Cooperation of admin. units		•	•
Project team			•
Organisation			•

Table 14.3: Instruments of Lower Saxony's new structural policy and their requirements

and led by external management know-how, that is, a management consultancy, the cost of which the state governments is willing to fund up to one third. Fourth, a PPP organisation should be set up to turn the business plans into practice. While these requirements are clearly taken from McKinsey's principles outlined above, the fifth point may be attributed to the state government's long-term goal of regionalisation. Regional growth concepts have to be proposed by more than one county or county-free town, and these inter-municipal alliances should reflect industrial value chains crossing administrative boundaries: wherever a value chain is located in more than one administrative unit, their co-operation is required in order to receive structural policy support from the state government. The new structural policy also offers support to less ambitious localised efforts such as growth co-operations lacking a formal project team and organisation, or growth projects which can be pursued by a county or county-free municipality alone. Table 14.3 summarises the three instruments of Lower Saxony's new structural policy and their respective requirements.

In addition to these five requirements, the state government prescribes the phasing of regional growth concepts as follows. The first phase of mobilisation may take between six months and two years. This is followed by five months during which the growth concept is drafted in the form of a business plan. The founding of the organisation marks the beginning of the first project cycle, during which communication and the start of the first projects are the main tasks. After 9–12 months, the organisation is up and running and expected to continue its work for approximately ten years. Hence, regional growth projects are designed for a limited lifespan only.

From growth projects via local growth co-operations to regional growth concepts, the intensity and commitment of the endeavours has increased, along with the employment impacts expected by the ministry (NMWAV 2004). Following the hannoverimpuls pilot project and the reorientation of the state's structural policy, three regional growth concepts have been devised for different parts of the state. To allow for an evaluation of this new policy orientation, these further case studies merit a brief introduction.

14.4.4 Weserbergland AG

The Weserbergland region consists of the three neighbouring counties of Schaumburg, Hameln-Pyrmont, and Holzminden. Its economy is characterised by small and medium-sized enterprises (SMEs) in rather traditional industries. Together, they shed around 20,000 jobs between 1980 and 1999 in the face of increasing competitive pressure. In the following years, the region's growth rates were constantly below the state average (Bartsch forthcoming). To address this decline, the counties joined forces in 2002 to develop a regional development co-operation plan (REK Weserbergland 2001). Led by a McKinsey spin-off, a project team staffed by public administration, local businesses, trade unions and educational organisations drafted a growth concept for the region between November 2002 and March 2003. Twenty-two projects were drafted as business plans – some of them generic, some focusing on a set of eight industries.[7] By removing obstacles to growth, the consultants calculated that these projects would lift annual regional per-capita income growth to 3.8 per cent from an assumed base rate of 2 per cent, as well as creating 15,000 new jobs within a decade. To put this bold vision and the underlying project proposals into practice, the Weserbergland AG was founded in March 2004 as a PPP involving the three counties and 20 local businesses, the latter accounting for 68.4 per cent of the total equity (Möller 2004: 44).

With a rather small team of six, the Weserbergland AG is currently pursuing eight projects designed to promote the economic structure and employment growth in its region through the growth of existing firms, the promotion of start-ups, and the attraction of mobile firms to the region. Projects are assigned to three areas of activity, that is, services to businesses, services for public administration, and investment projects (cf. Bartsch forthcoming; Weserbergland AG 2006). Services to businesses include networking projects to pool firms' resources in the areas of purchasing, training and sales, individual consulting, and events. For public administration, the Weserbergland AG streamlines the three counties' start-up advice, organises a corporate growth initiative, installs service centres as one-stop interfaces between administration and businesses, and works with partners to promote the region as a tourist destination. At the time of writing, two investment projects are being pursued. The "innovative module house" encourages the region's construction firms to collaborate on modular building projects, thereby capitalising on an emerging market for affordable private housing. The "regenerative power" project builds on the region's only research facility of national importance, which focuses on solar power. Despite the eight target industries identified by the consultants, only a few of the projects actually pursued so far show a clear industry focus, that is, the module house, regenerative power, tourism, and to a certain extent network projects that tend to target relatively homogenous groups of firms.

As in the case of Hannover, the grand ambitions articulated by the consultants received a fair amount of criticism. Growth and employment targets were soon dropped

[7] Reflecting the region's existing pattern of specialisation, these industries include solar power, mechanical engineering, construction, tourism, electro-technical industry, chemical industry (scents and aromas), as well as the manufacture of glass and furniture (Bartsch, forthcoming).

and replaced by the more modest goals of strengthening the regional economy and maintaining employment at 2003 levels (Möller 2004: 45). As a local trade union representative put it: "Expectations were much too high, many promises nonsense" (TAH 2005). In an economic region with scarce cluster potential and more basic challenges such as skills shortages, SME finance, and demographics, it appears sensible that the Weserbergland AG should engage predominantly in generic economic development tasks rather than industry-specific cluster promotion. The organisation's general manager, Bartsch (forthcoming), explains that clusters could not be developed from scratch, and a successful cluster-based strategy for economic development would need to build on endogenous potential such as research and educational facilities or highly skilled workers, which are in short supply locally. Although it is a Regional Growth Concept approved and funded by the state government at its conception stage, the initiative may be better characterised as a "rural growth concept" rather than a case of cluster policy and indeed, the term "cluster" itself is hardly ever heard in the region. The Weserbergland AG is thus a good illustration of how Lower Saxony's New Structural Policy takes a much wider approach and extends well beyond implicit cluster policy, offering support for all its sub-regions to develop their potential rather than just "strengthening the strengths" as the cluster concept would imply.

14.4.5 Süderelbe AG

Cluster policy in the three north-eastern counties of Stade, Harburg and Lüneburg has been triggered not so much by acute threats to their economic base, but rather by what was going on in the neighbouring city of Hamburg, an economic powerhouse with 1.7 m inhabitants. As one of Germany's 16 Länder on its own, Hamburg revealed a long-term vision of a "growing city" in 2002, which drew on an earlier McKinsey analysis (McKinsey & Co. 2001; Hamburg 2002). As one might expect, that vision included the promotion of a set of internationally visible clusters,[8] as well as a "leap across the Elbe" to extend urban development south of the river. As the "growing city" concept openly aimed at retaining and attracting population and businesses within the city, to reverse long-term trends of suburbanisation, the southern neighbours were frightened at the prospect of becoming de-linked from metropolitan growth spillovers. To counter this threat, the three abovementioned counties teamed up with the City of Lüneburg, Hamburg's metropolitan district of Harburg, the two Länder involved, and some major local firms to launch a growth initiative for the area south of the river. The concept underlying the "regional business plan" Wachstumsinitiative Süderelbe followed the prescriptions of Lower Saxony's NSP, but was developed by a team led by McKinsey's competitors, Deloitte Consulting. It would be interesting to learn more about this peculiar clash of consultancies. This project team came up with 38 project proposals expected to create between 10,000 and 20,000 new jobs within ten years, between 1,500 and 2,000 of which are to be created by a single project alone, the "logistics growth initiative" (cf. Glaser, Läpple 2004: 49–51).

[8]These are aerospace, life sciences, port and related logistics services, ICT and media, nanotechnology, regenerative power, and competencies surrounding trade with China (Hamburg 2002: 31–45).

Süderelbe AG was established in January 2005 to put this concept into practice. The cluster promotion organisation targets logistics, mechanical engineering, automotive and engineering, chemicals, food processing and maritime systems. At the time of writing, shares are being held by 57 parties including eight municipalities, seven banks and local savings banks, and 42 local firms. Around two thirds of the shares are private-sector owned. In addition to cluster management, Süderelbe AG provides several generic economic development services, such as attracting firms into the region, start-up and innovation support, education and training, and support for R&D and technological development (Süderelbe AG 2006).

Among our case studies, Süderelbe AG is unique in that its territory covers parts of two states, Lower Saxony and Hamburg. Such a trans-state initiative implies higher transaction costs, but also fosters closer political integration and provides a more meaningful approach to regionalisation of economic development policy (cf. Glaser, Ringe forthcoming). Hamburg itself has a cluster strategy of its own, and its northern neighbours in Schleswig-Holstein are trying to follow the Süderelbe example. In fact, Süderelbe AG's constitution allows for a future expansion to include territories north of Hamburg. Once again, demonstration effects and fears of losing out to clustering competitors become evident. According to Glaser and Ringe (forthcoming), the concept's main innovation is the combination of entrepreneurial know-how, PPP funding and a network of business and public administration. This gives the organisation's limited resources disproportionate leverage to benefit local economic development across administrative boundaries.

Glaser and Läpple (2004: 53 f.) acknowledge that the growth initiative helped stimulate and accelerate joint regional planning and economic policy between Hamburg and Lower Saxony. It also provides a possible counterweight to Hamburg's own cluster strategy, though it remains doubtful if an even division of labour can be achieved. On the other hand, the authors question if the Süderelbe AG's employment target is realistic; in any event it is impossible to corroborate it based on publicly available information alone. As a consequence, Glaser and Läpple demand a more thorough and transparent set of success criteria for evaluating and selecting project proposals. For example, it remains unclear why certain projects are being pursued, for example, for the already well developed local aerospace industry, while other key industries such as mechanical engineering remain rather neglected. Süderelbe AG faces a first evaluation of its activities at the end of 2007, a second one is due two years later. The results will determine the future of the organisation (Glaser, Ringe forthcoming).

14.4.6 Projekt Region Braunschweig

At the turn of the century, Lower Saxony's "second city" Braunschweig and its surrounding municipalities suffered from above-average unemployment, weak economic growth performance, continuing structural change and uneven levels of start-up activity. Although more than 100 concepts had accumulated over time for sub-regions, industries or particular firms, none had ever had any major impact (Warnecke forthcoming). As a first response to the ineffectiveness of previous efforts, the cities of Braunschweig, Wolfsburg and Salzgitter intensified their co-operation with the five counties in the region and initiated a regional development co-operation akin to that of the Weserbergland (Bezirk Braunschweig, Reson, ZGB 2001). Inspired by Wolfsburg's AutoVision and Lower Saxony's new structural policy, the abovementioned municipalities except Wolfsburg teamed up with the state government, major local firms, SMEs and trade unions to initiate the development of a regional growth concept. These agents commissioned McKinsey & Co. and their spin-off to lead the development of 16 business plan-style project proposals that promised to create 12,000 new jobs within a decade; the total costs of the projects are estimated at €31 m (Prätorius 2004).

Founded in February 2005, the project organisation was equipped with a guaranteed annual budget of €2.5 m for five years by a remarkably broad set of shareholders including eight municipalities, three large local firms, a pool of over 60 SMEs organised by the regional employers' association, and the IG Metall, a powerful trade union. Besides the union's investment, it is worth underscoring the involvement of the city of Wolfsburg – which had not been involved at the initiation stage – and VW, whose financial services and leasing arm is headquartered in Braunschweig. The project organisation integrates two pre-existing economic development organisations, the regional development agency for south-east Lower Saxony region, which is now the research and knowledge management unit, and the regional marketing agency DIE REGION GmbH (Projekt Region Braunschweig GmbH 2006a). Like the other case studies, the Braunschweig project promotes a number of target industries, but also provides generic economic development services through cross-sectional projects. The dominant automotive industry has been made the focus of cluster promotion, plus related activities like ICT (especially telematics and technologies to improve traffic safety), mechanical engineering and materials research. The organisation is also targeting seemingly unrelated fields such as environmental technologies, financial services and tourism. Traffic safety is not tied exclusively to VW, but also rather to major research facilities like the University's Institute for Traffic Safety and Automation Engineering, a site of the German Aerospace Centre, and Braunschweig's research airport. The latter became the focus of one of the first projects, the Co-operation Initiative Research Airport Braunschweig, which networks 15 SMEs around the facility. The region's research infrastructure is an asset local economic development can build upon (cf. Warnecke forthcoming). Indeed, a recent Eurostat survey ranked the former district of Braunschweig atop Europe's NUTS 2 regions in terms of R&D intensity (7.11 per cent compared to the EU-25 average of 1.93 per cent in 2002) and in terms of R&D personnel as a share of total employment (4.01 per cent vs. 1.44 per cent). Although this top ranking is attributable largely to VW concentrating its global R&D efforts at its Wolfsburg headquarters (evident from an unsurpassed business enterprise sector R&D intensity of 5.25 per cent), the region also scores fourth on government sector and seventh on higher educational sector R&D intensity (Götzfried 2005). During its first year of operation, the organisation also ventured into chemicals and micro production. The non industry specific projects deal with corporate growth, innovation and succession, regional purchasing, a one-stop service centre, as well as education and training (Prätorius 2004: 57). Out of twenty proposed growth projects and research co-operations, the cluster organisation launched five within its first year of operation and prepared the launch of a further eight (Projekt Region Braunschweig GmbH 2006b).

From an evolutionary perspective, the Braunschweig project can be seen as part of an ongoing regionalisation that integrates the region's cities and counties more closely in the face of structural change and locational competition; for an appraisal of this process, see Löb, Fürst (2004). As evident by the set of shareholders, the Braunschweig project managed to assemble a broad coalition of agents behind its vision for the region's economic development. It remains to be seen if this is an asset in terms of high governance capacity, or a liability in terms of high conflict potential. Another peculiarity is that the project's territory covers the city of Wolfsburg, which pursues its own cluster policy through the Wolfsburg AG. Although both the city of Wolfsburg and VW are shareholders in both projects, common focus industries such as automotive, ICT and leisure/tourism produce an intriguing mix of co-operation and competition between them. Both projects compete head-on for mobile firms (for example, automotive suppliers) and founders, but also for tourist and consumer spending. Their relationship will be interesting to watch in the future. Finally, as with all the other case studies except Wolfsburg, the Braunschweig project's original employment targets are deemed grossly exaggerated and have already given way to more realistic expectations. Furthermore, Prätorius (2004: 56) accuses the consultants of opportunistically overstretching the cluster term, thus publicly discrediting an otherwise useful concept.

14.4.7 Comparative Evaluation

Lower Saxony is a member of the grey mass of "normal" regions that neither exhibit a clear high-tech nor old-industrial specialisation. Informed by McKinsey & Co., the state government invites its sub-regions to develop business plan-style regional growth concepts with no explicit cluster reference other than the call for regional alliances to be forged in accordance with the localisation of value chains. Table 14.4 summarises the main features of the five case studies from a comparative perspective. Defined by the launch of the cluster organisation, the timeline shows the diffusion of the cluster approach to local economic development in Lower Saxony across time and space. Demonstration and learning effects clearly played a role here, catalysed by McKinsey & Co. and their spin-off consultancy, and leading to a convergence of approaches. Hence, the case studies display a set of common features. They all aim at increasing the competitiveness of their local economies, especially with reference to employment. They all acknowledge the role of knowledge transfer through external management know-how. And the fact that the McKinsey blueprint was adopted with only minor modification by the state government led to a set of rigid top-down guidelines such as organisation in PPP format, a highly standardised sequencing and timeframe, and the use of business plans as a tool for planning, governance and assessment.

However, structural and institutional differences in the sub-regions provide some resistance to strong convergence, as used by Gertler (2001). This has resulted in a number of notable differences between the case studies. Most programmes were initiated by local government alone, with the obvious exception of VW's company town Wolfsburg, and the less obvious one of Braunschweig where a broad range of agents

	Wolfs-burg	Hannover	Weser-bergland	Süder-elbe	Braun-schweig
Launch of co.	07/1999	04/2003	03/2004	01/2005	02/2005
Initiative					
County/town	•	•	•	•	•
State		•	•	•	•
Large firms	•				•
Shareholders					
County/town	•	•	•	•	•
Large firms	•		•		•
SMEs			•	•	•
Unions					•
Industry focus					
Automotive	•	•			•
ICT	•	•			•
Leisure, tourism	•		•		•
Mech. engineering				•	•
Health services	•				
Optical technologies		•			
Life sciences		•			
Manufacturing technology		•			
Construction			•		
Regenerative energy			•		
Logistics				•	
Aerospace				•	
Chemicals				•	
Food processing				•	
Maritime industries				•	
Financial services					•
Environmental technology					•
Cluster orientation	very high	high	low	medium	medium

Table 14.4: Local cluster policies in Lower Saxony at a glance

was involved in pushing the project early on. It is worth noting that local government has been involved in the initiation and funding in all cases, while the state government played an important role in initiating the programmes from its pilot project in Hannover onwards, funding one third of consultancy fees for concept development. However, its policy has been to withdraw thereafter and leave the ownership and operation of schemes to local shareholders. Here again, the Braunschweig project has the broadest set of shareholders, which even includes trade unions, followed by the Weserbergland. Both regions could build on alliances of agents forged in the process of designing regional development co-operations, or concepts. On the other hand, the state capital failed to tie private equity into its cluster organisation, hannoverimpuls. The cluster programmes' industry foci reflect the regions' traditional patterns of specialisation, which are relatively similar in Wolfsburg, Hannover and Braunschweig. As sites of VW plants, these places are all shaped by car and component manufacturing, albeit to varying extents. Süderelbe, with its close association to Hamburg's aerospace engineering and maritime industries, displays different patterns of specialisation than Weserbergland. In addition to these traditional strengths, the lists of target industries also include the usual suspects of high-tech manufacturing, which are always in high political demand. These include ICT, optical technologies, and life sciences. Examining the ratio of industry- or technology-specific projects to generic economic development projects, Wolfsburg clearly shows the highest cluster orientation, followed by hannoverimpuls. Conversely, the Weserbergland is least focused on particular industries or technologies. Especially for the four younger initiatives influenced by the state government, this difference in cluster orientation illustrates the flexibility of Lower Saxony's new structural policy and its willingness to cater to the specific needs of all sub-regions, including more rural ones such as the Weserbergland. In a sense, this reflects the preference for spatial equality over growth that continues to dominate thinking among many regional policy-makers in Germany.

All cluster programmes have contributed to accelerating local economic development policy and focusing it more strongly. The combination of consultants' management know-how and the initiative of private shareholders engaging in PPPs were clearly beneficial in this respect. However, our comparative analysis shows that "critical mass" of cluster potential as a precondition for successful cluster policy is not ubiquitously available – hence the varying cluster orientation of the five regional growth concepts. Despite the state government's theoretically informed call for local alliances to be forged around localised value chains, the projects and their underlying alliances are still delineated according to administrative boundaries and political constellations – cluster policy is still essentially politics after all. This flaw is best illustrated by the automotive industry, which is independently targeted in Wolfsburg, Hannover, and in the Braunschweig regions despite the fact that they are all tied together by VW's production system. Although a network analysis of the automotive industry in the Hannover region identified significant interactions with firms in Braunschweig (Brandt 2002: 62–71), co-operation between the respective cluster organisations is still absent. Critics go on to argue that the state government's top-down intervention and the consultants' input of largely standardised knowledge neglect local institutions and social capital (cf. Revilla Diez 2004: 76–78). For instance, there is no theoretical nor practical reason why concept development should take exactly five months, or why ten years were chosen as the complete timeframe – most narratives tell us that successful clusters need much more time to evolve. Another point of concern frequently voiced is that PPPs introduce a serious lack of democratic legitimacy and public accountability into local economic development. Our case studies provide evidence of a lack of transparency on at least four accounts. First, none of the regional growth concepts, or "business plans for the region", has been published. Second, the selection of target industries for cluster promotion has not been made public either. It would be important to know if proper use has been made of the toolbox available for identifying cluster potential, and how the results of this cluster mapping translated into policy-making. Has there been an honest appraisal, or has political rationality dominated sound empirics to produce wishful-thinking clusters after all? Third, the consultants commissioned to develop concepts are not responsible for their functioning and impact in practice, that is, they write the recipe but leave the cooking to others. Despite introducing problems of moral hazard, their early exit ignores the evolutionary character of cluster development, as well as the impacts of an ever changing external environment more generally. Constant monitoring, preferably informed by theory, is thus needed throughout the process. Fourth, the business plan format allows for internal controlling of cluster projects, which all organisations do. However, even if some of them issue annual reports on top of it, this is no substitute for the publicised independent evaluations that are clearly required. Nevertheless, the evaluation of cluster policies still poses tremendous methodological challenges stemming from the holistic character of the cluster concept: apart from the problem of tracing a particular outcome back to a specific policy instrument, cluster policy evaluation would also need to take the interaction of various measures into account. There is little evidence that such a scientific evaluation is politically desired; instead, most initiatives tend to resort to auditors and business consultancies for evaluation once again. To conclude our exploratory survey of cluster policies in Lower Saxony, we suggest that policy can foster the development of local industry clusters if certain building blocks are already in place, but independent in-depth evaluations have yet to be made.

14.5 CONCLUSION AND OUTLOOK: MOVING CLUSTER POLICIES INTO THE RESEARCH FOCUS

The boom of cluster initiatives around the globe has already far exceeded the number of working clusters each industry could potentially sustain in the long run. There is a clear danger of public funds being sunk into policy-driven or even wishful-thinking clusters. Cluster policy has not only surged ahead of cluster potential, it has also outpaced our theoretical and empirical understanding of the cluster phenomenon. Consequently, cluster policy tends to suffer from a lack of sound theoretical foundation. Even worse, it may rely on implicit theorising to justify what is politically desirable. One facet to illustrate the gap between cluster theory and policy is that the latter commonly equates clusters with networks and co-operation, completely ignoring the horizontal cluster dimension in which competition provides a powerful source of external economies. Regional scientists should not leave the task of informing policy-making to consultants who are free to pick whatever suits them from cluster theory, rewrap and amend it at their pleasure, or even ignore it altogether. Instead, they should engage more actively and directly in the design and evaluation of public policy.

Our exploratory look at cluster policies in Lower Saxony shows clearly that, more effort needs to go into the conceptualisation of cluster policies, especially when it comes to empirical cluster policy research. The distinction between public vs. private agency and explicit vs. implicit reference to the cluster concept proposed by Fromhold-Eisebith and Eisebith (2005: 1256) is clearly a useful point of departure, but still insufficient to capture the full complexity of the cluster policy phenomenon. We therefore suggest five dimensions that any attempt to delineate cluster policy should take into account:

Agency: Cluster promotion may develop from purely public or purely private initiatives. However, public-private partnerships (PPP) are emerging as an increasingly common way to initiate and fund cluster policies. Within this PPP continuum, some form of public impetus would be needed for an initiative to qualify as cluster policy. The challenge remains where to draw the line.

Cluster reference: Cluster policy may explicitly refer to the cluster concept by using the term. However, policy efforts may be designed to promote the development of specialised industrial agglomerations without explicitly referring to clusters – these may be called implicit cluster policies. On the other hand, many policy attempts eagerly use the term for marketing purposes only, with little or no actual cluster orientation.

Cluster orientation: This dimension denotes the extent to which a policy programme focuses on cluster promotion. Looking at a policy package at the regional scale, the ratio between industry-specific and generic projects may serve as a proxy to gauge that programme's cluster orientation. Our case studies show a clear link between regional cluster potential and the cluster orientation of local economic development packages.

Complexity: Policies to promote clusters may range from single instruments such as innovation centres, industry networks or business plan competitions to complex programmes such as location development programmes or integrated location management schemes that include a broad set of measures. Since the cluster concept is an intrinsically holistic notion, empirical research on cluster policies may be well advised to focus only on those efforts that integrate more than one single measure for cluster promotion.

Time: Finally, the temporal dimension informs us how long a policy programme is in operation, how much progress it has made, and if and when it is supposed to terminate. This implies that a cluster policy is 'born' when it officially becomes operational, either by a launch or the foundation of a dedicated cluster organisation. However, from an institutional and political-economy perspective it may be even more intriguing to look at embryonic cluster policies that never reach the operational stage, having been aborted for conceptual or political reasons.

Comparing the state of cluster theory, empirical evidence and policy practice, the political desire to promote clusters has moved far ahead of our scientific understanding of the underlying economic processes, strongly accelerated by consultants selling the concept. If policies are conceived and implemented this way, there is a clear danger for implicit theories governing policy action (cf. Hofmann 1993), or in Lovering's words,"that the policy tail is wagging the analytical dog and wagging it so hard indeed that much of the theory is shaken out" (Lovering 1999: 390).

This paper suggests ways for regional cluster research to regain policy relevance, the first step being to shift cluster policies into the research spotlight. As one of three strands of cluster research, cluster policy research must move beyond a mere identification and diffusion of best practice to situate cluster policies within their institutional environments. These environments condition the political processes that often lead to outcomes not predictable with economic rationality alone. Industry targeting might be a good case to illustrate this divergence. Research should focus on the acceptance and interpretation of clusters in policy and practice, as well as on the bargaining and lobbying processes. Borrowing from the varieties of capitalism approach that has attracted much attention recently (Hall, Soskice 2001), we may conceive the cluster concept as a standardised response to pressures of globalisation and locational competition that force institutional convergence at the international, national and local scale. However, structural and institutional variety tends to set limits to strong convergence (Gertler 2001) and leads to distinct adaptations of an otherwise uniform conceptual apparatus. Comparative cluster policy research should therefore be sensitive to industry, firm size and spatial structure, as well as to varying institutional environments that may express themselves in the set of agents initiating and funding cluster promotion. One way to account for this institutional influence would be to contrast cluster policies in different broad types of regions, such as high-tech regions, old industrialised regions promoting clusters for structural change, and the grey mass of so-called 'normal' regions that are so often neglected in economic geography and regional science. In essence, an institutional and political-economy perspective appears well-suited to reconcile cluster theory and policy.

REFERENCES

Acs, Z.J. (2002), *Innovation and the Growth of Cities*, Cheltenham/Northampton: Edward Elgar.

Andersson, T., S. Schwaag-Serger, J. Sörvik et al. (2004), *The Cluster Policies Whitebook*. Malmö: IKED.

Barnes, T.J. (2001) 'Retheorizing economic geography: from the quantitative revolution to the "Cultural Turn"', *Annals of the Association of American Geographers*, **91** (3), 546–565.

Bartsch, C. (forthcoming), 'Die Weserbergland AG: Neue Wege in der regionalen Wirtschaftsentwicklung des Weserberglands'. In: L. Schätzl, M. Kiese (eds.), *Cluster und Regionalentwicklung: Theorie, Beratung und praktische Umsetzung*.

Bathelt, H. (2005), 'Geographies of production: growth regimes in spatial perspective (II) – knowledge creation and growth in clusters', *Progress in Human Geography*, **29** (2), 204–216.

Bathelt, H., J. Glückler (2002), *Wirtschaftsgeographie: Ökonomische Beziehungen in räumlicher Perspektive*, Stuttgart: Ulmer.

Bathelt, H., A. Malmberg, P. Maskell (2004), 'Clusters and knowledge: local buzz, global pipelines and the process of knowledge creation', *Progress in Human Geography*, **28** (1), 31–56.

Benneworth, P., M. Danson, P. Raines et al. (2003), 'Confusing clusters? Making sense of the cluster approach in theory and practice', *European Planning Studies*, **11**

(5), 511–520.

Benneworth, P., N. Henry, (2004), 'Where is the value added in the cluster approach? Hermeneutic theorising, economic geography and clusters as a multiperspectival approach', *Urban Studies*, **41** (5–6), 1011–1023.

Bergman, E.M., E.J. Feser (1999), *Industrial and Regional Clusters: Concepts and Comparative Applications*, www.rri.wvu.edu/WebBook/Bergman-Feser/contents.-htm (2006-05-08).

Bezirk Braunschweig, Reson, ZGB (2001), *Regionales Entwicklungskonzept für Südostniedersachsen*, Braunschweig: Regionale Entwicklungsagentur für Südostniedersachsen e.V.

Boschma, R.A. (2004), 'Competitiveness of regions from an evolutionary perspective', *Regional Studies*, **38** (9), 1001–1014.

Brandt, A. (2002), 'Perspektiven der Mobilitätswirtschaft in der Region Hannover', Beiträge zur regionalen Entwicklung, **97**, Hannover: NORD/LB.

Brandt, A., (2004), 'Hannover-Projekt - Ein Beispiel für erfolgreiche Clusterpolitik?' in: D. Scholich (ed.): *Integrative und sektorale Aspekte der Stadtregion als System*, Frankfurt a. M./Berlin/Bern: Peter Lang, 153–170.

Brandt, A., T. Klodt, J. Kramer et al. (2001), 'Regionalwirtschaftliche Effekte der Expo 2000 - Eine Schlussbilanz', Beiträge zur Regionalen Entwicklung, **88**, Hannover: NORD/LB/NIW/Univ. of Hannover.

Bristow, G. (2005), 'Everyone's a 'winner': problematising the discourse of regional competitiveness', *Journal of Economic Geography*, **5** (3), 285–304.

Bruch-Krumbein, W., E. Hochmuth (2000), *Cluster und Clusterpolitik: Begriffliche Grundlagen und empirische Fallbeispiele aus Ostdeutschland*, Marburg: Schüren.

Bucksteeg, M. (2005), 'Ideen brauchen das richtige Klima - Die regionale Verankerung von Kompetenzfeldern', in: H. Meffert, P. Steinbrück (eds.): *Trendbuch NRW: Perspektiven einer Metropolregion*, Gütersloh: Verlag Bertelsmann Stiftung, 209–222.

Budd, L., A.K. Hirmis (2004), 'Conceptual framework for regional competitiveness', *Regional Studies*, **38** (9), 1015–1028.

Bundesregierung (2004), *Jahresbericht der Bundesregierung zum Stand der Deutschen Einheit 2004*. Berlin: Bundesregierung.

Camagni, R. (2002), 'On the concept of territorial competitiveness: sound or misleading?' *Urban Studies*, **39** (13), 2395–2411.

Cooke, P. (2002), 'Biotechnology clusters as regional, sectoral innovation systems', *International Regional Science Review*, **25** (1), 8–37.

Cooke, P., K. Morgan (1993), 'The network paradigm: new departures in corporate and regional development', *Environment and Planning C*, **11** (5), 543–564.

Dodt, A., L. Stein, S. Strack (1999), 'Do-it-yourself Silicon Valley: using business plan competitions to spur economic development', *The McKinsey Quarterly*, (3), 61–69.

Dohnanyi, K. von, (2005), 'Unification, reconstruction and federalist reform in Germany', *CESifo Forum*, **6** (4), 23–27.

Dohse, D. (2000), 'Technology policy and the regions – the case of the BioRegio contest', *Research Policy*, **29** (9), 1111–1134.

Enright, M.J. (2003), 'Regional clusters: what we know and what we should know', in J. Bröcker, D. Dohse, R. Soltwedel (eds): *Innovation Clusters and Interregional Competition. (Advances in Spatial Science)*, Berlin/Heidelberg/New York: Springer, 99–129.

Feldman, M.P. (2000), 'Location and innovation: the new economic geography of innovation, spillovers, and agglomeration', in G.L. Clark, M.S. Gertler, M.P. Feldman (eds): *The Oxford handbook of economic geography*, Oxford: Oxford Univ. Press, 373–394.

Feldman, M.P., D.B. Audretsch (1999), 'Innovation in cities: science-based diversity, specialisation and localized competition', *European Economic Review*, **43** (2), 409–429.

Feser, E.J. (1998), 'Old and new theories of industry clusters', in Steiner, M. (ed.), *Clusters and Regional Specialisation: On Geography, Technology and Networks*, London: Pion, 18–40.

Feser, E.J., M.I. Luger (2003), 'Cluster analysis as a mode of inquiry: its use in science and technology policymaking in North Carolina', *European Planning Studies*, **11** (1), 11–24.

Fontanari, M. (1996), 'Kooperationsprozesse in Theorie und Praxis', Betriebswirtschaftliche Schriften, **138**, Berlin: Duncker & Humblot.

Fromhold-Eisebith, M., G. Eisebith (2005), 'How to institutionalize innovative clusters? comparing explicit top-down and implicit bottom-up approaches', *Research Policy*, **34** (8), 1250–1268.

Fuchs, G., S. Wassermann (2005), 'Path dependency in Baden-Württemberg: lock-in or breakthrough?' in G. Fuchs, P. Shapira (eds): *Rethinking Regional Innovation and Change: Path Dependency or Regional Breakthrough*, (Economics of Science, Technology and Innovation, 30). Berlin: Springer, 223–248.

Gertler, M.S. (2001), 'Best practice? Geography, learning and the institutional limits to strong convergence', *Journal of Economic Geography*, **1** (1), 5–26.

Glaeser, E.L., H.D. Kallal, J.A. Scheinkman (1992), 'Growth in cities', *Journal of Political Economy*, **100** (6), 1126–1152.

Glaser, J., D. Läpple (2004), 'Wachstumsinitiative Süderelbe – Eckpunkte einer Clusterstrategie', *Neues Archiv für Niedersachsen*, (2), 49–54.

Glaser, J., B. Ringe (forthcoming), 'Die Wachstumsinitiative Süderelbe AG: Ein Cluster-Projekt im Süden der Metropole Hamburg', in L. Schätzl, M. Kiese (eds.), *Cluster und Regionalentwicklung: Theorie, Beratung und praktische Umsetzung.*

Götzfried, A. (2005), 'R&D expenditure and personnel in the European regions', *Statistics in Focus - Science and Technology*, 6/2005. Luxembourg: European Communities.

Grabher, G. (1993), 'The weakness of strong ties: the lock-in of regional development in the Ruhr area', in G. Grabher (ed.), *The Embedded Firm: On the Socioeconomics of Industrial Networks*, London: Routledge, 255–277.

Grabher, G., R. Hassink (2003), 'Fuzzy concepts, scanty evidence, policy distance?' Debating Ann Markusen's assessment of critical regional studies, *Regional Studies*, **37** (6–7), 699–700.

Grote Westrick, D., D. Rehfeld (2003), *Clusters and Cluster Policies in Regions of*

Structural Change - Comparing three Regions in North Rhine-Westphalia, Paper presented to the International Conference of the Regional Studies Association, 12-15 April 2003 in Pisa, Italy.

Hahne, U. (1986), 'Changes in the international division of labour and prospects for endogenous development', in Bassand, M., E.A. Brugger, J.M. Bryden, J. Friedmann and B. Stuckey (eds), *Self-Reliant Development in Europe*, Aldershot: Gower, 90–102.

Hall, P.A., D. Soskice (2001), 'An introduction to varieties of capitalism', in P.A. Hall, D. Soskice (eds), *Varieties of Capitalism: The Institutional Foundations of Comparative Advantage*, Oxford: Oxford Univ. Press, 1–68.

Hamburg (Freie und Hansestadt Hamburg, staatliche Pressestelle) (2002), *Leitbild: Metropole Hamburg - Wachsende Stadt*, 2002-07-11.

Hayek, F.A. von (1978), *New Studies in Philosophy, Politics, Economics and the History of Ideas*, London: Routledge & Paul.

Heinecke, H. (forthcoming), 'Clusterentwicklung in Wolfsburg - ein Blick aus naher Distanz', in L. Schätzl, M. Kiese (eds.), *Cluster und Regionalentwicklung: Theorie, Beratung und praktische Umsetzung*.

Henn, G. (ed.) (2001), *Autostadt Wolfsburg: The Automotive Theme World*, Munich, London: Prestel.

Herlyn, U., W. Tessin (2000), *Faszination Wolfsburg: 1938 – 2000*, Opladen: Leske & Budrich.

Heuser, T., P. Kraljic, M.R. Stuchtey (2001), 'A plan for German job creation: a partnership between Volkswagen and the regional government in Wolfsburg, Germany, shows how to build an economic cluster', *The McKinsey Quarterly*, **3**, 16–18.

Hofmann J., (1993), 'Implizite Theorien in der Politik: Interpretationsprobleme regionaler Technologiepolitik', Studien zur Sozialwissenschaft, **132**, Opladen: Westdeutscher Verlag.

Jung, M., J. Kluge (2006), 'Die Gemeinschaft neu begründen', *Frankfurter Allgemeine Sonntagszeitung*, **7**, 19.02.2006, 42.

Kitson, M., R. Martin, P. Tyler (2004), 'Regional competitiveness: an elusive yet key concept?' *Regional Studies*, **38** (9), 991–999.

Koschatzky, K. (2002), 'Regionsorientierte Innovationspolitik und innovationsorientierte Regionalpolitik: Zwei Wege in die gleiche Richtung?' in Gesellschaft für Regionalforschung (ed.), *Seminarberichte: Beiträge zum Sommerseminar vom 24. bis 25. September 2001 in Bremen*, Heidelberg: GfR, 7–30.

Krätke, S., C. Scheuplein (2001), *Produktionscluster in Ostdeutschland: Methoden der Identifizierung und Analyse*, Hamburg: VSA-Verlag.

Krugman, P.R. (1994), 'Competitiveness: a dangerous obsession', *Foreign Affairs*, **73** (2), 28–44.

Krugman, P.R. (1996), 'Making sense of the competitiveness debate', *Oxford Review of Economic Policy*, **12** (3), 17–25.

Küpper, U.I. (2005), 'Zwischenbilanz des "Dortmund-projects" aus der Sicht des Wirtschaftsförderers', *Informationen zur Raumentwicklung*, **9/10**, 627–636.

Küpper, U.I., S. Röllinghoff (2005), 'Clustermanagement: Anforderungen an Städte und regionale Netzwerke', *Deutsche Zeitschrift für Kommunalwissenschaften*, **44** (1), 60–93.

Lagendijk, A. (2000), 'Learning in non-core regions: towards intelligent cluster; addressing business and regional needs', in F. Boekema, K. Morgan, S. Bakkers and R. Rutten (eds), *Knowledge, Innovation and Economic Growth: The Theory and Practice of Learning Regions*, Cheltenham/Northampton: Edward Elgar, 165–191.

Lagendijk, A. (2003), 'Towards conceptual quality in regional studies: the need for subtle critique – a response to Markusen', *Regional Studies*, **37** (6–7), 719–727.

Löb, S., D. Fürst (2004), 'Schwachstellen und Perspektiven der institutionellen Kooperation in der Region Südostniedersachsen/Region Braunschweig', in D. Scholich (ed.), *Integrative und sektorale Aspekte der Stadtregion als System. (Stadt und Region als Handlungsfeld, 3)*. Frankfurt/Berlin/Bern: Peter Lang, 219–243.

Lovering, J. (1999), 'Theory led by policy: the inadequacies of the "New Regionalism" (illustrated from the case of Wales)', *International Journal of Urban and Regional Research*, **23** (2), 379–395.

Malecki, E.J. (2004), 'Jockeying for position: what it means and why it matters to regional development policy when places compete', *Regional Studies*, **38** (9), 1101–1120.

Malmberg, A., P. Maskell (2002), 'The elusive concept of localization economies: towards a knowledge-based theory of spatial clustering', *Environment and Planning A*, **34** (3), 429–449.

Markusen, A. (1999), 'Fuzzy concepts, scanty evidence, policy distance: the case for rigour and policy relevance in critical regional studies', *Regional Studies*, **33** (9), 869–884.

Marshall, A. (1890), *Principles of Economics*, London: MacMillan.

Martin, R., P. Sunley (2003), 'Deconstructing clusters: chaotic concept or policy panacea?' *Journal of Economic Geography*, **3** (1), 5–35.

Maskell, P. (2001), 'Towards a knowledge-based theory of the geographical cluster', *Industrial and Corporate Change*, **10** (4), 921–943.

Massey, D., P. Quintas, D. Wield (1992), *High-tech Fantasies: Science Parks in Society, Science and Space*, London: Routledge.

McKinsey & Co. (2001), *Hamburg Vision 2020: Vom nationalen Zentrum zur europäischen Metropole*, Hamburg: McKinsey.

McKinsey & Co. (2002), *Das Hannover-Projekt: Verstärkung der wirtschaftlichen Leistungsäfhigkeit der Region Hannover*, Unpublished report, Hannover.

Möller, K.P. (2004), 'Die Weserbergland AG: Partner für die Wirtschaft in den Landkreisen Hameln-Pyrmont, Holzminden und Schaumburg', *Neues Archiv für Niedersachsen*, **2**, 44–48.

Morgan, K. (1999), 'Reversing attrition? The auto cluster in Baden-Württemberg', in T.J. Barnes, M.S. Gertler (eds), *The New Industrial Geography: Regions, Regulation and Institutions*, (Routledge Studies in the Modern World Economy, 22). London/New York: Routledge, 74–97.

Moulaert, F., F. Sekia (2003), 'Territorial innovation models: a critical survey', *Regional Studies*, **37** (3), 289–302.

Natzmer, W. von (forthcoming), 'Regionale Wachstumskonzepte - eine Methode des Clustermanagements in der Praxis', in L. Schätzl, M. Kiese (eds), *Cluster und Regionalentwicklung: Theorie, Beratung und praktische Umsetzung*.

NMWAV (Niedersächsisches Ministerium für Wirtschaft, Arbeit und Verkehr) (2004), *Regionale Strukturpolitik für Wachstum und Arbeitsplätze: Eckwertepapier und Handreichung zum Eckwertepapier*, http://cdl.niedersachsen.de/blob/images/C-9483120_L20.pdf (2007-11-07).

OECD (1996), *The Knowledge-based Economy*, Paris: OECD.

OECD (ed.) (1999), *Boosting Innovation: The Cluster Approach*, Paris: OECD.

Piore, M.J., C.F. Sabel (1984), *The Second Industrial Divide: Conditions for Prosperity*, New York: Basic Books.

Pohl, J. (2005), 'Urban Governance à la Wolfsburg', *Informationen zur Raumentwicklung*, **9/10**, 637–647.

Porter, M.E. (1990), *The Competitive Advantage of Nations*, New York: Free Press.

Porter, M.E. (1998), 'Clusters and competition: new agendas for companies, governments and institutions', in M.E. Porter (ed.): *On Competition*, Boston: The Harvard Business School Publishing, 197–287.

Pralahad, C.K., G. Hamel (1990), 'The core competence of the corporation', *Harvard Business Review*, **68** (3), 79–91.

Prätorius, G. (2004), ' "Projekt Region Braunschweig" – Kooperatives Wachstumskonzept für die Region', *Neues Archiv für Niedersachsen*, **2**, 55–59.

Priebs, A. (2002), 'Regionalreform als Innovation', in H.-U. Jung, A. Brandt (eds.), *Wirtschaftsstandort Region Hannover - Regionalreport 2002: Auf dem Weg in die Wissensgesellschaft*, Hannover: Region Hannover, 254–260.

Prognos AG (2004), *Zukunftsatlas 2004 - Deutschlands Regionen im Zukunftswettbewerb*, http://www.prognos.com/zukunftsatlas/p_zukunftsatlas_04.html (2006-05-08).

Projekt Region Braunschweig GmbH (2006a), http://www.projekt-region-braunschweig.de (2006-05-08).

Projekt Region Braunschweig GmbH (2006b), *'Die Region im Aufbruch – ein Jahr Projekt Region Braunschweig GmbH'*, Press release, 2006-01-31, http://www.projekt-region-braunschweig.de (2006-05-08).

REK Weserbergland (2001), *Regionale Entwicklungskooperation Weserbergland, Stand August 2001*, Hameln: REK Weserbergland.

Revilla Diez, J. (2002), 'Innovative Cluster: Beispiele technologischer Kernkompetenzen', in H.-U. Jung, A. Brandt (eds), *Wirtschaftsstandort Region Hannover - Regionalreport 2002: Auf dem Weg in die Wissensgesellschaft*, Hannover: Region Hannover, 172–195.

Revilla Diez, J. (2003), 'Hannover after the world exhibition EXPO 2000: an attempt to establish an ICT-cluster', *European Planning Studies*, **11** (4), 379–394.

Revilla Diez, J. (2004), 'Regionale Wachstumskonzepte in Niedersachsen - Eine Bewertung aus regionalökonomischer Sicht', *Neues Archiv für Niedersachsen*, **2**, 65–81.

Roelandt, T.J.A., P. den Hertog (1999), 'Cluster analysis and cluster-based policy making in OECD countries: an introduction to the theme', in OECD (ed.): *Boosting*

Innovation: The Cluster Approach, Paris: OECD, 9–23.

Rupprecht-Däullary, M. (1994), 'Zwischenbetriebliche Kooperation: Möglichkeiten und Grenzen durch neue Informations- und Kommunikationstechnologien', Gabler-Edition Wissenschaft: Markt- und Unternehmensentwicklung, Wiesbaden: Gabler.

Sautter, B. (2004), 'Regionale Cluster: Konzept, Analyse und Strategie zur Wirtschaftsförderung', *Standort - Zeitschrift für Angewandte Geographie*, **28** (2), 66–72.

Schätzl, L. (1994), 'Wirtschaftsgeographie 3: Politik', UTB für Wissenschaft, 1383, Paderborn/München/Wien/Zürich: Schöningh.

Schumacher, H. (2005), 'Missvergnügen im Freizeitpark', *Wirtschaftswoche*, **23**, 18.

Sheppard, E. (2000), 'Competition in space and between places', in E. Sheppard, T.J. Barnes (eds), *A Companion to Economic Geography.* (Blackwell Companions to Geography, 2), Oxford: Blackwell, 169–186.

Siebert, H. (2006), 'Locational competition - a neglected paradigm in the international division of labour', *The World Economy*, **29** (2), 137–159.

Sölvell, Ö., G. Lindqvist, C. Ketels (2003), *The Cluster Initiative Greenbook*, Gothenburg: Ivory Tower AB.

Stadt Wolfsburg (2005), *Statistisches Jahrbuch 2003-2004*, Wolfsburg: Stadt Wolfsburg.

Stein, L., M.R. Stuchtey (2003), 'Strategische Entwicklung von Regionen - Silicon Valley ist überall', in H. Hungenberg, J. Meffert (eds): *Handbuch Strategisches Management*, Wiesbaden: Gabler, 561–578.

Steinle, C., H. Schiele (2002), 'When do industries cluster? A proposal on how to assess an industry's propensity to concentrate at a single region or nation', *Research Policy*, **31** (6), 849–858.

Sternberg, R. (2004), 'Technology centres in Germany: economic justification, effectiveness and impact on high-tech regions', *International Journal of Technology Management*, **28** (3–6), 444–469.

Sternberg, R., M. Kiese, L. Schätzl 2004: 'Clusteransätze in der regionalen Wirtschaftsförderung: Theoretische Überlegungen und empirische Beispiele aus Wolfsburg und Hannover', *Zeitschrift für Wirtschaftsgeographie*, **48** (3), 159–176.

Sternberg, R., U. Brixy, J.-F. Schlapfner (2006), *Global Entrepreneurship Monitor - Unternehmensgründungen im internationalen Vergleich: Länderbericht Deutschland 2005*, Hannover/Nürnberg: Univ. of Hannover/IAB.

StMWIVT (Bayerisches Staatsministerium für Wirtschaft, Infrastruktur, Verkehr und Technologie) (2006), *Bayerische Clusterpolitik*, Munich: StMWIVT.

Stoiber, E. (2006), *Speech of Bavarian Minister-President to Congress "Cluster-Offensive Bayern"*, Munich, 2 February, 2006.

Strambach, S., A. D'Lorio, C. Steinlein (2001), 'Innovation Clusters and Innovative Processes in the Stuttgart Region', in J.M. Simmie (ed.): *Innovative Cities*, London: Spon Press, 54–94.

Stuchtey, M.R. (2003), *Von der Kunst, Regionen wie Unternehmen zu führen*, Vortrag vor der InnoRegio-Klausurtagung, Leipzig, 15.05.2003.

Süderelbe AG (2006), http://www.suederelbe.info (2006-05-08).

TAH (2005), 'Wollen uns nicht aus der Fläche zurückziehen', *Täglicher Anzeiger*

Holzminden, 18.05.2005, http://www.tah.de/SEARCH/index.php?id=1108107-&showstoriesphp=ja (2006-05-08).

Thurow, L.C. (1992), *Head to Head: The Coming Economic Battle Among Japan, Europe, and America*, New York: Morrow.

Tichy, G. (2001), 'Regionale Kompetenzzyklen: Zur Bedeutung von Produktlebenszyklus- und Clusteransätzen im regionalen Kontext', *Zeitschrift für Wirtschaftsgeographie*, **45** (3–4), 181–201.

Turok, I. (2004), 'Cities, regions and competitiveness', *Regional Studies*, **38** (9), 1069–1083.

VDI Technologiezentrum GmbH (2004), kompetenznetze.de - Networks of Competence in Germany 2004-2005. Düsseldorf: VDI.

Warnecke, D. (forthcoming), 'Projekt Region Braunschweig: Ein Erfolgsmodell für die Regionalentwicklung?', in L. Schätzl, M. Kiese (eds), *Cluster und Regionalentwicklung: Theorie, Beratung und praktische Umsetzung*.

Weserbergland AG (2006), http://www.weserbergland-ag.de (2006-05-08).

Widuckel, W. (2002), 'AutoVison: Regionalentwicklung durch Kooperation', *RegioVision - Newsletter der NORD/LB Regionalwirtschaft*, **4**, 6–7.

Wolfsburg AG (2005a), *AutoVision - Konzept zur Halbierung der Arbeitslosigkeit und Steigerung der wirtschaftlichen Leistungsfähigkeit*, Unpublished presentation, Wolfsburg, 17-18 January, 2005.

Wolfsburg AG (2005b), *Statusbericht*, Stand September 2005, http://www.wolfsburg-ag.com/01_wag/unternehmen/statusbericht.shtml (2006-01-06).

Wolfsburg AG (2006), *Kurzprofil Wolfsburg AG*, http://www.wolfsburg-ag.com/sixcms-/media.php/606/ProfilWolfsburgAG_2005.pdf (2006-05-08).

Ziesemer, A. (2004), 'Strategische Stadtentwicklungsplanung im Ruhrgebiet: Eine Analyse am Beispiel der Städte Duisburg und Dortmund', Duisburger Geographische Arbeiten, **25**, Dortmund: Dortmunder Vertrieb für Bau- und Planungsliteratur.

Index